ULTIMATE
UNOFFICIAL
GUIDE
to the
MYSTERIES
of
HARRY POTTER

To all of our fellow Harry Potter fans, and to J.K. Rowling for sharing the magic with us.

ULTIMATE UNOFFICIAL GUIDE

to the

MYSTERIES

of

HARRY POTTER

Galadriel Waters
assisted by
Prof. Astre Mithrander

Wizarding World Press

Published in the United States by Wizarding World Press
8926 N. Greenwood Ave., Suite 133
Niles, IL 60714

LIBRARY OF Congress Cataloging-in-Publication Data available at the Library of Congress

ISBN 0-9723936-0-9

Printed in the United States of America
Limited Edition – Uncorrected Proof
First Edition, September 1, 2002

Uncorrected Proof

Ultimate Unofficial Guide to the Mysteries of Harry Potter

Limited Edition

Galadriel Waters
assisted by
Prof. Astre Mithrander

Wizarding World Press

FORWARD

I don't often make public appearances anymore, so for those of you who may not know me, my name is Merlin. I am best known for helping that lad, Arthur, become King and leader of the Knights of the Round Table (round was a new concept back then).

Unfortunately, there were a couple of scandals and I had a nasty run-in with the Lady of the Lake. It was Zeus' luck that this really kind wizard, Prospero, came along. He had just gotten back from an island excursion and managed to free me from my cursed enchantment. So I am now hanging out in the local wizarding town and attending wizard councils.

I must say, that literary sorceress, J. K. Rowling, has done an outstanding job of documenting the comings and goings of modern-day wizards. That's how I keep up with this whole (you-know-what) affair. However, even for me, it can be quite vexing trying to figure out all those secret and mysterious clues she keeps dropping. I am very thankful that the Wizarding World Press has put out this Guide. Now I spend many hours (I have a lot of time) going back over J.K.R.'s parchments, trying to see what else I may discover. We even get into debates over the clues at the local Pub, and I'm afraid I even lost a favorite amulet over a bet I made about the solution to that poison bottle puzzle in Book 1.

Even though there is no new news about Harry lately, discussions about him are a big event again around here. Wizard folk thought they already knew all the information, but now that they saw this Guide, they are running out to the wizard bookstores to buy J.K.R.'s accounts. It seems that we wizards missed a lot when the news first came out.

As a wizard of some strategic experience, I feel that you will surely find this Guide makes the stories about Harry even more exciting (if that is possible). Take my word, the more clues you see, the more mysterious it all becomes. The only downside is that my nails have gotten shorter since I read this Guide. I am finding the wait for J.K.R.'s 5th installment to be bloody excruciating.

Merlin

P.S. That kid, Rupert, from the WB movie looks awfully familiar (yes, I popped-in on the movie) – I could swear he's really got wizard blood in him....

Message to J. K. Rowling:

You say you don't know how the Harry Potter story came to you, since it sprang from your head, fully-formed. Did not Athena, daughter of Zeus, spring from Zeus' head in full armor? We know what you think about coincidences....

This was the most fun (and most work) we have ever had when reading books. No matter how many times we read them, or how many clues we had already spotted, we somehow couldn't put them down (maybe we'd better inform Mr. Weasley's department). Even when re-reading a passage for the twelfth time, we were still getting so caught-up in the dialog and writing that we'd forget we were supposed to be paying attention to clues! At this rate, we're going to need to borrow Dumbledore's glasses since our eyes are going buggy (of course, then there wouldn't be any more mystery, would there?).

The primary author, Galadriel, started this guide over a year ago when she was out of work (you can relate to that). She saw that fans were eager to ferret out more clues while they waited for the next book. Yet they were usually unaware of your maze of devious hints still hiding in what they already had - if only they knew where to look (tell Ariadne we need more thread). Your plan is working - the more we uncover, the more thrilling it becomes. When we discuss these clues with other fans, they get soooo excited, and go running back to your books to re-read them all! You left us with a lot more homework than we had realized, didn't you? Glad you left us with more time!

We are your fans, and we hope that you will appreciate the good intentions of our analysis (including the parodies). To quote a couple of our fellow fans from Linlithgow,* "Please don't kill us."

* http://www.whitten.demon.co.uk/potter/main.htm

INTRODUCTION

Are you starting to quiver like Quirrell from waiting for the fifth Harry Potter book to hit the shelves? Well, we can help you!

Did you know that you really haven't finished reading the first four books? J.K. Rowling has stated in interviews that she purposely writes books that "the reader won't necessarily get completely on the first reading."* The Harry Potter series is actually an Epic Mystery, and there's still a lot more fun and secret clues hiding in the pages than you probably ever imagined! Do you know how to look for those clues? Her books are packed with so many subtleties in the form of puns, satire, puzzles, and mysteries of epic proportion, that even those who have read them multiple times will confirm that they get even better *if you know what to look for!*

This Guide will show you what you missed when you read any of the books the first time(s). You will find easy-to-understand explanations for mysterious events and discover that very little of J.K. Rowling's text is there just for establishing characters or scenery. Seemingly insignificant comments or descriptions are often key clues buried within linguistic tricks and parodies. Of course, J.K.R. will also "play" with us too, so it is often difficult to figure out if she has a hidden meaning, or if she is just giving us a smokescreen. It's a literary "trick or treat."

You say you've read the stories so long ago that they are starting to get fuzzy in your brain? We provide summaries of the mystery elements as we discuss the first four Harry Potter books. Therefore, you can use this as a reference to help locate specific clues in the original books, or to refresh your memory of the unsolved mysteries before the next exciting volume hits the shelves!

Whether you have read only the *Philosopher's (Sorcerer's) Stone,* or the entire series many times, it is difficult to catch all the allusions. This Guide:

* clearly explains complex concepts which many readers find confusing,

* adds new insights to ponder for those who are already experts at trying to solve J.K.R.'s riddles, and

* brings out cauldronfuls of J.K.R.'s hints about the rest of the books.

You will find yet more excitement in the Harry Potter septology as you discover what she still has hiding up her sleeve!

For instance: In chapter 16 of Book 1, J. K. Rowling writes that Harry "watched an owl flutter toward the school across the bright blue sky, a note clamped in its mouth." Even after reading the book several times, it still catches readers by surprise when they realize that this note was the message used to trick Headmaster Dumbledore into leaving the school for a trip to London. That clue doesn't help us solve the plot of the book and it was never explained or mentioned again, but when we then see a similar clue in Book 4, we need to pay much closer attention! Look for yourself – it's awesome!

This Guide will unveil the Rowlinguistics of Harry Potter for you. You will have fun finding out what cool information she has camouflaged within her text, and discovering how to best sleuth a Harry Potter story for the most enjoyment. How good an HP Sleuth™ are you? Take a look....

Interview with the Sydney Morning Herald

SPECIAL NOTE: For those who have not yet read the whole Harry Potter series – this Guide is organized chronologically by book and chapter, so it does NOT give away any plot elements before J.K.R., herself, does.

SPOILER WARNING

Even though we have very carefully avoided exposing the plot in advance, this is a mystery plot analysis. Therefore, whenever something is revealed, we discuss it (disclosing patterns), and when we get to the ending, we openly talk about it!

Just like with any storybook, do not turn to the ending if you are not ready to read it!

In the Restricted Area: Future plot probabilities and speculations about the ending to the whole series are discussed – based on known information and existing clues.

TABLE OF CONTENTS

WWP HELP DESK

ᕹ What is an Ultimate Unofficial Mystery Guide? (...and What is an "HP Sleuth"™?)

ᕹ When Should I Read this Guide?

ᕹ What is a Septology?

ᕹ What do the Odd-Sounding Names and Words Mean (and What is a Rowlinguistic?)

ᕹ What is the Location of Hogwarts and Other Places Mentioned in the Magical World?

ᕹ Why Must We Wait So Long for J.K.R.'s Next Book?

ᕹ How Reliable is the Information in this Guide?

ᕹ How Was the First Movie ("Harry Potter and the Philosopher's/Sorcerer's Stone") Different from the Book?

What is an Ultimate Unofficial Mystery Guide?
(...and What is an "HP Sleuth"™?)

THIS IS NOT A CHEAT BOOK to give away or help skip over any parts of the original stories – in fact, you will probably find yourself going back to re-read in disbelief what you missed the first time! The plots are discussed chronologically in order to reveal at each point only what the author has revealed. The primary objective of this Guide is to show readers how to look for the hidden clues, and then have fun speculating about what will really happen.

This is an Unofficial "Mystery Guide," to the Harry Potter™ stories by *Wizarding World Press*. It is not authorized by J. K. Rowling, Warner Bros., Bloomsbury Publishing, or Scholastic Inc.. Nonetheless, since we like what they have done for us fans, we hope that this Guide will create new excitement for Harry Potter (plus new book and merchandise sales), when everyone discovers the truly sophisticated mystery hiding in the Harry Potter stories.

The Harry Potter septology is an Epic Mystery and is considerably more intricate than it appears. This Guide specifically highlights these *mystery* aspects, including all of the puzzles and brain-teasers that J. K. Rowling has painstakingly hidden within her story line. She has divulged that she purposely concealed clues along the way, and challenges us readers (we call ourselves "**HP Sleuths**"™) to discover them.

Use this Guide as a quick refresher of the clues, or to investigate the mystery in depth. It goes through each of J.K.R.'s books, chronologically, giving a quick summary of the mystery plots as it explains complex events, and analyzes as many of the story-line and septology clues as WWP has been able to identify (can you find more?).

The goal of this Guide is to show HP Sleuths what to look for since there are so many clever references that can slip by us (even on a third or fourth reading!). This Guide does not presume to have answers for anything that has not yet been published. Its purpose is to present reliable evidence in order to generate entertaining discussions. We encourage HP Sleuths to use this as a starting point for new theories and debates.

From the moment you uncover your first hidden clue, you will see how much fun it is being an HP Sleuth. *The HP Sleuth Club*™ *is now in Session!*

When Should I Read This Guide?

Whether this is the first time you will be reading J. K. Rowling's books, or after you have already read the books several times, you will find that there are many good times to use this Guide:

As You Are Reading One of the Harry Potter Books

Reference this Guide chapter-by-chapter, as you read each book. You will really enjoy the way it brings out all of the clever allusions and greatly enhances your reading experience. That way, you won't have to go looking for the book each time we mention something you've missed.

When You Have Just Finished Reading a Harry Potter Book

It's great to go through this Guide when you've read one of the Harry Potter books and want to see if you picked up on everything. (Don't blame us if you end up wanting to read the book all over again!) Of course, once you've read one of the Harry Potter books, this Guide helps so much to make sure you are totally prepared before going on to the next book.

Before the New Harry Potter Book Comes Out

This Guide is really handy when you need a refresher, or if you've forgotten about the books for awhile and want to remember all the subtleties. We provide a summary of the mystery as well as highlighting critical hints that will impact the rest of the septology. Not only does it help to refresh the clues, but keeps your sleuthing skills sharp for Book 5.

If you have worn out your HP Books and Have Started on Your Sister's Copies

If you're an HP Super-Sleuth™ already and want to research all your hunches, this is the Guide for you! It's a perfect reference while you wait for Book 5 – and much better than chewing on Ron's sheets....

This Guide is not intended as an alternate for J.K. Rowling's wonderful works, and is far less enjoyable if you do not actually experience J.K.R.'s ingenious writing style and see the passages that we reference. It is recommended that you either read her books first or concurrently with this Guide.

The Harry Potter series is a mystery, and in order to have the most fun with a mystery, it is best to have all the characters, clues, and key references ready and top-of-mind. Yet, with an epic mystery of this magnitude, it is difficult to absorb it all – let alone remember everything that happened 1,500 pages ago! Using this Guide, you can get quickly back up to speed from the plot summaries while learning to become an HP Super Sleuth!

What is a Septology?

There are many well-known three-volume series called "trilogies." According to J. K. Rowling, the Harry Potter stories will span a seven-volume series. As it is clearly an aggregate work (**not** just sequels), we decided we don't want to keep calling this simply a seven-volume series, therefore, we are calling it a *septology*. We think it deserves that recognition.

What do the Odd-Sounding Names and Words Mean?
(and What is a Rowlinguistic?)

If you have ever come across a name, magic spell, or other word in J. K. Rowling's books and said to yourself "Gee, this sounds like the word......," then you have encountered a Rowlinguistic. Many times those strange names and words in the Harry Potter books have been made up by J.K.R. from French, Latin, or other derivations. It is no coincidence that the names seem to relate directly to the personality of the character or the purpose of a spell.

Some Rowlinguistics are straight-forward, such as her spell to extinguish a wand light is "Nox," which means *night* or *darkness* in Latin. However, others are more subtle and contain secret clues, such as the name of Mrs. Figg (the crazy old lady with all the cats who babysat Harry). It is obvious that her name comes from the word "fig" or "fig leaf," but one of the definitions of a fig is "not literal" (meaning what you see **isn't** what you get), plus a fig leaf is used to "conceal or camouflage." That could be a clue about that character.

J.K.R.'s books are full of Rowlinguistics. We will only give background on names which relate to the mysteries, however, HP Sleuths can have fun figuring out all the other meanings of names and spells – they all seem to have significance!

What is the Location of Hogwarts and Other Places
Mentioned in the Magical World?

J. K. Rowling does not want to say where many of the places in her story are specifically located. That may be because it impacts the mystery, although it is more likely that she prefers to leave it non-specific (wizards are sensitive about making things like that public, you see).

Why Must We Wait So Long for J.K.R.'s Next Book?

Once you have read this Guide, you will start to understand the immense complexity and brilliance of J. K. Rowling's works. It will help you to gain a perspective about why it takes so long for her to write these masterpieces. Almost every sentence is there to hide a clue. J.K.R. makes use of multiple techniques (character names, dialogue, scenery, etc.) in order to imbed hints in each and every paragraph about both the immediate plot, as well as the whole septology. Since this Guide exposes those techniques, HP Sleuths can now see and appreciate the astounding detail that goes into just one of J.K.R.'s stories. You will never again question "why so long," but instead, marvel at how fast!

If we demand that J.K.R. put out books too quickly, then she may have to sacrifice the best part – the subtle mystery clues. Therefore, it is really good for us readers that she has taken the time to focus on Book 5 and beyond (even if we are "shivering with anticipation"). It should be an awesome masterpiece!

How Reliable is the Information in this Guide?

Even though this is an unauthorized Guide, all observations are based solely on what J. K. Rowling has written in her books (#1-4 and *Comic Relief*), what is contained on the *Bloomsbury* Web site (www.bloomsbury.com), the *Scholastic* website (www.scholastic.com), the *Warner Bros.* website (www.harrypotter.com), and/or what has been personally stated by J.K.R. in public interviews.

Accuracy and supported evidence are highly valued by *Wizarding World Press*.

Please remember - we are not revealing any proprietary information as all our insights are strictly from careful literary detective work on her published works.

How Was the First Movie ("Harry Potter and the Philosopher's/Sorcerer's Stone") Different from the Book?

This was a difficult movie to make successfully. In addition to all the special effects that were needed, it is a very demanding story line since it spans the complete realm of genres. The Movie captured the awesome characters, atmosphere, action, adventure, humor, and even the realism of the magical world incredibly well. We really liked the Movie (we saw it multiple times and we bought the video!).

The movie, however, could not possibly capture all the nuances while being true to the book and have a running time under 5 hours. Due to theatrical constraints, there are two elements the film was not able to capture: the more complex emotions motivating the characters, and the incredibly complex mystery. The screenwriter and director did not attempt to get into the highly intricate mystery. Therefore, it is important to realize that the movie had to omit or change some things that are specific to the mystery aspects of the stories.

In certain cases when we felt that the movie made a strong impression where information was altered that would impact the mystery, we mentioned the discrepancies. Otherwise, we liked the movie the way it was - so enjoy the movie for it's wonderful action, adventure, and atmosphere, and let us guide you through the mystery.

See you at the opening of the next movie!

How to Read This Guide *(Very Carefully)* ☺
(WWP Help Desk)

Navigating this Guide

This Guide is clearly organized for easy comprehension of both Plot & Analysis sections.

If you need a quick review of the mystery plot elements...
...you can skim through the plot notes to find what you need.

If you just want to read the mystery analysis...
...you can do that easily – the analysis is clearly identified and highly entertaining.

If you want the whole exciting experience...
...you can sit back and enjoy every word of this not-so-brief (but definitely-cool)
Wizarding World Press' Ultimate Unofficial Guide to the Mysteries of Harry Potter.

SPOILER WARNING

Even though we have very carefully avoided exposing the plot in advance,
this is a mystery plot analysis. Therefore, whenever something is revealed,
we discuss it (disclosing patterns), and when we get to the ending, we openly
talk about it!

Just like with any storybook, do not turn to the ending if you are not ready to read it!

In the Restricted Area: Future plot probabilities and speculations about the
ending to the whole series are discussed – based on known information and
existing clues.

A Clue About Clues

There are two kinds of clues that can be found in the Harry Potter books:

A story-line clue - which is specific to the book in which it is found.
An example of this is that Harry's scar hurts at certain times during Book 1.

A septology clue - which is not resolved by the end of the book. That kind of
clue relates to the whole seven-volume mystery, and will not be revealed by
J.K.R. until after Book 4 (the current HP book as of the time of this writing). An
example of this is the secret behind why Voldemort wanted to kill Harry even
though he was just a baby.

Abbreviations

Book Numbers

Throughout this Guide, to make the analysis easier (and to keep our typist sane), we will be referring to the Harry Potter books by number. Therefore, just in case, here is a cross-reference list of the books by title.

Book 1:   *Harry Potter and the Philosopher's (Sorcerer's) Stone*

Book 2:   *Harry Potter and the Chamber of Secrets*

Book 3:   *Harry Potter and the Prisoner of Azkaban*

Book 4:   *Harry Potter and the Goblet of Fire*

Book 5:   *[Harry Potter and the Order of the Phoenix]* (unreleased)

J.K.R.

J. K. Rowling's name is quite short (as authors' names go); however, given the number of times we reference her name, we will use her initials (J.K.R.). We mean no disrespect with this abbreviation. We hope you understand, Ms. Rowling.

WWP

This is us. This is also what is called an acronym. It stands for *"Wizarding World Press"* – the virtual pressroom where we spend real hours bringing you all these goodies.

HP SLEUTH HOME PAGE

The WWP Magical Toolkit

Toolkit Contents

HP Sleuths have some useful tools to help them as they read. In the spirit of J.K.R.'s own humor, we have had a little fun with satire for these. Here is your box of magical mechanisms:

* **The HP Hintoscope** – This is a very delicate device that detects J.K.R.'s hints and clues about the story-line plot. When it gets near an important hint, the HP Hintoscope makes a noise to alert HP Sleuths that a hint is being detected. The more annoying it gets, the bigger the clue.

* **The WWP Sleuthoscope** – This is a super sensitive sensor that can sniff-out cleverly disguised Septology clues. It alerts by flashing and various motions. The brighter it gets and the faster it moves, the greater the Septology implications.

* **The WWP Rememberit** – This is a really remarkable recording quill. It automatically transcribes all key clues and brain ticklers (Rememberits), and annoys us with rude reminders until we solve them.

HP Sleuth Suggested Supplies & Recommended Reading

* WWP Toolkit

* HP Sleuth detective quill and parchment -12 rolls (or an official Harry Potter notebook)

* Textbook: *Fantastic Beasts and Where to Find Them*, by Newt Scamander

* Background Reading: *Quidditch Through the Ages*, by Kennilworthy Whisp

* At least one of the Harry Potter books:

    Book 1 - *Harry Potter and the Philosopher's (Sorcerer's) Stone*

    Book 2 - *Harry Potter and the Chamber of Secrets*

    Book 3 - *Harry Potter and the Prisoner of Azkaban*

    Book 4 - *Harry Potter and the Goblet of Fire*

* Mythology, Alternate Reality, and Classic Literature Resources:

    ◦ *The Hobbit and The Lord of the Rings*, by J.R.R. Tolkien

    ◦ *Chronicles of Narnia*, by C. S. Lewis

    ◦ *Wizard of Oz*, by L. Frank Bauhm

    ◦ *Alice in Wonderland*, by Lewis Carroll

- ☾ Shakespeare's Plays

- ☾ *Dr. Who* TV Series (Tom Baker as the Doctor – Adric companion)

- ☾ *Wizards*, animated film by Ralph Bakshi

- ☾ *Star Trek, Deep Space Nine* TV Series

- ☾ *Nancy Drew* mysteries, by Carolyn Keene

- ☾ Jane Austen's novels

- ☾ *The Iliad* and *The Odyssey*, by Homer

- ☾ Mythology references by Irad Milkin, Michael Grant & John Hazel, and Edith Hamilton

✳ Hermione's favorite tools - the biggest (and heaviest) English-language dictionary (preferably International) that you can find, and a reference library.

✳ (Optional) – The Harry Potter TCG (Trading Card Game) by a company with truly awesome people (don't tell them we said that), Wizards of the Coast (www.wizardsofthecoast.com)

Special Request to HP Sleuths

The key word is "respect." Some people prefer to be surprised. If you are captivated by mysteries and puzzles, you may not understand those who are not interested in the mystery aspects of Harry Potter, but at least respect them. Please do NOT discuss or post these or your own clever theories about what might happen in the future with those people who don't wish to try guessing in advance. There are plenty of us HP Sleuths out here who like to dig for clues, so only reveal insights to those who want to know. We certainly are willing to discuss them with you. www.wizardingworldpress.com

Secrets of the HP Super Sleuth

(HP Sleuth Home Page)

WWP's Rules of Constant Vigilance

We have uncovered the "secret" to being an HP Super Sleuth. If you want to consider yourself a good HP Sleuth, there are 4 rules to keep in mind about the way J.K. Rowling writes:

Rule #1

IF SHE REINFORCES IT, SHE MEANS IT – HP Sleuths need to focus on these kind of clues. Like everyone else, J.K.R. is not flawless, and she has made a few minor errors in her books. Unfortunately, a few people may try to put special meaning on those or use those to debunk her intentional, masterful clues. The general rule here is to ignore conflicting or a one-time questionable reference. However, if she repeats a reference/clue (no matter how subtle), she means for us to take it seriously. We do.)

Rule #2

IF SHE SUDDENLY INTERRUPTS SOMETHING, SHE'S HIDING A KEY CLUE! – What was that? If Harry misses a lesson, if a character gets cut off while saying something, or even if someone forgets to ask a question, it's probably because we are being tormented by J.K.R. HP Sleuths should take note that if we know that we missed out on something, it is almost as good as knowing the information itself – especially if you like mysteries.

Rule #3

THERE'S NO SUCH THING AS A COINCIDENCE - When a character conveniently shows up at the right time (or wrong time), or when the same topic keeps mysteriously popping up over and over, it is a clue begging for attention. In her magical world, J.K.R. has put a high emphasis on fate, plus there is often a good reason why things that look like coincidences happen. Yet, she also has a mischievous sense of humor, so HP Sleuths have to work hard to also avoid the red herrings. Often, her red herrings are just incomplete clues, so that if we pick up on all the "real" clues, we find that she has actually given us enough information to sort it out accurately.

Rule #4

DON'T TAKE A CHARACTER'S WORD FOR IT - Characters often interpret events for us in her books. That is what characters are supposed to do. However, their analysis will be colored by their own personality and their particular perspective of the events. Just because the character has an explanation does not mean it is correct. J.K.R. constantly uses this technique to throw us off the trail, and a good HP Sleuth must be wary of that trick.

CONSTANT VIGILANCE! ☺

The Pocket Version

WWP's Rules of Constant Vigilance

Never let your guard down with J.K.R.

These are The Rules to remember for HP Sleuths:

1) If she reinforces it, she means it (and wants us to remember it).

2) If she suddenly interrupts something, she's hiding a key clue!

3) There's no such thing as a coincidence.

4) Don't take a character's word for it.

BOOK 1 MYSTERIES

About Book 1

Statistics

Book 1 Title - *Harry Potter and the Philosopher's Stone*
aka *Harry Potter and the Sorcerer's Stone* - by J. K. Rowling

Facts & Statistics:
- First U.S. Printing, October, 1998
- First British Printing, June 30, 1997
- Date J. K. Rowling started writing - 1990
- Published in the United Kingdom by Bloomsbury
- Bloomsbury paid $10,000 for *Harry Potter and the Philosopher's Stone*
- Published in the United States by Scholastic, Inc
- Scholastic paid $105,000 for *Harry Potter and the Sorcerer's Stone*

Awards & Records:
- Nestlé Smarties Gold Medal Book Prize (9-11years), 1997
- Birmingham Cable Children's Book Award 1997
- Young Telegraph Paperback of the Year 1998
- National Book Award - Children's Book of the Year 1997
- Sheffield Children's Book Award 1998
- Parenting Book of the Year, 1998
- New York Public Library Best Book of the Year, 1998
- FCBG (Federation of Children's Books Group) Children's Book Award -
  Overall winner and in Longer Novel Category, 1997
- ALA Notable Book
- *New York Times* Bestseller
- *USA Today* Bestseller
- *Booklist* Editor's Choice

Movie Stats:
- Warner Bros. signed contract: October, 1998
- Movie Release date: November 16, 2001

Theatre/Box Office
- US film revenue $317 million ($216.6 million)
- UK film revenue $64 million ($93.5 million)
- World film revenue $649 million ($926 million)

Video
- Video (VHS/DVD) sold 1.6 million copies in the first month
- Fastest selling DVD in UK history
- 2nd biggest selling DVD in UK history
- HP DVD release responsible for 280% spike in UK DVD player sales

Key Mystery Characters

STUDENTS
Crabbe (Slytherin)
Seamus Finnegan   (Gryffindor)
Marcus Flint (Slytherin)
Hermione Granger   (Gryffindor)
Lee Jordan   (Gryffindor)
Neville Longbottom   (Gryffindor)
Draco Malfoy (Slytherin)
Harry Potter   (Gryffindor)
Dean Thomas   (Gryffindor)
Goyle (Slytherin)
Fred Weasley   (Gryffindor)
George Weasley   (Gryffindor)
Percy Weasley   (Gryffindor)
Ron Weasley   (Gryffindor)
Oliver Wood   (Gryffindor)

RELATIVES
Cousin Dudley Dursley
Aunt Petunia Dursley
Uncle Vernon Dursley
Longbottom Relative – Neville's Gran
James Potter
Lily Potter
Charlie Weasley
Ginny Weasley
Mrs. Weasley

TEACHERS & STAFF
Prof. Binns (History of Magic)
Prof. Albus Dumbledore (Headmaster)
Argus Filch (Caretaker)
Prof. Flitwick (Charms)
Rubeus Hagrid (Groundskeeper/
Keeper of the Keys)
Madam Hooch (Flying Instructor/
Quidditch Referee)
Prof. Minerva McGonagall
(Deputy Headmistress/Transfiguration)
Madam Pince (Librarian)
Madam Pomfrey (Nurse)
Prof. Quirrell (Defense against the Dark Arts)
Prof. Severus Snape (Potions Master)
Prof. Sprout (Herbology)

OTHER HUMANS
Lord Voldemort ("You-Know-Who")
Mr. Ollivander
Mrs. Figg
Nicolas Flamel

CREATURES & ENTITIES
Bloody Baron (Slytherin Ghost)
Fang the boarhound
Fat Friar (Hufflepuff Ghost)
Fat Lady Portrait
Firenze, Ronan, & Bane the Centaurs
Fluffy the dog
Hedwig the owl
Sir Nicolas de Mimsy-Porpington
(see Nearly-Headless Nick)
Nearly-Headless Nick (Gryffindor Ghost)
Norbert the dragon
Mrs. Norris the cat
Peeves the Poltergeist
Scabbers the rat
Trevor the toad

Bits and Rememberits

These are tidbits that HP Sleuths should keep in mind as they read Book 1. Keep alert for more evidence....

Interesting Tidbits

Why Are There Two Names for This Book/Movie?

J. K. Rowling's title for her first book (released initially in Britain) was "Harry Potter and the Philosopher's Stone." In the United States, the word "Philosopher" conjures up images of boring, stuffy old men, while a Sorcerer is an exciting Merlin-type wizard. The problem is, the Stone was supposed to have truly existed, and it was called the "Philosopher's Stone," but most people did not know about that. Therefore, J.K.R. and her American publisher came up with the cool name "Sorcerer's Stone" for the U.S. printing.

The first book also was "translated" somewhat for U.S. readers because they would not have understood or related to some British terms. For instance, the British "Mum" was translated to "Mom" and "jumper" became "sweater." Now, however, the texts have been "unified" by making slight adjustments only when necessary so that all words are understandable to U.S. and British readers. For instance, in Book 4, both versions now use "sweater," while "dustbins" (which is not difficult to figure out) is used in both editions rather than changing it to "trash cans" for U.S. readers. From now on, of course, the titles will also be the same in both countries.

What HP Sleuths Have to Notice in Book 1

J.K. Rowling gives new meaning to "reading between the lines." She makes up many of her characters' names, explaining in a chat on *Barnes and Noble* how her use of foreign language-based words "gives readers a chance to work out clues along the way." Her books are so meticulously written that almost no word is there just for conversation. Even the most sublime comments and/or descriptions often hold special meanings – and usually keys to the whole septology mystery! J.K.R. uses running bits, comic relief, satire, and literary techniques to enhance her stories, but the joke's on us, as her comedy can be used to throw us off track or camouflage those important clues. HP Sleuths – CONSTANT VIGILANCE !

WWP's Rules of Constant Vigilance!

Never let your guard down with J.K.R. These are The Rules to remember for HP Sleuths:

1) **If she reinforces it, she means it (and wants us to remember it).**
2) **If she suddenly interrupts something, she's hiding a key clue!**
3) **There's no such thing as a coincidence.**
4) **Don't take a character's word for it.**

(see WWP Help Desk FAQs for full explanation)

Clues

The story takes place just outside London, England, at the home of the Dursleys, a very "normal" family. Vernon Dursley is a Director at Grunnings, a drill manufacturer, and he lives with his wife, Petunia, at number four, Privet Drive – a very normal street....

> ...Or so they think. Looks can be deceiving. "Normal" can be deceiving. Even names can be deceiving! This very first sentence of the first book contains a double-entendre (double meaning) that appears to be a clue to the mystery. The seemingly innocent word, privet, is a typical *Rowlinguistic*. "Privet" means an *ornamental shrub*, which perfectly describes the appearance of the neatly-pruned, hedge-lined street. However, in French (which J.K. Rowling taught), Privet would be pronounced like "privé" meaning *confidential* or *private life*. That is a grand clue, since Privet Drive is hiding many septology secrets that are yet to unfold, and the trail begins here...

Vernon Dursley had a (mostly) normal day at work, but there have been very unusual events going on all over the country, and especially here at Privet Drive – where two people are meeting at midnight. A cat that has been lurking around the house transforms into Professor Minerva McGonagall. She greets Professor Albus Dumbledore, who has silently materialized out of thin air. Dumbledore uses a Put-Outer to magically extinguish the 12 surrounding street lamps, concealing their abnormal presence.

> Can you imagine if the Dursleys had seen all that! Hope you HP Sleuths saw that number twelve. J.K. Rowling has fun with numerology (arithmancy) in her stories. She uses the traditional superstitious numbers (7,13) to designate key items and events. Since 12 is a number that is not usually considered superstitious, there is something very important about the number twelve that will happen in the future. This is a clue – but it is more like a destiny. The event is being foretold with every mention – it is as if we cannot escape that number. (Shudder)

Professor Dumbledore has long white hair and beard, bright blue eyes, and a crooked nose, on which he wears half-moon glasses. He checks his watch, which has 12 hands and looks more like a miniature orrery than a clock.

> There are actually a number of themes that span the whole septology. Noses, eyes ears, fingers, and other body parts seem to have significance. Clocks and watches are also winding up in the Harry Potter stories all the time. In this passage, they appear to be related to the predictions of twelve, but that is not definite elsewhere. Clocks are the timepieces of destiny, and are something that HP Sleuths need to watch!

As Dumbledore pulls out a sherbet lemon drop, he tells Professor McGonagall why he is here at Private Drive.

> This small, seemingly insignificant candy is actually a key to understanding Professor Dumbledore and the overall message of the Harry Potter series. Although sherbet lemon drops are not wizard food, Dumbledore eats them because he likes them. Dumbledore likes and respects what is good – no matter what its origin. Remember his affinity for sherbet lemon drops and other non-magical things.

Dumbledore is waiting for the delivery of a one year-old baby boy named Harry Potter. The Dursleys are to receive that surprise bundle on their doorstep (along with a note from Dumbledore). Harry is the son of James and Lily Potter (Petunia Dursley's sister). Although the Dursleys know the Potters have a son, his approximate age, and even his name, they have never seen Harry. This is because the Potters were a real witch and wizard, and the Dursleys do not associate with their type (even paranoid that someone else might find out). Tragically, the Potters were murdered the previous night by a Dark Wizard, and Harry is now an orphan.

> For some reason, even though the tragedy took place the previous night, Harry Potter is just now being delivered to the Dursleys. This timeframe is unaccounted for, is not explained by J.K. Rowling (as of Book 4), and is a favorite debate by those who are convinced that J.K.R. never does **anything** without a reason. Could it have just been a very long trip from wherever they lived, or did Privet Drive have to be secured before bringing Harry there? Is it possible the baby Harry received some special spells and protection during that period before being delivered? If this seems a bit picky to you, you will soon see that J.K.R.'s writing is so detailed that no information is too trivial or too subtle to be ignored. HP Sleuths – CONSTANT VIGILANCE!

The Dark wizard (Lord Voldemort) had terrorized the magical community for 11 years and was so feared, that he is only referred to as "You-Know-Who" (or "He-Who-Must-Not-Be-Named"). However, the Potter's one-year-old son, Harry, had miraculously survived the lethal attack at their home in Godric's Hollow, so he is being left at the Dursleys – who Dumbledore says are his only remaining relatives. Professor McGonagall has been watching the Dursleys all day and is alarmed, but Dumbledore insists that Harry should grow up shielded from his unintentional fame.

> This little issue about why Voldemort found it so important to kill the infant Harry is THE mystery around which the whole Harry Potter septology revolves. That subject alone can keep an Internet Discussion Board busy for twelve months. Everyone knew that Voldemort is after the Potters, however, the Potters must have been more than just enemies – as Voldemort was focused on killing their baby Harry. So why was Voldemort so intent on killing him? We are sure that J.K. Rowling will be keeping us guessing on that one until the final book – but she is teasing us with all sorts of clues! The small reference to Godric's Hollow is even a clue, and it is prowling the pages of this mystery.

Professors Dumbledore and McGonagall hear the sound of an engine from the sky as Hagrid, a giant man, arrives on a flying motorcycle. Whereas Professor McGonagall questions the integrity of such a character, Dumbledore emphatically states that he would "trust Hagrid with his life."

> A woman who can turn into a cat questions the integrity of someone who rides a flying motorcycle? Well, Hagrid is as loyal as a big, fluffy dog, and he always carries out Dumbledore's instructions precisely. It is highly likely that we need to remember just how much Dumbledore trusts Hagrid

Hagrid lands, with Harry wrapped in blankets in his arms. Hagrid tells Dumbledore how he got Harry out of the Potters' almost-destroyed house just before the Muggles (non-magical people) came to investigate.

> Now that's timing. How did Hagrid get there so soon? How did Dumbledore know about the attack on the Potters, and how did Dumbledore contact Hagrid so quickly? We need to be educated by the Professor.

Harry was the first ever to survive an attack by Voldemort. He had not only repelled the *Killing Curse*, but had somehow deflected it right back to the evil wizard, defeating him instead. That ended Voldemort's eleven-year reign of terror, which is being celebrated by wizards everywhere. The assault, however, had destroyed the home and left a lightning-shaped scar on the infant's forehead where the spell had hit him.

> The fact that the house was destroyed in the massacre is actually quite odd as Voldemort supposedly was only on a murder mission. It is reinforced later, so we know that the house was, indeed, damaged, but since this is J.K.R., we must not make assumptions as to what (or who) caused it.

Professor McGonagall wants Dumbledore to remove the nasty scar, but Dumbledore thinks the scar could be useful, as he has one of his own above his knee in the shape of the London Underground.

> If you can't easily see how a scar can be useful either, then you now have witnessed the eccentric personality of Albus Dumbledore. Does Dumbledore know something about this scar? Would it be a means of identification, or a badge of courage? Knowing Dumbledore, he could be jesting about his own scar, although that could be useful in an emergency. It should be noted that the famous Odysseus (Ulysses) of Greek mythology fame also had a scar just above his knee – used to identify him as the legitimate king upon his return home from the Trojan War.

Hagrid takes off to return the bike to Sirius Black, Professor McGonagall transforms and slinks off on all fours, and Professor Dumbledore disappears with a swish of his cloak. A gentle breeze blows across the hedges of Privet Drive.

> Sirius is an interesting name. There is a very bright star called that. Seems like

a nice guy as he let Hagrid borrow his bike. Gentle breezes are also very interesting – are those just the wind?

The Dursleys already have a 1-year old son, Dudley, and are as non-magical as can be (the ultimate Muggles). In a cruel twist of fate for everyone, they now have become the legal guardians of their famously magical nephew. They are extremely upset about having to care for and support yet another child – especially a child of "freaks."

The Dursleys aren't really mean, they're just personality-challenged... (Not). It is this very intolerant, close-minded attitude that causes friction among Muggles as well as wizards. So what's Petunia's problem anyway? Her sister was a witch, so why would she be so intolerant of wizards? There is a lot more to this family than we see here....

Oblivious in his new environment, the baby Harry Potter does not even know how to talk yet, but he is already a celebrity in the Wizarding World.

Rowlinguistics

✴ **Potter**? Interesting choice of name for an author who told us in interviews that her first book (age 6) was called *Rabbit*. A very famous Potter in England was Beatrix Potter, an exceptional woman who wrote the *Peter Rabbit* stories. She was an artist, a nature scientist, and conservationist. Potter was also the name of J.K.R.'s childhood friends. The word "Potter" relates to a *potters field* (a burial ground) for people of unknown identity and without money, and Harry is seemingly a penniless orphan.

✴ The definition of "harry" means to *assault* or *torment*. Guess if you're Voldemort, that's appropriate. The name **"Harry"** is also a nickname for *Henry*. Without further clues, there are too many Henrys or Harrys to be able to speculate if there is any significance to that. We did learn in a J.K.R. interview with Scholastic that Harry's middle name is *James* - after his father. Do any HP Sleuths have a theory?

10

- **Albus Dumbledore** (who is presumably intended to resemble Merlin and/or J.R.R. Tolkien's Gandalf) has an interesting name. His first name, Albus, is Latin for *white* – a tribute to his silvery hair and beard. According to a J.K.R. interview with Lindsey Fraser in *Conversations with J.K. Rowling*, his last name comes from an olde English word *bumblebee*, which J.K.R. said she chose because she likes to think of him "always on move, humming to himself." (We also know those busy bees have stingers if threatened....)

- For **Minerva McGonagall**'s name, J.K.R. uses alliteration, a technique she obviously likes a lot. Minerva is the Roman name for *Athena*, the Greek goddess of learning, wisdom, war, and crafts. Athena also just happens to have a famed reputation for morphing herself and others into clever disguises. Her symbols are the owl and the olive tree. We can assume that Minerva McGonagall is intelligent and a formidable opponent, and she is likely to be proud of her clan.

- **Petunia**'s name is that of a flower. Petunias represent *anger* and *resentment* (guess that's a hint!).

- **Lily**'s name is also from a flower, but is associated with *purity* or *fragility*. Some lilies bloom only for a short time (sniff), and some lilies grow on water. J.K.R. has now revealed in an interview with Scholastic that Lily's maiden name was *Evans* (snave backwards).

- A very popular **James** in Britain is King James, who is famous for uniting England and Scotland. Could James Potter somehow be responsible for re-uniting the wizards?

- In the French translation of Book 1, non-wizard humans are called "**Moldu**." Do any HP Sleuths know what the play-on-words or intended translation of that might be?

Curiosities

- In Britain, there is a lemon candy called a "sherbet lemon." Since most U.S. readers did not know what those are, Dumbledore's Muggle treats were called "lemon drops" in the U.S. version the first two books. By Book 4, all versions used *sherbet lemon*. To help with confusion, we use the name *"sherbet lemon drop."*

Other Oddities

- Ted, the TV newscaster, seemed like he might be aware of what was really happening with all the owls and odd sightings of stars, while the weatherman predicted rain (guess he was wrong?).

- Why was Hagrid flying over Bristol with Harry? Is that at all significant?

- The morning after Voldemort's demise, a "large tawny owl" flies by the Dursleys' window. Was that a convenient route, or is someone else getting an Owl Post in the Dursleys' neighborhood?

Chapter 2 Analysis

--- Clues ---

The story picks-up 10 years later, during Dudley's (Harry's cousin's) birthday. Dudley, had grown very large in all directions, and makes sport of punching Harry, who is a small, skinny kid. Dudley (the Dursleys "real" son) receives many presents, as usual, for his birthday – including a gold watch. Although Harry knows the date of his own birthday, the Dursleys never celebrated it, and he never received more than an old pair of socks or some other mean-spirited gift (and he doesn't even own a watch). In fact, Harry's clothes are all Dudley's baggy hand-me-downs.

> Socks are a *running bit* as well as another theme throughout the Harry Potter series. They usually carry positive (and humorous) connotations, but like the number 12 and watches, there seems to be a destiny for someone concerning socks. Harry eventually does manage to get himself a watch, but there was no specific mention of how he got his hands on it.

Harry has bright green eyes and black hair that won't grow neatly no matter what he does. The Dursleys treat Harry Potter as an abused step child "...like a slug." They detest his hair, using that as one of many excuses to belittle and mistreat him. The bedroom that they provide for him is a closet under the stairs – which he shares with the resident spiders. Harry has never been told the truth about the circumstances surrounding his parents' death, his own fame among magical people, or even that he, himself, is a wizard. He had been told that his parents died in a car crash, that he got the scar on his forehead from that crash, and that he is an unwelcome burden. Occasionally, Harry seems to have flash-backs to the fatal "accident" in which he remembers an intense green light, as well as some very odd dreams, but he is not allowed to ask questions.

> Well, avoiding questions is probably easier for a Dursley than trying to think up answers (hehe). Yet more running bits. Spiders, which are sometimes good and sometimes bad, and slugs, which J.K.R. has confirmed that she considers to be one of the epitomes of disgusting critters. Those spiders in Harry's cupboard may not be just ordinary spiders – you never know, since that's all part of the mystery in J.K.R.'s world.

Every year, the Dursleys take Dudley out somewhere special on his birthday, leaving Harry with "mad old" Mrs. Figg who lives two streets over. The Dursleys leave Harry behind both to keep Dudley happy, and to avoid "problems" from Harry. It seems that "strange things happen" whenever the Dursleys bring Harry out to public places.

> The word "fig" means *not literal,* and of course, a fig leaf is *something that conceals or camouflages.* What's going on with Mrs. Figg?

Harry really hates going over to Mrs. Figg's. Her house smells like cabbage and Harry is always forced to look at photos of her many cats (like Tibbles, Snowy, Mr. Paws, and

Tufty). This year, Mrs. Figg had broken her leg, so Harry ends up with a rare treat – being brought along to the zoo.

> Rowlinguistics tells us that Mrs. Figg is hiding a big secret. She probably has a much more interesting life than it appears on the surface. The dull, boring descriptions of her companion cats may yet turn out to be essential to the plot. Does Mrs. Figg want Harry to be able to easily recognize those cats for a specific reason? The most critical evidence here is a very tiny mention, but is probably a key clue to the septology – that Mrs. Figg's house smells like cabbage. HP Sleuths – sniff out those cabbage references – this is a potente clue!

While in the reptile house at the Zoo, Harry has a conversation with a boa constrictor. He finds out the snake is from Brazil, but had been bred in the zoo. Upon seeing the snake awake and moving, Dudley and his friend Piers Polkiss shove Harry to the floor to get a better look. Somehow, the glass partition on the front of the snake's tank vanishes, and among the panic, the snake slithers off – hissing "Thanksss amigo" to Harry as it heads off to see Brazil....

> Harry can talk to snakes, but there is no indication that he ever talked to a cat, dog, or other animal. Therefore, that seems to be a bit unique. In fact, it is a slippery clue to the entire septology. Harry clearly hears the snake thank him, and may be very glad he helped out this "amigo" when battling the Dark side!

Because of the snake "incident," Harry is again in big trouble with the Dursleys.

Rowlinguistics

* The French names of Mrs. Figg's cats seem to have some meaning. Did J.K.R. have input in those translations? Instead of a wintery name, **Snowy** becomes "Patounet," which seems to be a mutation of the phrase "not very clear/distinct (pas tous net)" **Tufty** becomes "Mignonette," which may refer to lace or ground pepper (?). More questions than answers.

Curiosities

✳ How does Harry know the date of his birthday? Did Aunt Petunia know? Did Dumbledore tell them?

Other Oddities

✳ Piers Polkiss is described as having "a face like a rat." J.K.R uses this rat-like appearance to depict a negative character profile.

✳ The *Harry Potter and the Philosopher's / Sorcerer's Stone* movie may have inadvertently given the impression that Harry had control over the vanishing glass at the Reptile House. In the books, wizarding children do not know how to focus their wizarding powers, and without a wand, their magic just sort of "slips out" only when they get highly emotional – such as when they get extremely upset or fearful. It's not conscious.

✳ We are being inundated by even the multiples of 12 and 13. The number of presents Dudley receives is 36, then 39. That is 3 x 12, then 3 x 13.

✳ We are a bit mystified as to why the movie changed the origin of the snake from Brazil to Borneo. The largest tree-dwelling boa does, indeed, come from Brazil, while Borneo is known for pythons, plus it is unlikely that anything from Borneo would speak Spanish. Anyone know why?

Chapter 3 Analysis

(THE LETTERS FROM NO ONE)

Clues

Harry is banished to his cupboard until summer (his worst punishment yet) for the boa constrictor incident. When he is finally released, he finds out that Dudley had run into Mrs. Figg with his racing bike as she was crossing Privet Drive on her crutches. Harry also gets some good news – that Dudley is being sent off to Uncle Vernon's old private alma mater, Smeltings, while Harry will be going on his own (yea!) to Stonewall High.

> Mrs. Figg seems to be around a lot. She does not live on Privet Drive, so was it just coincidence in this first book that she was the one hit by Dudley? (We're being hit by Rule #3.) Was she for some reason keeping a close watch on Harry who had been confined to his cupboard? Only the storyteller knows for sure.

One July morning, Harry receives a letter addressed to himself, "Mr. H. Potter, The Cupboard under the Stairs," bearing a lion, eagle, badger, and snake, in a coat of arms. However, before he has a chance to read his letter, Uncle Vernon confiscates it. Alarmed, Uncle Vernon moves Harry upstairs into Dudley's spare bedroom. Nonetheless, letters keep arriving addressed to Harry in "the Smallest Bedroom." The letters are even smuggled into the house inside eggs from the milkman, but Harry still does not have a chance to see who is writing to him or why.

> We have tried to imagine the strange sight of a letter stuffed inside each of those eggs (hope the gooey insides were removed first!). Is the milkman part of the conspiracy to contact Harry, or an innocent bystander?

They leave Harry in the upstairs bedroom, while Uncle Vernon boards up the mail slot and all the cracks around the doors. However, the letters start pouring out of the chimney, and Uncle Vernon is so spooked that he whisks the family off to a motel. Yet the letters somehow seem to follow. As a last resort, Uncle Vernon borrows a small boat from a "toothless old man," and rows them to a ramshackle cabin, atop a small island out in the sea. A huge thunderstorm rolls in. While Harry lies there in the cabin listening to the rain and thunder, it occurs to him that the next day would be his eleventh birthday, and watches the clock as it approaches midnight.

> Neither rain, nor sleet, nor Uncle Vernon can stop the Owl Post – this is really special delivery! This is also some storm. Wonder what it means? There are more clues ahead. HP Sleuths – hope you've got a long roll of parchment!

At midnight, a sudden loud knock on the remote cabin door breaks through the sounds of the storm.

Other Oddities

✳ The "toothless old man" who lent Uncle Dursley the boat is a bit reminiscent of Charon, the ferryman over the river Styx. Harry is, indeed, about to cross into a whole new world.

✳ This strange, persistent delivery method of the Letters has not been repeated in any of the books up to Book 4, so we know nothing of the magic behind it.

✳ We now have seen many references to 12, including a dozen, midnight, and 36. HP Sleuths might have fun going back to the book, itself, and seeing how many twelves they can spot.

✳

Chapter 4 Analysis

Clues

A gigantic man bursts into the Dursleys' remote cabin at the stroke of midnight on Harry's 11th birthday. The man hands Harry a birthday cake from out of his pocket, and introduces himself as "Rubeus Hagrid, Keeper of Keys and Grounds at Hogwarts." He remarks how Harry looks just like his dad, but has his mother's eyes.

> Does that mean Harry's mother also had green eyes? Is there anything else about her eyes that we should know?

Hagrid is upset when he finds out that the Dursleys never told Harry "anything" – especially that he's a wizard. Hagrid informs Harry how his parents really died when You-Know-Who (he's afraid to say Voldemort's name) attacked them on Halloween.

> For a wizard's holiday, Halloween certainly doesn't seem to be very lucky for Harry.

Hagrid tells how the Dark Wizard killed others too (the Bones, McKinnons, Prewetts), and how he "vanished." While some people think Voldemort died, Hagrid says that's "Codswallop."

> Hagrid is probably right. In French, the Dark wizard's name (vol de mort), means *flight from death*, as in robbing or depriving death, so Voldemort has no intention of dying. Some of the names of the murdered people that Hagrid mentions come up later. Like Harry, we would expect their children to be fearsome enemies of Voldemort.

Aunt Petunia admits that she knew all along that her sister, Lily (who would come home with pockets of frog spawn and changed teacups into rats), was a wizard. While their parents were proud of Lily, Petunia says she was the only one who "saw her for what she was – a freak!"

> But Lily was a nice freak.☺ Why were Lily's parents so proud of her being a witch – what did they know? Was either Lily or Petunia adopted? Where did Lily Potter get her magical heritage? If they are blood sisters, could Aunt Petunia possibly have some magical powers, but be in denial of them? Were Lily's parents truly Muggles, or were they hiding wizarding identities?? HP Sleuths are starting to see the complexity of the mystery that J.K.R. is brewing.

Hagrid finally delivers Harry's letter personally, which is an invitation to attend "Hogwarts," the most prestigious school for wizards. Hagrid explains that Albus Dumbledore, the Hogwarts Headmaster, had mentioned that he might have trouble gaining access to Harry.

Doesn't look to us like Hagrid would have trouble gaining access to anything.☺ How did Dumbledore know he'd have trouble? This is evidence that Dumbledore has somehow been keeping a very close watch on Harry at Privet Drive.

Hagrid tells Harry that while Voldemort was in power, the only person Voldemort had feared was Dumbledore. Hagrid explains that Voldemort wouldn't have dared to try taking control of the school, "not just then, anyway."

Ahem – we caught that "not just then" comment. Talk about ominous statements.... Why does Voldemort fear Dumbledore so much? It could be as simple as Dumbledore is an incredibly powerful and brilliant wizard (indeed), or it could be as obscure as there being a mysterious relationship between the two. Fantasy stories such as "Wizards," the movie by Ralph Bakshi, are famous for ultimate battles between the allies of two powerful brothers (one who has gone bad). No matter what the reason, Voldemort would like to seize Hogwarts. HP Sleuths – CONSTANT VIGILANCE!

When Uncle Vernon says that the school's revered headmaster is a "crackpot old fool," and that he will be teaching Harry "magic tricks," the loyal Hagrid loses his temper, pulls out a pink umbrella, and conjures a real pig's tail to sprout from the rear end of the porky Dudley. After performing the spell, Hagrid asks Harry not to mention it ("I shouldn'ta") – as Hagrid had gotten expelled from Hogwarts, and is not allowed to practice magic.

Why was Hagrid expelled from Hogwarts? Well, it certainly was not for lack of loyalty! Hagrid may look intimidating, but he is a very sensitive giant of a guy, whose fragile emotions can get away from him at times – usually causing him to break into tears. Emotions are Hagrid's weakness, and play an important role in all of the books' mysteries. This was just a "small" demonstration that **no one** should insult Dumbledore in front of Hagrid, and that HP Sleuths should never doubt Hagrid's fierce devotion to Dumbledore. (Do we get to find out why?)

Hagrid hands Harry his coat for warmth – warning that he might have left dormice in his pocket.

If dormice sound familiar, that's because *Alice in Wonderland* encountered them. It could be our imagination running away with us, but Alice also seemed to always be encountering watches (time) and rabbits. We'll see if Harry grows or shrinks....

Harry goes to sleep under Hagrid's coat that wriggles with a pocketful of dormice.

Rowlinguistics

✴ Nasty how **Voldemort** robs others of their life, yet wants to be immortal.☺ The phonetics of his name create an image as well. Many of the Danish kings (long history of brutal conflicts with England) had the surname Valdemar and Shakespear even drew from them to create his character name Voltemand.

✴ Ironically, Hagrid's title of "**Keeper of the Keys**" in the French version ("Le Gaurdien des clés") could also be translated as "Keeper of the Clues." Hagrid's first name, Rubeus, is a phonetic variation of "rubious," which means a red or ruby color. Seems like in J.K.R.'s world, the good guys wear red. The name **Hagrid** may be a derivation of haggard (hagard in French or hagrid in olde English). The name also conjures up images of Chris and Dik Browne's *Hagar the Horrible* comic strip. Hagar is a burly, intimidating Viking warrior, who (other than some plundering and pillaging for his day job) is a regular family man, powerless around females, and loves his dog and tankard. Is that Hagrid?

✴ In an interview with the *Sydney Morning Herald*, J.K.R. said she first heard the word "**Hogwarts**" as a species of lily. We also think it is a play on frog warts (no apparent relationship to "Pressed Rat and Warthog"). In the French translation of the Harry Potter books, Hogwarts is called **"Poudlard."** That is a combination of *poudre* (powder/dust) and *poulard* (foul/bird). (It is probably magical dust). Wonder if there is a tie to phoenixes?

Other Oddities

✴ Hagrid is described as having eyes "like black beetles." Another crawling critter reference to drive us buggy.

✳ According to a J.K.R. interview with Scholastic, whenever a wizard is born, their name is recorded in a master book by a magical quill. Upon their 11th birthday, they are sent their invitation to wizarding school. It is unclear as to whether all wizards get this invitation, and whether Hogwarts is the only British school for wizards (we know that it is the most prestigious). We'll have to wait for more from J.K.R..

✳ James and Lily were Head Boy and Head Girl, meaning that they were smart, powerful, and role models.

✳ The motto of the Hogwarts school, "Draco dormiens nunquam titillandus," is imprinted under its crest. HP Sleuths can see that on official Hogwarts merchandise, and Headmaster Dumbledore quotes it in *Fantastic Beasts and Where to Find Them*. It is Latin for: *Never tickle a sleeping dragon*. Interesting school.

Chapter 5 Analysis

Clues

The morning that Harry has turned 11, Hagrid sits in the cabin with him and explains all about the world of wizards – such as the Ministry of Magic, the *Daily Prophet* newspaper, Owl Post, and the only wizarding bank, Gringotts.

> Interesting sounding bank. The name Gringotts is a clever combination of the French word "gringou" – meaning a skinflint or miser, and the word "ingot" which is a nugget of precious metals (as in gold ingot). Anyone thinking of Scrooge?

Harry's parents have left him money that is stored there. This strange bank is run by goblins, has high-security vaults, and is protected by dragons.

> Yes, dragons probably are more effective than alarm systems – especially when they're hungry. (gulp) Keep in mind that there is only one wizarding bank, and it is run by goblins. As long as the goblins stay neutral during conflicts, there is no problem, but that is a potential hazard if the goblins ever take sides. The goblins' obsession with money and gold will probably keep them neutral, as they don't care what color their money is. But what might be the consequences if goblins can be bribed?

Hagrid mentions that people wanted Dumbledore to take the position of Minister of Magic, however, Dumbledore would not leave Hogwarts. Therefore, the bungling Cornelius Fudge is currently Minister.

> As we see here, Hagrid is not very quick to criticize those in authority, and he also mirrors Dumbledore's opinions. So when he ridicules Fudge (or anyone), we know we need to scrutinize that person carefully. Why wouldn't Dumbledore leave Hogwarts? Was that an excuse not to get involved in the politics of the Ministry - does Dumbledore prefer a scholastic environment, or is there something (or someone) tying Dumbledore to Hogwarts?

Hagrid tells Harry that Gringotts is the safest place in the world for storing something (except Hogwarts). He also warns Harry to "never mess with goblins."

> Did HP Sleuths hear that? Hogwarts is considered an even safer place than Gringotts to stash something. It will not only be important to us as a story-line clue, but throughout the whole septology. Hagrid's advice to not mess with goblins is also a good septology lesson. He is portraying goblins as powerful creatures, and warning that you would not want to get on their bad side. As boring as it may seem, HP Sleuths should pay attention to goblins throughout this series, and don't fall asleep during history class!

Hagrid and Harry go to shore in the Dursleys' rowboat, "powered" by Hagrid's pink umbrella. They catch a train to London, where Harry is to buy the books and school supplies which are required for his first year at Hogwarts. They enter a barely noticeable (to Muggles) pub called "the Leaky Cauldron." The pub turns out to be a portal from the Muggle world into a hidden section of London known only to magical people, called Diagon Alley. Harry, whose scar is immediately recognizable, is greeted by numerous witches and wizards who are thrilled to meet him. He begins to get a taste of the extent of his notoriety in the wizarding world. One of the people he meets is the nervous, stuttering, Defense Against the Dark Arts teacher from Hogwarts, Professor Quirrell, who mutters that he is getting a book on vampires.

> Wonder how fast Professor Quirrell can run? Those HP Sleuths who are reading Book 1 for the first time, take special note of the nervous Quirrell. Notice how he is dressed, the way he talks, the circumstances under which Harry meets him, and his reaction to Harry. Wonder why he needs to read up on vampires?

Hagrid and Harry go to Gringotts Bank, a towering white building, where Harry gets to see goblins. The goblins are almost a head shorter than Harry, with long fingers and feet. Hagrid empties his pockets searching for Harry's vault key. As Hagrid pulls out some moldy dog biscuits, the goblin wrinkles his nose.

> Follow those noses – they're a prominent lead. Now, here is the first mention of long fingers on creatures with powerful magic, and it's far from the last. Check those long fingers – they may be pointing HP Sleuths to key evidence. Talking about keys – how did Hagrid get the key to the Potter's vault? (Another clue, maybe?)

The money vaults are not only guarded, but just to get to them, Harry, Hagrid, and their Goblin escort, Griphook, have to ride a roller-coaster-like cart deep underground through a maze of passages. On the way, they even pass a subterranean lake with stalagmites and stalactites.

> Of course, fantasy literature fans are already aware that goblins are famous for their tunneling skills. It is also possible the underground lake may be more than just a passing comment, so remember it's there. As to stalagmites and stalactites, we are sure that a teacher who is familiar with caves and dungeons could solve that mystery. It's easy to recognize a stala<u>ctite</u> – they're the ones hanging from the ceiling that are always "holding on tite" so they don't fall.☺

Upon opening his parents' vault, Harry discovers that his parents had left him a "small fortune," about which the Dursleys had no knowledge.

> Wow! Harry's not only famous – he's rich and famous. Where did the Potters get all that money? On an AOL chat, J.K.R said that James inherited it, but she refused to tell us anything about his career. Bet there's more to that story.... FYI – according to the WB Movie, Harry's vault is # 687 (which adds up to 21).

Hagrid also has to run an errand for Dumbledore, so they visit another vault (713) that has no keyhole, and is clearly top security. Griphook, opens it by stoking the door with his long finger. Hagrid takes "a grubby little package wrapped up in brown paper lying on the floor" and stashes it in his coat.

> We see that Dumbledore has entrusted Hagrid with multiple critical errands. This is obviously a vital package if it is guarded so heavily. It also reveals Dumbledore's wit and understanding of human mentality – that he has such a valuable piece of property look so innocent by being wrapped in common brown paper.

Hagrid brings Harry around to the various shops in Diagon Alley. The Apothecary smells like bad eggs and rotted cabbages.

> The WWP Sleuthoscope is spinning and flashing brilliantly! Here's that cabbage smell again. Note that it's associated with an Apothecary – not with food. Hmmm. That reference to Mrs. Figg's house smelling like cabbage may be due to magical herbs and not because she likes to eat cabbage. HP Sleuths should start learning your potion ingredients if you want to solve this clue.

While in Madam Malkin's robe shop, Harry meets another Hogwarts "first year" who is extremely snobbish, and talks all about which "house" he will be in (hoping it's Slytherin). Hagrid, however, comments that all the Dark witches and wizards, including "You-Know-Who," came from Slytherin house, while Hufflepuff house is a bunch of "duffers." Harry is surprised to learn that years ago Voldemort, himself, had attended Hogwarts.

> Those Hufflepuffs sound somewhat "wimpy," however, it may be Hagrid's loyalties to his own house that make him a bit more vehement about Hufflepuff's weaknesses. In a chat on Barnes&Noble.com, J.K.R. confirms that Hagrid was in Gryffindor. There is no mistaking Hagrid's allegations against Slytherin. He is probably exaggerating, but he should be heeded.

According to the school list, students are allowed to bring an owl, cat, or toad, but Hagrid warns Harry that toads are old-fashioned (and that he'd be laughed at). Since cats make Hagrid sneeze, he buys Harry a birthday present of a snowy white owl as an animal companion.

> As of Book 4, we haven't been told if there is any special significance to having an animal companion. A potentially important clue is that **cats make Hagrid sneeze.** If J.K.R. is true to this piece of information, we should expect to see Hagrid sneezing any time he comes into contact with cats. However, we must follow Rule #1, and so far there is no confirmation of this. We now know, though, that toads are definitely nerd things.

Harry and Hagrid go to Ollivanders wand shop ("Makers of Fine Wands since 382 B.C."), to get Harry a magic wand. A single wand on a faded purple cushion is displayed in the window. The hair prickles on the back of Harry's neck – just as the proprietor appears unexpectedly, making even Hagrid jump.

> Alerting all HP Sleuths! This is not a random itch. This prickling seems to be one of Harry's accurate warning sensors. When Harry feels prickling, even if nothing is apparently there (especially is nothing is there), take heed for it is not his imagination – it usually means someone is lurking.

The shopkeeper is Mr. Ollivander, himself. He is a bit spooky and skeletal, with long, white fingers and non-blinking moon-like eyes. He discusses Hagrid's poor wand that was broken when Hagrid was expelled (and that Harry suspects is concealed within the pink umbrella he is carrying).

> Even though Mr. Ollivander is probably a descendent of the shop founder, one cannot help getting the impression that we are being led into at least contemplating that he may be the original proprietor. No matter what, we can tell that Mr. Ollivander definitely has power, and this is already another indication that J.K.R. may be associating wizarding power with long fingers. As to Hagrid's wand being concealed within his umbrella, does anyone doubt that?

Mr. Ollivander immediately recognizes Harry – reminiscing about how Harry has his mother's eyes. He remembers that Lily's first wand was excellent for charm work, and his father's wand was well-suited for transfiguration (Mr. Ollivander remembers every wand he ever sold).

> WWP Sleuthoscope started flashing bright green! Here we go – we will get quite tired of hearing that Harry has his mother's eyes. Let's just say, that is J.K.R.'s method of "hitting us over the head" with a clue! Interesting how James Potter's wand was specifically well-suited for transfiguration and Lily's for charms – is that just the musings of an old shopkeeper, or is that J.K.R. dropping subtle clues?

Mr. Ollivander has a difficult time finding a wand that responds to Harry. He explains that a wizard will never get as good results with another wizard's wand, and notes that Harry is right-handed.

> Even though it is evident throughout the series that any wizard can use any wand, Mr. Ollivander warns us there could be issues. We have not yet seen a wizard handicapped by using another's wand, so we do not even know in what way they would lose performance (though there may be a subtle hint in Book 4). The clue to keep in mind here is that Harry is right-handed. We have not been told if a wizard keeps their tendency in transfiguring, or how it might be influenced by lineage. Did anyone happen to notice if Professor McGonagall was left-pawed or right-pawed?

After trying an entire pile of wands with various cores (including dragon heartstring and unicorn hair), the wand that Harry finally is able to activate is made from a phoenix tail feather. It feels warm in Harry's fingers and bursts forth with gold and red sparks when he waves it. Mr. Ollivander finds it all so "curious...curious..." as the only other feather taken from that bird was used to make the wand of Lord Voldemort – the very wand that gave Harry his scar.

> Scary coincidence. HP Sleuths – what does Rule #3 say about that? That just might be a special phoenix, and this is definitely a special wand. Does everyone get a "warm" feeling when they try the right wand? Look at those gold and red sparks – they could be interpreted as phoenix colors, but they may relate to Harry's ancestry and/or destiny. Are the people who have wands with any phoenix core linked in some way? Wonder if there's going to be anything about that in Book 5?

Mr. Ollivander tells Harry that "we must expect great things from you..."

Rowlinguistics

-✳- Geometric patterns (such circles, pentagons, and pyramids) have always been symbols of wizards. **Diagon Alley** (a parallel world that intersects the Muggle world "diagonally") and circles, seem to be the only specific references to significant shapes we've seen so far.

-✳- Mr. **Ollivander** is described as having pale or moonlike eyes. In French, the word "olivatre" means sallow or olive-colored, which is very descriptive. In German, "van der" means from the [olive]. Could the olive reference be related to ancient Athens (Greece), or something else? So, what "great things" is Mr. Ollivander inferring? That's not a leading statement, is it?

-✳- The name **Quirrell** seems to come from the Professor's queer (as in odd) appearance and nervous twitching, which is very squirrel-like (and possibly squirrelly?)

-✳- **Malkin** is a funny name for a clothing shop, as it is slang for a poorly-dressed woman, or dust-rags. It is also the name of a well-known scholar of Greek Mythology (Professor Irad Malkin). However, the name may also hold clues about Madam Malkin since it can mean a cat or rabbit as well.

Curiosities

✳ Let's see, very old wand shop, very old wand, resting on the color of royalty. Since the shop has been around for centuries, does this imply that Ollivanders might have supplied the great Merlin or some similar Egyptian celebrity with the old wand?

✳ Mr. Olivander exclaims "curious... curious," like Alice (from *Wonderland*) who finds things "curiouser and curiouser." (So do we.) What other hints might be hiding in that source?

✳ If the rail car in the tunnels at Gringotts conjures up mining scenes from *Snow White and the Seven Dwarves*, then you are not alone. And where do goblins get all their money? Those small, yet powerful and ruthless, money-hungry goblins are metaphorically akin to the Ferengi, as portrayed in *Star Trek* (go ask a Trekkie).

Other Oddities

✳ At the end of this chapter, Hagrid seems to have magically disappeared. Does Hagrid know how to do that, or did he use some other magic?

✳ While on the train, Hagrid was knitting a "canary-yellow circus tent." We never saw it finished. What in the world was that for, J.K.R.?

✳ Harry's glasses no longer seem to be broken. It is likely that Hagrid might have done some work on them back while the boat rowed itself, or that Harry *willed* them into being repaired (the brat in the robe shop did not comment on them). It is also possible that it happened the way we saw it in the movie (thanks Hermione) ☺.

Clues

Uncle Vernon brings Harry to King's Cross Station to catch the train since he is driving to London anyway to have Dudley's pig tail removed at the hospital. There is no visible sign of Platform Nine and Three-quarters, and with only 10 minutes to go plus starting to panic, Harry overhears the word "Muggles," and meets the red-haired Weasley kids (Ron, Ginny, Percy, and the twins - Fred & George) who also attend Hogwarts. Mrs. Weasley kindly explains how to walk through the dividing barrier between platforms nine and ten. Harry takes his cart, piled up with his trunk and owl (who he named Hedwig), and runs straight into the barrier. Amazingly, he passes right through it to the waiting Hogwarts Express.

Percy might be a nickname for Perseus, the famous hero from Greek mythology who slew the Medusa (the ugly one with snakes for hair and whose looks turned men to stone). We think it more likely that it is short for Perceval, which was the name of a famous knight in the legend of the Holy Grail. In spite of his power as a warrior, Perceval was naïve, and through his ignorance, was supposedly responsible for the death of his mother and his uncle. He also missed the key opportunity given to him to heal the King of the Grail. Now, Percy Weasley wouldn't be that inept, would he?

On the train, Ron Weasley meekly tells Harry how his robes used to belong to his brother Bill, and his sleepy, old pet rat (called Scabbers), is a non-magical hand-me-down from his brother Percy; while Harry relates how he also always had hand-me-downs and never even a real birthday present. It is mutual curiosity and mutual friendship.

There are two curious issues here. One of them is that in just the previous chapter, we are told that students are allowed to take only a cat, owl, or toad to school, yet Ron has a rat. It is possible that it was an oversight by J.K.R., but the odd part is that she has not justified this discrepancy as of Book 4 (guess it's not important). The more crucial issue is where exactly did gullible Percy get this rat...and why (especially if it has no visible powers)? Also, who gave him that yucky name?

A witch brings by a cart of very unusual candies and treats. A favorite of wizarding kids are the chocolate frogs, which contain a *Famous Witches and Wizards* (FW&W) collectible card in each one. Harry gets a "Dumbledore" card. A picture of Dumbledore with his white hair and beard is on one side of the card, and his stats are on the other. It says that the Hogwarts Headmaster is considered to be the "greatest wizard of modern times." It explains that Dumbledore is famous for defeating the Dark wizard, Grindelwald, in 1945.

J.K.R. likes to mess with our brains. She has clearly implied here that the problems the wizards had in 1945 were somehow linked to the horrors of World War II (let us hope that Dumbledore can again help us out of the current world trouble).

For those who might be wondering now, according to a chat on BBC Online, J.K.R. has told us that Dumbledore is 150 years old (but don't tell Harry - he doesn't know this yet).

Dumbledore is also famous for discovering the 12 uses of dragon's blood, and for his Alchemy work with his partner, Nicolas Flamel.

> Here is an example of always being alert for the subtle clues. Why the 12 uses? Does that only relate to the other twelves, or has Dumbledore found a 13th use that will be key to this story? J.K.R. wouldn't make it that subtle if she wanted us to figure it out right now, but she may be leaving a trail. We see that Nicolas Flamel is his partner. Could that be where the baby Harry went during that missing day - with Flamel? We don't know, but an HP Sleuth doesn't rule anything out.

The FW&W card also mentions that Dumbledore enjoys chamber music and 10-pin bowling. When the image of Dumbledore leaves the picture frame and then returns with a small smile, Harry discovers that wizard pictures move.

> An old man with a long, white beard who likes 10-pin bowling? Can we say "Rip Van Winkle"? Although we learn it is common in J.K.R.'s magical world for the picture versions of people to leave the frame completely, one cannot help but wonder if one of those images of Dumbledore might have been the real person (!). J.K.R. mentions music a lot - this is definitely a story-line clue as well as a noteworthy septology clue.

Harry and Ron look out the window as the train passes cows and sheep in the fields. Ron informs Harry that the *Daily Prophet* newspaper reported that someone had somehow managed to break into a high-security vault at Gringotts, but it did not appear that anything was taken.

> This is a fairly obvious "coincidence" (review Rule #3) concerning a high security vault at Gringotts, but it reveals the pattern of how J.K.R. writes clues into the story. If it is important enough to generate conversation, it is safe to assume it is a key element of the plot.

Neville, a boy who has been looking for his lost toad (Trevor), stops by with a bossy, know-it-all girl named Hermione Granger. She tells Harry how she has read all about him in history books. It is embarrassing to Harry to find out that everyone else knows more about himself than he does.

> Hermione is not a common name, in fact, J.K.R. has made a point to tell us in an interview with Lindsey Fraser in *Conversations with J.K Rowling*, that she took the name from a character in Shakespeare's *The Winter's Tale*. Do any of you HP Sleuths happen to be Shakespeare scholars?

Draco Malfoy, the snob Harry had met in the robe shop in Diagon Alley, also stops by along with his two sidekicks, Crabbe and Goyle. When Malfoy makes it clear that he considers himself better than Ron because of his elite social status, Harry snubs him. For that, Malfoy purposely makes trouble, but when Goyle starts to grab for some of their food, Scabbers chomps on Goyle's finger, which effectively chases them off. Scabbers then goes back to sleep.

> Way to go Scabbers! But why did Scabbers bite Goyle? There has been nothing as of Book 4 to indicate motive for the otherwise listless rat. As to that slippery toad, based on what Hagrid told us about toads, we are to assume Neville is a nerd. Nevertheless, assumptions are exceptionally good for camouflaging J.K.R. clues.

The train arrives at Hogwarts - where Hagrid greets all of the first years. He leads them down to a lake that they cross in small boats... to an entrance of a great castle. They duck their heads as they pass under some ivy and enter a hidden dark tunnel. They find themselves in a sort of underground harbor.

> Wicked. Wonder what this "underground harbor" is used for? Bet there's lot of secret passageways and other scary stuff in this castle.

As they get out of the boats to walk up a passage to the entrance of the castle, Hagrid discovers Trevor, the toad, hiding in a boat.

Rowlinguistics

✳ The name **Weasley** sounds like *weasel* – which are crafty little fur balls that are very good at getting out of inconvenient situations (they also have a famous talent for being able to eat the insides out of an egg while leaving the shell almost untouched). Thought we'd mention it – you never know....

✳ **Draco Malfoy** is truly bad news as his name suggests. His first name, Draco, is Latin for serpent (or dragon) and a very famous Draco in history is from Greece. Draco (or Drakon) was the first law-giver of Athens, whose laws were famous for promoting the
Taking from French once again for his last name, J.K.R. combines the word "mal" (bad, evil, or sick), with the word "foi" (faith or trust), to be *bad* or *evil faith*. The French translation even took it one step further by adding the letter "e" – so it becomes Malefoy. That makes it sound close to malefique, which is definitely evil.

* **Crabbe** and **Goyle**, Draco's sidekicks, also have "complimentary" names - Crabbe, which sounds like a mean or irritable crustacean (crabby/crab), and Goyle, being a portion of the word "gargoyle," which are grotesque stone beasts from the dark ages used to guard things.

* Harry says he got **Hedwig**'s name out of *A History of Magic*. In reality, according to J.K.R. in an interview on eToys.com she got the name from Saint Hedwig, who was well-know for her charity work. She is the patron saint for a religious order that helps abandoned and orphaned children.

* Hermione's last name, **Granger**, is the name of the leader of the living books from the forest in Ray Bradbury's *Fahrenheit 451*. That would be a great name for a bookworm, but we are not sure if that is the source, or if it is hiding other clues.

* If **Percy** is named after Perceval of the Holy Grail, we might want to stash away some where that the derivation of the name Perceval is from French (Perce à val), and means *pierce the valley*, or to *take a middle road.*

* **Scabbers'** name in French, "Croutard," is a fabricated word from croute (scab) and translates to the same yucky name as the English. It also has a phonetic similarity to a real word, *moutard* (small boy).

Curiosities

* It doesn't appear that anyone ever tattle-tailed about what Hagrid had done to Dudley since the Dursleys had to go the hospital to have the curl removed. We find out later that there is a whole team of wizards who handle magical reversals to fix mistakes like this, but no wizards came by to undo *Hagrid's spell.*

* It seems that this vision of the cows and sheep from the train may be the one J.K.R. saw when she conceived of the Harry Potter story while gazing at fields from her own train ride.

* It's probably nothing, but we will remember Ron has Bill's old robes - especially since Bill will get very interesting in later books.

Other Oddities

* The U.S. book version said there was a train "conductor," while the U.K. version specifically called that person a "driver."

Chapter 7 Analysis

(THE SORTING HAT)

Clues

Professor McGonagall leads the first years into the Great Hall, where they will be "sorted" into one of the 4 Hogwarts houses which will be their affiliation for all seven years: Gryffindor, Hufflepuff, Ravenclaw, and Slytherin. The Great Hall is lit by thousands of candles floating in mid air over four long tables set with golden plates and goblets. Hermione (who has already read the complete *Hogwarts, a History*) remarks that the incredible ceiling is "bewitched" so that it always duplicates the conditions of the sky outside. The students are unnerved as approximately 20 ghosts suddenly emerge out of a wall and float around them.

> The ghosts may seem to be secondary characters, but they don't let a little thing like death kill their character development. HP Sleuths should be aware that ghosts have access to the whole castle (yes, even secret passages - only spells can keep them from hidden or locked places). Ghosts have been part of the castle for so long that they are probably crucial allies (or serious threats) to the headmaster. So far, we have not yet had a complete explanation as to why only a few people return as ghosts, but they appear to be "troubled spirits" – usually associated with a tragic life or death.

The Sorting Ceremony is performed by a patched and frayed, talking wizard's hat (Sorting Hat).

> Although the Sorting Hat is very old, it is a ceremonial hat, and is presumably handled and stored carefully - so why is it so patched and frayed? (Maybe one of the students didn't like the way he was sorted?) Does the Hat serve some other purpose? Although still quite a mystery all the way through Book 4, we will see in Book 2 the Hat is not all talk.

The Sorting Hat sings a song describing the qualities of each noble House: Bravery for Gryffindor, Intelligence for Ravenclaw, Loyalty for Hufflepuff, and Ambition for Slytherin. The Hat is set on the head of each student, slipping down over their eyes, where it searches their minds as it evaluates the proper place to put them ("There's nothing hidden in your head the Sorting Hat can't see").

> J.K.R. puts a lot of significance into the choices of the Sorting Hat, so it is important to keep in mind the qualities of the house into which the students are sorted. Even if those qualities do not appear strong on the surface for a person, it should be remembered that the Sorting Hat has "inside information." Did you get the Oz-type reference? We have bravery (the Lion), intelligence (the Straw Man), and loyalty (the Tin Man). So does that mean that Slytherin is the Wicked Witch and Dumbledore is the man behind the curtain?

It took the Sorting Hat almost a full minute before placing Seamus Finnegan in Gryffindor. It took a long time with Neville Longbottom as well. Susan Bones ends up in Hufflepuff, while Malfoy is (expectedly) quickly sorted into Slytherin. Ron and Hermione are thrilled to be sorted into Gryffindor.

> So why does the Sorting hat take so long with Seamus and Neville? In spite of his nerdiness and seeming ineptness, Neville is sorted into Gryffindor, which is a big clue. An even bigger clue might be the Longbottom name. *Lord of the Rings* fans may remember that Longbottom Leaf, which was found in the stores of Sauruman (an enemy and traitor), was a hidden link that later exposed Sauruman's evil plot. Could Neville have a hidden link? HP Sleuths might want to chaw on that one for a bit

When it is Harry's turn to be sorted, the Sorting Hat profiles Harry as "plenty of courage, not a bad mind, talent, and a nice thirst to prove himself." It suggests that he would do well in Slytherin, but when Harry protests, it places him in Gryffindor. Harry joins the Gryffindor table - happy to have avoided Slytherin.

> Notice that the very first thing that the hat sees in Harry is courage - the primary quality of Gryffindor. There will be many more references to his courage, ad nauseam, and he doesn't seem like the Slytherin type to us. So, why did the Sorting Hat want to put him in Slytherin? Is this a clue, a red herring, or some other ploy by the author? HP Sleuths should keep your pointed thinking caps on.

Harry meets Nearly Headless Nick, the resident ghost of Gryffindor tower, who points out Slytherin's ghost - the Bloody Baron. The Bloody Baron is drenched in ghostly blood, but Nick isn't sure why, since he never felt quite right about asking him. Harry recognizes Headmaster Dumbledore from the FW&W card. With a word from Dumbledore, their plates and goblets are instantly and magically filled with food and drink.

> There are numerous conflicting references in the books about how long Nick has been a ghost, but that only means to us that the date is not crucial since J.K.R. is extremely specific whenever it is an important clue. She may zing us with something later if she wants to justify the discrepancies, but we should just concentrate now on the circumstances surrounding his death. Those circumstances are still a mystery to us Readers as of Book 4. We do, however, want to keep in mind that although Nick seems a bit pathetic at times, he is (what's left of him is) a Gryffindor. Now, the Bloody Baron is purposely mysterious - not even the ghosts seem to know how he got so bloody.

The Gryffindor students discuss their family backgrounds. Seamus is half-and-half (witch mother, Muggle father), while Neville lives with his wizarding grandmother. Neville's relatives had started getting worried that he might not be at all magical. Neville tells the story about how his Great Uncle Algie (who bought him his toad), was dangling him from an "upstairs" window, but then dropped him when distracted by a delicious-looking meringue. When Neville bounced, they were so thrilled to find out he was a wizard.

Besides Trevor, it seems that Neville's acquiescent Uncle may have also given him some other qualities, which become more prominent in Book 4. Wonder what happened to Neville's parents? If Neville's background seems a bit fishy, that's because Harry is certainly not the only one with a mysterious past.

Up at the High Table where the professors are seated, Harry sees a teacher with greasy black hair, a hooked nose, and sallow skin. He is seated next to Quirrell who is wearing a large, peculiar-looking, purple turban. When that dark professor looks past Quirrell at Harry, a sharp, hot, pain shoots across the scar on Harry's forehead.

Keep in mind this description of the dark Professor - he may be more than ugly. A typical J.K.R. ruse - there is obviously something wrong here, but what? On careful reading, it is possible to hypothesize, but she is very clever. Harry's scar is definitely some form of sensor. Also, what's with the turban? Is there any significance to it?

The dark teacher is Professor Snape, the Potions Master and head of Slytherin House, who Percy says is after Quirrell's job (Defense Against the Dark Arts).

Notice that the information that Snape wants Quirrell's job comes from Percy. Has anyone else in the school ever corroborated this information? HP Sleuths - review Rule #4 - this could be a septology red herring.

The students are warned that Mr. Filch, the caretaker, will enforce the school rule of no magic being used between classes. Dumbledore reminds them that the Forbidden Forest is, as usual, out-of-bounds to everyone, as is the third floor corridor this year - on pain of death! Harry thinks Dumbledore is probably joking, however Percy says the forest is forbidden because there are beasts in it, but he can't figure out why a corridor would be forbidden. Everyone sings the school alma mater (in their own style), and Professor Dumbledore comments that "music is a magic beyond all we do here."

This third-floor corridor rule is an example of both a blatant and subtle storyline clue (watch for J.K.R. to do that a lot). The blatant part is that we now know there is something mysterious about the third floor corridor. The subtle part is that no one is sure if Dumbledore is joking about the death thing. J.K.R. continues playing with our brains as Dumbledore's love of music is emphasized again.

The Gryffindor students are led up to their house by Percy Weasley, who is a Prefect. On the way, they are assaulted by Peeves, a peevish Poltergeist, who suddenly materializes as he pelts them with walking sticks. Percy tells them that the Bloody Baron is the only one who can control Peeves.

From what we've seen of the Bloody Baron and what Nick said, the Bloody Baron seems to have control over most of the non-humans. The most puzzling (ghost) of all is Peeves, a poltergeist, who is solid and therefore able to move and hold things, as well as become invisible. Although he creates complete havoc with both living and non-living creatures, Hogwarts' pet Peeves is allowed to remain at Hogwarts, so it seems that someone must want him sticking around.

From the Gryffindor common room, Harry and Ron climb a spiral staircase to the boy's dormitory. They sit on four-poster beds, hung with deep red velvet curtains, and talk about the wonderful feast. Ron has to stop Scabbers from chewing on the sheets as they drift off to sleep.

Poor Scabbers - all that food talk would drive any creature to chew the sheets...

In the middle of the night, Harry wakes from a nightmare in which Professor Quirrell's turban was speaking to him, telling him he should transfer immediately to Slytherin because it is his destiny. When Harry awakes the next day, he has forgotten the dream.

This nightmare is a subtle story-line clue (possibly an overall septology clue) - how and why did Harry have the dream? We still don't have the answer to that, and it is odd that he forgot it. Not that people can't forget dreams, but Harry tends to remember them when they cause him to wake up. Was this really a dream? Could someone have made sure he forgot it?

Harry cannot forget his concern over almost being put in Slytherin.

Rowlinguistics

✴ For those who never had to clean a fish tank or a boat, "algae" (pronounced al-gie), are seaweed or moss-like plants that build up in water containing water creatures. So, it makes sense to us that **Uncle Algie** buys Neville a toad

✴ In a interview on eToys.com, J.K.R. says she took **Snape**'s name from a town. We also think it sounds a bit like "snipe" which is what he does to Harry with his mean attacks. The French version just calls him Professor "Rogue" (arrogant). In another interview with BBC Online, J.K.R. reveals that Snape is either 35 or 36 years old.

✴ We still do not know much about **Seamus Finnigan** by Book 4 except that when others seem to be losing their heads, both he and his friend Dean Thomas have a good grasp of reality. *Finnigan's Wake* is a famous book by James Joyce, and an incredible pun. The title is a multi-level pun – meaning *wake*, as in a funeral, as in the wake of an ocean, or as in *awake* (not asleep). Finnigan is *fin again*, where "fin" translates to *end* in French, so it would mean *end again* - which is appropriate since the last sentence of Joyce's book is the same as the first sentence (the book just starts all over again!). With J.K.R.'s sense of humor, we are wondering what might be awaiting Seamus's character.

✴ We find it interesting that **Quirrell** was never given a first name. Wonder what it is?

✴ Someone really used their head when they translated into French the name of the **Sorting Hat**. In French, the word for *selection/choice* is "choix," and the word for *hat* is "chapeau." They put the two together so that the word "chapeau" (shah-poh) became "choixpeau" (shwah-poh), a very select hat.

Curiosities

✴ We know from Hagrid (Chapter 4) that Susan Bones probably is a relative (if not the daughter) of people who were murdered by Voldemort, but so far, we have not yet met her personally. She may be important since, of all the non-primary characters in Books 1-4, the movie script highlighted her sorting into Hufflepuff.

✴ It is interesting that the style of the school song is not the same as any of the other poems and verses throughout J.K.R.'s books. Just an opinion here, but we wonder if it's hiding some significance that has eluded us.

✴ J.K.R. has given us a perspective that few authors offer their readers. We have the whole psyche of our hero (along with many supporting characters) handed to us in the words of the author via the Sorting Hat.

✴ It is apparent that Harry sees the turban on Quirrell's head for the first time here. Unlike portrayed in the movie, Quirrell could not have been wearing it at the Leaky

> ✦ Cauldron, or Harry would not have been so surprised at it's "peculiar" appearance when he saw it at the Sorting Ceremony. We would not mention it except that it may also be a septology clue.

> ✦ The ghost of Hufflepuff house is the Fat Friar (monk). We can't help but wonder if he was one of Robin's merry men.

Other Oddities

> ✦ The first words Dumbledore announces are: "Nitwit, Blubber, Oddment, Tweak." Although these may be just Dumbledore's strange wit, they could also be an anagram or some clue to the septology (so far, we could not find any). HP Sleuths with LOTS of time on their hands may want to experiment to see if anything is hidden in those words (but we doubt it).

> ✦ This is the complete list of the new students that we saw sorted:

Hanna Abbott	Hufflepuff
Susan Bones	Hufflepuff
Terry Boot (male)	Ravenclaw
Mandy Brocklehurst	Ravenclaw
Lavender Brown	Gryffindor
Millicent Bulstrode	Slytherin
Justin Finch-Fletchley	Hufflepuff
Seamus Finnigan	Gryffindor
Hermione Granger	Gryffindor
Neville Longbottom	Gryffindor
Morag MacDougal	(House not given)
Draco Malfoy	Slytherin
Moon	(House not given)
Nott	(House not given)
Parkinson	(House not given)
Patil (female twin)	(House not given)
Patil (female twin)	(House not given)
Sally-Anne Perks	(House not given)
Harry Potter	Gryffindor
Dean Thomas	Gryffindor
Lisa Turpin	Ravenclaw
Ron Weasley	Gryffindor
Blaise Zabini	Slytherin

Clues

Since Ron Weasley and Hermione Granger ended up in Gryffindor with Harry, they attend all the same classes. Most classes are shared with at least one other house. Wizarding studies include Charms, Herbology, Potions, Transfiguration, Defense Against the Dark Arts, History of Magic, and Astronomy (which is held on Wednesdays at midnight).

> That Astronomy class seems to have wandered into a big Black Hole, since so far (as of Book 4), nothing about it has leaked out to us. A midnight class can't possibly be boring, but all we can figure is that no matter her original reason was for not telling us about it, she has wanted to keep that class a dark secret. She even gives us some hints about the class later on that magnify our curiosity.

While trying to find their way around the castle, Harry and Ron get sort of lost. Argus Filch, whose cat (Mrs. Norris) is somehow able to instantly alert Filch of any wrongdoing, catches them unwittingly trying to open the door to the out-of-bounds corridor. Thankfully, Quirrell, who was passing, rescues them from Filch.

> Quirrell to the rescue. Nice person. Hope HP Sleuths take good notes.

Hedwig delivers Harry's first ever Owl Post - inviting him for a cup of tea at Hagrid's cabin that afternoon. During their first Potions class, Professor Snape constantly targets Harry and does everything he can to make Harry look bad. He penalizes 2 points from Gryffindor because Harry didn't notice that Neville was in the process of melting Seamus's cauldron. It is obvious to Harry that Snape hates him.

> Now, maybe Snape thought the other teachers would question if he took off too many points from Harry on their first day, or maybe J.K.R. was not as aggressive at first with the way teachers deducted points, but we now know that two points is trivial. It is odd that Snape only deducted two points when he probably could have taken off 10 or more if he really wanted to. He seems to have been trying to create an impression - but on whom? On Slytherin? On Harry? On the class in general? On us readers? (If so, it worked! - we don't like him either.)

Harry and Ron visit Hagrid at his cabin, where they are slobbered on by Fang, Hagrid's boarhound, and have tea and rock cakes. Harry sees a story in Hagrid's copy of "The Daily Prophet" reporting about the break-in at Gringotts – it was the day he was there with Hagrid. It mentions that nothing had been taken since the vault had been emptied earlier that day.

> Here she goes again - there are actually two story-line clues here. J.K.R. gives us the obvious one to mask the subtle one. We now know that Hagrid's errand for Dumbledore at Gringotts was directly related to this news article. Since we also know the day it happened, we know who and what the characters saw on that

day, so we can then try to figure out the much more subtle clues as to who might have been involved.

The day of the attempted robbery was July 31st. Harry exclaims to Hagrid that was his Birthday, the day they were there. Hagrid quickly changes the subject.

Gee, Harry's birthday just **happens** to be J.K.R.'s own birthday as well. It also happens to make him a Leo. HP Sleuths – follow those tracks....

Harry is now extremely intrigued by this mystery.

Rowlinguistics

★ **Argus Filch**'s first name is perfect for a watchful guardian. In Greek mythology, the monster, Argus, had 100 eyes and was used as a guardian by the legendary gods. Except for Filch's confiscating of illegal items, we do not get any other clue from his last name. The French version calls him "Rusard," a trickster, or sly one.

★ **Mrs. Norris** is Miss Teigne in the French version. That is pretty funny, as it translates to *Miss Ringworm* or *Miss Vixen*.

Curiosities

★ Snape seems to consider the questions he asked Harry to be extremely important. As expert sleuths, we should all keep in mind Snape's lesson. He taught us that Asphodel & Wormwood [A&W] are the ingredients for "Draught of Living Death," that bezoar comes from the stomach of a goat and can save one from "most" poisons, and that Wolfsbane=Aconite=Monkshood [WAM], which are poisonous plants.

★ Peeves plays pranks because he enjoys chaos. One of his tricks is to invisibly grab students' noses and yell "Got your conk!" It is obnoxious and it's also another "nose" reference.

Clues

Malfoy's eagle owl constantly delivers treats from home, while Neville receives a Remembrall (a glass ball that turns red if you forgot something) from his grandmother. It turns red. Gryffindor and Slytherin have their first flying lesson together with Madam Hooch, a teacher with short gray hair and yellow eyes like a hawk. Neville (of course) falls off his broom, and has to be brought to the hospital, while the rest of the class is emphatically instructed to stay off the brooms. Malfoy spots Neville's Remembrall on the ground, and since the teacher is away, takes off into the air with it. Harry jumps on his broom and instinctively flies after him, but at 50 feet in mid-air, Malfoy purposely drops the glass Remembrall. Harry dives after it, catching it barely a foot from the ground - just as Professor McGonagall comes out to the field.

> An excellent example of one of J.K.R.'s famous subtle clues: Malfoy uses an eagle owl. Just remember...*birds of a feather...* applies to both humans and their winged companions. Neville would have trouble remembering that advice since something seems to be a bit wrong with his memory (not to mention his coordination).

Harry thinks he is a gonner, but Professor McGonagall brings him to see Oliver Wood, the Gryffindor Quidditch Team Captain, and introduces Harry as their new "Seeker." She shocks everyone by bending the rules prohibiting first years from being on a team. Wood informs him that he is the youngest house player in a century. McGonagall comments that Harry's father (also a Quidditch player) would have been proud. Fred and George Weasley, who are also on the team, congratulate Harry as Lee Jordan drags the twins off to see a new secret passageway (hoping it's not the one they already found behind the statue of Gregory the Smarmy).

> The Weasley twins and Lee Jordan seem to really know their way around the castle, and they obviously know of several secret passageways. Wicked. ☺

Malfoy, Crabbe and Goyle harass Harry and Ron, challenging them to a wizard's duel at midnight in the trophy room, which is never locked.

> The information about the unlocked trophy room seems like a clue, but there has been enough confusion to cast doubt about the reliability of any information about that room. For instance, in this chapter the trophy room is located on the third floor, but by Book 4, it is definitely on the 6th floor (see Rowlinguistics and Curiosities). We'll remember that the trophy room (wherever it may be) is never locked - which might be important later on in the septology.

Hermione overhears Harry and Ron, and is determined to stop them from sneaking out, but then gets locked out of the tower, herself. Fuming, she ends up tagging along with them. She is upset that they might get caught and lose the points she got for knowing all about *Switching Spells*.

What are *Switching Spells*? What gets switched? Is it body parts, one's identity or something else? HP Sleuths had better study hard since J.K.R. makes constant references to this, and we do know what Rule #1 is....

On the way to the trophy room, they find Neville, who had forgotten the password to get back in (is anyone surprised?). He joins the growing troupe on their midnight mission.

No need to remind anyone that this memory lapse is to help reinforce that we remember Neville's forgetfulness.

In the trophy room, Malfoy and Crabbe never show up. Instead, Mr. Filch arrives accompanied by Mrs. Norris, his cat, obviously having been tipped off by Malfoy. The four students flee down the hall and escape through a locked door (that Hermione opens with a spell), and without realizing it, end up hiding in the forbidden corridor. As Peeves teases Filch in his sing-song voice just outside the door, Neville advises Harry (through desperate tugs on his sleeve) that the corridor is also occupied – by a massive, ferocious, 3-headed dog, that Harry figures was caught off-guard when they entered. In sheer terror, they bolt straight back to their common room. Hermione points out that the dog was standing on a trap door - obviously guarding something.

This is the big neon sign type of story-line clue that is covering up a teeny little story-line clue. The blatant clue is: it is now evident what is forbidden about the corridor, that it holds yet more intriguing clues, and that what is in there can, indeed, inflict a painful death. The incredibly subtle clue is that they stood there listening to Peeves' taunting of Filch but did not happen to notice that the beast sat fixed behind them.

Harry concludes that the 3-headed dog is guarding the package Hagrid picked up from vault 713.

Rowlinguistics

✳ **Hooch** is a humorous name for a flying teacher. It is slang for bathtub brews, which are famous for causing light-headedness and that high-flying feeling. Her name is "Bibine" in French version, but that translation just flew over our heads. Do any HP Sléuths understand that one?

✳ **Oliver Wood**'s last name is obvious. The French Version adds just a little by calling him "Dubois" (of the wood, or from the wood)

Curiosities

✳ J.K.R. has cleverly explained the discrepancy concerning the Trophy Room location in interviews by noting that the castle rooms will move around just to be difficult. It is best to stick with reinforced information, however, we will keep these references in our notes just in case.

✳ Neville was not on the Midnight Duel adventure in the Movie, but just in case, we should mention for the septology that he was there.

Chapter 10 Analysis

Clues

Harry's new Nimbus 2000 racing broom is delivered by Owl Post, much to the dismay of Malfoy. Harry goes to Quidditch practice where he tries out his new broom and learns the rules of the game. Hermione is still so upset at Harry and Ron over the midnight duel that she stops speaking to them (suits them fine). Hermione and Ron are partners for Charms, which annoys both of them, as Hermione is exasperatingly adept at doing levitations while Ron struggles at it. Flitwick, the Charms Professor, instructs them with their wrist movements - "swish and flick." After class, Ron spouts off to Harry that it is "no wonder" Hermione does not have any friends, but Hermione overhears him and runs off.

> Professor Flitwick is an interesting character. He is the head of Ravenclaw house, and is portrayed as extremely knowledgeable in his field, so we can trust his information. He does have some fascinating quirks. He is extremely tiny and tends to squeak out words, which make him seem very elf-like. He is also a bit effeminate - both in his emotions and his mannerisms (wrist movement).

When Harry and Ron get to the Great Hall for the Halloween feast, they hear that Hermione has been crying in the girls' bathroom. During the feast, Professor Quirrell dashes in and gasps out that there is a Troll loose in the Dungeons, and faints. Harry and Ron go to alert Hermione, and on their way, spot Professor Snape headed for the third floor. After getting past Snape, they smell the Troll, then spot it entering a doorway. Ron and Harry run and slam the door behind it, trapping it. However, upon hearing a scream, they realize it's the girls' bathroom, and bolt back inside to rescue Hermione. Harry jumps on the troll's back, while Ron impulsively uses the levitating charm - causing the Troll's club to rise in the air and fall back on top of its head, knocking it out. Professor McGonagall arrives on the scene, followed by Snape and Quirrell.

> Looks like Ron finally got that "swish and flick"! There are more questions here than there are answers, and they all revolve around story-line clues. Who let the troll into the castle? What was Quirrell doing in the dungeons? Why was Snape heading for the third floor? Why did all the teachers get there at the same time? What do all these events have to do with each other or with what is being guarded on the third floor? These may be clues, but J.K.R. has started to throw some red herrings at us, and this is one big fish fry.

Harry and Ron are astonished as Hermione lies to Professor McGonagall to cover for them, and upon returning to the common room, they thank each other, and become close friends.

Curiosities

* The players on a Quidditch team are:
  3 Chasers (offensive), 2 Beaters (defensive), 1 Keeper (goalie), and 1 Seeker.

* The balls used in Quidditch are:
  1 Quaffle (red), 2 Bludgers (black), and 1 Snitch (golden with wings)

* There are 3 hoops on each side of the Quidditch field (pitch).

* (If you want to know more, check out *Quidditch Through the Ages*,
  by Kennilworthy Whisp.)

* We are a bit curious as to where and how Harry got his Nimbus 2000 broom, but it is
  probably not important.

Chapter 11 Analysis

Clues

Harry, Ron, and Hermione are outside when Snape passes by them, visibly limping. As a diversion from his injury, he confiscates Harry's book (*Quidditch Through the Ages*) with the excuse that library books are not allowed outside the castle. That evening, Harry goes down to the Staff Room to ask Snape for his book back. He walks in on Filch bandaging up Snape's leg which is bloody and mangled, as Snape grumbles about "all 3 heads at once." Harry tells Ron and Hermione he'd bet his broomstick that Snape let the troll in as a diversion so he could get to the dog.

> A blatant story-line clue that Snape has encountered the 3-headed monster. Seems that Snape was not quite tasty enough (probably because the menu called for red herring). A possible subtle septology clue is that it was Filch, and not Madame Pomfrey, who was treating Snape. We know that Madame Pomfrey can magically cure a broken wrist in minutes, so why did Snape not go to the hospital just for flesh wounds? Why also is Filch his partner in crime? Very strange.

Harry's first Quidditch match is against their arch-rival, Slytherin. The Slytherin team captain is Marcus Flint, who seems to have troll blood in him.

> J.K.R.'s description of Marcus Flint is a clue about the whole magical world. She is communicating that wizards have inter-married with other species and that it is possible for humans to be descended from other creatures - including beasts. Those wizards would also be expected to exhibit some of the traits of their heritage – so could Professor Flitwick have elf blood in him or Madam Hooch be related to bald eagles? What other creatures might be in the background of the human characters?

For the Quidditch match, Dean Thomas, who is artistic, creates a team banner. It has an image of a Lion, the Gryffindor team mascot.

> For some reason, J.K.R. has made it a point to mention that Dean Thomas has artistic ability. This talent could come in handy for numerous yet unknown possibilities. Brave Gryffindor has a lion for a mascot (of course). Harry is brave, he is a Leo, and he was placed in Gryffindor. Are we starting to see a trend here? Bookmark Rule #3.

During the match, Harry's broomstick is being cursed by someone, and keeps jumping perilously higher while trying to buck him off. As everyone watches in horror, Hagrid exclaims that he can't figure out what could possibly be doing it since only "powerful Dark magic" could affect a Nimbus 2000. Ron and Hermione spot Snape muttering spells directly at Harry from across the stadium, so in a panic, Hermione runs through everyone to stop him, knocking over frail Professor Quirrell on the way. She executes a *Fire Spell* to distract Snape, and when Harry safely regains control of his broom, she scoops the fire back into a jar. Harry does a rapid dive back down to the field, and unexpectedly inhales the Snitch into his mouth - which is ruled a legal catch, beating Slytherin.

> Something very fishy happened here (this may not be what it seems). Since this is definitely a story-line clue - read carefully, as you might be upset with yourself later on if you miss this one. Also note that Hermione always seems to have a jar handy for holding fire or anything else she needs to control.

After the game, Harry, Ron, and Hermione have tea at Hagrid's hut, while they try to convince Hagrid that Snape is behind a lot of the incidents. They also find out that the 3-headed dog belongs to Hagrid, that his name is Fluffy, and he came from a Greek "chappie." Hagrid tries to insist that they should not be meddling in things concerning Professor Dumbledore and Nicolas Flamel ("I shouldn'ta told yeh that").

> Fluffy? (Maybe he is to another giant 3-headed dog!) The plot thickens.... Now the kids have some real story-line clues to work with, although they realize that they cannot put all the clues together without knowing more about Flamel. Hagrid bought the dog from a Greek, so we assume this is Cerberus, or a descendent of Cerberus - the dog from Greek Mythology that guards the gates of Hades (how many 3-headed, Greek dogs can there be?). That information may be important in helping to solve story-line clues.

Harry, Ron, and Hermione now have a mission - find out about Nicolas Flamel.

Rowlinguistics

* The name **"Gryffindor"** is a combination of the words griffin d'or – which means a golden griffin (the mythological beast with the head and wings of an eagle and the hind quarters and tail of a lion). It also would make sense that the mascot of brave Gryffindor is a lion (as in *The Wizard of Oz*), and that it is a red lion, as is Aslan, in the *Chronicles of Narnia*.

Curiosities

— One of our favorite additions to the Harry Potter story that was done in the the movie of the *Philosopher's (Sorcerer's) Stone* was Hagrid's running bit of "I shouldn'ta told yeh that!" The reasons we liked it was because it's funny, it used J.K.R.'s joke and turned it into a running bit (just like she might have done). It also captured the spirit of what J.K.R. had intended with the character – well meaning, but a little loose-lipped.

— Marcus Flint is portrayed as a bit dim-witted, which may influence his ability to graduate.

Chapter 12 Analysis

(THE MIRROR OF ERISED)

Clues

This is Chapter 12.

Besides being an important chapter to the plot, there seems to be something extra special about this chapter in reference to the entire septology. When J.K.R. was asked what are her favorite parts of her books, she replied "Chapter 12 in Book 1" - which could mean a reference within this chapter in particular, or could be her way of hinting that the number 12, in general, is significant (or both). Do authors usually remember their chapters by number?

Harry and the Weasley kids are all staying at Hogwarts for the Christmas holidays. Fred and George get into holiday mischief by sending bewitched snowballs to pursue Quirrell and pelt his turban from behind. Ron, Hermione, and Harry had been searching the library to find out about Nicolas Flamel, but didn't want to arouse suspicion by asking the librarian, Madam Pince, for help. They still haven't found anything, so Hermione asks them to keep looking while she's at home for the holidays. Harry knows he saw the name, but can't remember where he saw it. When not in the mood to look for Flamel, Ron teaches Harry how to play wizard chess with a set he had inherited from his grandfather. In wizard chess, the chess pieces are "alive" and interact with the human players as they move (or argue about moving) and slay their opponents.

If you have all been good little HP Sleuths, you will already know where Harry had seen the name Nicolas Flamel, so you don't need our help on that, right? No cheating by going back and looking! (Spells have been put on the pages of the HP books so you won't be able to find it anyway.) Note that Ron is portrayed as an excellent chess player.

On Christmas day, Harry awakes to discover that he actually has a pile of real presents. Hagrid has given him a wooden flute that sounds "a bit like an owl," Hermione has given him Chocolate frogs, and Mrs. Weasley had knitted a Weasley sweater for him, like she does for all her children. There is a mysterious gift, which turns out to be an Invisibility Cloak. It includes an anonymous note, written in "narrow, loopy" writing, saying it had belonged to Harry's father.

Hermione's gift is sweeter than she thought, while Hagrid tends to give very useful gifts (which is recommended to keep in mind throughout the septology). And you never know, Mrs. Weasley's famous Christmas sweaters could become important. Harry's mystery gift-giver has loopy writing - although not a story-line clue, it is a septology Rememberit for diligent HP Sleuths.

The note from the Cloak also says that Harry should "use it well," so he (of course) has to try it. That night, Harry goes under cover to the restricted section of the library to see if he can find information on Flamel. Since Hogwarts does not teach Dark Magic, these books are only accessible with a teacher's permission. Harry senses a "faint whispering" (he thinks from the books) and feels prickling on the back of his neck. The very first book he pulls out falls open and starts shrieking non-stop.

> There's Harry's prickly neck – someone was definitely there, but it was not obvious who, and it was never explained. We have one theory that will be discussed as the plot is revealed. The faint whispering is very mysterious, and was also not explained. Harry was encouraged to use the Cloak, so the person who gave it to him definitely intended that Harry investigate the castle and "come across" things.

In Harry's attempt to run and hide, he slips into a room and finds an unusual mirror. There is a strange inscription on it that says "Erised stra ehru oyt ube cafru oyt on whosi."

> The inscription tells the secret of the mirror. Clever Sleuths would know that it is written in mirror language. With a little reflection, anyone can figure out mirror language.

In the mirror, Harry is startled to see not only himself, but also his lost family - including his parents. He sees his father's untidy hair that he inherited, and his mother's dark red hair and bright green eyes. He sees a crowd of other ancestors and relations who all share his features.

> The WWP Sleuthoscope is going bonkers! It is a virtual family reunion and a real whopper of a septology clue. Harry now sees for the first time what his family looked like. He sees where his physical traits come from, including (yes!) those bright green eyes of his mother. Note also his mother's dark red hair - this could be a very meaningful septology clue. Since there are numerous people in the mirror, Harry can see that his family had been fairly large. So, what happened to them all? Are there any still alive? Where are Aunt Petunia and "Dudders" in this mirror? Harry sees his mother's side - so is this proof that Aunt Petunia is NOT a blood relative? Now, if he truly is looking at all his immediate relatives (live and dead), then this Mirror also answers some other questions. It has been proposed that Dumbledore or Voldemort are relatives of Harry's, but if they do not appear in the mirror, does it mean that's not true? We cannot assume anything! CONSTANT VIGILANCE

Harry is so excited, he brings Ron back the next night to see them. Ron doesn't know what to expect - joking that maybe it only shows dead people.

> Ron jokes about the mirror only showing dead people, but Ron has weird stuff happen when he jokes, so we're not laughing. In fact, in this case, we're wondering if he could somehow be right.

On the way, they pass the ghost of a tall witch. There is no indication that the ghost saw them.

We know that J.K.R. rarely puts in anything just for effect. This ghost is there for a reason. Is she monitoring the halls and informing Dumbledore who is wandering around? Is she connected to Dumbledore, a former Headmistress, or the as yet unidentified Ravenclaw ghost? Can ghosts see through invisibility cloaks? As of Book 4, she is the only ghost Harry has encountered while under the Cloak, and she's not telling...

Ron does not see his parents, but sees himself as Prefect and captain of their Quidditch team. Harry and Ron are talking so loudly that they attract the attention of Mrs. Norris. They throw the Invisibility Cloak over themselves and hold their breath as they mercifully discover that the Cloak works on animals as well.

So far, the Invisibility Cloak has worked on all the animals encountered, although it may not work on a Demiguise. (If you don't know what that is, we recommend you brush up on your creature knowledge by checking out a copy of *Fantastic Beasts and Where to Find Them*, by Newt Scamander. You can get one from Madam Pince, Flourish and Blotts, or your local bookstore).

Ron doesn't trust the mirror, but Harry is captivated and returns a third night to sit and view his family. Dumbledore appears in the room and sits down on the floor to talk with Harry. He relates to Harry how he had observed Harry and Ron there the previous night, as he does "not need a cloak to become invisible."

The WWP Sleuthoscope is phasing out of sight! We have some crucial septology information about Dumbledore. We learn here that he can move invisibly around the castle at will. So, Dumbledore has lots of silvery hair and doesn't need an Invisibility Cloak to become invisible. We mentioned we are suspicious that he may have some Demiguise in his ancestry. We also now know that Dumbledore does wander around and sees what is happening at night, and apparently has even somehow intentionally led Harry to view this Mirror. Just how much is Dumbledore in control of events here (or do we dare ask)?

Dumbledore explains to Harry that this is the "Mirror of Erised" and that it only shows the viewer their heart's deepest desires, yet does not necessarily show the truth or the future. It therefore has been known to completely mesmerize viewers and even drive them mad with beguiling possibilities.

So, it could be possible that since Harry assumed all of his *true* relatives were dead, that he only **desired** to see his deceased relatives!? Wow!

Dumbledore claims that when he looks into the Mirror, what he sees is himself "holding a pair of thick, woolen socks."

Although the running bit with socks spans all four Books, this is the reference that can drive an HP Sleuth to Ogden's Old Firewhiskey. According to Dumbledore, thick woolen socks are his deepest desire, and although he is probably joking in the way he described it, his jokes are usually based in truth or to make a point. There is definitely something about wool, socks, or thick socks that factors into his greatest desire, but we do not yet seem to know enough to solve this mystery. Based on some future references, a hypothesis is that the socks represent retirement or freedom for him, or that he uses woolen socks and gowns for other activities, - but that is in lieu of hard evidence.

Dumbledore lets Harry know that the Mirror will be moved and that Harry should remember its power should he ever encounter it again.

Curiosities

✴ Does the call of a phoenix sound at all like an owl? Probably not, but Harry had not yet heard a phoenix, and since Book 5 relates to phoenixes, we were wondering if that's what the flute might sound like.

✴ Presumably Ron's grandfather, from whom he inherited his chessboard, was quite skilled, and it is possible that Ron may have inherited other special skills.

Other Oddities

✴ When Malfoy meanly taunts Ron (yet again), Ron swears "one of these days, I'll get him –" We think he just might get a chance sometime.☺

✴ Dumbledore sits on the floor to talk – Harry think he acts a lot younger than his years and the kids do not see him as an "old man."

✴ The author of *Fantastic Beasts and Where to Find* Them is Newt Scamander. Scamander is the river god that Homer talked about in his tales of the Trojan War. It was also the name of the river that flowed by the city of Troy.

Chapter 13 Analysis

Clues

This is chapter 13.

Welcome to Whodunit13. HP Sleuths will have noticed by now, that there are clues hiding wherever there is a significant number. J.K.R., therefore, could not resist the temptation to have the culprit or his fiendish plot make a *cameo appearance* within chapter 13 of each book. This is a trend that so far has held true through Book 4. The following are the key story-line events that take place in this chapter - we leave it up to HP Sleuths to decipher whodunit. Don't worry, if you can't solve it here, she always tells-all at the end of each book.☺

To his dismay, Harry learns that Snape will be refereeing at the next Quidditch game. After Malfoy "practices" a *Leg-Locker Curse* on Neville, Harry gives Neville a chocolate frog to make him feel better. Neville gratefully offers Harry the FW&W card out of it - it's another Dumbledore card, and Harry sees that this was where he had read about Nicolas Flamel.

All HP Sleuths who had remembered where Harry first saw the name "Flamel," raise your hands (going back and peeking doesn't count!)...only 13 of you? Don't worry, that is typical of how J.K.R. is so clever at getting us to read carefully the things she wants us to notice, and ignore as trivial the things she wants to slide by us. Almost everything she writes is an integral part of the septology mystery. If it does not impact the plot of a particular book, and even if it was not a clue when she first used it, she will most likely bring it into the mystery somewhere at a later time. HP Sleuths must have CONSTANT VIGILANCE!

Hermione looks Flamel up in an "enormous old" reference book where it was written that he was 665 years old as of "last year." It also states that he is a "noted opera lover."

J.K.R. is having fun playing with numbers here - if Flamel was 665 years old the previous year, then that means he was celebrating the big 666 in the year the biography was written. As that was written in an "enormous old book," we cannot possibly know how old Flamel really is (see Curiosities). What we do know is that he is yet another music lover! If you think that's just a coincidence, Neville's got a slightly used cauldron you might be interested in.

The old book says that Nicolas Flamel is the owner of the "Philosopher's (Sorcerer's) Stone." The Philosopher's Stone transforms any metal into gold and also "produces the Elixir of Life which will make the drinker immortal" (thus explaining Flamel's great age). The kids realize that Dumbledore is probably hiding the Philosopher's Stone in the trap door under Fluffy.

Who is looking for the Philosopher's (Sorcerer's) Stone and why? Also, how did Dumbledore know to move the Stone in time? (Seems as if that one is an unanswered question for the septology!) Another septology question is whether the Philosopher's Stone has any relationship to the pile of gold sitting in Harry's parents' Gringotts vault.

In their next Quidditch match, Gryffindor plays Hufflepuff. Although Snape referees, the game is one of the shortest games ever played, as Harry catches the Snitch less than 5 minutes into the match. After the game, Harry happens to witness Severus Snape holding a secret meeting with Quirrell in the forbidden forest. A hooting owl obscures part of the conversation, but Harry hears enough to know that Snape is asking Quirrell if he has found out how to get past Hagrid's dog, and that Quirrell is obviously scared of Snape.

What is going on between those two in the forest? (Rule #2 for one thing.) Let's just say that this is like the *ones that got away* - a real big fish story.

Harry, Ron, and Hermione are afraid that Quirrell may not hold up against Snape for long.

Curiosities

 It should be noted that Nicolas and Perenelle Flamel were real people who had really worked on an actual Philosopher's Stone in the 14th century, A.D., and were reputed to have truly discovered the Elixir of Life. So this obviously implies that they have made it to the present. According to the Harry Potter stories, we do not know how old Flamel **really** is. His age was listed as 665 in the **old book** Hermione found, and books don't typically look old for at least 50-100 years. This would mean he would have to be over 700 years old, and faked his "original" birth! Not sure if this is meant to be a clever twist or some other ploy.

 We learn that Snape's first name is Severus. There have been several famous people, including some nasty Roman emperors and a saint, with that name. Which one did J.K.R. have in mind, and what clues might that hold? Could the name just be a play on "sever us"?

Chapter 14 Analysis

Clues

As nothing had yet happened, it seems that Quirrell "must have been braver than they'd thought." However, Harry, Ron, and Hermione did notice that he was apparently becoming paler and thinner.

> J.K.R.'s just confusing us here with more facts. We are being told that Quirrell's personality may not be what it seems. We are also shown that whatever strain Quirrell is under, it is taking a physical toll on him.

While in the Library, Harry, Ron, and Hermione see Hagrid in there acting very mysterious about something. After he leaves, Ron discovers that Hagrid was looking up information about the care and feeding of dragons. Ron explains that it is illegal to keep and/or breed dragons, since the Ministry has a hard enough time putting *Memory Spells* (so they don't remember) on Muggles who constantly encounter wild ones.

> HP Sleuths may recall that Harry forgot the "dream" that he had about Slytherin his first night at Hogwarts. Could someone have used a *Memory Spell* on him? Are *Memory Spells* common?

Harry, Ron, and Hermione visit Hagrid in his cabin to learn that Professors Sprout, Flitwick, McGonagall, Quirrell, Dumbledore, and Snape had all cast different spells to protect the Stone. While there, they discover that Hagrid has won an illegal Norwegian Ridgeback dragon's egg from someone in a game of cards and is in the process of hatching it over a fire.

> While knowing who has cast spells adds to our information, it is marginal clue help. Since no teacher is specifically included or excluded, we do not learn anything except that all the primary teachers know about the Stone. The more intriguing story-line information is that Hagrid was very lucky to win something he had always wanted – a real dragon's egg. Wicked! (Should we check Rule #3?)

Through some slip-ups, Malfoy overhears Harry, Ron, and Hermione talking about the dragon in the Great Hall. Malfoy sneaks down to the cabin where he spies on them and apparently sees the illegal dragon hatching. They now need to get rid of the baby dragon (who Hagrid has affectionately named Norbert). Ron writes to his brother, Charlie, who agrees to rendezvous at midnight on Saturday in the tallest tower. Ron unfortunately leaves his letter in a book that Malfoy borrows, so Malfoy knows the time and place.

> The Malfoy incident is a bit confusing from a story-line perspective. He is so quick to tattle on anyone every other time, so why not this time - especially if he has the letter as evidence? Is it because it involves an adult, no one would believe him, or is this literary convenience? Until further notice, we'll settle for writer's license...

Using the Invisibility Cloak, Harry and Hermione haul Norbert in a crate up to the top of the tallest tower. On the way, they are ecstatic to see that Professor McGonagall has caught Malfoy who was sneaking around looking for them. Four of Charlie's friends arrive on broomsticks with a special harness used to transport Norbert away.

> This tallest tower is an interesting place. It is the location of their Astronomy classes, which we still have not observed as of Book 4, and is shrouded in mystery. We will be focusing more on this one throughout the septology.

In their glee from having disposed of Norbert and the thought of Malfoy in trouble, Harry and Hermione get careless, forget the Invisibility Cloak, and Filch catches them coming back down the stairs.

Rowlinguistics

★ Hagrid has a unique philosophy for naming his pets:
Fluffy & **Norbert** = nice name, nasty creatures
Fang = nasty name, harmless creature

Curiosities

★ Maybe to make up for the odd behavior of Malfoy in the book, the movie just had Malfoy run to Professor McGonagall to tell on Hagrid right away (makes sense to us). However, the movie also shows us that Filch and Dumbledore knew about the dragon, and implied many others also found out about it (that would mean that pretty much the whole castle knew). This is a discrepancy which should probably be clarified since Hagrid would not only have been in extremely big trouble, but it takes away from an important clue where Dumbledore later hints that he might have somehow found out about Hagrid's encounter with the dragon.

Clues

Filch brings the renegade students to Professor McGonagall, where she has also caught Neville (who had been trying to find and warn them that Malfoy was after them). She takes off scads of points and gives them detention for being in the tower - an area that is out of bounds except for classes. She also scolds them for walking around at night "especially these days - it's very dangerous."

> Ahem! What does Professor McGonagall know - or what is she implying that is so dangerous "these days"? Is that supposed to be the Stone or a story-line clue? And what goes on in the Astronomy tower that is so important that it is off-limits except for classes? This is a major septology question that has yet to be answered. Even the dungeons are accessible. Who (or what) might live in the Astronomy tower besides a few bats?

The rest of the school is not talking to Harry, Ron, Hermione, or Neville for losing so many house points that Slytherin is back on top, and Harry swears off interfering. They start studying for final exams - cramming information such as the dates of the goblin rebellions. As they look at the vast collection of library books, they wonder if there is a book that describes how to get past a huge, three-headed dog.

> For those who know their Greek legends, there are, of course, a number of books that tell how to get past a three-headed dog. Check the HP Sleuth Reading List if you want to do your own research. The boring goblin rebellions might have been introduced here to help us relate to the tedium and work required by some of the classes, however those rebellion studies have taken on a life of their own. They have become a running bit for comic relief, but they also hold septology clues. Just like real history classes, the goblin rebellions are important lessons that may impact current events. Tolkien scholars already know the importance of goblin-wars. We will be seeing a lot more about goblins and goblin rebellions, so HP Sleuths had better start studying too.

From inside a classroom, Harry overhears Quirrell giving in to someone and sobbing. Harry is about to investigate who is in there, when he remembers his promise to himself to stay out of things. He watches as Quirrell leaves the room, straightening his turban. Harry is sure it was Snape who was in there - he would have wagered 12 Philosopher's Stones on it. The kids are now bummed that Quirrell has at last given in and told Snape how to break his spell, but that Snape still does not know how to get past Fluffy.

> This is story-line stuff all the way. How convenient that Harry resists temptation to see who's there just as Quirrell gives in (see Rule #2). What exactly happened in that room? Notice that oh so subtle comment about Quirrell straightening

his turban as he leaves. We are denied evidence for a reason. The only clue we are given is that pesky number 12.

Harry, Hermione, Neville, and Malfoy are assigned their detention. They are to accompany Hagrid into the Forbidden Forest, which unnerves Malfoy. As a gentle breeze blows through their hair, Hagrid explains that they need to track a wounded unicorn (a rare injury, as unicorns are protected by powerful magic).

This is a very strange detention. Did Dumbledore orchestrate it to expose Harry to the forest and dangerous events that are occurring? Note the story-line clue that it had to be something Dark and powerful to have injured a unicorn, and it is now roaming the forest. Also, what's with that breeze? Is that just the wind again?

Hagrid splits them into two groups - Malfoy chooses to go with Fang and Neville, while Harry and Hermione go with Hagrid. Hagrid cautions Malfoy that Fang is a sissy and they are to "keep ter the path." The kids are instructed to send-up green sparks if they find the unicorn, or red sparks if they get into trouble. Hagrid assures them that "there's nothin' that lives in the forest that'll hurt yeh if yer with me or Fang."

So, nothing in the forest will hurt them as long as they are with Fang? Is that really true? Didn't he just tell us that Fang is a sissy?

Harry's group comes across two centaurs, Ronan and Bane, who warn of Mars shining especially bright. They do not speak plainly, talking about foreboding signs and that "the innocent are the first to die." After the centaurs leave, Hagrid explains that those creatures know things, but are always cryptic.

As many people know from watching mythology-oriented shows on TV, Mars (Ares) is the ancient Greek/Roman god of war. It is a reddish planet (blood-red to some), and portends conflict and challenge. The most important aspect of this encounter is that we are given some septology clues. One of them is that the centaurs DO know what is in the stars (as in seeing the future), but have been sworn to not change destiny. That means they do give accurate hints - even if they don't speak plainly (so it is probably true that more innocent lives may be in peril). The other clue is that this brightening of Mars has been ongoing, and is not just a solitary event.

They go on, yet Harry is convinced they are being followed. Hermione suddenly spots red sparks, and Hagrid sprints off to help the others. Fortunately, it was only Malfoy sneaking up on Neville, but Hagrid splits them up again - putting Harry, Malfoy, and Fang together. Harry and Malfoy go off, sticking to the path as Hagrid had told them.

Knowing the care that everyone in the school has taken to protect the students, it is illogical that they would then allow Harry (or any students) to wander alone and unprotected in the Forbidden Forest. Therefore, Harry's instincts are probably correct – they are most likely being followed - but it is friend (not foe) who tails them.

Harry's group finds the unicorn shining sadly in a clearing where it recently died. They hear a slithering sound and witness a cloaked figure crawl across the ground and drink from the fatal wound. Malfoy and Fang are spooked, and bolt. The figure raises its head and looks straight at Harry. Harry's scar suddenly pierces his head with blinding pain, and he falls to his knees as hooves gallop over him, charging at the figure. It is a centaur, but a different one, who rescues Harry. His name is Firenze, and he is concerned about getting Harry back to Hagrid.

> HP Sleuths should beware that the hooded figure was described as "slithering" across the ground. The centaur's presence and quick action were almost certainly not a coincidence. Firenze called Hagrid by name, knew who Harry was, was not at all surprised to find Harry there, and even knew where in the forest to find Hagrid. Sounds like Rule #3 to us.

Firenze places Harry on his back. Ronan and Bane arrive and are upset that Firenze is carrying a human on his back and interfered by saving Harry. Firenze is upset with them for not being more concerned about the events they just witnessed, and is willing to align himself with humans to fight it.

> This is a really interesting scene. Ronan and Bane think that Firenze might have altered something that was told to them in the stars. Did Firenze get in trouble for it, or was it not an issue since he was entrusted to protect Harry this night? It is apparent that they are aware of a monumental impending threat and consider it serious – bigger that just Book 1....

As Firenze gallops off with Harry to find Hagrid, he explains to Harry that unicorn blood is used to keep someone alive (even at the brink of death), but it is a cursed, half-life. However, the Elixir of Life from the Philosopher's Stone, which is currently "hidden in the school," can be used to bring the person back to full strength, plus then they never die. It could be worth drinking the unicorn blood to survive until then.

> WWP Sleuthoscope is glowing deep red. How did Firenze know that the Stone is in there? Because of magic, the stars, or is he a friend?

Firenze helps Harry to realize that the not-quite-dead Voldemort could possibly be the one feeding on unicorns and trying to get at the Stone.

> Well, for HP Sleuths, this new information was a bit anti-climatic. We had already figured that Voldemort was somehow involved, but we still don't know exactly how he is in communication with anyone. It does raise the stakes a lot now that we know why the Stone is so important and what Voldemort plans to do with it; but we're still back where we were - trying to figure out how to convince anyone that one of the teachers wants to get to the Stone.

Harry tells Ron and Hermione about the Centaurs and their fortune-telling. Hermione advises them that Professor McGonagall informed them that is a "very imprecise branch of magic."

> This is not the only time Professor McGonagall will tell us about the shortcomings of fortune telling. Is she personally very sensitive to it, or are we being told for a reason?

When Harry goes to his dorm, he finds the forgotten Invisibility Cloak returned to him on the bed.

> We don't think Harry sewed his nametag into the Invisibility Cloak, so it must have found its way back to whoever gave it to him. Who would have picked it up in the tower, and did whoever it was see Norbert flying off?

There is a short note attached to the Cloak: "Just in case."

Curiosities

✳ We have only been told a few things about unicorn magic - so expect there will be more about unicorns later in the septology.

✳ How does J.K.R. define a "cursed life" from the unicorn blood? Are they cursed because they are forever trapped between life and death, or are there other ramifications?

Clues

The students have their exams, which are given with quills that have been bewitched with *Anti-Cheating Spells*. Harry's scar keeps bothering him with stabbing pains, and he keeps having his nightmare of flashing light and pain. After finishing exams, they are crashed out on the grass, watching Fred, George, and Lee Jordan sitting on the edge of the Hogwarts lake, tickling the tentacles of the Giant Squid.

> The Giant Squid seems friendly enough, and apparently may even *know* some of the students by sight. If that's true, it could come in handy to have a great creature like that on your side. Harry's scar is telling him of danger, but he is not correlating it well. He does realize that the danger is real, yet exams have also been very painful and very real.

Harry sits gazing at an owl flying toward the school with a note in its mouth. As he thinks about Hagrid, Harry suddenly realizes that Hagrid could have slipped. He runs down to the cabin with Ron and Hermione on his heels.

> This is the ultimate in subtlety. While in most books this scene with the owl soaring overhead would have been there just for atmosphere, in a J.K.R. book, that owl is carrying an extremely important letter.

Harry asks Hagrid all about the person from whom he had won the dragon's egg, and what he talked about. Hagrid explains that the stranger was hooded and did not show his face. The stranger kept buying him drinks while keeping him talking until Hagrid seemed to slip and let out that the dog could be sedated with music. (He shouldn'ta told them that!)

> Ahhh, music - of course. Talk about subtle...Yep, Fluffy's got Cerberus' blood in him, alright. Cerberus was sedated by music in the Greek myth of Orpheus. If you are a mythology fan, you might have also guessed a piece of meat or drugged cake as used by the ancient sorceress, Sibyl, to get by Cerberus. However, we were given all those wonderful allusions to music. Remember back in Chapter 9, when they first encountered Fluffy - Harry thought it did not attack because their sudden appearance surprised it? Wrong. The reason it didn't attack was because Peeves' singsong voice was keeping it a bit sleepy! We can see how J.K.R. purposely drops clues like that. However, don't forget all these music lovers now - musicians are highly skilled at pattern recognition and would be the kind to bury codes within music in the future. By the way, who was that hooded figure that sold the egg to Hagrid?

Harry, Ron and Hermione run immediately to talk to Dumbledore, but Professor McGonagall informs them that Dumbledore has just been summoned to London on an emergency, and won't return until the next day. They realize it is a ploy to get Dumbledore away from the school grounds so Voldemort can steal the Stone. Since it is obvious that there is no time, as it will probably happen that night, they tell McGonagall about the Stone being stolen. She does not believe that it is possible, and shoos them off, threatening to take off more points if she catches them near the corridor.

> Remember the owl with the note in its mouth that Harry watched earlier in the afternoon? That was the note calling Dumbledore to London. Harry could not have known it was the deceptive message, but that is yet another way that J.K.R. loves to mess with our brains.

Frustrated and desperate, they all agree to try to retrieve the Stone before Voldemort does. As they are leaving the Gryffindor common room that night, Neville tries to stop them from getting Gryffindor into yet more trouble. As a last resort, Hermione has to place a full *Body-Bind Spell* on the poor kid. Harry checks the grandfather clock, and they exit nervously.

> Not only is this another clock - it's a **grandfather** clock. Guess it's time for a big event. Grandfather clocks are known for stopping when someone dies, and as portals to other worlds. They also have great big faces. High septology potential here.

Harry, Ron and Hermione arrive at the third-floor corridor.

- ☾ Using the flute that Hagrid made for Harry, they put Hagrid's dog, Fluffy, to sleep and then drop down through the trap door.

- ☾ They land in Professor Sprout's "Devil's Snare" of dark, damp plants that entwines and tries to suffocate them, but Hermione is able to free them with a jet of warm, bright flames.

- ☾ In Professor Flitwick's room, Harry has to fly a broomstick to catch the one key that opens the next door from hundreds of evasive, flying keys flittering above the room.

- ☾ In the next room, Professor McGonagall has transfigured a wizard chess set into life-size chessmen, and the three kids need to assume the places of three chessmen and win a dangerous game of wizard chess. Ron must sacrifice himself to a queen before winning spectacularly so they can move on. (Harry and Hermione have to leave Ron behind, unconscious.)

- ☾ Quirrell's room has a troll lying on the ground, already knocked out, so Harry and Hermione do not have to deal with him.

- ☾ In Snape's room a wall of fire springs up in each doorway as they enter, trapping them inside, and a table of potions includes a riddle to solve. The riddle states that some of the potions will let the drinker move ahead through the fire, or go back, but 3 are poisonous. Hermione solves the riddle, but there is not enough potion in the teeny bottle for both of them to move onward, so Hermione drinks the potion to go back and summon help, while Harry drinks the potion which allows him to proceed into the next room.

When reading the Harry Potter book, there are actually 2 solutions to Snape's riddle. The bottle that they needed (the Forward bottle) turned out to be the "smallest bottle," so it's position cannot be absolute without seeing the **size** of the bottles. If we want to know the real solution, it requires knowing the size of each bottle (especially one of the poison bottles and the forward bottle), which is not given in the book. Without knowing the sizes of those two, they are interchangeable - so there are 2 possible solutions. Below are the two solutions that satisfy the requirements as we know them from the book.

In this solution, there is no poison on the right of any nettle, although the verse only said that there was always a poison on the left - it never said the poison couldn't be also on the right:

Poison	Nettle	Forward	Poison	Poison	Nettle	Back

This is the alternate solution:

Poison	Nettle	Poison	Forward	Poison	Nettle	Back

According to the images on the *Wizards of the Coast* TCG, the correct solution is the second one (alternate solution).

When Harry arrives in the next room, there is, indeed, someone already there, but it is not Voldemort or Snape standing there.

Other Oddities

✳ Harry is reminded of Gringotts by the way the stone passageway slopes down. We also are reminded of goblin tunneling. Who built these tunnels? Where do they go? What were they for originally? Is the last room truly the last room?

✳ In Professor Flitwick's room of keys, Harry, Ron, and Hermione "each seized a broomstick and kicked off into the air," grabbing at the keys. This is just a minor reinforcement that Hermione does, indeed, know how to fly.

✳ In the movie, they show Fluffy drooling heavily on Ron. That is not only gross, but would have been potentially deadly to Ron. Legend tells us that the spittle of Cerberus (Fluffy's ancestor) was the origin of the deadly poisonous plant, aconite (remember Snape's first lecture?).

✳ The "Full-Body Bind" on Neville has a really wild French translation. When Harry asks Hermione what she did to poor Neville, she replies that she used the "evil spell of the large, dry sausage" on him!

Chapter 17 Analysis

Clues

Quirrell is the traitor. Harry bemoans that he was so sure it was Snape. Quirrell agrees that Snape was an excellent decoy the way he was always "swooping around like an over-grown bat," but it was Quirrell all the way. Quirrell explains to a confused Harry that he was the one who broke into Gringotts with Voldemort's help. He also was jinxing Harry's broom during the Quidditch match until Hermione knocked him over on her way to get to Snape, which interrupted his curse that they thought Snape was casting.

> Wow! Look how intricate J.K.R. has made this. Remember - Harry met Quirrell at the Leaky Cauldron that day? (Hmmmm... Harry also saw Draco.) Also, back at the Sorting Ceremony when Harry's scar hurt, Snape was right next to Quirrell. So it wasn't Snape (but Snape does drive even Quirrell batty). Do we assume then that it was a hooded Quirrell who gave Norbert's egg to Hagrid, or could someone else have been helping him?

Quirrell was also responsible for Snape being attacked by Fluffy and for the troll on Halloween. However, Quirrell was unable to do anything whenever Dumbledore was watching.

> This is something that has been true through at least Book 4 - no matter who the foe is, they are always afraid to act in sight of Dumbledore. Dumbledore is clearly a very powerful wizard. There is also a lot of mystery still surrounding Dumbledore.

The room in which Harry and Quirrell confront each other contains *Dumbledore's Spell*, in the form of the Mirror of Erised. As Quirrell looks into the Mirror, he sees himself presenting the Stone to Voldemort, but cannot find the actual Stone. A voice, which seems to come from inside Quirrell, tells him to use Harry. Harry is aware of the strange smell coming from Quirrell's turban as he sets Harry in front of the Mirror.

> Did HP Sleuths notice what was always in the Mirror of Erised – no matter who was looking in it? Can HP Sleuths remember what it is that everyone (Harry, Ron, Dumbledore, and Quirrell) has seen? The one thing that is present in everyone's "deepest desires" is: themselves.

Harry sees the Stone being placed into his reflection's pocket at the same time that he feels the weight of the Stone enter into his own pocket. When asked what he sees, Harry claims he sees himself winning the Quidditch Cup, but the voice from the turban insists he lied and demands that it speak directly to Harry. Quirrell unwraps his turban, and on the back of his head is the ashen face of Voldemort, who is alive in Quirrell and addresses Harry.

That two-faced excuse for a Professor...it was the turban! At the Sorting Ceremony, when Harry thought that Snape zapped his scar, he hadn't thought about Quirrell's turban there next to Snape. Also, that means the Voldemort/Quirrell combination was the thing they saw drinking the unicorn blood when Harry collapsed from the pain in the forest. Looks like Harry's scar is a Voldemort sensor. There is also a powerfully strong septology clue here. Voldemort seems to be able to detect when someone is lying, and is adamant that he knows when people lie to him. From what we've seen, we won't argue.

Voldemort tells Harry that his parents were begging for mercy when they died, but he then changes his story when Harry calls him a liar.

Voldemort speaks with forked tongue (groan). He may have lied to Harry to try to intimidate or weaken him, but it still means that Voldemort will alter facts to suit his purpose. Therefore, we are forewarned that we cannot completely believe what Voldemort says (Do we look stupid?).

Voldemort says he values bravery and that Harry's parents were brave - Voldemort first killed Harry's father after a valiant struggle.

Here's some septology information – Voldemort says he killed Harry's father first. (No obvious reason to lie about that, yet we can't be sure.) Then, even Voldemort has to get into the act - confirming that the bad guys consider bravery a definite Potter family trait. HP Sleuths on safari – we're going lion hunting.

Voldemort is emphatic that Harry's mother died only because she insisted on protecting Harry.

Okay, given what you know about Voldemort, how much would **you** trust him if he said he would leave you alone (even if he wasn't about to kill yet another person in your family)? Still, Voldemort has now emphatically stated that he specifically wanted to kill the infant - that his attempt on Harry's life was not just part of a general killing spree. Also, why was Voldemort (supposedly) willing to spare Harry's mother? The mystery is just beginning....

Voldemort asks Harry to give him the Stone from his pocket (he knew). Harry tries to run, but Quirrell grabs him. Harry's scar sears with pain, but he then sees that he is inflicting great pain on Quirrell too. Harry grabs at Quirrell, who breaks out in horrible blisters wherever Harry touches his bare skin. Just by touching Quirrell (and Voldemort) Harry sees that he can fight back. As Quirrell tries to kill him, Harry grips tight and holds on until he eventually blacks-out from his own trauma.

That scar is going to be a real pain in the head, but it could definitely be useful if Harry is trying to track or elude Voldemort. We also find out that Voldemort is in for a rude surprise if he tries to lay even a virtual hand on Harry.

Harry awakes in a hospital bed with Dumbledore looking over him. Dumbledore explains that he arrived back just in time to save Harry by pulling Quirrell off, but Voldemort escaped - leaving Quirrell to die. Dumbledore also claims that the Stone has been destroyed, as agreed by Flamel and his wife.

> J.K.R. has such a talent for being ambiguous. She is so descriptive but somehow avoids the precise facts. So, Quirrell was left to die, and Dumbledore says that **particular** Stone was destroyed. Was that **the** Stone? Could there have been more than one – or something even better now? And, of course, Voldemort is true to his name – as he obviously had managed (like Tolkien's Sauron) to escape death, and **may not even be capable of dying.** We learned our lesson from Sauron that Dark Lords can rise again "stronger than ever." Do not expect Voldemort to be easy to defeat permanently, which could give the good guys a lot of grief!

Dumbledore tells Harry, "your mother died to save you." Dumbledore also lets Harry know that the protection his mother gave him from her powerful, loving, spell is still with him - in his very skin.

> The WWP Sleuthoscope is pulsating like a quasar! Back in Chapter 1, Dumbledore said "we may never know" how Harry survived. We now have a statement by Dumbledore that Harry was protected because of a powerful charm his mother used on him. That may have been true, but how does Dumbledore know about her spell or what happened at all that night **if he wasn't there before she died?** Or was he? Or was someone else? Now we're the ones with a headache....

Dumbledore will not yet explain to Harry why Voldemort had wanted to kill him. He tells Harry that he will find out when it is time, although he impressed on Harry the importance of not being afraid of using Voldemort's name.

> Grrrrrr! Yes, it's rule #2 - to the extreme. This is it, of course - this is THE MYSTERY QUESTION. All other questions, clues, and events focus on this one controversy - why DOES Voldemort consider it so important to kill Harry then and now? Based on the way he said it, Dumbledore surely seems to know the answer. J.K.R. had better have a really good reason for this one if she is going to make us wait 7 volumes to tell us! No matter what, Dumbledore does not want Harry to be afraid of using Voldemort's name. Dumbledore is not afraid to use it. Remember that - if Dumbledore ever refers to Voldemort as "You-Know-Who," be immediately suspicious....

Dumbledore does admit to giving Harry his father's Invisibility Cloak at Christmas (which he recalls was used mostly for sneaking food from the kitchens). He also explains that Professor Snape hates Harry because Harry's father (who Snape detested) saved his life.

When we are told that James Potter used the Cloak to get food, we should know better than to think that Harry's dad would just be hungry. There is a story behind that - it will be told in Book 3. We also find out in Book 3 more about the friction between Snape and Harry's father. As usual, there's a lot more to it. By the way - why (how) did Dumbledore (the guy with loopy handwriting) end up with James's Invisibility Cloak? Did James leave that and their Gringott's key with Dumbledore because they were afraid something would happen?

Dumbledore jokes with Harry as he explains what happened. Dumbledore mentions that he is proud of his idea to use the Mirror for the Stone - and is amused by his own cleverness with the concept.

We are convinced that although Hermione's personality is based on J.K.R. as a kid, Dumbledore is J.K.R. now. J.K.R is speaking through Dumbledore and controlling events through Dumbledore.

Dumbledore clarifies that the reason Harry was able to find the Philosopher's Stone was because he was only looking for the Stone, itself - NOT the powers it would bring.

Those HP Sleuths who have not yet figured out how to read the inscription on the Mirror - just *think like a mirror* (the words are displayed as if they are reflected back in a mirror). If any HP Sleuths still need help deciphering it – check the Rowlinguistics and Intriguing Info at the end of this chapter.

Also, don't feel badly if you are still not completely clear about how that "deepest desire" thing works. Lots and lots of people didn't quite get exactly why Harry could get the Stone but Quirrell could not. There are also many inaccurate explanations being circulated. The real explanation is:

* One sees in the Mirror **exactly** what their heart desires.If they seek the Stone for its elixir, they don't see how to obtain the Stone, but instead see themselves drinking the elixir from it.

* If they seek the Stone for another person (such as Lord Voldemort), again, they do not see how to obtain the Stone - they only see themselves being rewarded as they hand it to their master.

* However, if they are only looking to obtain the Stone itself, with no other purpose except to have it in their hand, then they see themselves holding the Stone - and thus, they do so.

So simple, yet so paradoxical. It is so clever, in fact, that when Dumbledore comments that he considers it "one of my more brilliant ideas" and that "my brain surprises even me sometimes," we are sure that J.K.R. is actually speaking through her character. It was a stroke of brilliance and she is having fun with it, herself - especially since the Mirror is hiding septology secrets we still haven't solved!

Ron and Hermione visit Harry in the hospital, and Harry hypothesizes that Dumbledore purposely gave them the chance to go after the Stone and face Voldemort if they desired. In fact, it is Harry's opinion that Dumbledore pretty much knows everything that goes on in the school.

> This idea that Dumbledore knows most everything that goes on is quite possible and we see a lot of evidence of that in all the stories. It is likely that between teachers, ghosts, portraits, suits of armor, elves, students, and his own incredible powers, that Dumbledore does have the ability to monitor (if not control) a good portion of activity. It's mind-boggling. It's probably so complex, it's not even worth us trying to figure out how he's doing it all....

Hagrid comes to visit Harry, sobbing over his blunder in spilling the secret of Fluffy. Hagrid gives Harry a present of a photo album filled with pictures of his mother and father, obtained from their old school buddies.

> Yet more to ponder. Who and where are all these old friends of Harry's mother and father? Some of this will be addressed in Book 3, but there's still plenty of mystery about that too!

At the end-of-year feast, Slytherin House thinks they have won the House Cup, but Dumbledore awards extra points. Ron gets points for his big chess game, Hermione gets points for her logic with the potions, Harry got his for nerve and courage (roar), and even Neville received points for bravery at standing up to his friends. Hermione, of course, tops the class with her grades.

> Yes, Harry gets the lion's share of the award for (what else?) nerve and courage. This profiles the personalities of the kids well. Expect them to live up to their "reputations."

Gryffindor has won the House Cup! Dumbledore magically transforms the decorations in the Great Hall from Slytherin green and silver to Gryffindor scarlet and gold.

> Remember Harry's wand (back in Chapter 5) sent out red and gold sparks when he first tested it? Curious. And he's a Leo. Very curious. And he's a very bravehearted Gryffindor. Very curious indeed!

Back at platform nine and three-quarters, a "wizened old guard" is responsible for regulating the students' re-entry into the Muggle station.

> Now this guy is really subtle but potentially important. He obviously must be there not only to regulate flow of traffic, but most likely to perform *Memory Spells* if there is an *oops*, and possibly to keep an eye out for undesirables (like escaped prisoners maybe). The trouble is, we have not seen him since, so we do not know for sure if J.K.R. has any plans for him, but we do know he had better be on our side....

Harry returns to the Dursleys and Privet Drive - but he knows he is a wizard and has the advantage this time!

Curiosities

✳ Quirrell was not only two-faced, but he (and his Voldemort façade) remind us of Janus, the two-headed mythological character after which the month January is named – as it looks both back at the previous year while looking forward to the new year. Is Voldemort Harry's past and future?

✳ Where is Fluffy now?

✳ The inscription at the top of the Mirror of Erised is written plainly if you view it from a mirror's perspective – that is, it reads right-to-left:
"Erised stra eh/ru oy/t ub/e caf/ru oy/t on wohs/I"
Knowing that, HP Sleuths can see that the inscription says:
I show not your face but your hearts desirE

✳ Where is the Mirror of Erised now?

✳ We have seen several references to a smell supposedly coming from Quirrell's turban. A strange clue to go with a strange smell. The reason for the smell is not ever explained. It is probably not significant since there are many other times when J.K.R. could have explained it, but HP Sleuths should stash that in your cap, just in case.

Other Oddities

✳ A famous quote from a famous bad guy: "There is no good and evil, there is only power and those too weak to seek it."

✳ The Philosopher's (Sorcerer's) Stone is described as "blood red" in color

✳ It has been reinforced in both the book and the movie that Dumbledore hates Bertie Bott's candies because he always gets pukey ones (such as vomit and ear wax flavors).

✳ Goyle is portrayed as the most stupid in their class.

✳ Hagrid takes the first years to the boats again when they leave.

Key Rememberit Clues from Book 1

(HARRY POTTER AND THE PHILOSOPHER'S/SORCERER'S STONE)

Book 1 Mysteries Not Yet Solved

- ☾ Why did (does) Voldemort want to kill Harry?
- ☾ What happened the night Harry's parents died, and why was the house destroyed?
- ☾ How did everyone all know about and communicate the events that took place the night Voldemort attacked the Potters?
- ☾ Voldemort says he killed Harry's father first – Voldemort's a liar, do we believe him?
- ☾ How did Dumbledore get James' Invisibility Cloak, and how did Hagrid get the key to the Potter's vault?
- ☾ Did Hagrid bring the infant Harry somewhere else before Privet Drive?
- ☾ Is Dumbledore in control of events?
- ☾ Who is Dumbledore, what does he know, and what is his past?
- ☾ Why won't Dumbledore leave Hogwarts?
- ☾ What is the history behind Lily and Petunia?
- ☾ Why did Harry not see any living relatives (like Petunia) in the Mirror of Erised?
- ☾ What is so special about Harry's eyes?
- ☾ Can all wizards talk to animals?
- ☾ What is Harry's relationship to the Gryffindor?
- ☾ Why did the Sorting Hat want to put Harry into Slytherin?
- ☾ Why did the Sorting Hat take so long with Seamus and Neville?
- ☾ Why did Harry not remember the dream about Quirrell's turban?
- ☾ Why does Snape hate Harry so much?
- ☾ Why did Filch bandage Snape's leg instead of Madam Pomfrey?
- ☾ Why haven't we seen an Astronomy class or the tallest tower?
- ☾ Who gave Norbert's egg to Hagrid?
- ☾ Why was Hagrid expelled?
- ☾ What was that "faint whispering" Harry heard in the Hogwarts library?
- ☾ Who is the Ravenclaw ghost?
- ☾ Who was the ghost Harry and Ron saw on their way to the mirror?

- ꙅ Why is Peeves allowed to remain at Hogwarts?

- ꙅ Can ghosts see through Invisibility Cloaks?

- ꙅ Where did Percy get Scabbers (and why was Ron allowed to take him to school)?

- ꙅ What are *Switching Spells* and how do they work?

- ꙅ What is the magic behind Owl deliveries?

- ꙅ Why was an owl flying through the Dursley's neighborhood?

- ꙅ Is there a reason that Mrs. Figg's house smells just like an Apothecary?

- ꙅ Who planted Harry's letters in the eggs?

- ꙅ Why can't Dumbledore tell Harry why Voldemort wanted to kill him?

BOOK 2 MYSTERIES

About Book 2

Statistics

Book 2 Title - *Harry Potter and the Chamber of Secrets* - by J. K. Rowling

Facts & Statistics:
- First British Printing, Bloomsbury Publishing, July, 1998
- First U.S. Printing, Scholastic, Inc., June, 1999

Awards:
- Nestlé Smarties Book Prize - Gold Medal 9-11years, 1998
- Scottish Arts Council Children's Book Award 1999
- British Book Awards - Children's Book of the Year 1998
- North East Book Award 1999
- North East Scotland Book Award 1998
- The Booksellers Association / The Bookseller Author of the Year 1998
- FCBG (Federation of Children's Books Group) Children's Book Award - Overall winner and for Longer Novel Category, 1998

Movie Stats:
- Movie Release date: November, 2002

Key Mystery Characters

STUDENTS
Millicent Bulstrode (Slytherin)
Penelope Clearwater (Ravenclaw)
Crabbe (Slytherin)
Colin Creevey (Gryffindor)
Justin Finch-Fletchley (Hufflepuff)
Seamus Finnegan (Gryffindor)
Goyle (Slytherin)
Hermione Granger (Gryffindor)
Lee Jordan (Gryffindor
Neville Longbottom (Gryffindor)
Draco Malfoy (Slytherin)
Harry Potter (Gryffindor)
Dean Thomas (Gryffindor)
Fred Weasley (Gryffindor)
George Weasley (Gryffindor)
Ginny Weasley (Gryffindor)
Percy Weasley (Gryffindor)
Ron Weasley (Gryffindor)
Oliver Wood (Gryffindor)

RELATIVES
Cousin Dudley Dursley
Aunt Petunia Dursley
Uncle Vernon Dursley
Mr. & Mrs. Granger
Neville's Gran
Lucius Malfoy
James Potter
Lily Potter
Mr. Arthur Weasley
Charlie Weasley
Mrs. Molly Weasley

TEACHERS & STAFF
Prof. Binns (History of Magic)
Headmaster Armando Dippet
(Former Headmaster)
Prof. Albus Dumbledore (Headmaster)
Argus Filch (Caretaker)
Prof. Flitwick (Charms)
Rubeus Hagrid (Groundskeeper/
Keeper of the Keys)
Prof. Gilderoy Lockhart (Defense against
the Dark Arts)
Prof. Minerva McGonagall
(Deputy Headmistress/Transfiguration)
Madam Pince (Librarian)
Madam Pomfrey (Nurse)
Prof. Sinistra (Astronomy)
Prof. Severus Snape (Potions Master)
Prof. Sprout (Herbology

OTHER HUMANS
Lord Voldemort ("You-Know-Who")
Tom Marvolo Riddle
Cornelius Fudge
Mr. & Mrs. Mason

CREATURES & ENTITIES
Aragog
Bloody Baron (Slytherin Ghost)
Dobby
Errol the owl
Fang the boarhound
Fat Lady Portrait
Fawkes
Turquoise Ford Anglia
Hedwig the owl
Sir Nicholas de Mimsy-Porpington
(see Nearly Headless Nick)
Moaning Myrtle
Nearly-Headless Nick (Gryffindor Ghost)
Mrs. Norris the cat
Peeves the Poltergeist
Scabbers the rat
Weasley Ghoul

Bits and Rememberits

These are clues and unsolved mysteries from the previous book that HP Sleuths should keep in mind as they read Book 2. Keep alert for more evidence....

Rememberits

Running Bits That May Be Clues

Body Parts
- Noses
- Eyes
- Ears
- Feet
- Heart
- Stomach
- Hands and Fingers
- Untidy and/or long Hair

Creatures
- Slugs
- Spiders
- Beetles, Cockroaches, and Scarabs
- Flies and Bugs in general

Numbers
- The number 12 and Chapter 12s
- The number 13 and Chapter 13s

Woolies
- Socks
- Mrs. Weasley's Sweaters

Wonderland
- Watches and Clocks
- Hares and Rabbits

Miscellaneous
- Ogden's Old Firewhiskey
- Orphans
- Banging noises

Questions Still Bugging Us...

- Why did (does) Voldemort want to kill Harry?
- What happened the night Harry's parents died, and why was the house destroyed?
- Voldemort says he killed Harry's father first – Voldemort's a liar, do we believe him?
- Why can't Dumbledore tell Harry why Voldemort wanted to kill him?
- Is Dumbledore in control of events?
- Who is Dumbledore, what does he know, and what is his past?
- Why won't Dumbledore leave Hogwarts?
- Why did Harry not see any living relatives (like Petunia) in the Mirror of Erised?
- What is the history behind Lily and Petunia?
- What is so special about Harry's eyes?
- What is Harry's relationship to *the* Gryffindor?
- Why did the Sorting Hat want to put Harry into Slytherin?
- Why does Snape hate Harry so much?
- Why was Hagrid expelled?

- Who gave Norbert's egg to Hagrid?
- Where did Percy get Scabbers? (And why was Ron allowed to take him to school?)
- Can all wizards talk to animals?
- Can ghosts see through Invisibility Cloaks?
- Who is the Ravenclaw ghost?
- Why haven't we seen an Astronomy class or the tallest tower?
- Is there a reason that Mrs. Figg's house smells just like an Apothecary?
- Why was an owl flying through the Dursley's neighborhood?
- Who planted Harry's letters in the eggs?

Interesting Tidbits

The Choices You Make Define Who You Really Are (...and How You Should Be Judged).
As J.K.R. described in an interview with *The Sydney Morning Herald*, a major theme of Book 2 is to establish the effect of choices and actions taken by Harry and the other characters. No matter who they are or what kind of background they came from, each character is faced with choices that define who they are and what they will become. Those choices will also impact the lives of all the characters and are at the heart of this mystery. The Sorting Hat gave Harry a choice: Slytherin and power, or Gryffindor and morality. Harry took Gryffindor.

What HP Sleuths Have to Notice in Book 2
Back in Book 1, there were constant references to music, Harry's eyes, the number twelve, and other *running bits* – both obvious and subtle. We did not point out every mention (some of you will thank us). We showed the first few times they appeared and once you got the idea, we only drew attention to later key instances. In Book 2, there will be more running bits and we will use the same procedure. For those who want the challenge, you can pick your favorite running bits and go back and see how may occurrences you can spot. It is mind-boggling how many hints J.K.R can slip into any one chapter!

WWP's Rules of Constant Vigilance!
Never let your guard down with J.K.R. These are The Rules to remember for HP Sleuths:

1) If she reinforces it, she means it (and wants us to remember it).

2) If she suddenly interrupts something, she's hiding a key clue!

3) There's no such thing as a coincidence.

4) Don't take a character's word for it.

(see WWP Help Desk FAQs for full explanation)

Chapter 1 Analysis

(THE WORST BIRTHDAY)

Clues

The Dursleys are so paranoid of young wizard Harry Potter, that he now sleeps in his Cousin Dudley's spare bedroom upstairs. However, they have locked all of his wizarding books and supplies in his former closet down under the stairs. Hedwig (his owl) has also been locked in her cage, so Harry has not been able to send word to Ron or Hermione all summer. Strangely, he has not received anything from them either. The Dursleys are unaware that Harry is under edict not to practice magic while away from school, so they have forbidden him from practicing magic while at their house. This has not stopped Harry from teasing Dudley or threatening to use it when they start to bully him. One morning, Harry is sitting on the garden bench just staring into the bushes. He is startled upon noticing that "the hedge was staring back"! Hidden in the hedge, a pair of large, green eyes are looking right at him, but before he can investigate, Dudley interrupts him.

> The HP Hintoscope is humming in our ear - it spotted Rule #2 (already an interruption). Oh, look, it's also another J.K.R. running bit. There is something very creepy about the way eyes are staring and glaring at us.... (wink)

It is Harry's 12th birthday, but the Dursleys completely ignore it and concentrate on Uncle Vernon's scheduled dinner party for an important client (the Masons). Harry has been ordered to go up to his room and pretend that he is not there....

> Pretend he's not there? That might work in theory, but this is Harry Potter we are talking about. Even Professor Snape knows better than to assume that "famous Harry Potter" can avoid being noticed. Harry can pretend all he wants, yet somehow things still always seem to make Harry stand out. Also, Harry may not be getting bullied, but he is obviously not much better off this summer, and there is definitely an air of foreboding here. Is Harry's 12th birthday the twelve that J.K.R. has been hinting about all through Book 1? We will watch for further clues.

As Harry quietly closes his door and turns to sit down on the bed, he suddenly discovers that it is occupied.

Other Oddities

✳ In this first chapter, J.K.R. reviews the events from Book 1 for people who may not have read it or might have forgotten. In her review, she defines Muggles as "not a drop of magical blood in their veins." She also tells us that "Voldemort's powers had been destroyed the instant he failed to kill Harry." Should we take her literally?

Clues

Harry finds himself staring into "bulging-green eyes the size of tennis balls." He realizes it was this creature with "bat-like ears" who had been watching him from the bushes earlier that day. This little guy seems to be wearing an old pillowcase, and bursts into tears when Harry invites him to sit down with him "as an equal."

> Talk about uninvited guests dropping in! Looks like Harry's going to have to play host too. More staring and bulging eyes. Is it some kind of story-line clue (like music in Book 1)?

The creature says his name is Dobby, and he explains to Harry that he is a house-elf servant, which means that he is "bound to serve one house and one family forever." The only way to leave is if the family sets him free, which will never happen. In fact, Dobby says that the wizard family he serves is not aware that he is there. He is extremely honored to meet Harry.

> Okay, why is Dobby here? Did someone send him? Did he come on his own? Who is his family? This is all the big story-line mystery, so don't get your hopes up for a quick answer. J.K.R. is careful to show us through the dialog that Dobby is very much in awe of Harry - minimizing any negative suspicions we may have. Yet, he isn't exactly up-front either. We also learn that house-elves are bound to one **house** and family. The Rememberit Quill just started scribbling.

Dobby tells Harry that someone is plotting "terrible things" for Hogwarts, but Dobby keeps interrupting himself by hitting his head against Hedwig's cage and other loud self-inflicted punishments, whenever he starts to let slip more information. He warns Harry not to return to school, but he is so cryptic with his warnings, that instead of being informed, Harry is even more confused. Harry asks if it has to do with "He-Who-Must-Not-Be-Named," or if "You-Know-Who" has a brother, but Dobby shakes his head "no," opening his eyes wider in such a way as if that, itself, were a clue.

> Yet more eye-openers from another little guy with a big headache. Although we're not getting very much from Dobby (check Rule #2), he is an interesting character and he knows a lot about something important. (Is everyone **sure** Voldemort doesn't have a brother?) The only clue he gives us is that it's something to do with the fact it has nothing to do with Voldemort. Ugh. Our advice: don't bother trying to figure this one out in advance - not worth it, and don't try to understand house-elf logic. You'll just get a headache trying.

Dobby describes Dumbledore's powers as equal to Voldemort's at his best. He also implies that there are Dark powers that Dumbledore will not use (even though he could), which would make him more powerful yet.

Because of their unique situation, house-elves are very well informed. Therefore, if Dobby has heard that Dumbledore's powers rival those of Voldemort at the peak of his power, then he probably would know. In Book 1, Professor McGonagall also claimed that the only reason Dumbledore was not as strong as Voldemort was because he would not use Dark magic (yep, that's Rule #1). We can assume that Dumbledore is as great as the Famous Witches and Wizards card says.

Dobby reminds Harry that his "friends" have not been writing to him - which immediately tips off Harry that Dobby had been intercepting his mail. Dobby pulls all Harry's letters from inside his pillowcase, and tries to blackmail Harry into saying that he will not return to Hogwarts in exchange for the letters. Harry, indeed, spots the handwriting of each of his friends, and chases Dobby all the way down into the kitchen.

Exactly how has Dobby been intercepting Harry's mail? Is it difficult to intercept people's mail? Did he use magic, or is he well-connected in the owl community? Since we are told what everyone's handwriting looks like, we should keep them in mind in case of attempted impersonations (although we don't need a handwriting analyst to figure these out):

Hermione - *Neat writing*

Ron - *Untidy scrawl*

Hagrid - *Scribble*

Harry enters the kitchen to see that Dobby has Aunt Petunia's dinner pudding magically suspended in mid-air, and is threatening to drop the pudding if Harry does not agree to stay away from Hogwarts. Harry cannot do that, and Dobby lets the pudding crash to the floor, while disappearing with a crack like a whip. Then, a huge barn owl suddenly swoops in and drops a letter on Mrs. Mason's head, sending her screaming from the house. Harry is in hot water.

There's lots of really strange things happening here (strange even to Harry) that have possible septology implications. Notice that Dobby can appear and disappear at will. House-elves must be pretty powerful. Then there's this unexpected letter delivery. We know that owls always attempt to deliver directly to their recipients - that is their responsibility. So why does the owl dump the letter on the guest's (Mrs. Mason's) head? In fact, why did they send an Owl Post in front of Muggles (or were they)? Harry has not been sending letters all summer and poor Hedwig has been locked in her cage. Someone might have wanted to check up on them. Could be just writer's license, but makes you wonder....

The letter says that the *Improper Use of Magic Office* received "intelligence" of a *Hover Charm* being used at their house. It reminds Harry that according to the *Decree for the Reasonable Restriction of Underage Sorcery*, under-age wizards are not permitted to perform spells outside school, and that he could be expelled if there are further infractions. Uncle

Vernon swoops down on Harry, enraged that he "forgot" to mention that he is not allowed to use magic at home. Armed with that new information, Uncle Vernon giddily installs bars on Harry's room and locks him in permanently, pushing his food through a cat-flap in the door and letting him out only twice a day to use the bathroom.

> Just how did that *Hover Charm* get reported so quickly? Is that typical, or is that because Harry is being closely monitored? Why did they not know Harry didn't do magic (or did they)? Do all kids get owls every time they break the rules? Does the Ministry have a flock of owls assigned to Fred and George? It feels like there might be something more to this, but nothing was reinforced, so we'll just have to wait and see.

One night, Harry awakes to hear Ron Weasley rattling the bars outside his window.

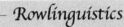

Rowlinguistics

✳ **Dobby** is an uncommon variation used to describe a hobgoblin. Quite appropriate for this puckish house-elf.

Curiosities

✳ It seems that almost all forms of materializing and de-materializing are accompanied by a sound effect. House-elves make one of the louder noises - like the "crack of a whip." Dumbledore appears without a sound (Book 1). What makes some louder than others? Does Hagrid disappear with a sonic boom? Is it related to their power or maybe their finesse?

✳ Dobby has green eyes – the Rememberit Quill is just taking notes.

Clues

Ron, Fred and George Weasley have a turquoise Ford Anglia automobile parked (in mid-air) just outside Harry's window, waiting to rescue him. Ron says he wrote to Harry at least 12 times during the summer, but got worried when Harry didn't write back. Then they heard about the *Hover Charm*, so they "borrowed" their father's car to check things out for themselves.

> Another year and another 12 reference. HP Sleuth detectives are going to need another bottle of ink....

They take a rope attached to the car, tie it to the bars, and yank them off the window. Using a hairpin from his pocket, George picks the lock on Harry's bedroom door (Muggle style). They are convinced that is a useful Muggle skill.

> The Weasley bandits obviously appreciate the finer Muggle attributes. This training also could be important in the future when confronted with an inconvenient situation.

Fred and George then sneak down to the closet under the stairs to retrieve Harry's belongings. Harry warns them that the bottom stair creaks.

> Is that a hint? Not important for this story line, but knowing about that creaking stair might make the difference in the septology. HP Sleuths – watch your step!

Fred and George retrieve Harry's trunk and other wizarding belongings, which they load into the car through the window. Hedwig seems to understand to stay quiet, but when Harry forgets her, she screeches out. Uncle Vernon awakes, and checks to see what is going on. Upon seeing Harry getting away, Uncle Vernon grabs at Harry's ankle, but the Weasleys pull Harry up into the flying car and take off. Ron unlocks Hedwig's cage with the hairpin and lets her fly along with them.

> Hedwig will put up with a lot, but being left at the Dursleys is clearly not one of them. She is quite aware of what is going on around her - far more so than just delivering letters. Her intelligence indicates she has a valuable role in the septology. Notice that Ron shares his brothers' appreciation for useful Muggle talents.

Harry recounts the Dobby incident to the Weasley kids, who think it odd and that the visit might even be a set-up. They are suspicious that it could be tied to Draco Malfoy. They inform Harry that house-elves serve rich families, and "have powerful magic of their own," but only use it with their master's permission.

> So who do we know that is apparently rich, would treat servants like a slave, and has it in for Harry? (Is this a tough one for anybody?) However, the suggestion that Dobby's visit could be a set-up does not correlate with what we saw of Dobby, though, does it? Also note, J.K.R. is making sure we get the clue from the Weasleys, who state outright that house-elves have powerful magic, but normally cannot use it without their master's permission. How did such powerful creatures become so subservient to human wizards? There is a very big septology story here waiting to be told.... Perhaps Hermione can find it in one of her big books?

The Weasley kids explain that their father works in the *Misuse of Muggle Artifacts Office* of the Ministry of Magic, along with an old warlock by the name of Perkins. Their mum is always concerned that Mr. Weasley's fascination (and tinkering) with Muggle items (like the flying car) could jeopardize his job. The Weasley kids also mention that their parents do not know they have "borrowed" the car to rescue Harry. When they land the car at the Burrow, Mrs. Weasley comes out ripping mad, looking like "a saber-toothed tiger."

> Perkins... now he's an interesting character. This is one of the few references to "warlock," and we have not yet been given a specific definition of a warlock. How does it differ from a wizard? Perkins may have some major secrets of his own. "Perkin" was the first name of a famous British imposter, *Perkin Warbeck.* Could that mean Perkins might be an imposter? Hope he's a good guy.

As punishment for flying the car, Fred, George, and Ron have to *de-gnome* the garden, so Harry helps. Mrs. Weasley greets her husband, Arthur (a thin, balding man with glasses), as he returns home from work. He doesn't mind having gnomes.

> Did she say Arthur? As in King Arthur – from the same legends as Perceval? Maybe there is something to that Percy/Perceval thing after all. Even though Mr. Weasley doesn't mind them, de-gnoming gardens could be important. In a chat on Scholastic.com, J.K.R. explains that gnomes not only leave mounds of earth as they devour plant roots, but are a giveaway that wizards live in a house.

Mr. Weasley complains about his hard night at work - how Mortlake was questioned about some odd ferrets in his possession, and how when his back was turned, Mundungus Fletcher attempted to put a hex on him. Mrs. Weasley is as upset with her husband for enchanting the car as she was with her children for flying it. Harry also meets the youngest of the Weasley children, Ginny, as she flees from the kitchen, and then again as a pair of eyes staring from behind a door. She is very shy around him, and it is clear she has a crush on him.

> We are learning that we should never disregard any character - no matter how seemingly insignificant. Mundungus Fletcher is one of those to remember. He does not appear to be highly ethical, but in the magical world, looks are often deceiving... Ginny's fascination with Harry is not a mystery, yet her character still is.

Mrs. Weasley cooks breakfast while listening to Celestina Warbeck on the wizarding "wireless."

> Remember that imposter, Perkin Warbeck? Now we have Celestina Warbeck. Since both names appear in the same chapter, it is reasonable to assume that was an intentional hint by J.K.R. to correlate the two. Nonetheless, we should not assume that they are both bad imposters.

Ron shows Harry his room, which is decorated in late Chudley Cannon-style (his fave Quidditch team). Harry looks around and sees Ron's magic wand lying on a tank of frog spawn next to Scabbers, his rat.

> Remember Aunt Petunia mentioned that Lily Potter also messed around with frog spawn? What exactly does anyone do with frog spawn? There is probably some little message being sent to us, but we're not sure what it might be. Is there a reason why J.K.R. would point out that Ron's wand, Scabbers, and frog spawn are together? Was there some magic going on in Ron's room? Ron didn't mention anything, and we have not been given a lesson on frog spawn as of Book 4. Once again, where did Percy get Scabbers?

Ron says apologetically that his room is a bit small and is located under the ghoul in the attic (who bangs on the pipes and groans all the time). Nonetheless, he is clearly hopeful that Harry will like his room.

> The ghoul can't be any worse than Dudley's snoring, and he's probably not as mean. Or is he? Traditionally, ghouls don't tend to be the friendly type – hope this one is a loyal pet.

Harry tells an embarrassed Ron that he thinks it's "the best house I've ever been in."

Rowlinguistics

✴ **Mundungus** is a disgusting name for a disgusting type of person. The dictionary meaning is foul-smelling tobacco, and he is definitely an unsavory character. His last name, **Fletcher**, is a tradesman who puts feathers on shafts to make arrows. HP Sleuths keep your sights on Mundungus Fletcher – he is a septology target.

✴ Is **Ginny** a nickname? If it is a nickname, what is her proper name? (Guenivere? Ginger?) Could be a clue. (Somehow we can't imagine a relationship to gin.)

✴ The name **Mortlake** is made up of two parts, "mort" *(death)* and "lake" - meaning *death lake.* That guy doesn't sound very pleasant.

Chapter 4 Analysis

(At Flourish and Blotts)

Clues

Life at the Burrow is interesting. **Nothing** acts "normally." Even the mirrors talk back. Harry receives his second-year letter from Hogwarts, as Mr. Weasley marvels at how Dumbledore, who "doesn't miss a trick," already knew Harry was at the Burrow. Ginny is starting at Hogwarts this year, and the Weasleys ponder how they are going to afford all of the books and supplies that Ginny will be needing (Harry feels self-conscious about his own pile of gold). Percy, who aspires to become Minister of Magic (according to Ron), had received an exemplary 12 O.W.L.s (Ordinary Wizarding Levels) on his exams. Ron's oldest brother, Bill, also got 12 O.W.L.s. He is in Egypt, working for Gringotts.

> Even Mr. Weasley seems to be awed at the way Dumbledore is so much on top of Harry's whereabouts. This says something about Dumbledore's network of people, something about what tricks he may be using to keep track of Harry, and a lot about the guard that has been established to keep Harry safe while not at school. All hints we have been given seem to be intentional. Why would anyone (besides wicked Queens) want to buy or enchant a mirror to talk back to them? We figure it had to be a present from Fred and George (or one of their experiments).

Using Floo Powder, the Weasleys bring Harry and the kids to Diagon Alley. Following Mrs. Weasley's instructions, Harry takes a pinch of glittering *Floo powder,* throws it into the fireplace flames, and steps in. He swallows some hot ash - causing him to stutter out the name "D-Dia-gon Alley." His journey ends abruptly as he falls onto the stone floor of Borgin and Burkes (a shop devoted to the Dark Arts), breaking his glasses. Harry sees that the shop has many curious and questionable objects, such as a *Hand of Glory,* evil-looking masks, and a "staring glass eye."

> Wicked. Is that an evil eye? It is definitely a staring eye. We see we are still being followed by those hints.

Before Harry is able to get out of there, he spots Draco and his father coming in the door, so quickly hides in a cabinet in the back of the shop. He overhears Lucius Malfoy selling off some illegal potions to Mr. Borgin, the owner, who clearly knows him well, and mutters "darkly" about Lucius.

> We had assumed that the snobbish bully, Draco, has similar-in-kind parents, but this is a confirmation that Mr. Malfoy is certainly not an upstanding citizen either. As a regular customer of Mr. Borgin, it is unlikely that Lucius is only admiring his Dark possessions - he is probably (willingly) capable of using them. In fact, Mr. Borgin is quite convinced that Lucius has plenty of interesting Dark items in his possession (anything in particular?). No matter what, we are starting to get a good idea of the character of Lucius Malfoy.

Lucius mentions that he is on his way to some important business, and quickly finishes his transaction with Mr. Borgin.

> Lucius is going to some important business? Time to wake up HP Sleuths! Notice how subtly J.K.R. sneaks that one in - so typical.

After the Malfoys leave, Harry goes out onto the street, but realizes he has no idea where he is. He is lost on a strange street called Knockturn Alley. Fortunately, Hagrid happened to be in the area looking for some flesh-eating slug repellent for the school cabbages. He helps Harry find his way back to Diagon Alley and the Weasleys.

> Look out, it's yet another one of them slug clues (and another mention of cabbages). This particular species sounds disgustingly scary. So why was Hagrid looking for that stuff? Was it really for cabbages, or was he on the lookout for Harry (Rule #3)? Unlike most slug references, these here sound moderately dangerous and having repellent seems like a real good idea....

Hagrid and Mrs. Weasley brush the soot off of Harry while Mr. Weasley magically repairs Harry's glasses. Hermione Granger spots them, and they all go into Gringotts where she has them meet her parents. Mrs. Weasley has to clean out the family's meager savings to pay for this year's school supplies, while Harry tries to obscure his embarrassing pile of gold as much as possible.

> As of Book 4, we still do not know much more about Harry's parents than we did at the beginning of Book 1, except for J.K.R.'s comments that the Potters' money was inherited. As a comparison, the Weasley's financial plight is made quite apparent here.

They discover that Gilderoy Lockhart, the blond wavy-haired heart-throb of female witches, is making a personal appearance at Flourish and Blotts. He is dressed in "forget-me-not" blue robes, selling his autograph and his autobiography, *Magical Me.* When Gilderoy spots Harry in the crowd, he recognizes Harry, rudely grabs him, and insists that the *Daily Prophet* photographer take pictures of them together. Gilderoy also makes an announcement that he will be taking up the vacant post of Defense Against the Dark Arts at Hogwarts this year. Harry is then presented with a complete set of Gilderoy's books, but is so disgusted with Gilderoy's abrasive, self-serving manor, that he dumps the books into Ginny's cauldron saying that he will buy his own.

> It doesn't take an HP Sleuth to understand that Lockhart is an opportunist and egomaniac. What is especially notable is that Lockhart seemed to have recognized Harry from a bit of a distance in the midst of a large crowd. He was either expecting to see Harry, or was well-versed concerning Harry's physical appearance. This is not relevant to the story line, so it is probably what would be expected of Lockhart, yet maybe worth noting for later in the septology (if anyone's memory is still good by then).

Draco Malfoy, who is also in the shop, harasses Ginny. Ron needles him about Harry managing to make it to Diagon Alley, but Draco doesn't react. Then Lucius Malfoy comes over to Mr. Weasley, scoffs at Ginny's used and battered school book, and insults her family and the Muggle Grangers. Mr. Weasley reacts by lunging at him, and a scuffle occurs. As Hagrid breaks them up, Lucius hands Ginny back her book, along with a final insult.

> At least he gave Ginny's book back - even if it was rudely. So Lucius Malfoy got back to the bookstore already. Where was his important business? HP Sleuths should not rule out the small possibility that his business also involved a septology-related meeting with someone in this bookstore. Was Draco surprised to see Harry there? Was that his house-elf?

Harry reluctantly uses Floo Powder to return to the Burrow.

Rowlinguistics

* The name **Gilde-roy** could be interpreted as meaning a *gilded king*. Something that is gilded would have a veneer of gold, but be plain metal underneath – as in fake gold jewelry. "Roi" is *king* in French. So far, we only know that Gilderoy is an egomaniac, but what is under that façade? Also, he comes across as a ladies' man, but he may remind older readers of a similarly flamboyant (but not so arrogant) celebrity pianist called "Liberace" (that's a hint too).

* **Arthur** is an extremely well-known name in fantasy – that of King Arthur, famous for his Knights of the Round Table. However, the name Arthur Weasley also rolls off the tongue to sound just like Arthur Wellesley – the 1st Duke of Wellington (also know as the "Iron Duke"). Like J.K.R.'s Arthur Weasley, he worked in government, and was an important General.

✳ **Lucius** – an appropriate name for an evil-like bad guy like Mr. Malfoy. It sounds very much like Lucifer (a devilish name). However, it also coincidentally (Rule #3) was the name of Pope St. Lucius I, who became Pope when the exiled St. Cornelius died. Could the Minister of Magic, Cornelius Fudge, be facing a similar fate? Another namesake would be Lucius Verus, a Roman general who became co-emperor. So many possibilities....

✳ We already know **Borgin** and **Burkes** is not a nice place. Additionally, the word "burke" derives from a famous criminal, *William Burke,* who murdered people by strangulation in order to get bodies that he could sell for dissections.

✳ The name **Knockturn Alley** is a play on *nocturnally* in the same way that Diagon Alley is a play on *diagonally.* Wonder if it's just a street for Dark Arts, or if something goes on there at night?

Curiosities

✳ Harry's glasses were easily fixed ("good as new") by Mr. Weasley - just more evidence that they had been fixed in year 1 before he even reached Hogwarts.

✳ In case anyone's looking for it, note that the Weasleys keep the Floo Powder in their flower pot.

✳ Although we are being told by Ron that Percy wants to be Minister of Magic (Rule #4) – from everything we've seen of Percy, we have no reason to disagree, and are quite convinced it is true.

✳ J.K.R. demonstrates with her Lockhart character that she understands demographics exceptionally well.

Chapter 5 Analysis

Clues

The morning that Harry and the Weasleys are leaving to catch the Hogwarts Express is very busy and they are running late. Mrs. Weasley looks all over for spare socks, and everyone seems to have forgotten something - including Ginny who goes back at the last second for her diary.

> Almost forgetting a diary is not very important. ...Or is it? There are those darn socks again too, but we don't have enough to link them to anything yet.

The Ford Anglia has been magically expanded (without Mrs. Weasley's knowledge) to fit all their luggage plus 7 passengers comfortably. Mr. Weasley drives the car (on the road) to London.

> This has science-fiction overtones. Somehow, this fantasy is starting to span the sci-fi genre in which space/time is being warped. We will watch these extra dimensions very carefully.

At King's Cross Station, the rest of the Weasleys pass quickly through the barrier at platform nine and three-quarters, leaving Ron and Harry to go last. With only 5 minutes to get to the train, Harry and Ron try to go through, but the barrier gateway has been sealed and they hit solid wall. They watch as the clock counts down - trying desperately to get through, but it will not budge. They have been sealed off from the train and are fearful that Ron's parents, who know how to Apparate (disappear and reappear somewhere else), have possibly been trapped on the other side. Upon realizing they have missed the train, they are desperate to find alternative transportation to the school.

> Now this is a first - kids desperate to go to school? We finally have proof this is a fantasy book.☺ That barrier problem is a solid story-line clue. How did it get sealed, and why? We never did hear what happened on the other (train) side - what did Mr. and Mrs. Weasley do to try to get to Ron and Harry? Not explained, thus considered not important (at this time).

The flying car is parked outside of the station, and Ron convinces Harry that it would be okay in an emergency to borrow it. The *Invisibility Booster* works fine, and they become only a "pair of eyeballs" as they take off. However, the Booster fails momentarily and Ron has to zoom into the "woolly" clouds to escape detection.

> Eyeballs? Did we see some eyeballs again? We were probably just seeing things - from staring at the woolly clouds (another running bit).

Flying through the clouds, they follow the train to Hogwarts castle, which is exhilarating at first, but soon becomes a boring, long, uncomfortable ride. It is getting dark, and just as they get to Hogwarts, the car's engine suddenly dies. As the car loses altitude, Ron tries frantically to steer it, but ends up crashing into a tree (and breaking his wand). The "ancient" tree that they have run into starts unexpectedly attacking them. The car restarts it's own engine, backs away from the tree, ejects Harry, Ron, Hedwig, and all of their belongings, and rumbles off.

> Why did the engine die? Was the car truly tired or fed-up - or was there another reason? We later learn that Muggle electronics do not work on the castle grounds, yet, it also says that the engine re-started here - or is that a *different* kind of re-start or a magical kind of engine? This is not a reinforced clue, so we do not know, but the kind of magic used on that car may be important later on in the septology.

Hedwig's cage bursts open and she flies off on her own, while Harry and Ron drag their trunks up to the castle. As they look through a window at the sorting ceremony (unable to spot Ginny being placed in Gryffindor), Snape discovers them. A cold breeze ripples his black robes as he escorts them down to his dungeon office, where the fireplace is "dark and empty."

> Was that just another breeze? Too bad we didn't see the Sorting Hat sort Ginny or any of her classmates (wonder how long it took the Hat to sort her?). Wonder if that falls under Rule #2. Also, how does Hedwig's cage manage to burst open? Was that caused by Hedwig herself, or something else?

Snape's questions give Harry the impression, once again, that Snape could read minds.

> This reference to Snape being able to read minds is soon explained this time, but Harry's instincts tend to be good. Does Snape maybe have some ability in this area, and if so, what gives him that ability?

Snape shows Harry and Ron a copy of the *Evening Prophet* reporting that they had been seen by Muggles in the flying car, and is convinced they will be expelled. Professor McGonagall and Headmaster Dumbledore, himself, come down to talk with them. Although extremely disappointed, Dumbledore does not expel them (which bums out Snape). Since term had not yet started, Professor McGonagall does not remove any points from Gryffindor House (whew!), but Harry and Ron do get detentions.

> Snape is always overly anxious to get Harry expelled - he must be holding an awfully large grudge against Harry. And by the way, what was Snape doing out on the grounds that evening? Was he specifically awaiting their arrival or was this a chance encounter? Put that in your septology parchment notes just in case.

When Harry and Ron reach the Gryffindor entrance, they realize they don't know this year's password. A disgusted Hermione emerges, telling them "it's Wattlebird," ... "but that's not the point," but is cut-off as the other Gryffindors drag them inside.

> Let's see, put together "wattle" + "bird," and that probably means cock (rooster). Since Hermione was cut-off (Rule #2), we know it's a clue, but we're not really sure if that was the "point," or just bird dinner (fish).

In the Gryffindor common room, Harry and Ron are greeted by a cheering crowd of envious classmates who inform them that the tree they had run into is the *Whomping Willow*.

Curiosities

* When the Invisibility Button fails, the car re-appears with a popping noise. So even cars make noise when they appear or disappear.

* If the Whomping Willow is "ancient," where did it come from? Is it related to the Ents from *The Lord of the Rings* or the Fighting Trees in *The Wizard of Oz?*

* According to an interview by Lindsey Fraser in *Conversations with J.K. Rowling,* J.K.R. says that her choice of a turquoise Ford Anglia was influenced by the one her friend had that rescued her from teenage boredom.

Other Oddities

* Harry said the Dursleys had not given him pocket money for about 6 years – why did they ever, and did something happen 6 years ago to change that?

* We get reinforcement in this chapter that Slytherin turned out more Dark Wizards than any other house. We knew that Hagrid was exaggerating when he said "all," but it wasn't by much.

Chapter 6 Analysis

Clues

At breakfast on the first day of classes, Ron receives a *Howler* letter from his mother. It turns crimson, smokes, and hollers out loud at him in a booming projection of Mrs. Weasley's voice that the whole school hears. The letter fumes about the disgrace and embarrassment that Ron caused his family - specifically his father, who is now under inquiry by the Ministry of Magic. Gilderoy Lockhart is just as unwelcome that morning, as he keeps lecturing Harry about always being in the spotlight - as if Harry is purposely doing it. Their first class is Herbology, where Harry meets Justin Finch-Fletchley (a Hufflepuff). Justin tells them how glad he is to be at Hogwarts in spite of doubts from his Muggle mother. The students learn how to re-pot Mandrakes, which are used as restoratives for people who have been cursed or transfigured (but whose cry is fatal to anyone who hears it).

> This is a bummer of a first day - starting out bad and just gets worse. A lot of text has been spent on telling us about some plants that can kill or restore, so they must have purpose in the story line. Not a good sign.

Ron had Spellotaped his wand back together, but is having trouble with it working properly. During lunch-break, a new first year, Muggle-born Colin Creevey, pleads with "famous" Harry to have his picture taken with him (giving both Lockhart another chance to lecture Harry, and Draco another chance to snigger). For their first Defense Against the Dark Arts class, Gilderoy pops a quiz in which he divulges that his ideal birthday gift, peace among all creatures, is written in chapter 12 of his book, *Wandering with Werewolves*. He also has a secret desire to market hair care products. Lockhart then releases some pixies into the classroom, which proceed to trash the room and create havoc. Gilderoy instructs Ron, Harry and Hermione to gather the pixies back into their cage as he tactfully leaves at the end of class.

> Hair care products? Do we doubt this guy's orientation? He may smile sweetly, but Gilderoy Lockhart does not strike us as having a peaceful type of personality, so his stated desire for peace is a hint to look more closely at his sincerity. The chapter 12 reference is still going. Is that supposed to be a hint about **all** the Chapter twelves, a specific Chapter 12, or Harry's twelfth year (this year)? Is Gilderoy's werewolf book at all significant?

While Harry and Ron are of the opinion that Gilderoy is inept, Hermione is enamoured with him and his legendary feats.

Rowlinguistics

* Here is a fun Rowlinguistic. In Britain, the brand name for adhesive (cellophane) tape is *Sellotape* – so Ron uses "**Spellotape**" to tape his wand back together J

* We are not sure about the **Creevy** name. It sounds a bit like *creepy,* and it also looks a bit like the French creve (break), or the Latin crevi (understand). If J.K.R. is giving us hints, we don't understand. Do any HP Sleuths have a theory?

Curiosities

* Mandrakes have appeared in folklore for centuries. The cry of the Mandrake is referenced by Shakespeare as well – in *Romeo and Juliet.* Remember that mandrakes work for both curses and transfigurations

Other Oddities

* Colin says his dad is a milkman. Wonder if the Dursley's are on his route? (Remember the letters in the eggs in Book 1?)

* Venomous Tentacula are dark red, spiky plants with long feelers.

* Gilderoy said if he could not obtain peace, he'd take a bottle of Ogden's Old Firewhiskey. Is Ogden's Old Firewhiskey just a running bit or a clue?

Chapter 7 Analysis

(MUDBLOODS AND MURMURS)

Clues

Colin Creevey follows Harry down to the Quidditch practice field with his camera clicking. Oliver Wood had booked the field for their own use, but the Slytherin team shows up, with their captain, Marcus Flint, who has a "look of trollish cunning" (and they see why). The Slytherins have brand new *Nimbus Two Thousand and One* brooms, which have been donated to the team by Lucius Malfoy. They also have a new Seeker - Draco Malfoy (an interesting coincidence).

> This is a reinforcement that Marcus Flint may be part troll - HP Sleuths should log that just in case. J.K.R. is again letting us know in subtle ways that wizards have inter-married with other species. That will be addressed even more openly in the future. Guess that broom "donation" helps to classify the Malfoys into the "rich" category.

Ron and Hermione, who had been watching from the stands, walk over, and when they hear the Slytherins insulting the Gryffindors, Hermione stands up for her team. Malfoy calls her a "filthy little Mudblood," to which all the Gryffindors become extremely upset. Ron tries to hex Malfoy, but his damaged wand explodes out the wrong end – back into his own stomach and Ron starts belching up slugs. Alarmed, Harry and Hermione drag Ron off to Hagrid's nearby cabin, where they see Lockhart was just leaving. He had been giving Hagrid his famous "advice" on how to get kelpies out of a well.

> Kelpies are interesting. This is the only mention of them so far, yet, they are listed in the *Fantastic Beasts* handbook, are in *the Wizards of the Coast Harry Potter Trading Card Game*, and have a prominent legend in the British Isles. So, we are expecting to see more of those steeds. (If you don't know about kelpies, you still haven't done your HP Sleuth recommended reading (shame) - consult your favorite bookstore for a copy of *Fantastic Beasts and Where to Find Them*, printed for *Comic Relief*.) Notice the emotions this Mudblood thing causes. It is an intolerance that runs very deep in the wizarding community, and at the heart of this mystery.

Hagrid says there is nothing much to do, except to wait for the slug effect to stop. He gives Ron a large basin to spit the slugs into as they come up. Hermione and Harry learn that the term "Mudblood" is used to mean "dirty blood" - a foul term to describe Muggle-born Witches and Wizards. Ironically, if wizards hadn't intermarried with Muggles, they would have become extinct.

> Since Muggle intermarriage was critical to wizard survival, the Mudblood thing is a very strange resentment. It is likely that it might not be as much a prejudice as an excuse for creating an underclass and foe in the same way that Nazis created their enemy through *ethnic cleansing*. Watch for more references to this bigotry - and HP Sleuths should keep track of who might be sympathetic to that belief.

94

While Ron continues to puke up slugs, Hagrid discusses how unimpressed he is with Lockhart. He tells the kids that Lockhart was the **only** one willing to take the Defense Against the Dark Arts job - as people now think the position is jinxed.

What? Jinxed? Why would anyone think that? (smirk) Of course, we were never told who (or how many) had the Defense Against the Dark Arts job before Quirrell came back from sabbatical in Albania, or what happened to **those** teachers (probably an interesting story)... As mentioned in Book 1, Hagrid does not like to speak badly about teachers or anyone in authority, so this is quite significant that he feels this way about Lockhart. Also don't forget that Hagrid's opinions mirror Dumbledore's opinions.

Hagrid shows the kids some abnormally large pumpkins he is growing for Halloween. His flowery pink umbrella is nearby - which most likely conceals his wand that was snapped when he was expelled. Hagrid says that Ginny had stopped by the day before while looking around the grounds, and suggests she might have had something else in mind (like running into Harry).

Reinforcement of the pink umbrella theory (Rule #1) - guess it's a bit beyond theory by now. As to Ginny, HP Sleuths pay attention. This is a prime example of how J.K.R. gives us a hint and immediately distracts us. She tells us that Ginny was down looking around the grounds, but before we have a chance to wonder why, Hagrid tells us he figures she was looking to run into Harry. Was that what she was doing? Could be, but could also be Rule #4.

Harry and Ron do their detention for the Whomping Willow incident late into the night. Ron reports to Filch, the Caretaker, to polish silver in the trophy room, while Harry reports to Gilderoy Lockhart, to help answer fan mail. When Harry is about finished addressing envelopes, he suddenly hears an ice-cold, venomous voice saying, "Come...come to me...Let me rip you...Let me tear you...Let me kill you...." Lockhart does not hear it, and thinks that Harry is getting drowsy and hallucinating, so he finally sends him to bed. Harry waits for Ron to return from scrubbing silver all night, and tells him what he heard.

This is obviously a story-line clue here. This is not a happy voice - this is a dangerous voice, and for some reason Harry heard it and the teacher did not. Believe it or not, we **do** have enough septology information to this point in Book 2 to guess what the nature of it might be. If you guessed what could be causing this without reading ahead, then you are surely an HP Super Sleuth. However, our evidence would not even be enough for a jury right now, so we must await further clues and hard evidence no matter what.

Neither Ron nor Harry can figure out what it was or why Harry heard it while Lockhart didn't.

Rowlinguistics

✳ **Marcus Flint**'s first name may possibly relate to Marcus Antonius (Mark Antony) of Cleopatra fame. The Captain Flint part definitely makes one think of the savagely mean, powerful, (and dead) Captain Flint from Robert Louis Stevenson's Treasure Island (it was his treasure map). Of course, Long John Silver's annoying parrot also had that name (Yo-ho-ho). We also noticed that the names of the rival Quidditch captains are Wood and Flint. We find it very amusing that the material, flint, ignites wood.

Curiosities

✳ More slimy slugs coming up.

✳ We now know that there is at least one well on the Hogwarts property. Those tend to be a good place to hide things (including secret passageways).

Clues

The weather is miserable, and the students are catching colds. Ginny is looking pale, so Percy bullies her into taking some nasty *Pepperup potion.* Harry is covered with mud from a wet Quidditch practice when he comes upon Nearly Headless Nick, who is upset from being turned-down by the *"Headless Hunt."*

> This is a little taste of Percy's personality. He is a control freak and believes in rigidly obeying rules. It does not necessarily mean he is a bad person, but his personality does cause him to infringe on others under his domain. This will become more and more important in the books, and may be a key in the septology. We are told Ginny is looking pale, and if Percy has to bully her into taking some potion, she took it quite **unwillingly.** Is that because she doesn't like the potion, or was she pale for some other reason?

As Harry and Nick are talking, Filch's cat, Mrs. Norris, sees Harry dripping mud all over the floor, and somehow summons Filch immediately to the scene. Filch escorts Harry to his office, which has a "faint smell of fried fish." As Filch is in the process of writing out a punishment (for mud?), a big "bang" on the ceiling of his office interrupts him, and he runs out of the office to try to catch Peeves.

> Filch is tied very closely to his cat, who seems to somehow be able to alert him of misdeeds. It is highly possible that Mrs. Norris has some Kneazle in her (see *Fantastic Beasts*), or is hiding other magical powers. If this is the case, she could be an important character to the septology - especially if true undesirables (not just rambunctious students) enter the walls of the castle. What's with the fish smell? Is this simply Mrs. Norris's dinner, has Filch been frying up some red herring, or is J.K.R. wafting a clue under our noses somewhere in here? What do HP Sleuths think?

As Harry waits, he notices a large, purple envelope on Filch's desk that says: "Kwikspell - A Correspondence Course in Beginners' Magic." Intrigued, Harry opens it and reads how the course has helped various people who had poor wizarding skills. When Filch comes back to the room, he notices that the envelope was moved, and is so embarrassed that he immediately shoos Harry out (without any punishment). As Harry hurries back up the corridor, Nick finds him and asks if his having Peeves crash the vanishing cabinet had worked to stop Filch from punishing him. Harry says it did, wishing he could return the favor.

> Ghostly capabilities are highly significant, but as of Book 4, have not yet been addressed. We still do not know how a ghost becomes a ghost and why most ghosts cannot move solid objects while a few of them can. Since Nick had to ask Peeves to drop the cabinet, we assume that Nick cannot do that on his own - which would mean that Nick is not capable of moving objects. The ability by

specific ghosts to be able to move (or not move) things is reinforced and a potentially powerful clue for the septology.

Nick will be holding a Deathday Party on Halloween to celebrate the 500th anniversary of his death, and asks if Harry, Hermione, and Ron would attend. Harry agrees, and on Halloween, while everyone else is at the Hogwarts party in the Great Hall, they go down to a very *cool* dungeon ghost party. Unfortunately, the ghosts (especially the morose Moaning Myrtle) are depressing, plus the kids get very get cold and discomforted from all the frigid ectoplasm. When the party becomes a bit rowdy, they gracefully leave to go up for what is left of the Hogwarts Halloween party.

> There has been a lot of discussion on the Internet about Nearly Headless Nick's ghostly career. J.K.R. makes several references to how long he has been bodiless (and mostly-headless), but they tend to contradict one-another. However, most references are more anecdotal (like the last time he tasted food), and never reinforced by J.K.R. Therefore, HP mystery Sleuths can ignore those confounding "clues" - at least until we are given some reinforced hints. As we've seen, Halloween has never been a good day for Harry. Looks like it's not much better for Nick.

On their way back upstairs, Harry suddenly hears the cold, murderous voice he had heard in Lockhart's office. It seems to be moving straight upward, and though he does not see anything, he runs upstairs, following the voice. In a deserted passage on the second floor, Harry, Ron, and Hermione see a message written on the wall that says "THE CHAMBER OF SECRETS HAS BEEN OPENED. ENEMIES OF THE HEIR, BEWARE." They almost trip on a big puddle of water as they move closer to find Mrs. Norris, Filch's cat, stiff with eyes staring, and hanging by her tail from a torch bracket.

> Clues floating all over the place. Whatever happened to Mrs. Norris is now linked to the voice that Harry heard. We bet it's also linked to her staring eyes. Harry may not have seen anything, but now we know the voice is real. What's with all the water? It may just be water, but there is nothing to indicate that the corridor normally has a big puddle in the middle of it - so HP Sleuths should reflect on this clue.

As Harry, Ron, and Hermione are about to run from the scene, hoards of students start filing into the corridor from the feast that has just ended – it looks bad for the three of them.

Curiosities

✳ What is a "Vanishing Cabinet?" What vanishes? Is it the cabinet, the contents, or something else?

✳ Ghosts they meet at the Deathday Party:
- ☾ Moaning Myrtle
- ☾ Gloomy Nuns
- ☾ Ragged man wearing chains (Ghost of Old Morley, Scrooge's ex partner?)
- ☾ Knight with an arrow sticking out of his forehead
- ☾ Wailing Widow from Kent
- ☾ Sir Patrick Delany-Podmore and the *Headless Hunt*
- ☾ Bloody Baron (who is given a wide berth) - reinforcement (Rule #1) that the Bloody Baron is shunned by other ghosts.

✳ Nick banged the cabinet. There seems to be an increase in banging noises as the septology continues.

✳ Nick (nearly) lost his head about the time that Columbus sailed to the Americas.

Chapter 9 Analysis

(THE WRITING ON THE WALL)

Clues

Filch accuses Harry of killing his cat because Harry had found out he is a Squib (born into a wizarding family but without magic powers). Lockhart is eager to be in the center of attention so donates his office (which is close by) for the investigation.

> The HP Hintoscope is wailing mournfully. There are starting to be some captivating coincidences with these events (Reference Rule #3). In addition to staring eyes on Mrs. Norris, how fascinating that the location of the voice is approximately the same both times (general vicinity of Lockhart's office). Once again, Halloween is not much of a party for Harry.

Dumbledore looks over his crooked nose and prods Mrs. Norris with his long finger, as he and Professor McGonagall examine the cat carefully. They determine that the cat is still alive, but petrified by powerful Dark Magic. Professor Dumbledore reassures everyone that Professor Sprout will restore Mrs. Norris when her Mandrakes have grown to full size.

> Hmmmm. There's obviously something we are supposed to notice about Dumbledore's long nose and HP Sleuths need to investigate those references to long fingers! There are two gripping possibilities. One is that (as with house-elves) long fingers are a physical sign of great magical power, or the other is inheritance. Verrry interesting either way. As expected, Professor Sprout's Mandrakes will be needed.

Ginny seems especially distraught over Mrs. Norris and the whole incident (Ron explains that Ginny really loves cats). Filch tries, in vain, to remove the writing with "Mrs. Skower's All-Purpose Magical Mess Remover."

> Guess this is more of a Special-Purpose mess. Ginny is interesting. Her brothers keep saying that she is normally outgoing, yet she seems to be a bit frail at Hogwarts. Ron thinks she's upset because of the cat, but we are thinking about Rule #4.

In their History of Magic class, Hermione asks Professor Binns to tell them about the Chamber of Secrets. In a rare deviation from the ghost Professor's boring lessons, he tells them how Hogwarts school was founded by four powerful Wizards: Godric Gryffindor, Rowena Ravenclaw, Helga Hufflepuff, and Salazar Slytherin. According to legend, Slytherin left the school after a serious argument with Gryffindor over half-bloods about 1,000 years ago. It was Slytherin, himself, who started the pure-blood bigotry. It was said that Slytherin had built a hidden chamber in the castle of which the other founders knew nothing, and had sealed the Chamber so no one could open it until his true heir arrived at the school. There is supposed to be some kind of monster within, that only the Heir of Slytherin can control. Professor Binns doesn't believe it, since none of the esteemed faculty have found anything in 1,000 years.

Seems this bad blood thing between Slytherin and Gryffindor wasn't just a bad heir day. So what does an heir of Slytherin look like - anyone we know? What do we know about Slytherin to help us identify someone who might be powerful enough to control its monster? These are story-line clues, but are septology teasers as well.

Harry, Ron, and Hermione investigate the corridor where the attack occurred. Since Dumbledore wasn't able to cure Mrs. Norris, Hermione feels that Mrs. Norris was not attacked by a human. Harry sees scorch marks on the floor, while Hermione sees spiders scurrying out a crack in the window. Ron, however, stands back in fear - as he informs them he has a phobia of spiders.

Based on Hermione's comment, we could infer that Dumbledore can counter any spell a human casts. We are waiting for reinforcement of that one.

The water they had seen that night has been mopped up. There is a girls' bathroom nearby with an "Out of Order" sign on it, which Hermione explains is haunted by Moaning Myrtle. They all go in and try to ask Myrtle if she saw anything that night, but she is, as usual, very sensitive and upset-able, and huffily splashes back into her toilet. They do not get any information from her.

Other than the fact that she is haunting a bathroom, there is something very strange about Moaning Myrtle. As we mentioned previously, it is highly unusual for a ghost to be able to move solid objects - even water. What gives Myrtle this special ability? This is certainly important to the septology, since it shows us that some ghosts can alter the physical world. As to story-line clues, there is not much to go on except spiders and a high-strung ghost.

As they exit the bathroom, however, they are discovered by Percy. He is upset that the boys were in there, and describes how Ginny has been upset and crying. Ron accuses Percy of not being as concerned about Ginny as he is about having his chances messed up to become Head Boy.

Ron is convinced that Percy is so focused on his career that Percy would be willing to hurt his own family in pursuit of advancement. Is this another red fish? It is definitely true that Percy is too rigid with rules, and that he is overly ambitious, but we have not been given proof that he would sacrifice his family over a job. Ron tends to interpret things wrong (unless he is joking), but it is true that Percy is a control freak and could be dangerous in his own right. HP Sleuths – just don't turn your back on Percy.

Harry, Ron, and Hermione do conclude that it is likely Malfoy is the Heir of Slytherin, and is responsible for the attack (Harry has not told Ron and Hermione that the Sorting Hat almost put him in Slytherin). They agree on a plan to brew up some Polyjuice Potion to change themselves into 3 Slytherin students so they can sneak into Slytherin house and interrogate Malfoy personally.

As of Book 4, Harry still has not owned-up to Ron and Hermione that he was almost sorted into Slytherin. Is this a septology clue or not a big deal? Knowing J.K.R., it's certainly suspiciousssss.

The biggest problem with brewing Polyjuice Potion is that the recipe is from a book (*Moste Potente Potions*) in the restricted section of the library, and they need a teacher's signed note of permission to check it out.

Rowlinguistics

✳ The word **"squib"** means a *firework that just fizzles* – in other words, a *dud*. So Filch is a wizarding dud (snigger).

✳ **Myrtle** plants signify marriage, home, and love. That seems to be the antithesis of this Myrtle. Maybe J.K.R. was thinking more about the fact that myrtle is from the genus of poisonous plants.

Curiosities

✳ We now learn that Hogwarts is about 1,000 years old, which means it was founded during the period of European history called *The Dark Ages*, even before the time of Merlin and King Arthur.

✳ The scorch marks that Harry sees on the floor are interesting to HP Sleuths since those are not well explained at the end.

✳ Who wrote *Hogwarts, A History* and when was it written/revised?

Chapter 10 Analysis

--- Clues ---

Hermione easily sweet-talks Lockhart into signing a permission note so they can check out the restricted book with the Polyjuice Potion recipe. After holding Lockhart's signature up to the light to check for a forgery, Madam Pince hands her *Moste Potente Potions*. Ron, Harry, and Hermione take the book to Moaning Myrtle's Bathroom where they look over the ingredients (lacewing flies, leeches, fluxweed, knotgrass) and realize that some items, *like powdered horn of bicorn* or *shredded skin of boomslang*, are not easily available (translation: they will have to steal them). Hermione estimates that the potion will take about a month to brew.

> HP Sleuths are instructed to memorize those ingredients. You **will** be quizzed later! (No, we're not joking.) Also note that the potion takes about a month to brew, depending on the phase of the moon when the potion is started. This has not been reinforced again, but that is a very long time – so it's not an option if you need a quick disguise (unless you happen to keep some lying around in a jug).

During their Quidditch match against Slytherin, Gryffindor realizes that one of the Bludgers has been tampered with to constantly attack Harry. Oliver Wood doesn't understand how, since they were locked in Madam Hooch's office. The Snitch (which seems to have a sense of humor) positions itself next to Malfoy, who is too busy taunting Harry to see it. Harry is distracted by Malfoy, so does not notice the "Rogue Bludger," which slams into him, breaking his arm. Harry dives at Malfoy and catches the snitch anyway, with his good arm, winning the game. When Harry slumps to the ground, Lockhart insists on helping, but instead of fixing the bone, his spell removes all of the bones from Harry's arm! Ron and Hermione bring Harry up to Madam Pomfrey who tells Harry that she can re-grow the bones, but it will take all night and be very painful.

> If we thought Lockhart might have been a bit incompetent, we do not need any further proof now. Is he just a bimbo, or is there more to him (remember Quirrell)? Overall, there have been some really weird events in this book. Closing the barrier was difficult, and getting at this Bludger was not easy. Couldn't be they are related could it?

In the middle of the night, Harry awakens to find Dobby at his bedside. Dobby explains that wearing a pillowcase is the mark of a house-elf's enslavement. A house-elf can only be freed if his master presents him with clothes, so his family is careful not to pass Dobby even a sock.

> There's that sock thing again. This time we see socks are related to freedom. Not much to go on - as any piece of clothing would do as well. But at least we know now that socks can do more than just keep feet warm...

Dobby admits to closing the King's Cross Station barrier and to tampering with the Bludger – in a misguided attempt to "save" Harry (Dobby's long, bandaged fingers reveal his self-imposed punishment for that deed). Harry, of course, still will not leave Hogwarts. Dobby also tells Harry that the Chamber of Secrets had been opened before.

> Aha! The butler did it! (well, he did...) Guess we gotta watch those house-elves. Well, those two mysteries are solved, yet the Chamber of Secrets is still a secret. The reference to the long fingers is interesting. We seem to have a tendency here. We are told that house-elves have powerful magic (which we saw with this Bludger and with the barrier back at King's Cross Station), **and** they have long fingers. Yes, we are starting to get the point.

Before Dobby can tell Harry anything more, he suddenly evaporates with a loud crack, as Dumbledore and Professor McGonagall enter the hospital. Harry, who had been holding Dobby's arm, is left clutching air.

> Did you see that? Dobby disappeared somehow. Nothing to do with the story line here, but HP Sleuths need to keep a good grip on this septology clue. Also, the sound Dobby makes when he Disapparates is louder than the one humans make. Is that because he is more powerful, less powerful, or because it is a different kind of spell? Whatever, we still lost our hold on him just as he was giving us some excellent insights, of course (Rule #2).

Harry sees the Professors placing the rigid body of Colin Creevey on a bed. Harry manages to get a glimpse of his "staring face." Colin had been found petrified with a bunch of grapes next to him, and they figured he was on the way to see Harry. Whatever attacked him had also melted his camera.

> Lots of juicy stuff here - like grapes for instance.☺ What was Colin doing with grapes? As we now know, J.K.R. never puts in details like that without a reason. Was he down in the kitchens? The story-line clue that the camera was fried is clearly due to a very powerful spell - but what kind of spell? Also, another septology clue concerns what Colin was doing wandering around at night at all - since Colin never told us. We are not convinced he was looking to visit Harry (Rule #4). Colin is extremely brave and he is having great fun being a wizard, so he might be having some of his own nighttime adventures. Wonder what he's been up to?

Dumbledore, wearing his woolly dressing gown and nightcap, had been on his way to get some hot chocolate. He just happened to discover Professor McGonagall and Colin on the stairs.

> Is J.K.R. trying to convince us that this was a coincidence? (We know a Rule #3 when we see one.) So, what was Dumbledore up to? We already know from Book 1 that Dumbledore gets around at night, and we can bet hot chocolate was probably not his main mission. Was he tipped-off about the attack? Was he

watching Colin? Lots to ponder. Make special note of that "woolly dressing gown" - it goes well with the "thick, woolen socks" that Dumbledore claimed would be his desire from the Mirror of Erised. What would make a grown man wear a woolly dressing gown? We know Dumbledore's eccentric, but we also know he's very ingenious....

Professor McGonagall is frustrated to know who is doing the attacking. Professor Dumbledore is adamant that it is not "who," but "**how**."

This tells us that there is no doubt in Dumbledore's mind who is behind the attacks. Is this because he has prior knowledge? Does he suspect Voldemort but does not know how he could be doing it in his defeated state, or does he think the person who did it last time is dead or being watched carefully?

No matter whether it's who or how, Dumbledore deduces that "the Chamber of Secrets is indeed open again."

Curiosities

✳ Interesting. Hermione has proposed that she, Harry and Ron break rules in order to spy on Malfoy using Polyjuice Potion. Hermione was obviously affected by this Mudblood bigotry (she is quite sensitive to intolerance, in general).

✳ Dobby tells Harry that when Voldemort was around, house elves were "treated like vermin." Dobby also refers to the house-elves as "lowly enslaved dregs of the magical world." How did they end up like that?

✳ Beware biblio-cleptos... Madam Pince may somehow be able to check signatures for forgery.

Other Oddities

✳ Gilderoy says he cured a werewolf with an "immensely complex *Homorphus Charm*." He seems to have a lot of run-ins with werewolves.

Chapter 11 Analysis

(The Dueling Club)

——— Clues ———

Ron and Hermione had heard the news about Colin Creevey, so had started on the Polyjuice Potion immediately. When Harry leaves the hospital, he finds them in Moaning Myrtle's bathroom, where Hermione has created a "portable, waterproof" fire (her "speciality") to simmer the potion.

> We are told outright that "portable, waterproof" fires are Hermione's "speciality." That is enlightening septology information to keep on the back burner.

Harry, Ron, and Hermione ponder how the monster could be moving around the school. Hermione suggests a chameleon ghoul, which can disguise itself, but without more evidence they are stumped. In order to obtain the restricted ingredients to add to their Polyjuice Potion, Harry tosses a Filibuster firework into Goyle's cauldron of Swelling Solution during Snape's class. While Snape is trying to restore calm and administer a Deflating Draft, Hermione slips into his office and plunders his private stores.

> We now know that chameleon ghouls exist. Hermione says it can disguise itself as a suit of armor, and we know there are plenty of armors around the castle (even ones that seem to move around at times). What we do not know, as of Book 4, is if ghouls can be friendly and helpful, just obnoxious, or even dangerous.

There is an announcement that a dueling club is being organized, so Harry, Ron, and Hermione decide to attend. Some students think Flitwick might be teaching it - as he supposedly was a dueling champion when he was young. Unfortunately, it turns out to be Lockhart.

> Flitwick was a dueling champion? Awesome. Sounds like the students had better behave in Charms class.

Lockhart has trouble dueling against Snape, who easily disarms him with the charm "Expelliarmus!" Snape, who comes "gliding over like a large and malevolent bat," picks Harry and Malfoy to demonstrate by facing off against each other. Lockhart tries to show Harry how to use a special wiggling motion with his wand as a defense, but manages to drop it instead, with the comment "Whoops! My wand is a little overexcited..."

> Did he say "Whoops"? How many of you are now convinced Gilderoy escaped from *The Bird Cage (La Cage aux Folles)*? Ohhhh, some of you think that's not correct. You say, he didn't escape - he was kicked out....

Draco doesn't play fair - he conjures a snake, which then threatens to strike at Justin Finch-Fletchley. When Harry sees this, he yells at the snake and it slumps to the floor in obedience. Instead of being grateful, Justin is angry, Snape is looking strangely at Harry, and everyone is muttering ominously. Ron and Hermione usher Harry away – telling him that he was speaking snake language, called Parseltongue and that it was not obvious he was trying to stop the snake from attacking. Harry is surprised that he can speak another language and not know it - he just knew he somehow communicated with the boa constrictor at the zoo (Book 1).

> Not only can Harry talk to snakes, it seems that they obey his bidding. Wicked. Wonder why? How did he get such a rare talent? This is definitely something to monitor. And Snape is still flitting around – driving everyone batty....

Harry does not understand why this snake thing would be so bad. Ron and Hermione explain how Salazar Slytherin was famous for being one of the few Parselmouths - which is why his house mascot is a serpent. Harry denies being related to Slytherin, but Hermione points out that would be difficult to prove since Slytherin goes back 1,000 years, and for all he knew, he could be.

> Is this why the Sorting Hat wanted to put Harry in Slytherin? Because he is a Parselmouth, or even possibly because he is a descendent of Slytherin himself? Hermione would certainly be interested in helping Harry trace his roots, but Harry is apparently too afraid to admit to the Sorting Hat's suggestion - even to his closest friends. Does that mean that deep inside he suspects something? It seems that Harry, himself, may not even want to know the answer.

Harry is even more bothered now - especially since he does not know anything about his wizard father's ancestry.

> HP Sleuths get out your fishing nets! Here's a septology red herring, and it's a big one. Notice how Harry quickly assumes that he should focus on his father's side of the family - a blatant J.K.R. trick. She is as good as telling us the information straight out by purposely pointing us in the wrong direction. Although Harry has not put it all together, we have seen that the clues all add up to his father being a descendent of Gryffindor. So where would the Slytherin lineage come from? What about Harry's (supposedly) Muggle-born mother's side? Ron has recently tipped us off that the reason wizards are born from Muggles is specifically due to previous inter-marriage, so that is one possibility. Another is that since we do not know anything of Lily's background, we shouldn't assume she is a blood relative of her parents or that her parents really were Muggles. Either way, HP Sleuths might want to start thinking about those "strikingly green eyes" that Harry has inherited from his mother...

Harry goes to find Justin to try to explain what really happened with the snake. He looks in the library where Ernie Macmillan is telling the other Hufflepuffs that Harry is probably the heir of Slytherin. Ernie is convinced of it because Harry survived Voldemort's original attack, and even thinks that is why Voldemort attacked Harry in the first place – Voldemort "didn't want another Dark Lord competing with him."

> Hope no one else starts believing him. Good thing these are just kids, right?

Harry runs into Hagrid, who was on his way to Dumbledore with a dead rooster, saying that this is the second one he has found. After Hagrid walks off, Harry goes upstairs where a "strong, icy draft" coming through a windowpane has blown out the torches. Harry discovers Justin lying on the floor, petrified, with a black and smoky Nearly Headless Nick floating immobile just above him.

> Harry just *happened* to run into Hagrid with some dead roosters right before discovering Justin and Nick. Hope all you HP Sleuths have learned Rule #3. Things don't just happen in a Harry Potter book. But what is the connection? That's still the hard part. Unless you are a scholar of mythology and legends, you probably do not have enough information to get this one, so don't strain your brains yet.

Before Harry can alert anyone, Peeves (who loves chaos) loudly announces the attack. It looks very incriminating for Harry. Professor Sinistra, the Astronomy Professor, helps take Justin and Nick to the hospital. Professor McGonagall takes Harry away.

> So we really do have an astronomy teacher, and her name is "Sinistra" - not a very friendly sounding name. And how did she happen to be in the area? HP Sleuths would be advised to never let her out of your sight. Funny how Peeves is always around and ready to whoop it up at the slightest disturbance. Come to think of it, he makes an awfully good intruder security alarm. Is that why Dumbledore keeps him around? Even if that's not the reason, considering how he loves to create chaos, he could probably foil any plan to take over the castle. (snigger)

Professor McGonagall leads Harry past a stone gargoyle (password "lemon drop"), and up a moving spiral staircase, to meet with Headmaster Dumbledore.

Curiosities

✳ Gargoyles are grotesque statues of carved stone that were very popular in the European Middle Ages. They are believed to ward off evil, but legends exist that they come to life at certain times and that they can be formidable protectors, as well as very nasty.

✳ In the movie version of *Harry Potter and the Philosopher's (Sorcerer's) Stone*, the Sorting Hat announces its desire to put Harry into Slytherin to the whole student body. From a mystery perspective, it makes a difference here that Harry is actually the only one who is aware of any ties he may have to Slytherin.

✳ That icy draft was awfully strong to have put out the torches in the corridor. Was that at all significant?

✳ Ernie Macmillan is descended from nine generations of witches and warlocks.

Other Oddities

✳ Millicent Bulstrode looks like a hag. Could she have hag blood in her?

✳ Ginny sits next to Colin Creevey in their Charms class. Bet Ginny must know some things about Colin that we haven't heard about yet.

Clues

This is Chapter 12.

Harry is twelve years-old in this Chapter 12. Is this the fateful twelve? Even though we are now in Book 2, the hints about 12 have continued, so they were not just story-line hints for Book 1 after all – we now know they are a septology clue. We will be looking for clues about the mysterious number 12 very carefully here.

As Harry sits alone, waiting for Dumbledore to call him into his office, he sees portraits of previous Headmasters hanging in the room.

Wonder what old Headmasters do for retirement (especially if they're just hanging around)?

Harry notices the Sorting Hat sitting on a shelf and can't resist the urge to try it on again. The Hat astutely asks ("bee in your bonnet?") if Harry has been wondering if it had put him in the right house. The Sorting Hat then reaffirms that Harry was particularly difficult to place, but that it stands by what it said before - Harry "would have done well in Slytherin."

J.K.R. has just done one of her reinforcement thingies. She wants us (and Harry) to know that the Sorting Hat meant what it said (Rule #1). The problem is, was that supposed to be a positive or negative reinforcement (or a red herring)? No matter what, we see the Sorting Hat has no trouble reading what's on people's minds. (We did notice that bee reference.)

A decrepit-looking bird in Dumbledore's waiting room suddenly bursts into flames. Harry is horrified, but Dumbledore walks in at that moment and has Harry observe his phoenix, Fawkes, being reborn out of the ashes. Dumbledore explains that phoenixes have special powers of healing in their tears, an ability to carry heavy loads, and are highly faithful pets.

This was a fairly traumatic event, so it has to be important to the story line or septology. HP Sleuths are advised to remember those three qualities of a phoenix. What Dumbledore does **not** mention is that, although phoenixes may be highly faithful, according to Newt Scamander in *Fantastic Beasts*, they also have a XXXX rating because few wizards have ever been able to domesticate them! Evidence of Dumbledore's power, compassion, or maybe even a mysterious link to these birds.

With the tips of his long fingers together, Dumbledore studies Harry as he states that he does not think Harry was responsible for the attacks. He does want to know, however, if there is anything that Harry would like to tell him. At this time, Harry is not ready to discuss anything with Dumbledore, and tells him "no."

Just a short comment here to point out Dumbledore's long fingers again.

Fred and George think the idea of Harry being Slytherin's heir is all very funny. George has great fun joking to everyone about Harry being dangerous and having a "fanged servant."

Wonder if George shares Ron's sense of humor....

On Christmas day, Hermione greets Harry and Ron with presents as she sits down next to Scabbers. Hedwig delivers to Harry a rude present of a toothpick from the Dursleys, while Mrs. Weasley has knitted Harry yet another famous Weasley sweater.

Scabbers always seems to be around whatever the kids are doing - doesn't seem motivated to go anywhere. He must be getting quite old by now. He deserves a scribble in the HP Sleuth investigation parchment.

Hermione lets Harry and Ron know that the Polyjuice Potion is ready. She informs them that they need to get a hair from Crabbe and from Goyle, and that she already has a hair from Millicent Bulstrode. After dinner, they leave two chocolate cakes with sleeping draught on the ends of the banisters, as bait for the greedy Crabbe and Goyle. When their victims have fallen for the bait and fallen asleep, Harry and Ron stow the two of them into a closet across the hall, plucking some hairs and taking their bigger shoes to use. Hermione has acquired some larger robes, and Harry loosens his watch. In Moaning Myrtle's bathroom, Harry, Ron, and Hermione mix in the hairs, and drink the potion that tastes like over-cooked cabbage.

IS J.K.R. SUBTLE OR WHAT? It's okay - those of you who fell over can get up now and recover. Those of you who kept sloppy notes, let us know when you have found all your cabbage references - especially the ones from Book 1 where it talked about Mrs. Figg's house smelling of cabbage. We now know what the cabbage smell might have been. Is Mrs. Figg or someone else brewing Polyjuice Potion in her house, and if so, why? Is Mrs. Figg also someone else? Or is there some other kind of potion being brewed in there?

Harry and Ron stare at each other in amazement as they see themselves transformed into Crabbe and Goyle. Hermione, however, refuses to come out of her stall, insisting that they go without her. They only have one hour before the potion wears off, returning them to normal.

That is the big drawback to Polyjuice Potion. You only have one hour unless you keep drinking that nasty stuff (yuck). That means if you wanted it to last longer, you would have to carry it with you - not too convenient for long-term transformations. You either have to get creative, or use a different spell. HP Sleuths should become experts on the making and use of Polyjuice Potion, since J.K.R. always has something brewing.

They have a difficult time finding and getting into the Slytherin Common room, encountering both a Ravenclaw girl and Percy along the way. Malfoy finally comes along and ushers them in.

> If by now you are aware that coincidences do not just happen with J.K.R., you should be wondering what both a Ravenclaw and a Gryffindor Prefect were doing down in the dungeon area near Slytherin. If you don't know, we aren't gonna ruin it for you...

Draco shows Crabbe (Ron) and Goyle (Harry) a *Daily Prophet* article reporting that the Ministry of Magic fined Arthur Weasley for bewitching a Muggle car. Draco mentions how his own father has some valuable Dark Arts items hidden under their drawing room floor. Although Draco disappoints them by admitting that he doesn't know who the heir of Slytherin is after all, he does mention the last time it was opened was 50 years ago, that it was kept quiet, and a "Mudblood" had died. The person who opened the chamber the last time had been caught and expelled, and he assumes is in the wizard prison, Azkaban. The Polyjuice Potion starts to wear off, so Harry and Ron have to split - running back to the bathroom, where they find out that the hair that Hermione thought was from Millicent turned out to be a cat hair. Ron backs into the sink in shock when he sees that Hermione has grown whiskers, yellow eyes, and a tail.

> (Watch your step, Ron – Hermione's hissing mad.) Not Draco – total bummer. We learn story-line clues that the last time the chamber was opened was 50 years ago, someone died, and someone was expelled. It is time to think about who might have died and who might have been expelled. We are given the hint that the person who died was Muggle-born, and we wonder how many students have ever been expelled from the school? (Fred & George are still attending, so it must not be tooo easy to get kicked out!)

Hermione's cat features did not wear off after the hour since the potion was not intended for animal transformations, so they bring a furry Hermione to the hospital.

Curiosities

✳ It should be noted for future septology reference that Millicent (or someone she hangs out with) has a cat.

✳ The Hedwig Christmas delivery of Harry's present is odd here and brings up other odd communication issues. How has the school been communicating with the Dursleys? Do they use Muggle Post, or Owl Post? A regular postman would not even be able to see the castle, Uncle Vernon won't use owls, and Aunt Petunia hates animals. So, are they forced to send owls at times like this, or does the school have a Muggle address that the Dursleys use?

✳ We never find out what Crabbe and Goyle thought happened to them. Maybe they were too embarrassed to admit it, or maybe they had too much holiday cheer, but waking up in a closet with their shoes outside the door had to seem a little odd even for dim-witted, greedy punks. This is not reinforced anywhere, so at this time we can ignore it.

✳ Phoenixes are very popular mythology creatures, associated with the Egyptian god of the Sun. Just like Fawkes, legends say they die in a pyre of flames and then are reborn out of the ashes. According to *Fantastic Beasts and Where to Find Them*, the song of the Phoenix will also boost courage in "the pure of heart" while instilling fear in "the impure." The *Chronicles of Narnia* mention a special horn with similar abilities. Fawkes' name is most likely inspired by the bonfires of Guy Fawkes Day in Britain. Could Fawkes, the phoenix, play a part in any conspiracies?

✳

Chapter 13 Analysis

Clues

This is chapter 13.

Welcome to *Whodunit13*. As HP Sleuths know, there are clues hiding wherever there is a superstitious number. J.K.R, therefore, could not resist the temptation to have the culprit and his fiendish plot make a *cameo* appearance within chapter 13. This is a trend that so far has held true through Book 4. The following are the key story-line events that take place in this chapter - we leave it up to HP sleuths to decipher whodunit. Don't worry, if you can't solve it here, she always tells-all at the end of each book.☺

Hermione needs several weeks to recover from the cat-hair Polyjuice Potion, so Harry and Ron visit her in the hospital. They notice that she is treasuring a get-well card from Gilderoy Lockhart, which is signed "Professor Gilderoy Lockhart, Order of Merlin, Third Class, Honorary Member of the Dark Force Defense League, and five-time winner of Witch Weekly's Most-Charming-Smile Award." Ron laments to her, over and over, that he was sure Malfoy was responsible for the Chamber of Secrets.

Poor Hermione - she may look like a cat, but we doubt she's purring (it must be difficult to turn pages with claws). HP Sleuths take heed of this Dark Force Defense League – it seems like comic relief now, but it's potentially serious for the septology. We are disappointed to see Hermione has been sucked-in by Gilderoy's game. Even for Hermione, emotions do have a way of obscuring one's vision. Then there's Ron - who is almost never right. He was so sure Malfoy was responsible - well, don't rule that out yet - this is Chapter 13.

In the corridor, Harry and Ron hear Filch shouting about cleaning up a huge flood from Moaning Myrtle's bathroom. As Filch leaves, Harry and Ron go in to find out what happened. Moaning Myrtle explains that she got upset when someone threw a book into the toilet at her. Harry retrieves what turns out to be a diary that is dated from 50 years ago, with the name T. M. Riddle.

Myrtle is very talented with water. This is a strong reinforcement that she can move large amounts of the stuff. So the question is, can she affect any other physical objects or is she limited to water? HP Sleuths should absorb this septology clue.

Ron is concerned about the diary being hexed. He mentions that his dad has seen books that burn peoples eyes out or that the reader always has their nose in, because they can "never stop reading it." It does not appear to be hexed, but there is nothing written inside the diary, and they can't get it to reveal any entries.

Uh oh, we have been getting all these hints about eyes and noses. Maybe this book does have something bad to do with eyes. Be careful Harry! (And we thought reading was a safe activity.)

Harry feels, however, there could be a lot of importance to the diary if someone was trying to ditch it. Harry keeps thinking the name T. M. Riddle sounds familiar - like "a friend he'd had when he was small."

The WWP Sleuthoscope just went wacko - bouncing off the castle walls and the Rememberit Quill is scribbling frantically. A friend? Familiar name? There's something awfully fishy here. Even as of Book 4, we have not had a full explanation about this "clue," but it's so blatant that we have not ruled it out as significant to the septology. Or did J.K.R. pull us in hook, line, and sinker?

Hermione thinks the diary could tell them a lot, but Ron jokes that would be a bit difficult since it's blank. However, the night he did detention in the trophy room, Ron had noticed that Riddle received an award for special services to the school. Ron and Harry wonder what the award might have been (Ron jokes that maybe Riddle received 30 O.W.L.s or was rewarded for doing everyone the favor of murdering Myrtle). Hermione deduces that if the chamber was opened 50 years ago, and Riddle (who was a student 50 years ago) received a special services award from the school, that he might have caught the heir of Slytherin.

The septology clues are getting more complex with each book, Ron's jokes are getting funnier, and Hermione's astute deductions are getting even more accurate. Hope HP Sleuths are also paying more attention.

They check the trophy room for more clues. They re-examine Riddle's gold shield "tucked inside" a corner cabinet, but can only find that Riddle also received a Medal for Magical Merit and was Head Boy.

Riddle seems like an important student. Do they usually keep awards for students stashed away inside cabinets? Maybe just not enough room?

The attacks seem to have stopped, and Lockhart is implying that he himself may be responsible for the cessation. On Valentines Day, Lockhart decorates the school with a Valentines theme to the dismay of many students and teachers (and embarrasses Flitwick by gushing about his *Entrancing Enchantments* and addressing him as a "sly old dog"). Gilderoy also provides a troop of ungainly dwarves dressed as cupids for delivering Valentine greetings.

This is a hint to all people who may want to send a friendly greeting to J.K.R. - she's most likely not into hearts and butterflies. Valentines Day does bring out the sissies, and along with that, more inferences as Gilderoy makes suggestive (and inappropriate), coy remarks about dainty (and modest) Flitwick.

In a crowded corridor on the way to class, Harry is approached by one of Lockhart's cupids. Embarrassed, Harry tries to escape, but the dwarf tackles and serenades him, ripping his book bag open in the process, spilling the inkbottle and everything all over the floor. As Harry scrambles to stuff the contents back into his bag, Malfoy grabs the diary, and teases Harry with it. Ginny, who was responsible for Harry's musical Valentine, stares "terrified" as Malfoy taunts Harry. Harry pulls out his wand and ejects the diary out of Malfoy's hands.

> What a mess - and we don't mean the spilled ink. In addition to helping Harry solve the mystery of the diary, there is another story-line clue in this incident. Notice the (as usual) carefully chosen word J.K.R. has used to describe Ginny's reaction. One would have expected dire embarrassment, but she reacts with "terror" (not to mention that stare). Something's up.

Harry notices that although everything else in his book bag has been drenched in ink, the diary pages are completely clean. Back in his dorm, Harry tests it by writing "my name is Harry Potter" on one of the pages. The ink is sucked into the page and vanishes. Harry actually gets a response as words magically write "My name is Tom Riddle...How did you come by my diary?" which then fade away. Harry writes to Tom all about someone trying to discard the diary and asks Tom to tell him everything he knows about the Chamber of Secrets. Tom Riddle tells Harry that when it was opened back in his time, the headmaster (then Professor Dippet) was so ashamed that a girl died at Hogwarts, Riddle was forbidden from telling anyone about it.

> We find out here that it was a female who died last time, and we know from previous clues that she was Muggle-born, but so far that is all. This Dippet sounds like a real dip - it seems that not all Hogwarts headmasters were of Dumbledore's caliber.

Riddle takes Harry inside his memory to actually witness the events as they occurred on June 13. When Harry drops in, Professor Dippet is reading a letter from Tom Riddle, and frets as he draws the curtain on his window. Tom, a prefect with jet-black hair like Harry's, arrives shortly thereafter. He tries to convince Professor Dippet to let him stay at Hogwarts, so he doesn't have to go back to a Muggle orphanage for summer holiday. They talk about Riddle's Muggle father (Tom) and grandfather (Marvolo) who he was named after, and about his witch mother. Dippet says Tom can't stay - that it is too dangerous since a number of students have been attacked and now one has already died.

> Yes, we are meant to see a resemblance between Harry and Tom, but we are not to let our imaginations get the best of us. That is both a story-line and septology clue, but HP Sleuths know you can't always believe what you see. Tom Marvolo Riddle? J.K.R. is overtly telling us there is a riddle to solve concerning Tom.

Harry then follows Tom down from Dippet's office, past the gargoyle, where he encounters a tall, auburn-haired wizard. It is Professor Dumbledore from 50 years ago, and he warns Riddle to be wary and get to bed.

> Now this is interesting. Dumbledore had auburn (brownish-red) hair. Lily Potter had dark red hair (Book 1). There's nothing to connect the two, but knowing J.K.R., it's worth a DNA sample.

In the dungeons, Riddle confronts Rubeus Hagrid, who (at that time) is a student in the school. Hagrid had been keeping a monster spider in the dungeons for a pet, and now that the student was killed, Riddle turns him in.

> Poor Hagrid. We now know why he was expelled. Do you at all doubt the evidence? But would Hagrid protect his spider if it truly had killed someone? Is Hagrid really the descendent of Slytherin? Yet, would they have expelled Hagrid if he wasn't guilty? This is Chapter 13, so all possibilities should be considered.

Harry returns to present-day where he delivers the sad news to Ron that it was Hagrid who opened the Chamber 50 years ago.

Rowlinguistics

✴ **Riddle**'s surname in the French translation is Jedusor, which seems to be a mutation of the phrase *jeu du sort*. It is a clever play-on-words, as it can mean a *game of chance*, *game of fate*, or *a pretend spell*. A similar phrase "jeu de mot" means *pun*! Then there's his middle name, which in the French version, is "Elvis." (Hmmm...) Tom is one big riddle.

Curiosities

✳ We see that the Gargoyle, which guards the entrance to the office of the Headmaster, has been there since at least Dippet's time.

✳ It may not be important, but we were wondering which side of the family Marvolo comes from.

✳ On a scratch piece of parchment, HP Sleuths might want to note that the day that Tom Riddle brings Harry into his memory to see Hagrid and his spider is June 13.

✳ Maybe this is just due to the events being from the perspective of Tom's memory, but note that after reading the letter, the only thing Dippet does is pull the curtains back, and Riddle appears.

✳ Another note for the scratch parchment - the Chamber was opened in Riddle's 5th year, and Hagrid's 3rd year at Hogwarts.

✳ Ron wonders if Riddle had received 30 O.W.L.s. That may be an exaggeration, but it tells us that 12 isn't the most you can get.

✳ If this little trip back in time through Riddle's memory seems familiar, you may be thinking of Charles Dickens' "Ghost of Christmas Past." Can this technique be used for other purposes?

Other Oddities

✳ Hermione used a "Revealer" (opposite of an eraser) to try to find the hidden words on a page.

Chapter 14 Analysis

(CORNELIUS FUDGE)

Clues

Hermione thinks they might have accused the wrong person 50 years ago. However, Harry, Ron, and Hermione all feel that they cannot comfortably ask Hagrid about the Chamber and the attacks, so since the attacks have stopped, they decide to let it go.

> There are two things we are learning about Hermione's analyses. The first is that she's almost always right. The second is that whenever she lets her emotions get in the way, she's almost always wrong. We hope we can trust her judgement here....

Harry, Ron, and Hermione spend time trying to plan their next year's classes. Everyone is giving advice, including Percy, who recommends Divination. Hermione takes no one's advice and just signs up for everything – explaining that "it could affect our whole future"!

> Look who recommended Divination! Should have known. If you are reading the books for the first time, you will understand shortly (in Book 3), that Divination is a bit of a joke (and that's not giving anything away). If you have already read all the books and wondered whatever motivated Harry and Ron to take such an absurd class, we have refreshed your memory (Percy). If HP Sleuths were paying close attention to Hermione just now, we are also being provided with a very subtle story-line hint for Book 3.

The night before their Quidditch match with the Hufflepuffs, Harry's room is broken into and the diary is stolen. Harry and Hermione realize that whoever stole it had to have been a Gryffindor. On the way to the match the next morning, Harry hears the Dark voice again - and Hermione suddenly figures something out - taking off to the library (as always) to investigate.

> Hmmm. Diary stolen, Dark voice. Is this another one of those coincidences that's not really a coincidence? (Check Rule #3.)

The Quidditch match never begins - Professor McGonagall cancels it. She orders everyone to return to their rooms; there has been another double attack. She brings Harry and Ron to the hospital, where they stare at Hermione's glassy eyes, for she and a Ravenclaw Prefect, Penelope Clearwater, have been petrified. (Penelope is the female that Harry and Ron saw when they were looking for the entrance to Slytherin.) Professor McGonagall has a small mirror that was found near the girls, but Harry and Ron do not know anything about it. Percy is quite in shock. Ron explains that's because Percy can't believe a Prefect could have been petrified. Lee Jordan wants everyone to notice that no one from Slytherin has ever been attacked and thinks they could be at the bottom of all this.

> Now this is out of character for Percy. Usually he feels quite at home helping to contain a crisis, but instead of taking control, he is in shock this time. Yes, that's

a hint (but beware of Rule #4). Staring eyes are also hints, but HP Sleuths knew that. Lee Jordan's information was somewhat anti-climatic, as we had already noticed the Slytherins seemed to be enjoying this. However, he still could be right about it being a Slytherin - even if Draco is not the specific culprit (Lee Jordan is usually fairly accurate). So have any HP Super Sleuths understood the reference to the compact mirror yet?

Ron and Harry decide they had better talk to Hagrid, so they go down to his cabin that night using the Invisibility Cloak. It was difficult enough to get out with all the teachers patrolling the corridors, but then Ron stubs his toe. If Snape hadn't sneezed just then, they might have been found out.

> Odd coincidence. We don't normally accept coincidences, but then again, who would have known in advance (or how?), that Ron was going to stub his toe? There is a minute possibility that just after Ron stubbed his toe (as he started to yelp), a quick *Sneezing Spell* could have been tossed in Snape's direction by an invisible observer (just one possibility). Since this was never explained, we consider it future-looking septology material to contemplate.

While Harry and Ron are visiting Hagrid at his cabin, Cornelius Fudge and Dumbledore arrive. The kids hide in a corner under the Cloak, listening and watching. Fudge tells Hagrid that due to political pressure, they must take him away to Azkaban.

> So this is the famous head of the Ministry of Magic - a political flunky? Guess even magic can't help politics! This is a crucial personality profile for the whole septology. Who does Fudge answer to? His constituents? His conscience? Maybe even bribes? HP Sleuths watch this guy really carefully. He has ultimate control over the whole wizarding society - which makes him a central figure as well as target by both good and evil.

Lucius Malfoy then stops by with an Order of Suspension from the 12 school governors to remove Dumbledore from his post of Headmaster. Dumbledore agrees to step down, stating though, that he will "only truly have left this school when none here are loyal to me" (his eyes glance toward Harry and Ron in their corner).

> The WWP Sleuthoscope is strobing wildly. Does this mean what we think it means? Not only can Dumbledore become invisible without an Invisibility Cloak, he can **see through** Invisibility Cloaks!? Is that one of Dumbledore's natural abilities, or are those half-moon glasses not just for old age? This comment about leaving the school is highly significant to the story line and especially the septology - as we worry about what will happen in Book 5.

Malfoy ushers everyone out of the cabin, but as they are leaving, Hagrid very loudly says that if anyone wants to find out some "stuff" that all they have to do is "follow the spiders"....

Curiosities

✳ If Hagrid was in 3rd year (age 13) 50 years ago, then he is 63 years old now.

✳ According to an interview with J.K.R. on Scholastic.com, McGonagall is 70.

Chapter 15 Analysis

Clues

Professor McGonagall has now taken over as head of Hogwarts in Dumbledore's absence. In Herbology class, Harry and Ron notice some spiders scuttling away toward the Forbidden Forest. They decide to follow Hagrid's clue, and take Fang into the forest that night (despite Ron's phobia), to see where they lead. In Harry's first year, Hagrid had warned them never to leave the path. But in order to follow the spiders, they end up doing so. In the depths of the Forest, they are startled as they stumble upon Mr. Weasley's car that is now roaming the forest wild.

> ...And you thought your car has a mind of it's own! Just what kind of spell did Mr. Weasley use on his car? This is not likely to be the last we see of it.

Just as their nerves begin to settle, giant "eight-eyed" spiders emerge and capture Harry and Ron. The monsters bring them to their spider father, Aragog - the very one who was accused, 50 years ago, of being Hagrid's creature from the Chamber of Secrets. Aragog's eyes, however, are all milky-white as he is now blind from old age. He tells Harry that Hagrid was good to him – even brought him a wife, Mosag. Harry explains that he and Ron are Hagrid's friends, and that Hagrid is in trouble, having been taken off to Azkaban under suspicion of causing the new attacks. Aragog insists that he never attacked any humans out of respect for Hagrid, and that the dead girl's body had been found in a bathroom while he kept to his dark, quiet cabinet. Aragog says that Hagrid was wrongly accused, but will not reveal the name or nature of the attacking creature, and will never utter its name to anyone, including Hagrid. Aragog is unmoved by Harry and Ron's friendship with Hagrid and gives permission to the spiders to eat them.

> The "staring eyes" clues probably don't refer to Aragog – since he not only isn't from the Chamber, but his eyes cannot stare. Now, either Hogwarts bathrooms are highly lethal, or we have a real good idea who died last time. The trouble is, if it wasn't Aragog, we still don't know what killed her. Then there's this big lesson here - don't expect much compassion from a monster spider (even a talking monster spider). We also were surprised Hagrid's friends didn't count more in Aragog's opinion.

Harry and Ron are saved at the last moment by Mr. Weasley's car roaring in with bright headlights, knocking spiders out of the way, driving them to safety.

> Good car, nice car - but waaay too convenient. What does Dumbledore do with all his time when he's on suspension from Hogwarts? Maybe a midnight cruise in the forest plus a little automobile enchantment? Or is this car actually a highly faithful pet of the Weasleys? Nothing yet explained as of Book 4, but it's "engine" seems to work fine.

So, Riddle has caught the wrong person, and now Harry and Ron do not know if it was the same person or a different one who has opened the Chamber this time. All they do know is that this seems like a monster version of Voldemort, as the other monsters will not say its name.

> In other words, it is a *You-Know-What*. Obviously, it is a danger even to other monsters, and it is somehow moving around the castle (gulp).

With the knowledge that she was found in a bathroom, Harry and Ron are able to deduce that the girl that was killed the last time must be Moaning Myrtle....

Rowlinguistics

✳ **Aragog** seems like it could be related to the word *arachnid* (a spider). When talking about some bad guys, the Bible mentions Gog and Magog, after which two hills in Cambridgeshire are named (sort of like Aragog and Mosag). The name also sounds very similar to Aragorn from *The Lord of the Rings*, and we wonder if, like Aragorn, Aragog may have descended from an ancient (and powerful) race.

Other Oddities

✳ To keep Fang from barking, Harry and Ron "glue" his teeth together with Hagrid's treacle fudge – never know when that clever trick might come in handy again. Also, remember Hagrid's treacle fudge is kept in a tin on his mantelpiece.

✳ It is mentioned that Ernie and Hanna of Hufflepuff, who are working together in Herbology, are friends.

Clues

At breakfast, Professor McGonagall announces that the mandrakes are of age, so the people who were petrified can now be revived. She hopes at least one of them will be able to describe what they saw. Ginny comes over to tell Harry and Ron something very important, rocking back and forth the way Dobby does as he is about to reveal a prohibitive secret. However, she runs off when Percy arrives. Percy asserts that what she was going to say had to do with him and an incident he asked her to keep secret.

A mystery always involves personalities as well as motives, and these two Weasleys are intriguing ones. Along with being rigid with rules and a control freak, Percy is quick to judge without all the facts, and clearly thinks the world revolves around him. Not a real pleasant guy. Then there's Ginny, who obviously does not trust her brother any more than Ron does. Just in case, we might want to remember that rocking motion for the future.

On their way to the bathroom to speak to Moaning Myrtle, Harry and Ron are intercepted by Professor McGonagall. To avoid punishment, they tell her that they were on their way to visit Hermione, so they must now sidetrack to the hospital. While visiting with a petrified Hermione, Harry notices that a piece of paper is crumpled in her fist. They secretly pry the paper out of her hand and see that it is torn out of a library reference book. It describes a King of Serpents called the Basilisk, which can live for hundreds of years. It kills with either venomous fangs or by a direct look into its eyes. It is the mortal enemy of spiders who flee from it, while a crowing rooster is fatal to it. Hermione had written the word "Pipes" down on the page.

As J.K. Rowling explains in the book:

Harry and Ron see that Hermione had figured out that the creature in the Chamber is this snake - which is why only Harry (a Parselmouth) is hearing it - and it has been moving around the castle through the plumbing. Harry realizes that the reason no one had died is because none of the people actually looked *directly* into the eyes of the snake...

- Colin saw it through his camera

- Justin saw it through Nearly Headless Nick

- Nick was already dead

- Hermione and Penelope used Penelope's small mirror

- Mrs. Norris only saw its reflection in the water on the floor

Additionally, Hagrid's roosters were being slaughtered because their crowing is deadly to it.

> Oooooo, staring eyes. We get it. It is so easy now to see how it all relates. Snakes with deadly stares are very common in legends - probably originating from the belief that a cobra can hypnotize its prey. There's even a snake Pokemon™, Arbok, who can do that. In the famous Greek myth of the Medusa, the Gorgon had snakes for hair and her gaze would turn men to stone. She was ultimately slain by Perseus, who used a highly-polished bronze shield to see her reflection in order to slay her without being affected - similar to how the reflection of J.K.R.'s Basilisk could be seen without dying. HP Sleuths might want to go back and re-view all of the "eyes" lurking throughout this book.

Harry and Ron speculate that the entrance to the Chamber may be right in Moaning Myrtle's bathroom, and decide to tell Professor McGonagall. They go down to the staff room where they overhear that Ginny Weasley has just been taken by the monster - leaving the message that "her skeleton will lie in the Chamber forever." Sensitive Professor Flitwick bursts into tears and Professor McGonagall is completely distraught. She starts to say "This is the end of Hogwarts. Dumbledore always said...", when Lockhart bounds in (totally oblivious to the tragedy). Lockhart is instructed to go take care of the monster, so that evening, Harry and Ron sneak off to his office to tell him what they know.

> WWP Sleuthoscope flashing furiously! Along with his other talents, Mr. Personality Lockhart definitely has a talent for entrances and a real knack for timing. Are we sure that Lockhart isn't doing this on purpose? Can Lockhart really be that brain-dead? Arrgh! Now we'll never know what Dumbledore "always said." Was it a prophecy or just an observation? Whatever it was, according to Rule #2, it was important for the septology. The HP Hintoscope is also moaning at us. HP Sleuths will remember that the first two times that Harry heard the Dark voice were in or right near Lockhart's office - which is also right by Myrtle's bathroom. You see, no such thing as a coincidence.

Harry and Ron discover that Lockhart is in the process of running away. Lockhart admits to them that he has not really performed any of the feats that he has written about. He impersonates others (like he did with the warlock who saved the village form were-wolves) by casting *Memory Spells* on them (his best talent) so they do not remember anything. Lockhart then tries to cast the same spell on the kids, but Harry disarms him.

> Looks like Lockhart has a talent for exits, as well. *Memory Spells* seem to be used a lot by magical people. Effective for Muggle issues, but also too convenient for corrupt wizards as we see here. HP Sleuths bone-up on your memory charms - much more about them in upcoming books.

Harry and Ron march Lockhart at wand-point to Moaning Myrtle's bathroom, where they ask her how she died. She tells them that she was hiding in the bathroom because Olive Hornby had been teasing her. She had heard a boy enter who spoke another language, but when she looked out to tell him to leave, she saw a "pair of great, big, yellow eyes" at the sink in front of her toilet, and then she died. She came back as a ghost because she was intent on haunting Olive. Upon inspecting the sink, Harry finds the image of a snake etched into the side of one of the copper taps that has never worked. By convincing himself that the snake is real, Harry eventually manages to hiss "open up" in Parseltongue, which causes the sink to fall away - exposing a big pipe.

> Talk about a grudge. Olive definitely got her due. However, grudges must only be one reason why some people become ghosts. Professor Binns, we are told, just got up one day to teach - leaving his body behind, so that whole issue is still nebulous. Okay, the entrance was under the sink. Based on Chapter 12, we might say that Ron has a way of backing into clues (tee-hee).

Harry and Ron push Lockhart down the pipe first and then follow after him. They end up in a slimy tunnel that appears to be beneath the lake. As they walk along the tunnel, Lockhart suddenly lunges at Ron, knocking him down and grabbing his wand. Lockhart raises the Spellotaped wand and yells *"Obliviate!"* However, Ron's broken wand backfires (as usual), exploding out the back end - zapping Lockhart's own memory while sending chunks of the ceiling down to the floor. Harry is cut off from the other two by a wall of rocks, so continues on alone. Ron starts to dig out an opening while he waits for Harry to return.

> With Lockhart on our side, who needs Voldemort? Or is he on our side? HP Sleuths should remember that he has no morals and that he is extremely ruthless if he would do this to 12 year-olds. Lockhart also has a bit of an advantage if his memory ever returns - as he now knows some personal information about Harry, Ron, and Myrtle.

Harry comes to a solid wall with a carving of two entwined snakes with strangely realistic eyes, and he has no trouble hissing "Open."

Curiosities

✳ Although it is not explained, we presume the scorch marks under the water, the camera melting, and Nick turning smoky, were because of the intensity of the spell from the Basilisk's eyes. Are there other eyes with that kind of power?

*✳ The Basilisk is referenced in literature and legends, and is also the name of a modern-day lizard.

*✳ What do we know about the *Dark Force Defense League*? Hope Lockhart is not a typical member.

*✳ One issue sort of bothers us: Why did Myrtle never see this big monster of a snake slither through her bathroom this year? We will assume for now it is literary license and not a clue since it has not been reinforced.

*✳ Book-loving Hermione normally wouldn't rip pages out of important library books - especially since Madam Pince threatens painful consequences for such actions (as stated on the checkout list inside the cover of *Quidditch Through the Ages*). Hope Madam Pince was able to re-affix that page (you never know who might be in need a basilisk reference 1000 years from now).

*✳ Myrtle now knows Harry is a Parselmouth.

Other Oddities

*✳ It was an "old Armenian warlock" who saved a village from werewolves (whose memory of it is now gone), and "The witch that banished Brandon Banshee had a hare lip" (whose memory is also now gone).

*✳ We really hate to bring this up, but while we know that there were running water and pipes in Ancient Rome, was there really a girls' bathroom 1000 years ago? If not, what used to be there, or did Riddle somehow move the entrance? If he moved it, where was it before?

Chapter 17 Analysis

(THE HEIR OF SLYTHERIN)

Clues

Harry enters the long Chamber of Secrets, where he finds Ginny lying unconscious next to Tom Riddle's diary at the foot of an enormous stone statue of Salazar Slytherin. Harry is careful to protect his eyes in case the Basilisk appears. He sees that Ginny is not petrified, but he cannot wake her. A blurry Tom Riddle appears before him to tell him that Ginny is not dead, but will not wake and is getting weaker. Harry had dropped his wand but Riddle has picked it up and is twirling it between his long fingers.

> First Ollivander, then Dobby, next Dumbledore, now Riddle - those long fingers do mean something. (powerful magic... heritage... both?)

Riddle laughs (a "high, cold laugh that didn't suit him") as he tells Harry how Ginny had been writing in his diary for months pouring out her soul, confiding in him all her deepest fears and darkest secrets. In turn, Tom has been pouring his soul into her, taking control of her. He brags that he has always been able to charm anyone he needed.

> Riddle explains how everything happened this year:
>
> ☾ Through Riddle's control, it was Ginny who opened the Chamber of Secrets this time.
>
> ☾ All attacks, including the writing on the walls and the killing of the roosters, etc., were done by Ginny under his control.
>
> ☾ Riddle found out from Ginny how Harry had defeated Voldemort 13 years ago, and again last year.
>
> ☾ Ginny became suspicious, realizing what was happening, and tried to ditch the diary.
>
> ☾ When Harry ended up with the diary, Riddle changed his focus from killing mud-bloods to killing Harry.
>
> ☾ When Ginny saw that Harry had the diary, she panicked and stole it back.
>
> ☾ Riddle forced Ginny to write her own fate on the wall and then come down to the Chamber so Harry would follow her and he could get to Harry.

Riddle admits to Harry that he framed Hagrid 50 years ago.

> Oh, wow. Riddle **did** murder Moaning Myrtle ☹ (Ron had joked that it would have merited an award, but considering how ornery her ghost is, Riddle didn't do anyone a favor.)

Dumbledore, the Transfiguration teacher, was the only one that did not seem to be fooled, and thought Hagrid was innocent. There is an "odd red gleam" in Riddle's eyes.

> Lesson Number One - You can't fool Albus Dumbledore. Lesson Number Two - Review Lesson One! So, Dumbledore used to teach Transfiguration? The current Transfiguration teacher, Professor McGonagall, can turn into a cat, and...well, who ever heard of a Transfiguration teacher that couldn't transform into at least one other *something*? So what can Dumbledore turn into, and have we already seen it? We know he likes woolly things, so maybe he's a sheep? We also know his name means *bumblebee*, therefore, it is very possible that he takes on the form of a bee or bug for at least one of his transfigurations, and has probably been flitting around a lot...! HP Sleuths - CONSTANT VIGILANCE!

Riddle reveals that his name, Tom Marvolo Riddle, is really an anagram (a scrambled version) of "I am Lord Voldemort."

> So that's Tom's riddle! And that's one huge anagram. But then, why has Harry's scar not hurt? Is it because Riddle is not real, is it because it's before he attacked Harry, or is this a clue?

Riddle started using the Voldemort name among his most intimate friends while at Hogwarts. Riddle says his mother was a full-blood witch. His father, a Muggle, supposedly abandoned her before Tom was born - having found out that she was a witch. She carried the blood of Salazar Slytherin, and died just after his birth, only living long enough to name him "Tom" after his father and Marvolo after his grandfather. He points out the similarities between himself and Harry:

- Half-bloods
- Orphans
- Raised by Muggles
- Parselmouths
- Similar appearance

> (But what color are his eyes??) HP Sleuths - do not fall for fish bait! Remember your Rule #4 to not take a character's word for anything. There may be a very distant blood relationship between Harry and Voldemort, but we might want to fish around a bit more before making any assumptions.

> You genealogy fans should be having fun right now. Although we are missing most of the family trees, what we've been told sure makes for interesting speculations! This is it so far:

Tom Riddle /
Voldemort: Jet-black hair, Long fingers (~70 years old)
Mother = Witch = Slytherin descendent (died ~70 years ago)
Father = Muggle = (lived 50-80 years ago) - named Tom
Grandfather (not sure which side) - named Marvolo

Dumbledore: Auburn hair, Long fingers (J.K.R. interview says 150 years old)
James Potter: Black hair (stands up in back), Wears glasses
               Mother & Father = Wizards (potential Gryffindor descendent)

Lily Potter: Dark Red hair, Green eyes (potential Slytherin descendent)
               Mother & Father = ? (supposedly Muggles - is she birth daughter?)

Why would Riddle's mother name him after the guy that abandoned her? Because she was still in love with him? Because Riddle is lying? Or maybe Riddle was never told the whole story? Who did tell him the story and how did that person know? Also, who were Riddle's "intimate friends" at Hogwarts?

Riddle (a.k.a. Voldemort), claims to be the greatest sorcerer in the world. Harry disputes him, saying that Dumbledore is not only considered the greatest, but Voldemort still fears him. At that moment, Fawkes, the phoenix, suddenly materializes in a burst of flames. Fawkes is carrying the Sorting Hat, and lands firmly on Harry's shoulder, his warm body against Harry's cheek. Fawkes sings a song that fills Harry's soul and vibrates within his ribs.

According to *Fantastic Beasts*, the phoenix can "disappear and reappear at will" (keep in mind that Fawkes did so from inside the castle). It also explains why the phoenix song is so empowering for Harry but does not inspire Voldemort.

Riddle has become much less blurry and a lot more solid as he continues to suck the life out of Ginny. He is intent on learning how Harry defeated Lord Voldemort. When Riddle hears that the love of Harry's Muggle-born mother was the powerful counter-charm, and that there is nothing special about Harry or his powers, Riddle summons the Basilisk from inside the mouth of Salazar's statue. Harry hears him hiss his instructions in Parseltongue to the snake.

This should make for interesting movie dialogue - two guys and a snake all hissing at each-other (hehee – will we get subtitles?). For some reason, it does not seem to occur to Harry to try to talk to the snake, himself. Probably because he figures that he is not the heir of Slytherin, and it's not his snake so it wouldn't listen, anyway. Even so, it couldn't hurt to try.... Maybe next time?

While Harry stumbles around with his eyes covered, Fawkes gouges out the deadly eyes of the Basilisk. Although the serpent is blinded, it can still smell Harry, and Tom commands it to keep lunging at Harry with its long, sharp, poisonous fangs.

Eyes are a weak point of all creatures and beasts - even magical ones. HP Sleuths should not lose sight of that.

In desperation, Harry pleads for help, and the tail of the Basilisk whips the Sorting Hat into his arms. Harry puts the Sorting Hat on, and it conjures up a ruby-encrusted, gallant sword for him. Taking the sword, Harry spears the serpent through the roof of its mouth, killing it, however, one of its poisonous fangs pierces and breaks off in Harry's arm as the serpent falls.

> Who, or what, was responsible for causing the serpent's tail to toss Harry the Hat? Did the Basilisk respond to Harry's "command," or was there another force at work here? That Sorting Hat gets around - which now explains why it is so patched and frayed. Wonder what other talents it might have?

Harry feels himself dying from the poison. Riddle sneers at Fawkes who is crying over Harry's injured arm, saying that Harry's mother only bought him 12 extra years. Riddle becomes suspicious as to why Harry is not dying faster, and chases Fawkes away, but not before its phoenix tears have healed Harry's arm. Riddle is now eager to finish Harry off, and as he raises the wand to attack, Fawkes grabs the diary and drops it onto Harry's lap, whereupon Harry instinctively grabs the Basilisk fang and plunges it into the book. Riddle screams and writhes... then disappears, at which point Ginny awakes.

> Guess for Riddle, the sword was mightier than the pen (groan). Note that Harry can (obviously) be poisoned. Fawkes not only healed the wound, but was also able to heal the poison in him. Interesting. Now about that 12 number - here is a credible possibility. We are being reminded that Voldemort will have been vanquished for 12 years as of Book 3 - a possible significance there.

With Fawkes in the lead, Harry escorts Ginny back to the cave-in, where Ron has opened up a hole big enough to fit everyone through. Ron explains that when his wand back-fired on Lockhart, Gilderoy's memory was completely erased (the bloke doesn't even know his own name).

> But the important question is - can he still smile and sign autographs? (If so, maybe no one will notice a difference?) J.K.R. has shown us here that memory charms can go too far and even ruin memories. HP Sleuths should be mindful of this critical clue!

Fawkes, whose wings emit a golden glow in the darkness, pulls them all up the pipe with a warm feeling of weightlessness, and then leads them to Professor McGonagall's office.

Curiosities

* Riddle's "high, cold, laugh that didn't suit him" - makes the "hairs stand up on back of Harry's neck." Hmmm – how did Riddle get this way?

* The "odd red gleam" in Riddle's eyes is quite devil-like. Voldemort, himself (what's left of him), seems to have red eyes all the time now. Is this because of the Dark magic he's been doing on himself or something else influencing him? It's not difficult to imagine Dumbledore vs. Voldemort as Good vs. Evil.

* Fawkes' wings emit a golden glow.

* Riddle is 16 years old in the diary.

* Pour notre HP Sleuths Francais, garcon

Other Oddities

* Riddle says it took him 5 years to find out information about the Chamber and to find it's entrance.

* Riddle tells us Hagrid tried to raise werewolf cubs under his bed, and sneaked off to the Forbidden Forest to wrestle trolls. According to a chat on Barnes&Noble.com, J.K.R. says that Riddle was telling lies about the werewolves. If HP Sleuths remember from Book 1, that's not the first time Voldemort has lied to Harry!

* Slytherin is described as "monkeyish," a long, thin beard, and enormous feet. To what kind of creature would he be related? Do HP Sleuths have any ideas?

* Ginny wrote in the diary how her brothers tease her – this obviously affects her. (She respects her brother, Bill, a lot.)

* Ginny is definitely worried that Harry won't ever like her.

Clues

Mr. and Mrs. Weasley are in Professor McGonagall's office as Harry, Ron, Ginny, Lockhart and Fawkes enter. Professor Dumbledore is also there "beaming" at them while everyone in the room is overwhelmed to see them alive. Dumbledore asks how Voldemort accomplished this deed since Dumbledore's "sources" are telling him that Voldemort is currently in Albania. When Harry shows them the diary, Mr. Weasley is shocked, reminding Ginny to "never trust anything that can think for itself if you can't see where it keeps its brain." Ginny explains to her parents that she thought the diary had belonged to them since she found it in a book her mum got her. Dumbledore sends Ginny to the hospital wing and Professor McGonagall to the kitchens to prepare an all-night feast in celebration.

> We did see that Fawkes obviously knew exactly where to lead them. That wouldn't have anything to do with the fact that while everyone else was surprised to see them, Dumbledore just stood there beaming? Now, who are these "sources" of Dumbledore's and how do they know where a Voldemort shadow is hiding out? Harry gets some excellent advice from Mr. Weasley about magical objects and their brains (that also might be useful when meeting certain people - hee-hee).

Dumbledore thanks Harry for the loyalty Harry showed him, which is why Fawkes appeared. Harry expresses concern about his own likeness to Riddle. However, Dumbledore feels that Voldemort (who he emphatically states is the last ancestor [descendent] of Slytherin) probably inadvertently transferred some of his own powers to Harry, which is why Harry can speak Parseltongue.

> Here in Book 2, Dumbledore says that Voldemort is the "last remaining **ancestor** of Salazar Slytherin." On first look, that seems to be a typo (confusion between descendent and ancestor), however, in an interview with scholastic.com, J.K.R. said it was a "deliberate" typo, but then they supposedly changed it to **descendent** in later editions (we haven't seen that one yet). In Book 4, J.K.R. made a Freudian slip when she used the wrong name for a character (her own typo). Could this also have been a Freudian slip?

Dumbledore assures Harry that although Harry may have Slytherin qualities, like resourcefulness and determination, "it is our choices that show what we truly are."

> Note the positive qualities of a Slytherin that the Sorting Hat did not yet tell us: Resourcefulness and Determination. Good to know Slytherins are not strictly cruel and ambitious – they can be resourceful about it too (ugh). Since Dumbledore usually is correct, we will have to strongly consider his statement in determining why Harry can speak Parseltongue. However, Harry does have "strikingly green eyes...."

The name engraved on the sword Harry pulled from the Sorting Hat is Godric Gryffindor - which Dumbledore assures him could only have been pulled by a "true Gryffindor."

> "Only a true Gryffindor" – did he mean that literally? Are we basically being told outright here that Harry is bloodline Gryffindor? And that name - Godric. It was Godric's Hollow (Book 1) where Harry's parents lived when Voldemort attacked. The evidence is overwhelming that Harry is somehow related to Gryffindor:
>
> ☾ The Potters lived in Godric's Hollow
>
> ☾ Harry is a Leo (the sign of Gryffindor house is the Lion)
>
> ☾ The Sorting Hat put Harry into Gryffindor House
>
> ☾ In Ollivander's shop, Harry's wand sent out red and gold sparks (the colors of Gryffindor) when he first waved it (Book 1).
>
> ☾ Everyone talks about how brave Harry is
>
> ☾ Dumbledore said that "Only a true Gryffindor" could have pulled Godric's own sword out of the Hat.

Lucius Malfoy storms into the office (with Dobby at his side) demanding to know why Dumbledore has returned to Hogwarts. Dumbledore explains that when Ginny Weasley was taken, the rest of the school Governors sent a "hailstorm of owls" demanding his return - indicating that they had suspended him in the first place due to threats from Malfoy. Dobby is frantically pointing back-and-forth between the diary and Malfoy, while constantly punishing himself. Harry makes the connection, and openly accuses Malfoy of having slipped the diary into Ginny's Transfiguration book at Flourish and Blotts.

> Back in Diagon Alley? J.K.R. also used that trick on us in the beginning of Book1, when Harry saw Quirrell in the Leaky Cauldron... and we fell for it again (sigh). In Chapter 13, when Ron kept insisting he was so sure that Malfoy was responsible for opening the Chamber, he was right - they just had the wrong Malfoy! There should be no question at this point that Lucius Malfoy is truly evil.

Lucius Malfoy is very upset, and as he turns to leave, gives Dobby a hard kick – sending the elf through the door, squealing in pain down the corridor. Harry takes off one of his own slimy socks, puts the diary in it, and runs after them to bring it to Lucius. Lucius is irate, saying Harry is just like his parents ("meddlesome fools"). Lucius Malfoy removes the diary from the sock, flinging away the sock, which is caught by Dobby. Dobby has been set free!

> A sock is truly now the symbol of freedom. While they definitely are freedom for house-elves, J.K.R. has not made it clear whether that is the only benefit of wool- ly socks. What exactly did Malfoy mean about Harry's parents being "meddle- some fools"? What did they find out before they died?

Dobby protects Harry from Malfoy's wrath at losing his house-elf. When Malfoy draws his wand, Dobby threatens him with a long finger, so Malfoy "had no choice" but to leave. Dobby hugs Harry and then disappears.

> Wow! Malfoy does not even attempt to retaliate against Dobby! In fact, J.K.R. very purposely says that he has "no choice." This is awesomely clear proof that house-elves have amazing power. That long finger characteristic has to be tied-in too. So what is Lucius going to do – will he get another house-elf? If so, will the elf be serving willingly or unwillingly?

Madam Pomfrey dispenses the Mandrake Juice, reviving Hermione and everyone who had been petrified. Dumbledore has Hagrid set free from Azkaban. Amazingly, Gryffindor secures the House Cup for the second year running, final exams are canceled, Harry and Ron receive awards for special services to the school, and Lucius Malfoy is kicked off the school governing board. But best of all, Professor Lockhart is unable to return next year - as he has to "get his memory back." That means (alas) Hogwarts needs yet another Defense Against the Dark Arts teacher.

> Good riddance, Gilderoy, you say? Think again. J.K.R. just told us Lockhart is in the process of getting his memory "back." However, in an interview with the BBC, J.K.R. said he is still in the hospital so she won't make promises. So is he gone for good or not? HP Sleuths should not assume that this is the last we see of Gilderoy Lockhart....

As they ride home on the Hogwarts Express, the kids all practice disarming each-other, mastering it quite well. Harry asks Ginny what she saw Percy doing that he didn't want anyone to know. Ginny divulges that Percy has a girlfriend, Penelope Clearwater, the Ravenclaw Prefect that Harry and Ron saw in the dungeons with Percy. Ginny had caught them kissing. That is why he was so distraught when Penelope was attacked.

> So that was Percy's big important adventure? His priorities are a bit con-fused. Talking about Penelope, there's something that still bothers us about the way that she and Hermione were attacked. Small mirrors that fit in a pocket or bag don't easily allow two people to see into it at the same time, and why would they? Why wouldn't Hermione or Penelope have checked first, and then if something happened, why would the other one also look instead of running for help? Harry just assumed that's how it happened, but we must assume Rule #4. There may still be some mysteries surrounding these attacks.

Harry gives his telephone number to Ron and Hermione, telling Ron that he taught Mr. Weasley how to use a telephone, and asks them to please call him during the summer.

Curiosities

✳ It is probably not important, but we are curious - how does one (Madam Pomfrey in particular) go about administering Mandrake Juice to a *ghost*?

✳ We were never told if any of the victims saw anything besides a pair of big yellow eyes. Did any of them see Ginny, or know of Ginny's involvement?

✳ Although Harry and Ron receive awards for special services to the school, there does not appear to be any announcement or awards ceremony. Is this because they do not want to draw attention to the circumstances surrounding it? Does this mean that the next time Ron polishes silver during detention, that he will have to polish his own plaque?

Other Oddities

✳ Dumbledore says Riddle was "probably the most brilliant student Hogwarts has ever seen." This is presumably accurate since Dumbledore says he taught Riddle himself. We can only hope Dumbledore didn't teach Riddle **everything**!

✳ Dumbledore says that very few wizards know Voldemort was Riddle – he underwent "many dangerous magical transformations."

Key Rememberit Clues from Book 2

Book 2 Mysteries Not Yet Solved

- What did everyone who was petrified actually see, and what were they all doing when they saw the Basilisk?
- How did both Hermione and Penelope become petrified with one small mirror?
- Why was Colin Creevey wandering around at night with grapes?
- Why haven't we seen an Astronomy class or the tallest tower?
- Why did the name T. M. Riddle sound familiar to Harry?
- Why did (does) Voldemort want to kill Harry?
- Is there a link between Harry and Slytherin?
- What is so special about Harry's eyes?
- What is Harry's relationship to the Gryffindor?
- Why did the Sorting Hat want to put Harry into Slytherin?
- What else can/does the Sorting Hat do?
- Why do some people seem like they can read minds (can they)?
- Why does Snape hate Harry so much?
- Why did Lucius Malfoy call Harry's parents "meddlesome fools" - what did they find out?
- Could Lucius Malfoy have had any other business in Diagon Alley?
- Why are house-elves subservient to wizards – how did that happen?
- How powerful are house-elves?
- What is the significance of long fingers?
- Is Dumbledore in control of events?
- Who is Dumbledore, what does he know, and what is his past?
- Can Dumbledore see through Invisibility Cloaks?
- Does Dumbledore Transfigure into something like McGonagall?
- What is it that Dumbledore "always said" about the "end of Hogwarts"?
- Who are Dumbledore's sources that are keeping track of Voldemort, and how?
- Who is keeping track of Harry and how?

- Why does everyone make different noises when appearing/disappearing?
- Who is the Ravenclaw ghost?
- Are Myrtle's special water skills unique for a ghost?
- What do wizards do with frog spawn?
- Why did the Ford Anglia engine die?
- Why did the Ford Anglia engine restart and keep running?
- How did the *Hover Charm* get reported so quickly?
- Will Gilderoy get his memory back?
- Is Voldemort the last remaining "ancestor" or "descendent" of Slytherin?
- Remember *Memory Charms*
  Don't forget *Memory Charms*
     "Obliviate!"
        Memory Charms????

BOOK 3 MYSTERIES

About Book 3

(Harry Potter and the Prisoner of Azkaban)

Statistics

Book 3 Title - *Harry Potter and the Prisoner of Azkaban* - by J. K. Rowling

Facts & Statistics:
- First British Printing, Bloomsbury Publishing, July, 1999
- Initial print run of 200,000 copies
- In the first 2 _ days after it's release, Prisoner of Azkaban sold over 68,000 copies
- First U.S. Printing, Scholastic, Inc., October, 1999
- For 16 weeks, the first 3 Harry Potter books simultaneously held the top 3 positions in the *New York Times* hard-cover bestseller list, and the #1 paperback.
- Due to the Harry Potter phenomena, the *New York Times* newspaper created a new and separate bestseller list for children's books.

Awards:
- Nestlé Smarties Book Prize - Gold Medal 9-11 years, 1999
- Whitbread Children's Book of the Year 1999
- British Book Awards - Author of the Year 1999
- FCBG (Federation of Children's Books Group) Children's Book Award - Overall winner and for Longer Novel Category, 1999

Key Mystery Characters

STUDENTS
Lavender Brown (Gryffindor)
Cho Chang (Ravenclaw)
Penelope Clearwater (Ravenclaw)
Crabbe (Slytherin)
Cedric Diggory (Hufflepuff)
Seamus Finnegan (Gryffindor)
Marcus Flint (Slytherin)
Goyle (Slytherin)
Hermione Granger   (Gryffindor)
Lee Jordan (Gryffindor)
Neville Longbottom (Gryffindor)
Draco Malfoy (Slytherin)
Parvati Patil (Gryffindor)
Harry Potter (Gryffindor)
Dean Thomas (Gryffindor)
Fred Weasley (Gryffindor)
George Weasley (Gryffindor)
Ginny Weasley (Gryffindor)
Ron Weasley (Gryffindor)
Percy Weasley (Gryffindor)
Oliver Wood (Gryffindor)

RELATIVES
Cousin Dudley Dursley
Aunt Marge (Marjorie) Dursley
Aunt Petunia Dursley
Uncle Vernon Dursley
Mr. & Mrs. Granger
Longbottom Relative – Neville's Gran
Lucius Malfoy
James Potter
Lily Potter
Mr. Arthur Weasley
Bill Weasley
Charlie Weasley
Mrs. Molly Weasley

TEACHERS & STAFF
Prof. Binns (History of Magic)
Prof. Albus Dumbledore (Headmaster)
Argus Filch (Caretaker)
Prof. Flitwick (Charms)
Rubeus Hagrid (Groundskeeper /
Keeper of the Keys)
Madam Hooch (Flying Instructor /
Quidditch Referee)
Prof. R. J. Lupin (Defense Against
the Dark Arts)
Prof. Minerva McGonagall
(Deputy Headmistress/Transfiguration)
Madam Pince (Librarian)
Madam Pomfrey (Nurse)
Prof. Sinistra (Astronomy)
Prof. Severus Snape (Potions Master)
Prof. Sibyll Trelawney (Divination)
Prof. Vector (Arithmancy)

OTHER HUMANS
Sirius Black
Cornelius Fudge
Macnair
Peter Pettigrew
Madam Rosmerta
Lord Voldemort ("You-Know-Who")

CREATURES & ENTITIES
Bloody Baron (Slytherin Ghost)
Buckbeak (Beaky)
Sir Cadogan the Portrait Knight
Crookshanks
Dementors
Fang the boarhound
Fat Lady Portrait
Hedwig the owl
Sir Nicolas de Mimsy-Porpington
(see Nearly-Headless Nick)
Moony, Wormtail, Padfoot, & Prongs
Mrs. Norris the cat
Peeves the Poltergeist
Nearly-Headless Nick (Gryffindor Ghost)
Scabbers the rat

Bits and Rememberits

These are clues and unsolved mysteries from the previous book that HP Sleuths should keep in mind as they read Book 3. Keep alert for more evidence....

Rememberits

Running Bits That May Be Clues

Body Parts
- Noses
- Eyes
- Ears
- Feet
- Heart
- Stomach
- Hands and Fingers
- Untidy and/or long Hair

Creatures
- Slugs
- Spiders
- Beetles, Cockroaches, and Scarabs
- Flies and Bugs in general

Numbers
- The number 12 and Chapter 12s
- The number 13 and Chapter 13s

Woolies
- Socks
- Mrs. Weasley's Sweaters

Wonderland
- Watches and Clocks
- Hares and Rabbits

Miscellaneous
- Ogden's Old Firewhiskey
- Orphans
- Banging noises

Questions Still Bugging Us...

- What happened the night Harry's parents died, and why was the house destroyed?
- How did everyone all know about and communicate the events that took place the night Voldemort attacked the Potters?
- Voldemort says he killed Harry's father first – Voldemort's a liar, do we believe him?
- Why did (does) Voldemort want to kill Harry?
- Who are Dumbledore's sources that are keeping track of Voldemort, and how?
- How did Dumbledore get James' Invisibility Cloak, and how did Hagrid get the key to the Potter's vault?
- Is Dumbledore in control of events?
- Who is Dumbledore, what does he know, and what is his past?
- Does Dumbledore Transfigure into something like McGonagall?
- Can Dumbledore see through Invisibility Cloaks?
- Who is keeping track of Harry and how?
- What is Harry's relationship to *the* Gryffindor?
- What is Harry's heritage on *both* sides?
- Why does Snape hate Harry so much?
- Why do some people seem like they can read minds (can they)?

- ◦ Can other wizards talk to animals?
- ◦ Where did Percy get Scabbers (and why was Ron allowed to take him to school)?
- ◦ Do cats really make Hagrid sneeze?
- ◦ What is the magic behind Owl Post and Owls?
- ◦ How did the *Hover Charm* get reported so quickly?
- ◦ What are *Switching Spells* and how do they work?

Interesting Tidbits

Some Not Too Trivial Trivia:

- ◦ In an interview on SouthWestNews.com, J.K.R. says that because Hagrid was cleared of all wrongdoing, and is now a teacher, he can legally do magic. However, since he never finished his education, he is not really good at it.

- ◦ According to a J.K.R. interview with scholastic.com, Azkaban is located in the northern (coldest) part of the North Sea. (Brrrr...)

What HP Sleuths Have to Notice in Book 3

- ◦ This is WWP's fave book of the first 4. It really stretches the imagination, puts the reader on an emotional roller coaster, and most importantly, raises the mystery to an ultimate level. Far more than the previous two books, HP Sleuths have to be on the constant alert here!

- ◦ J.K.R. was asked in an AOL chat if the animal one transforms into (e.g. Professor McGonagall turns into a cat) reflects their personality. J.K.R. assures us that it does. She comments that if she were to transform, she hopes it would not be into a "cock roach"! Even in her interviews she is bugging us with cockroach references...

- ◦ On a Scholstic.com chat, J.K.R. said her favorite characters are: Harry, Hermione, Ron, Hagrid, and the Book 3 Defense Against the Dark Arts Professor. We should watch this year's teacher very carefully.

WWP's Rules of CONSTANT VIGILANCE!

Never let your guard down with J.K.R. These are The Rules to remember (unless your memory is as bad as Neville's). Rules for HP Sleuths:

1) **If she reinforces it, she means it (and wants us to remember it).**
2) **If she suddenly interrupts something, she's hiding a key clue!**
3) **There's no such thing as a coincidence.**
4) **Don't take a character's word for it.**
   Corollaries
   4a) **Hermione is usually right (except when she gets emotional)**
   4b) **Ron is usually wrong (except when he makes a joke about it)**

(see WWP Help Desk FAQs for full explanation)

Chapter 1 Analysis
(OWL POST)

— Clues —

Wizard Harry Potter is back at the Dursleys this summer. The Dursleys have again locked away all Harry's magic belongings in the closet down under the stairs, but Harry creeps down to his closet, picks the lock, and brings his books upstairs.

> So Harry now knows how to pick locks? Fred and George seem to have an interesting influence on everyone (snigger). Proof here that Harry has benefited from Fred and George's wide range of skills. This particular talent with locks could get him out of other jams as well.

Harry has hidden his books under a loose floorboard in his current bedroom, so he can do his homework at night after everyone else has gone to sleep. He doesn't want to take a chance on the consequences of not handing in Professor Snape's essay on Shrinking Potions.

> Hope you HP Sleuths have done your homework and are ready to show what you've learned about sleuthing a Harry Potter book for J.K.R.'s mysterious brews. She is already pouring on the running bits here. Wonder if shrinking potions is a big clue?

Ron Weasley tries calling Harry on the telephone. Having never used a phone before, he shouts into the phone at Uncle Vernon, who is enraged that Harry had given out their phone number to a *wizard*, and insists that Ron not call again. On Harry's birthday, three owls arrive at night with Harry's first-ever birthday card and some presents. He opens them with "trembling" fingers. Ron has sent a Pocket Sneakoscope, which lights-up and spins if someone untrustworthy is around. Ron writes that Bill isn't sure those miniatures work, plus it alerted during the family dinner (but he was unaware that the twins had pulled a prank on Percy).

> Notice the "trembling" fingers. More running bits and more potential clues. We remember the music hints in Book 1 and the wide, staring eyes in Book 2. Fingers and hands seem to be a bit important, not to mention a bit injury-prone, and we have here another inference to sub-sizing. Harry's pocket-sized Sneakoscope seems to be in fine working order from what we can see, however, our HP Hintoscope is already purring with excitement! It detects J.K.R. up to her tricks - casting doubt on the reliability of the little Pocket Sneakoscope.

Hermione has sent Harry a Broomstick Servicing Kit. She had bought it by Owl Order and was relieved when Hedwig showed up in France (unbeknownst to Harry) where Hermione was vacationing. Hagrid has sent him a biting book (*The Monster Book of Monsters*) that really bites! The book is decidedly not very friendly, snapping closed on his hand. Harry has to tackle and constrain it with a belt.

147

See what we mean about fingers and hands? Guess Harry won't be thumbing through that book. Looks like catalog sales are big business with wizards too. We are told that Hermione bought Harry's present via Owl Order, which appears to be as common a practice among wizards as it is with Muggles. We have already seen that Hedwig and owls in general are quite intelligent, but this awareness of Harry's birthday confirms that Hedwig has unusual awareness of things. Is she getting help from someone in the neighborhood?

The Dursleys only give Harry a pair of Uncle Vernon's old socks for a birthday present.

It's those blasted socks! Once again, we start out Book 3 with a sock reference. So they did not end with Dobby's freedom sock. This is beyond hinting - to paraphrase Dumbledore, it's like getting hit with a sock hailstorm! (At least they're soft...)

Ron also sends Harry a newspaper clipping from the *Daily Prophet* - announcing that Arthur Weasley has won their annual Grand Prize Galleon Draw. It shows a picture of the whole Weasley family (including Ron - with his pet rat Scabbers on his shoulder) in Egypt in front of the pyramids.

Let's see, Harry and Ron help clear Hagrid's name, and Arthur Weasley just happens to win this year's drawing. Even though this is not a clue, it is still a coincidence, and HP Sleuths know from Rule #3 what we think about coincidences ;o) Notice how Ron is pretty attached to his pet rat and how much J.K.R. wants us to notice that....

Ron writes that they are visiting his brother Bill, who works as a curse-breaker for Gringotts. He also mentions that Percy has been named Head Boy at Hogwarts for this year.

Bill is an extremely interesting character. He is apparently very intelligent and presumably a powerful wizard - as it must be quite difficult (not to mention dangerous) to be poking around the curses of ancient Egyptian wizards! His exploits (translation: treasure-hunting) are funded by Gringotts - which we are told is "run" by goblins. J.K.R. does *not* say "owned" by goblins, so we do not know if the bank is privately owned by anyone (or who that would be), but we do know that Bill most likely works for (and closely with) goblins. Wonder what he knows? It's good to have connections with goblins since they are both powerful and in control of the bank.

Along with his presents, Harry receives a letter from Hogwarts informing third-year students that they are allowed to visit the wizarding village of Hogsmeade on designated weekends - but they must have a permission form signed by their parent or guardian in order to go.

Rowlinguistics

✳ **Hogsmeade** is a recreational town, so is appropriately named. A "hogshead" is a *barrel* (or *keg*), while "mead" is an *ale*. It sounds like a great place for partying, but are there other activities that go on there?

Other Oddities

✳ It is mentioned that Voldemort is the "most feared Dark wizard for a hundred years." If Voldemort was more feared than Grindelwald (who Dumbledore defeated), then what terrible wizard was around 100 years ago?

Chapter 2 Analysis

(AUNT MARGE'S BIG MISTAKE)

Clues

Harry views a report on TV with the Dursleys about a dangerous, escaped prisoner, by the name of Black. Aunt Petunia, who already spends her time spying on "boring, law-abiding neighbors," now becomes even more watchful.

> From what Harry has been allowed to observe, their neighbors appear boring, but this is also J.K.R.'s wry sense of humor. We have been led to believe that there's a lot more going on along Privet Drive than a nosy Muggle like Petunia will *ever* see.

Uncle Vernon's sister Marge, a large woman who breeds and owns 12 bulldogs, comes to spend a week with the Dursleys. Aunt Marge likes to bully and insult Harry. Since Harry wants to visit Hogsmeade at school, he makes a deal with Uncle Vernon that if he doesn't cause any "funny stuff" while Aunt Marge is there, Uncle Vernon will sign his permission form. Harry removes all evidence of his magical belongings and sends Hedwig back with Errol to stay with the Weasleys for the week. Harry also has to uphold Uncle Vernon's story that Harry is attending *St. Brutus's Secure Center for Incurably Criminal Boys.* ☺

> Oooh. More twelves. But now Harry has turned thirteen, so that means what happened in Book 2 while Harry was 12 years old was probably **not** the 12 that was being foretold. CONSTANT VIGILANCE!

Aunt Marge keeps bullying Harry and then snidely remarks that it isn't Uncle Vernon's fault that Harry turned out so "bad," since (just like breeding dogs), if there is something wrong with the parents, there will be something wrong with the offspring. Her wineglass suddenly shatters. Although Harry did inadvertently cause it, she thankfully thinks that it was her own fault - since she had just done the same thing the other day at Colonel Fubster's.

> The same thing happened the other day? HP Sleuths - can you say "coincidence"? Who is this Colonel Fubster? Is he a *fibster*? Is he yet another wizard watching over Harry? In a chat on Barnes&Noble.com, J.K.R. said that the Colonel is a Muggle. Just in case, we will maintain surveillance on this Colonel.

Aunt Marge provokes Harry some more by insulting his parents. She insists that his parents not only died in a car crash, but were drunk, then calls Harry ungrateful.... At this, Harry totally loses self control, and Aunt Marge swells up like a balloon and floats to the ceiling (another incident of breaking the *Restriction of Underage Wizardry* regulation).

> Yet another sizable clue. In this case, something got bigger, so it has to do with little things that are like big things, or big things that are like little things. So far, we have too little to go on.

150

Realizing that he is suddenly in a lot of trouble with the Dursleys (plus most likely going to be expelled from Hogwarts), Harry runs to his closet where the door magically bursts open.

Guess the Dursleys found out that just because a wizard doesn't have his wand, it doesn't mean he's safe. Maybe these were not difficult spells, but Harry obviously did not need a wand to perform either of them. We already know that under stress, wizard children will invoke magic, however, this is evidence that a very focused wizard could be somewhat powerful even without a wand.

Fearful and angry, Harry grabs all of his belongings and runs away.

Rowlinguistics

* The **St Brutus** name is most likely a parody on the most brutal of all brutes – the traitor, Brutus, who helped assassinate Julius Caesar.

Curiosities

* Bulldogs are known for their characteristic of sinking in their teeth and never letting go. We'd say that Marge's personality is a good fit with those dogs.

Other Oddities

* Aunt Marge lives in the country.

* Aunt Petunia hates animals.

Chapter 3 Analysis

Clues

After walking several streets, Harry stops for a few minutes to recover from dragging his trunk and to decide where he could realistically go now. He suddenly feels a funny prickling on the back of his neck, and spots something in the bushes that is massive and dog-like with "wide, gleaming eyes" - it frightens him.

> In Book 1, Harry felt a "prickling" before Mr. Ollivander suddenly appeared. He also felt a prickling the night of the *Mirror of Erised* when he was in the Restricted Section of the Hogwarts library, and it is highly reasonable that something could have been lurking there. Therefore, we are fairly sure that *something* was also here.

Harry staggers backward, tripping on his trunk, his wand arm whips up into the air, causing the wand to fly out of his hand. The purple *Knight Bus* suddenly appears with a loud "BANG" and blinding light. Stan Shunpike, the conductor, is under the impression that Harry has flagged them down.

> The Knight Bus keeps "banging." Our heads are already dazed with information, and we're not sure if all that banging might be a clue or not. Was it Harry's wand arm that flagged the Bus? Seems reasonable, but also a bit (shhh) coincidental.

Harry decides to take the bus to Diagon Alley. The ride is disconcerting as Ernie Prang, the bus driver (who wears thick eyeglasses), does not stick to the roads, so solid objects are constantly leaping out of its way to avoid being run over. While on the Knight Bus, Harry sees a copy of the *Daily Prophet* that has a report about the escaped prisoner, Sirius Black. Black is actually a wizard, and is so dangerous, his escape was reported to the Muggle Prime Minister, which is why it was on the Muggle news.

> Sirius Black? Hmmm, where have we seen that name before? HP Sleuths might want to unroll their whole parchment of notes to look for this one.... According to the newspaper, the Ministry of Magic is in communication with the Muggle Ministry. That sets the stage for complex implications in Book 5, and yet more coincidental ties with real-life Muggle events (similar to Dumbledore defeating Grindelwald in 1945).

There is a photo of Black, who Harry thinks looks "strangely familiar." Black's waxy-white skin gives him a vampire-like appearance. Stan says that Black allegedly murdered 13 people (a wizard and 12 Muggles) with a single curse just after the fall of Voldemort. Plus, this is the first time anyone has ever escaped from Azkaban. Ernie is really uncomfortable talking about the guards at Azkaban and asks Stan to change the subject.

> Black looked familiar? Is this is a red herring – or a red alert? Where would Harry have seen this derelict before? (HP Sleuths should at least know the name.) Also, if he is the first to break out of Azkaban, is he that powerful or did

he have help? As future information for the septology, if waxy-white skin can be attributed to vampires, then what does that say about *sallow* skin?

The bus drops Harry off at the Leaky Cauldron pub, where (of all people) the Minister of Magic himself, Cornelius Fudge, is waiting. Instead of expelling, or at least punishing Harry for what he did to Aunt Marge, Fudge spends the time reassuring Harry that everything was made all right. Ministry wizards even performed a *Memory Spell* on Aunt Marge so she won't remember anything. Fudge also sets Harry up with a room at the Leaky Cauldron, and is intensely concerned about Harry's safety and making sure that Harry has everything he needs (but evades Harry's questions). Harry goes up to his room where Hedwig had already arrived - only five minutes after Harry had disembarked.

Yet another indication that Hedwig is no dumb animal. How does Hedwig know? Does she visit someone to get info or instructions about Harry? Is she typical or special among owls? As of Book 4, the background and habits of wizarding owl messengers is still a complete mystery (and they are too domesticated to be listed in *Fantastic Beasts*). Fudge still acts quite pompous here - not a very straightforward person. He does not seem to be a highly credible clue source either (Rule #4).

Harry is checked into Room 11, where he will now amazingly be free of the Dursleys until he returns to school in two weeks.

Curiosities

* Notice how uncomfortable Ernie is just talking about Azkaban - wonder if he's really that sensitive or if he might even have personally encountered someone form there in the past?

* Don't know if it matters, but we saw that Harry is put in Room 11 at the Leaky Cauldron.

Chapter 4 Analysis

(THE LEAKY CAULDRON)

Clues

Harry is allowed to go wherever he wants as long as it's within Diagon Alley. He sees many strange and interesting things – such as hags, wizened wizards discussing articles out of *Transfiguration Today*, and a lunascope that gives the phase of the moon.

> The HP Hintoscope is howling at us. When J.K.R. gives us a lesson about strange and interesting things, that means it's time for HP Sleuths to pull out their quills.

Harry is most attracted by his favorite shop, Quality Quidditch Supplies - where the newest (and exceedingly expensive) racing broom, the Firebolt (each with it's own registration number), is on display. At the bookstore, Harry notices a book called *Death Omens: What to Do When You Know the Worst Is Coming.* It has a picture on the cover of a death omen: a "black dog as large as a bear, with gleaming eyes."

> What **do** you do when you think you've seen a death omen? Maybe Harry should have paid more serious attention to what the book says. Have HP Sleuths spotted a bunch of dog references lately? Is that another clue or are we just barking up the wrong tree? Check out that Firebolt (each with its own registration number) - cool. Anyone that has ever owned a limited or hand-built item with a registration number will know that those items are kept track of fairly carefully. The company who issues it usually knows all the details about it - including which shop sold it, and, of course, the buyer. Since the items are so special, much of that is for authenticity purposes, but then also for maintenance as well. Obviously, this is a very special broom.

Ron returns from Egypt, and Hermione returns from France. They are both staying overnight at the Leaky Cauldron, and the next morning, the Weasleys, Hermione, and Harry will ride together to King's Cross train station. Ron has a new wand, and Hermione has some money as a birthday present that she wants to use to buy an owl. At the Magical Menagerie, they see some very odd creatures, such as "custard-colored fur balls that were humming loudly" and a "gigantic tortoise with a jewel-encrusted shell." Ron has the shopkeeper look at his pet rat Scabbers, who he thinks has been looking ill since their trip to Egypt. The witch then tells Ron to "bang" Scabbers on the counter. She informs him that non-magical rats typically only live about three years, so it probably is just old age.

> HP Hintoscope – squeaking loudly! Look at all these story-line clues. Ron's rat is looking rattier than he usually does since they came back from Egypt. Was it something in Egypt or something when they got back? What is most intriguing is the shopkeeper's remark about the life span of non-magical rats. We know that Percy had Scabbers first, and this is Ron's third year at Hogwarts, so Scabbers should have checked into the Senior Citizen home (if not the morgue) by now...that is...unless he does have some hidden magic?

The witch checks out Scabbers with his missing toe and tattered left ear.

> It is probably an understatement to say that Scabbers does not seem to be much of a fighter, yet he has had some traumatic experiences that left these scars. Maybe he got those when running from cats?

A huge Ginger-colored cat suddenly lands on Ron's head, and spitting madly, lunges at Scabbers who scurries off. When Ron and Harry finally track down Scabbers, they see Hermione coming out of the shop holding that same big cat, called Crookshanks. Both Ron and Harry are not very happy that she decided to buy Crookshanks (who no one else had wanted).

> Was there not a whole cage full of delicious rats on the counter next to Scabbers? Why did Crookshanks pick on Scabbers? Guess Scabbers was the easy meal (though a bit boring if you're the kind that likes to play with your food).

That night at the Leaky Cauldron, Harry hears Mr. and Mrs. Weasleys arguing and, when his name is mentioned, he stops to listen. Mrs. Weasley does not think Harry should be burdened by knowing that Sirius Black is out to get him and that his life is in danger, while Mr. Weasley thinks Harry has the right to know and should be alerted. Mr. Weasley describes how Black had been talking in his sleep saying "he's at Hogwarts...he's at Hogwarts" and then breaks out of prison.

> Since Voldemort is still a bit indisposed, Black is getting to make the *bad guy house call* this year. HP Sleuths should be wary, though, that J.K.R. is up to something. She only tells us that Black was saying "he's at Hogwarts." Remember, Rule #4 is that we do not take characters' words for anything, and so far we can't be sure whether a half-asleep Black wants to kill Harry, bring him to Voldemort, drop in for a spot of tea, or why they're so sure it's Harry he's after. Obviously, there is something more her characters must know about Black's motives to make them so worried for Harry's safety, and she is teasing us with that.

Mrs. Weasley is convinced that as long as Albus Dumbledore is at the school, Harry is safe. She also feels that the extra protection from the Azkaban guards that the Ministry insisted on putting around the school is a benefit, but Mr. Weasley did not seem to like the guards being there. Harry now understands why Fudge was not at all upset with him, why he was to stay within Diagon Alley, and why he is being personally escorted by everyone in Ministry cars to the train. Harry is quite relieved to just learn why everyone has been acting so weird.

> As long as Dumbledore is at Hogwarts.... More reinforcement of Dumbledore's power and competence. It also seems fairly universal that Dumbledore has created a stronghold at Hogwarts. But this reference to Dumbledore is beginning to sound like Rule #1, and is beginning to make us uneasy.

Harry thinks again of that big dark creature he thought he saw, of the book on death omens, and starts convincing himself he is not going to be murdered.

Curiosities

✳ We're still not sure if it's anything important, but Scabbers is now banging on the counter. As it is a creature shop this seems very fishy.

✳ Those custard-colored humming (yarn-like) fuzz balls sound awfully similar to the Star Trek tribbles, but our handy *Fantastic Beasts and Where to Find Them* helps us identify them as Puffskeins. HP Sleuths who have done their suggested reading will know what those are. Harry obviously did not remember his homework, but HP Sleuths should know that those gigantic tortoises are *Fire Crabs*, which are important to remember.

Other Oddities

✳ Both Ron's and Mr. Weasley's ears go red when they are under pressure (possibly all Weasley males?).

✳ Mr. Weasley makes a joke about no one yet inventing self-spelling wands (Oh, George....)

✳ Fred and George changed Percy's badge to say "Bighead Boy" Yup, the size-related running bits are growing so frequent, they're hardly worth mentioning.

Chapter 5 Analysis

Clues

At the train station, Mr. Weasley covertly draws Harry away from the others and awkwardly tries to warn him about Black. However, Harry lets Mr. Weasley know that he overheard them, and already knows about Black's intentions. That makes Mr. Weasley feel better, but he still warns Harry to not "go looking" for Black.

> Not go looking for him? Why would Mr. Weasley say such a strange thing? They can't be misinterpreting Harry's personality that badly - this just confirms that the other characters know something more. But what? We must like getting teased by J.K.R. - we keep reading this stuff.

On the train, Harry, Hermione, and Ron settle in a compartment where their new Defense Against the Dark Arts teacher, Professor R. J. Lupin, is sound asleep. They see that the Professor's clothes are shabby and darned, his hair is pre-maturely gray, and he looks ill.

> Hagrid had said last year that no one wanted the job of Defense Against the Dark Arts because they thought it was jinxed - well by this year, Dumbledore may have had to stoop to an all-time low. Lupin is an interesting name (Latin, isn't it?). Wonder what the R. J. stands for? (No doubt the reason we don't know is that's Rule #2.) So how do we know Professor Lupin is sound asleep? We aren't taking the words of the characters are we? He would never be pretending...(cough).

They notice that Harry's Sneakoscope is whistling from within his trunk. Ron suggests that Harry bring it to Dervish and Banges in Hogsmeade to have it checked out. Ron thinks it is broken because it went off as he was tying it to Errol.

> This is a J.K.R. trick. We know that this poor Pocket Sneakoscope has already been wrongly accused, so is it malfunctioning now? But if it's working correctly, HP Sleuths should think carefully about the procedure of tying a package to Errol and why it might have gone off at that time. And why now? (Yes, we have theories... yes, we're confused.)

Harry informs Ron and Hermione that he could not get a signed permission to visit Hogsmeade. Hermione feels really badly for him – as it is an interesting place. Not only is it the "only entirely non-Muggle settlement in Britain," but the Hogsmeade Inn was used as the headquarters for the Goblin Rebellion of 1612.

> Why were there goblin rebellions? What exactly happened in the goblin rebellions? Hermione never says precisely *whose* headquarters it was, but assuming it belonged to the goblins, knowing goblins, couldn't there be something valuable hidden in there? No matter what, since it was a headquarters during a

conflict, also knowing goblins, there are most likely secret passages and other really cool things there. HP Sleuths should put the Hogsmeade Inn on your map.

The clouds move in and it starts to rain as they ride further north. The train suddenly lurches to a stop, luggage bangs to the floor, the lights go out, and Professor Lupin awakes. He illuminates the compartment with a magical flame, but before he can get to the door, a hooded figure enters.

> (Book 3 is a really noisy book.) So, Professor Lupin lights a flame and goes for the door. Hmmm...awfully alert for a sleepyhead. Let's see, the lights went out and then the hooded figure appeared. No coincidence here, right?

Harry sees a revoltingly slimy, scabbed hand protruding from the hooded creature's cape, which it quickly withdraws. He then hears it's "rattling breath." Everyone is inundated by an intense cold, but it completely overtakes Harry - causing him to faint and not regain consciousness until the train is already moving again.

> Uck. That hand was not only damaged, it was decayed. What is a dementor and where do they come from? Based on what we know of J.K.R.'s fantasy, it is highly likely that they may be created beings. No matter what, there is no question that they are Dark creatures.

Professor Lupin gives everyone some chocolate to eat, which warms them and makes them feel better. He addresses Harry by name, explaining that what they saw was an Azkaban dementor.

> How did Professor Lupin know Harry's name? Was he not asleep, or was there another reason? He didn't seem to react to Harry like other people have. He didn't stare at Harry's scar, didn't mention the resemblance to his dad, or his mother's eyes. This is the first of numerous Lupin septology clues – hope HP Sleuths aren't sleeping through this one!

Ginny and Neville did not faint, but are very pale. When Lupin leaves to "talk to the driver," the others tell Harry that Lupin pulled out his wand and told the dementor to leave. When it did not leave right away, he muttered some words and a "silvery thing shot out of his wand at it," then the dementor left.

> Looks like Lupin knows a bit more about Defense Against the Dark Arts than Gilderoy did. He knows enough at least to defend against dementors. What kind of "silvery thing" came out of his wand – what did it look like? That could be important. Now, who or what drives the Hogwarts Express, and what would Lupin want to talk about? This was never answered specifically and could even be an important septology clue. We assume he might have been logging his complaint with him (or her) about their *warm* reception by the dementors...

They arrive at the Hogsmeade station in the freezing rain.

Hogsmeade – that would make sense. We had erroneously assumed that the Hogwarts Express just stopped at a Hogwarts station. Of course, we didn't have to know the name of the station - it is being clarified for a reason. We now know that this is an express train specifically for Hogwarts students, and that there may be other trains that go to Hogsmeade. So, do many wizards or other magical beings normally take trains? Do they use trains for supplies? More septology data chugging through our brains.

Since they are not first years, Harry's class rides "horseless carriages," up to the castle through the heavy rain. The carriages have a faint smell of mold and straw, and Harry thinks they are drawn by invisible horses. Draco Malfoy starts harassing Harry about his having fainted, but Professor Lupin intervenes.

We are being told about that smell for a reason. Why would these carriages smell of mold and straw? What are they and how are they controlled? (We don't necessarily buy into the invisible horse explanation – Rule #4, you know). We also think these coaches are a bit vulnerable. Hope they all make it safely up to the castle every year.

Professor McGonagall takes Harry and Hermione away from the Great Hall and brings them to her office, where Madam Pomfrey checks Harry over. She is impressed that their new Defense Against the Dark Arts teacher knew enough to give the kids chocolate. Professor McGonagall then meets privately with Hermione for a few minutes about her schedule, after which Harry and Hermione are free to go back downstairs. Unfortunately, they have missed the sorting ceremony.

Hmmm... Professor McGonagall and Madam Pomfrey already know what had happened on the train. Was it Lupin who sent word ahead? Lupin not only earned our respect, but earned the coveted Madam Pomfrey stamp of approval (and that's not easy)!

Before the feast, Professor Dumbledore informs the students that there will be dementors guarding all entrances to Hogwarts. He warns them that, as dementors cannot be fooled by tricks, Invisibility Cloaks, etc., the students will be in grave danger if they try to get past a dementor without permission.

HP Sleuths will recognize the famous Dumbledore cunning sense of humor as he specifically references Invisibility Cloaks. As we have already seen, Dumbledore likes to drop personal jokes into serious remarks, which means that his comments often contain clues. Beware of Dumbledore double-talk.

Dumbledore makes an unexpected announcement that Professor Kettleburn is retiring, and that Rubeus Hagrid will take over as the new Care of Magical Creatures teacher (Hagrid got the position because Harry, Ron, and Hermione proved last year that he was wrongly expelled!).

Curiosities

✳ The "rattling breath" of the dementors appears to be how they suck in the warmth and positive emotions. If dementors are a created species, it is possible that part of their origin may be the creature called *Lethifold (see Fantastic Beasts and Where to Find Them).*

✳ Ginny and Neville reacted to the dementors almost as badly as Harry did.

✳ We do not learn the first name of Professor Kettleburn.

Other Oddities

✳ Hedwig is now reluctant to get into her cage – she is learning to dislike it (we don't blame her).

✳ We are told that Fred and George know "every secret passage out of the Castle." Even if they don't really know every single one, that's pretty impressive.

✳ J.K.R. says here that Dumbledore "though very old, always gave an impression of great energy." We have been told that at least twice now (Rule #1).

✳ We already know that Dumbledore has a crooked nose, but in this chapter, J.K.R. had emphasized that it is an "extremely crooked nose."

✳ The password into Gryffindor is "Fortuna Major." "Major" means *big*, which means we are getting a little overwhelmed with this running bit.

Clues

Ron looks at Hermione's timetable and thinks there is a mistake because she has several classes all scheduled simultaneously. He tells her emphatically "there isn't enough time," but she explains that Professor McGonagall has worked it out for her.

> Hermione had said that Professor McGonagall talked to her about her schedule, but it seems to need more than talk. HP Sleuths know that Ron has been known to not get clues, but this schedule may make Hermione's life a bit more hectic than planned. We'll have to see how it all works out in good time.

They go to find their Divination class, which is held in the North Tower. On their way there, they have to enlist the help of Sir Cadogan, a knight in one of the portraits. He falls off his horse, gets his own sword stuck in the ground, and can't seem to tell the difference between a student and a foe. However, he is inspired by their "quest" to find the classroom, and does lead them there.

> This Don Quixote-type knight is a ringer for the White Knight in Lewis Carroll's *Through the Looking Glass*. As inept as he was, the White Knight helped Alice to become a Queen. Sir Cadogan probably also can be of service in his own way.

Professor Sibyll Trelawney, their Divination teacher, is a stereotypical fortune teller. She wears shawls and bangles, and has the room overheated and heavily perfumed. She tells the students that in her class, books are not much help - as they need to rely on their "Inner Eye." Trelawney intersperses her lecture with ambiguous predictions - including an unambiguous prognostication that Harry will die. Ron and Harry think it is a big joke, and Hermione thinks it is rubbish.

> Sorry Hermione - books won't help (you're much too logical for Divination). In ancient mythology, the Sibyls were prophetesses, yet J.K.R. does not seem to put much credence in the kind of sideshow fortune telling that Sibyll Trelawney mimics. J.K.R. has carefully distinguished between the gifted centaurs (Book 1) and the melodramatic Trelawney. There is another famous Sybil - she suffered from Schizophrenia (multiple personalities). Wonder if Trelawney is at all like her and is hiding any other identities?

When they try to read tea leaves, Ron sees a blob that looks "a bit like a bowler hat." He jokes as he describes it.

> We know that J.K.R. borrows extensively from Greek literature. It may be far-fetched, but a bowler hat looks just like the Greek letter W *omega* (as in omen=omega or *last* maybe)... Yah, it's a stretch. Forget it.

Trelawney sees a number of foreboding images in Harry's cup - including a deadly enemy, an attack, danger in Harry's path, and a *Grim*. The other kids are extremely concerned - thinking it a definite death omen.

> HP Sleuths should watch Trelawney carefully! She may be a fraud only because of her ego and lack of an open mind. That causes her to either misinterpret or disbelieve her own vision when she is right, yet when she is wrong, she has herself convinced she is all-seeing. For instance, here Trelawney sees the black dog-like image in Harry's cup. Because she knows Harry is in constant danger, she jumps to the conclusion it was a Grim. Harry really did, indeed, encounter a black, dog-like image so she is actually right - but was it the Grim? Can we believe her?

In their next class, Professor McGonagall is lecturing about Animagi, but Harry is too busy avoiding stares from the other students who are convinced he is doomed. As an example, she transforms herself into her own cat form, and back into her human self with a "small pop."

> J.K.R.'s doing it again - she says Harry missed what Professor McGonagall was saying about Animagi (anyone have a spare Red *Lesson Card?*) HP Sleuths - don't miss Rule #2.

Professor McGonagall shows her own displeasure with the subject of Divination - explaining that Divination is an inexact science, and that "true seers are very rare." She lets them know that Professor Trelawney has predicted a student death every year since she's been at Hogwarts, and a student hasn't died yet.

> Not very good odds for Trelawney. Even teachers such as Professor McGonagall do not respect her. We now know for sure that Trelawney doesn't have a good track record, however, keep in mind that it is her close-mindedness that blinds her to what she sees.

While most of the kids are happy to see Hagrid teaching, Malfoy makes the rude comment: "This place is going to the dogs."

> Dogs, bulldogs, and big black dogs. A bunch of running doggy bits.

Hagrid brings Hippogriffs for his first Care of Magical Creatures class. He instructs that the students need to make eye contact, bow to them, and only if they bow back will Hippogriffs let them approach. Hagrid warns that it is also highly dangerous to insult a Hippogriff (they have very sharp talons). Harry is the only one brave enough of both Gryffindors and Slytherins to volunteer. Harry introduces himself to "Buckbeak," who allows Harry to fly on his back once around the paddock.

> Harry's bravery (a key quality of Godric Gryffindor) is reinforced again.

Malfoy, who was not listening, insults Buckbeak and is immediately slashed by him, so Hagrid has to schlep Malfoy to the hospital.

Curiosities

✳ The U.S. printing uses the word "schedule" for Hermione's classes rather than "timetable."

✳ Grim is probably from the same derivation as Grim Reaper, and is based on the leg ends of big black dogs that are said to haunt churchyards. One source is the kirkegrim, which is supposed to guard the graveyard against the devil. Many believe that the grim is truly a death omen.

✳ McGonagall transforms with a small "pop."

✳ If Hippogriffs can't understand language, how do they know if they are being insulted? We were expecting hippogriffs to somewhat understand language from this incident. Maybe it's that they understand emotions, but not words? Is this mystery or literary license?

Other Oddities

✳ Dean Thomas and Lavender Brown don't know about the Grim – it is possibly evidence that they come from Muggle families.

✳ When Professor McGonagall is miffed, her nostrils go white.

✳ Parvati Patil was told to "beware a red-haired man" (or did she mean red her-ring?)

✳ Professor Trelawney's appearance is described as a "large glittering insect." (More bugs.)

Chapter 7 Analysis

(The Boggart in the Wardrobe)

Clues

Malfoy keeps his arm bandaged and feigns continued pain (in spite of Madam Pomfrey's care). He has his father complain about Hagrid and Buckbeak to the school governors, and to the Ministry of Magic, where Lucius has a "lot of influence."

> Even though Lucius Malfoy was kicked off the school governing board in Book 2, he still seems to maintain a lot of control over them. He is corrupt, danger-ous, and up to his old tricks....

In their potions class, Snape makes Harry assist the *supposedly* handicapped Draco. Snape tests Neville's botched shrinking solution on his toad, Trevor, who successfully deflates down to a tadpole and is then restored.

> Jumpin' frogs legs! A Shrinking Potion doesn't make things shrink – it makes them get younger. Wow! The possibilities.... Do they remember everything from their adulthood, or do they start all over again? Has anything (or anyone) we know been subject to a shrinking solution? It's got huge possibilities.

Sirius Black is spotted by a Muggle in the Hogwarts area. Draco Malfoy derides Harry for not going after Black to get "revenge," but Harry is clueless as to what he is talking about, and Malfoy does not say. Ron does not know what he means either.

> There is now no question that some of the wizards know something about Black that they are not telling Harry. HP Sleuths should not waste time on this - since based on the information we have been given so far, we cannot possibly deduce what it is. J.K.R. is, as usual, teasing us.

Harry, Ron, and Hermione are talking when Ron suddenly notices that Hermione is not there, but spots her at the bottom of the stairs. As she is tucking something into the front of her robes, her overly stuffed book bag splits and Ron sees that she is carrying books for classes that she is not taking that day. Harry and Ron feel that there is something she is not telling them.

> Maybe it's just a running bit, but there is something mysterious about the time-ly comings and goings of Hermione and her overloaded class schedule. We are starting to get a few extra hints. For instance, Hermione is tucking something into her robes (we know it's not a letter from Gilderoy!). HP Sleuths should be suspicious.

For their Defense Against the Dark Arts class, Lupin brings them down to the teacher's staff room. On the way, Peeves, who is stuffing gum into a keyhole, greets Lupin with his sing-song "loony loopy Lupin."

Peeves talks a lot of nonsense, but it has been said, "fools and children speak the truth." (Hayes, 1537)

Professor Lupin gives the class their first ever Defense Against the Dark Arts practical lesson. He teaches them how to thwart a boggart that resides in dark, enclosed spaces - such as under beds, in grandfather clocks, and, like this one, in wardrobes. Lupin mentions that Neville lives with his grandmother and asks him to describe what she wears.

Hmmm. Lupin knew that Neville lives with his grandmother. Either Lupin is extremely sensitive to the orphans in the class, or Neville's background may be known in the wizarding community.

Lupin explains that a boggart is a shape-shifter - taking on the appearance of whatever most frightens the person it focuses on. Using Neville to lead, Lupin releases the boggart that first turns into Snape (the thing Neville fears most), but then with a ("Riddikulus!") charm the Snape figure is suddenly clothed in the funny hat, dress, and handbag that Neville's grandmother wears. The whole class breaks into laughter, and each of the other students step up to help dispel the boggart.

That's incredibly clever - the same boogie man for everyone, but different appearances due to shape-shifting. But then, that brings up an interesting question. What if the person either overcomes their fear or it is replaced by another fear? Do we assume that the boggart takes on the appearance of that new fear? HP Sleuths should hold that thought for later in the septology.

The boggart had become a spider for Ron, a banshee for Seamus Finnegan, a mummy for Parvati Patil, a severed hand for Dean Thomas, plus a rattlesnake, a bloody eyeball, and a rat. Everyone, including Neville, is proud of themselves.

Sounds like a movie matinee fright-fest. Note that while Ron likes his rat, some people are very wary of them. We are not sure why Seamus is so frightened of banshees, but we know it is fairly consequential because this isn't the only time he mentions them. The key clue here is Dean Thomas and his severed hand. Is that Dean's boggart because, as an artist, he fears the loss of a hand, or is it more sinister that that? There is something awfully creepy about severed hands in this septology.

For some reason, Professor Lupin does not give Harry a crack at the boggart, but instead moves up to the boggart himself. While Lupin is near it, it turns into a floating, silvery-white orb, and when he issues the charm, it dissolves into just a cockroach.

Don't know about you, but we don't see anything humorous about a cockroach. The point behind the spell is to turn it from something scary into something funny (not icky). Why would Lupin's orb become a cockroach? That was never answered and may be a septology clue. As to why Lupin's boggart turns into an orb is a much easier story-line clue to solve. HP Sleuths on the case.

Hermione wishes she could have had a try at the Boggart. Ron jokes that hers probably would have been a bad mark on her schoolwork.

> We will find out later why Lupin does not have Harry try the boggart, but we never get an explanation as to why he did not have Hermione try it. Now, the evidence is becoming overwhelming that when Ron tries to quickly analyze something, he is usually wrong, but if he jokes about an explanation, then he's usually right. So if Hermione were to go up against the boggart what might she see? Hmmmm....

They wonder what Lupin's own orb-like boggart image meant.

Curiosities

✳ We know you caught the inference (*The Boggart in the Wardrobe*) to the C. S. Lewis story, *The Lion, the Witch, and the Wardrobe*. J.K.R. has specifically mentioned that she really enjoyed reading that as a kid. For kids who may still be afraid, she has now supplied this *Counter-Spell* so they won't fear wardrobes.☺

✳ Shrinking Solution ingredients: daisy roots, shrivelfig, caterpillar, rat spleen, leech juice (a dash) – it becomes a bright-green potion.

Other Oddities

✳ Snape's sink has Gargoyles as faucets - where jets of water gush from their mouths (we already know that Gargoyles tend to come to life).

✳ The boggart changes with a noise like a whip crack (doesn't that remind us of some- one from Book 2?).

Chapter 8 Analysis

(FLIGHT OF THE FAT LADY)

Clues

Harry, Ron, and Hermione are studying Astronomy together in their common room. Ron asks Hermione to keep Crookshanks away from his bag where Scabbers is sleeping, but upon hearing that, Crookshanks attacks Ron's bag. Ron is upset, and thinks Crookshanks has it in for Scabbers.

> Cats do like to chase rats, but Ron is right - this cat has a fixation on Scabbers. No matter what the reason, it is eerie that Crookshanks seems to know what Ron is saying.

On Halloween, the rest of the third-years are to visit Hogsmeade, while Harry has to stay back at school. Dean Thomas offers to forge Uncle Vernon's signature, but Harry had already admitted that he was not able to obtain permission.

> We were told in Book 1 that Dean is a good artist, and we find out here for sure that his masterpieces are not restricted to pretty pictures. HP Sleuths are now alerted for the rest of the septology that forgeries exist and Dean is eager to show his talent!

While looking for something to pass his time alone, Harry comes across Professor Lupin, who invites him into the office where he is studying a grindylow. Professor Lupin says that Grindylows have brittle fingers. If you get in trouble with them, you break their grip. Harry considers telling him about the dog he saw in Magnolia Court, but decides that he did not want to seem too concerned.

> Wonder what Lupin would have thought about Harry's hairy dog? Would he have thought it a Grim? Do we think it's Rule #2? Also, didn't they just discuss more damaged fingers?

Without asking, Lupin knows what's bothering Harry. He explains that the reason he did not have Harry test the boggart was because he figured Harry might conjure up an image of Lord Voldemort and "people would panic."

> What people would panic? Since the kids don't even know what Voldemort would look like, is it possible Lupin doesn't even trust himself on this one? It seems that Lupin is one of a few people who give Harry the impression that they can read minds. It may be that those were just coincidences, but there is a possibility that at least one of them really has that ability. In Lupin's case, it may just indicate a closer link to Harry. HP Sleuths keep your minds open and alert!

Harry explains to Lupin that he actually most fears the dementors. Lupin is impressed as it indicates that what Harry fears most is fear, itself.

A wise person is aware that the fear of something is usually worse than the reality, and who else besides a brave Gryffindor would have fear as his worst fear? Lupin seems to relate to that. Add this to our pile of evidence that Harry is a bloodline Gryffindor....

What surprises Harry is that, like Dumbledore, Lupin calls Voldemort by his proper name.

Odd how the most respected wizards can say the name of Voldemort without flinching. Again, HP Sleuths should watch to make sure Lupin (and those wizards who do say his name) always use Voldemort's proper name.

While Harry is talking to Professor Lupin, Snape enters the room carrying a smoking goblet which, to Harry's horror, Lupin drinks down.

Let's just say that *we* would never wanna drink anything that Snape has made up. However, **so far** there is no indication that Snape has any intention of doing lethal harm to anyone, and we know that Lupin has been suffering from something. Remember - it was only on Percy's word that we make the assumption that Snape is after the position of Defense Against the Dark Arts, and HP Sleuths know Rule #4.

They all go to the Halloween feast, where the entertainment includes a reenactment by Nearly Headless Nick of "his own botched beheading." On the way back from the feast, the Gryffindors are dismayed to find that their hidden entrance, the portrait of the Fat Lady, has been slashed and mutilated. Percy calls for Dumbledore, who appears on the scene a moment later.

For 150 years old, Dumbledore gets around awfully fast. We assume he probably has a whole bunch of informants around the castle, but he may also have made it there quickly for other reasons that we do not yet know (even as of Book 4).

Peeves tells Professor Dumbledore that the attacker was Sirius Black, who had actually been in the castle, and gotten angry when the Fat Lady wouldn't let him in.

Curiosities

✴ So if they saw Nearly Headless Nick's nearly beheading, do they know how/why it happened and who (nearly) did it? We'd like to know. (Is this Rule #2?)

✴ So far, we haven't seen any correlation, but we all know that *good* witches and lions are known to be from the North and South, while *wicked* witches tend to live in the East and West. Divination is in the North Tower. Where is the Astronomy tower?

Chapter 9 Analysis

Clues

Upon learning that Sirius Black has been in the castle, Dumbledore immediately sends all the students to sleep in the Great Hall while the teachers do a complete search of the premises. Everyone in the Hall is formulating a theory as to how Black got in. Hermione informs Harry and Ron that, Hogwarts, a History, says the castle is protected with special enchantments that prevent people from entering by stealth ("you can't just Apparate [appear out of thin air] in here").

> Huh? What did she say - you can't? In Book 2, is what Dobby did in the hospital room not truly Apparating? Is what Fawkes did in the Chamber of Secrets not truly Apparating? Septology alert! HP Sleuths pull out your magnifying glasses and inspect those quick comings and goings. So, how does everyone appear and disappear and how did Sirius get in? We need more details.

Hermione points out that it's "lucky" that Black picked the night everyone was away for the feast. Ron is sure that, being on the run, Black probably lost track of time.

> Did Black really lose track of time? Remember - when Ron is trying to quickly figure things out, he blows it. (Watch out when he jokes, though - it's not so funny!)

They hear Snape telling Dumbledore that he thinks Sirius had help from the "inside," but he is cut-off by Dumbledore, who is firm, almost angry, that Snape would imply that. Percy wants to know if the dementors should be used, and is surprised when Dumbledore says they are not allowed in the school. Sir Cadogan, the only volunteer brave enough for the job, temporarily takes the place of the Fat Lady while her portrait is repaired.

> The story line is becoming a bit complex. Who does Snape think is helping Sirius Black? Thanks to Rule #2, we don't know. Dumbledore doesn't seem to need to ask him - so he obviously must know who Snape is implicating. We haven't had many hints about this, but Snape doesn't hide his feelings about anyone.

One day, when Lupin is sick, Snape substitutes for him. Snape is abusive and insults the Gryffindors' knowledge as well as Lupin's teaching method. Although they were not scheduled to cover the subject until the end of the semester, Snape insists on having the class study werewolves.

> Snape is at his meanest here. Why does he insist that they study an advanced subject? He does not seem to respect Lupin very much - of course, he doesn't seem to respect *anyone*.

The day of their first Quidditch match, Harry is wakened by a cold breeze on the back of his neck that turns out to be Peeves blowing in his ear. He asks Peeves why he did that, but Peeves just zooms out of the room. Harry cannot sleep, so he decides to go down to the common room. As he opens the door to his dorm, he has to stop Crookshanks from entering. While sitting in the common room, he continues to have to stop Crookshanks from heading up toward his dorm.

> Oh weird. What was Peeves doing? It was never explained at the end of this book, but it might have been directly related to the plot and Crookshanks' capers. Is this a septology clue that there might be some kind of communication there? Is Crookshanks still intent on attacking Ron's rat? He is assuredly well-fed, so what's the fascination?

The Hufflepuff team, which has a new Captain and Seeker, Cedric Diggory, has been substituted for Slytherin (with the excuse that Malfoy's arm is still injured). Harry finds Crookshanks still lurking outside the boys' dorm room when he leaves for the match.

> He's baaack... Crookshanks is scary and he's on a mission. This is more than just a playful puddy tat...

The match is held in a thunderstorm of pouring rain and high winds. Hermione helps Harry by putting a spell on his glasses that causes them to repel water, but the team is soaked, frozen, and constantly blown off-course. Harry thinks he sees the image of the enormous, black, Grim-like dog in the stands, and is distracted. As he starts to dive for the Snitch, Harry suddenly finds a crowd of dementors under him.

> Are HP sleuths noticing the weather turns stormy whenever dementors or other evil presences grow stronger? Also, how interesting that a bunch of dementors suddenly decide to invade the field at the same time Harry sees a Grim-like image. Is this a foretelling of doom in relation to the dementors, or is this one of those "coincidences" from Rule #3?

As the dementors close in, Harry starts to get flash-backs of his mother's voice pleading for his life to her attacker. Harry is overcome and faints, falling off his broom. What he hears is:

"Not Harry...Please not Harry."
"Stand aside you silly girl..."
"Not Harry, please no, take me, kill me instead..."

> The mystery surrounding the murder of Harry's parents is the key to the whole Harry Potter septology, yet we had been given almost no information about it. HP Sleuths are being treated to some new details here, sparse as they are. We now know for sure that Harry was targeted, that his mother offered her own life in exchange, and there was dialogue between his mother and at least one person. Harry is positive it was his mother, but no name was used for the attacker - so we do not yet know if Voldemort was working alone.

When Harry wakes, he is in a hospital bed surrounded by Hermione, Ron, and all his drenched teammates. They tell him that Dumbledore drove off the dementors and that Cedric had caught the Snitch. Although even Cedric wanted a re-match, everyone said that it was a fair catch, so Hufflepuff won the tournament.

This is our first indication that Cedric is a fair player. J.K.R. likes Cedric and she wants us to like him too.

It was the first time Harry did not catch the Snitch, the first time he lost a Quidditch match, and the last time he will see his Nimbus 2000 - as it had sailed off, run into the Whomping Willow, and was pummeled into toothpicks.

Curiosities

⁕ Dumbledore disperses the dementors by shooting "silvery stuff" at them like Professor Lupin did. Again, what did the stuff that came out of Dumbledore's wand look like? Was it the same as what came out of Lupin's?

⁕ So, Sir Cadogan was the only one brave enough (dumb enough?) for the job. Could the painted tin-can have been a Gryffindor many centuries ago?

⁕ Should we be questioning how a one-year-old can understand all of Lily's words? Maybe wizard children are advanced, or Harry's subconscious just retained it?

Other Oddities

⁕ According to our expert, Newt Scamander in *Fantastic Beasts*, Snape gave a wrong location for the Kappas – bet Lupin and the students had it correct (Japan).

⁕ Harry's glasses had not broken from the fall – Hermione's *Impervious Charm* was extremely impervious. Hermione – you may want to try it on the rest of Harry!

⁕ The fat lady was found hiding in a map of Argyllshire – a famous place for... socks.

Chapter 10 Analysis

Clues

Malfoy is so excited by Harry's embarrassment and Gryffindor's defeat that he finally removes his bandages and says his arm is healed. Also, Professor Lupin, who has recovered from his illness, is back teaching again. Lupin is sorry to hear about Harry's broomstick, relating how the Whomping Willow was planted the year he arrived at Hogwarts.

> So the Whomping Willow just happened to be planted the exact same time Lupin arrived at Hogwarts? Raise your hand if you think this was a coincidence... (Trolls are not allowed to vote.) What does Lupin know about the tree - and why would anyone want to plant a nasty tree like that at a school?

Harry tells Lupin about the dementors. He asks if Lupin thinks he is being weak, but before Harry can articulate the whole question, Lupin seems to have read his mind.

> That's the second time we see Lupin know what's on Harry's mind. According to Rule #1, we are intended to take special note of his mind reading, yet according to Rule #4, we shouldn't necessarily believe it. Then again, according to Rule #3, this is no coincidence, yet maybe Lupin just knows Harry well enough to second-guess him.... Are you getting dizzy? So is this a red herring or a great septology catch? Just how well does Lupin know Harry? A mega septology question for HP Sleuths.

Lupin explains that without a single cheerful thought left, even the strongest Azkaban prisoners go mad. The prisoners are trapped by their own destitute emotions as well as by the dementor guards surrounding them. Harry tells Lupin that when a dementor gets near him, he hears his mum being murdered by Voldemort. On hearing this, Lupin had made "a sudden motion with his arm, as though to grip Harry's shoulder, but thought better of it."

> Why would Lupin react this way? Why is he so affected? Did he know Harry's mum or dad, and if so, how well? This is a story-line clue and another Lupin septology clue.

Harry wonders out loud how Black was ever able to escape. Lupin looses his grip on his briefcase as he is also shaken, since the dementors are supposed to drain a wizard of his powers if he remains in there long. Lupin claims he is not very good at fighting dementors, but agrees to teach Harry how to make the dementor back-off like he had done on the train.

> No wonder all the wizards react so dramatically when hearing the name of Azkaban - it's no Niagara Falls! We are not told much about the long-term effects of the dementors. What if the prisoner is later found innocent? Can their powers come back? There's a lot of mystery surrounding the dementors.

Ravenclaw demolishes Hufflepuff in the Quidditch match, so Gryffindor is back in the running. On the morning of the last Hogsmeade field trip before the holidays, Fred and George give Harry a very generous Christmas present - it is an old piece of parchment. However, with the right words ("I solemnly swear that I am up to no good"), it reveals *The Marauder's Map*, created by "Moony, Wormtail, Padfoot, and Prongs." Fred and George had stolen it out of a file drawer in Filch's office a number of years ago, and had been using it for all their mischief.

> Who did Filch originally filch it from? How did Fred and George figure out how to use it? Did they have hints, or are they that talented?

The map is of the Hogwarts castle - and shows a secret passageway to Hogsmeade behind a third floor statue of a hump-backed, one-eyed witch. Most importantly, the map shows the name and exact position of every person, animal, (and poltergeist) in the castle in real-time as they move about. There are 6 other secret passageways displayed: one behind the mirror on the 4th floor that caved-in last year, another has the Whomping Willow "planted" directly over the entrance, and Filch knows about the remaining four.

> Secret passageways...secret maps...wicked! The only passageway that J.K.R. focused on was the one to Hogsmeade through the statue entrance. We must keep in mind that there are 6 others displayed - you never know when you might need a secret passage ;o) They just happened to plant the tree over that one passage (is that a coincidence?), and the one that caved-in last year – could Ron's old wand have had anything to do with that?

As he studies the Marauder's Map, Harry sees Dumbledore pacing his study, as well as the movements of Mrs. Norris and Peeves.

> Although it has not been specifically stated, we are led to believe that the way the map works is that you have to be moving around, otherwise you may not appear on it. If that is true, Harry (or anyone who has it) could still be caught by surprise in the future. For those of you clever enough to note, J.K.R. has demonstrated that animals and poltergeists also appear on the map. As of Book 4, however, WWP has not been able to find any evidence whether ghosts also appear on it or not. Have any HP Sleuths found anything?

Harry decides to go to Hogsmeade, and follows the passageway behind the statue that leads him to the cellar at Honeydukes. He surprises Ron and Hermione, who had been debating whether they should bring Harry back some Cockroach Clusters. Ron thinks it's cool Harry's there, while Hermione is concerned that may be how Black got into the castle.

> HP Sleuths know that Hermione is usually right. So, could Black be using one of those passages? How about the one that was caved in? Just because the Weasleys said it was not passable... remember Rule #4. Plus, if there are 7 secret passages on the map - could there be others that never made it to the map? (The Rememberit Quill is busy taking down GPS coordinates.) We also seem to be crawling with cockroach clues as well.

The three of them decide to go across the street for a butterbeer at the Three Broomsticks pub. While in there, Harry feels a breeze through his hair as some people come in the door. The kids are panicked to see Professor McGonagall, Professor Flitwick, Hagrid, and Cornelius Fudge have walked in and are headed for a table right next to theirs. Ron and Hermione quickly shove Harry down under their table while Hermione magically slides a decorated tree in front of them to obscure their presence. They hear the adults all order drinks - Flitwick gets a cherry syrup and soda (with an umbrella).

> A cute little umbrella? How sweet. Plus, we know from a British Muggle rock group that L-o-l-a drinks cherry c-o-l-a. This seems to be more reinforcement that Professor Flitwick is a very sensitive male.

Harry, Ron, and Hermione overhear them discussing Sirius Black with Proprietor Madam Rosmerta. She had known Black and could not ever imagine him going bad. Fudge tells everyone that Sirius was best friends with James Potter, was Best Man at his wedding, and named Godfather to Harry (under the table Harry goes into mental shock).

> Back on the Knight Bus, Harry had felt that Black looked familiar, but this is a little too familiar! Like any bar or pub, Madam Rosmerta probably knows her customers better than a psychiatrist, so she is a good source for personal information in the septology. If she was surprised that Black would defect, that is significant. Therefore, HP Sleuths should scrutinize the circumstances concerning Black's terrible deeds.

At one point, Dumbledore was tipped off by his spies that Voldemort was looking for the Potters, so he had warned James and Lily to go into hiding.

> Dumbledore must have one wicked spy network. Now why was Voldemort going after the Potters? Lucius Malfoy contends they were "meddlesome fools." Could that be related?

Professor Flitwick describes how much had been done to protect the Potters. The Potters had used an "immensely complex" *Fidelius Charm*, in which the location of a person is so secret that they cannot be found - even if they are within sight. The secret information was hidden inside a person (the Secret-Keeper) in order to hide the Potters. Black was their Secret-Keeper. But Dumbledore had been informed that someone in their own group had been leaking the information to Voldemort, and was wary.

> Oh, wow! That's really effective. Wonder if those charms are being used for anyone else?

Black is the one who betrayed them, and when Hagrid (who did not know this) arrived to rescue Harry, he recounts how Sirius "turns up" and tries to convince Hagrid to give Harry to him. When Hagrid refused, Black insisted that Hagrid take his motorcycle (since he wouldn't be needing it) to deliver Harry to his Muggle relatives. Hagrid realizes that should have made him suspicious.

WWP Sleuthoscope is shining mysteriously. HP Sleuths should think about this: If Voldemort was vanquished, Lily and James killed, and Black was not in communication with them, then who would have known that Harry lived in order to contact Dumbledore so Hagrid could come to rescue him? There is more to this story. We still don't know the order of events or who else might have been there, and what was Sirius doing "turning up" on his bike - does that mean he left and came back or is Hagrid missing something? Who informed Dumbledore?

Fudge portrays how Black had been ready to give up his role as double-agent and openly declare his loyalty to Voldemort. With Voldemort's powers gone, Black then has to run.

Does anyone hear a Sneakoscope going off? This conversation with Fudge is really strange and maybe not completely honest. This information about Black's motives was not made public, yet he is suddenly sharing it with these people. Is he telling them all this because he likes being important or is he telling them for some alternative reason?

However, when Peter Pettigrew, a pudgy, tag-along friend, tracks Black down, Black murders him in the street (along with 12 Muggles). Professor McGonagall weeps that Pettigrew (who was "never in their league talent-wise") was "always hopeless at dueling."

Interesting name – Petti (small) grew (got large). Gee, another growing/shrinking clue. We realize that it doesn't seem like it, but take our word for it – poor Pettigrew's skill at dueling may be important information to know for the septology.

Fudge claims that only a trained *Hit Wizard* from the *Magical Law Enforcement Squad* could have stopped Black. Fudge recounts how he was one of the first on the scene of the mass murder.

Do Hit Wizards wear sunglasses? That name sounds funny (and deadly). Fudge really likes to be in on the action. Maybe he was in the area at the time, or maybe it was bad enough that he received an emergency call, but how was it that Fudge just happened to be one of the first on the scene of the mass murder? Probably just doing his job, right? Probably. But HP Sleuths will be watching him more carefully now.

Black was taken to Azkaban, where he was guarded all the time by dementors. Yet, during Fudge's last inspection of Azkaban, he found Black to be shockingly normal - asking to read his newspaper. Fudge remarks, just like other wizards, that he does not like the dementors, but is adamant that their benefits outweigh their negatives.

This is a septology clue about the behavior and/or motivations of Fudge. Everyone else (including Dumbledore) is a bit uneasy about the dementors, but Fudge is comfortable to use them. Are they a symbol of his power in office, or is there a possible sinister reason for this? The story-line clue here is that not only was Black surprisingly normal, we now know he is also somewhat up on current events from that newspaper - reinforcing that Ron's assessment of Black having lost track of time was probably wrong.

When Fudge and the others have left the pub, Harry, Ron, and Hermione can only wordlessly look at each-other....

Rowlinguistics

✴ **Butterbeer** is a cool-sounding drink. It is also a very clever parody on Mr. Butterbur, the Innkeeper in Lord of the Rings.

Curiosities

✴ Guess Sirius didn't want his motorbike back after all (it was probably illegal anyway).

✴ Does the Marauder's Map actually "think for itself"? Does it need a brain or does it just reflect the images that exist?

Other Oddities

✴ Ginny sends Harry a get-well card she made herself – she is showing interesting magic and creative abilities (as well as still an interest in Harry).

✴ We are confused by the way the map showed Harry **in advance** tapping the statue and saying *"Dissendium!."* Will it do that for everyone at all secret entrances?

✴ Madam Rosmerta wears turquoise heels – does that relate somehow to the turquoise Ford Anglia?

Chapter 11 Analysis

Clues

In a daze, Harry returns to Hogwarts via the secret passageway. He wonders why no one had ever mentioned that his parents died because their best friend betrayed them, and is becoming obsessed with doing something about Black. Ron warns him how dangerous Black is. Ron heard from his father that after Black finished with Pettigrew, all that Pettigrew's mother got back was his finger (all that was left of him). When Harry thinks of Pettigrew, he is reminded of Neville Longbottom. The more he thinks about Black, the more he contemplates revenge (just like everyone feared).

> This is an example of how J.K.R. weaves a new septology element so smoothly into a story line. She had not prepped us for Black's betrayal in a previous book, so what else might she spring on us? We now know why everyone else can easily assume Black's after Harry, and why they kept thinking Harry might try to track down Black. Poor inept Pettigrew - and now Black is loose - hope they catch that rat!

Ron and Hermione go with Harry to visit Hagrid, and find him sobbing uncontrollably. The Ministry of Magic has cleared Hagrid of any charges with the Hippogriff incident, but is requesting an inquiry into Buckbeak's "instability" with the Committee for the Disposal of Dangerous Creatures. The kids assure Hagrid that they will help with Buckbeak's case, but Hagrid is sure that the Disposal department is under Lucius Malfoy's control and that nothing they might do will matter. Hagrid's troubles help Harry forget his own.

> Hagrid's opinions of people are highly influenced by Dumbledore, as well as his own experience, so we know that he probably has accurate information about Malfoy's influence on that Committee. We also know as a fact from Book 2 that Malfoy has no trouble threatening and controlling governing bodies in the magical world. We notice here that Hagrid (who said he's allergic to cats) does not seem to be sneezing from contact with Hermione. Maybe it's just a mild allergy.

Hagrid briefly mentions his own short stay at Azkaban, and makes it clear that he will never do anything that might make him have to go back there again. Even as an innocent man, his experience was horrible, since the dementors don't care about guilt - only that they have emotions on which to feed. Thankfully, all of Hagrid's positive emotions came back when he was released.

> Well, at least the effect of the dementors was not permanent. These dementors are leeches (slug things), and have no morality or reasoning. They do not seem to serve much purpose, which is a further indication that they may have been created by someone and that their allegiance would be to the Dark side.

Harry, Ron, and Hermione spend their holiday searching through the library for previous cases that would help them defend Buckbeak, but they do not find anything. They also discuss Lupin, who Ron knows was not in the hospital, so they are confused as to where he went when he was supposed to have been sick.

> J.K.R. is such a tease! This is probably a big hairy story-line hint, but it is so vague. We know that Lupin was not faking his sickness, so maybe he was just recuperating in his room? Too simple.

On Christmas morning, Harry awakes to find that someone has given him a gift of an authentic professional Quidditch Firebolt broomstick - complete with golden registration number on the handle. There is no note and no one can figure out who gave it to him. Hermione, however, is sure that Black has sent it to Harry, and is concerned that it could be jinxed.

> Okay class, what do we know about Hermione's analyses? That's right - she's usually correct. Now we're scared.

Crookshanks goes after Scabbers again, ripping Ron's pajamas; so Ron takes a kick at Crookshanks, but connects with Harry's trunk instead; the trunk gets knocked over as Ron yells from the pain; then the Sneakoscope goes wild, falling out of the Dursley sock. Ron stashes Scabbers safely away – ordering Hermione to remove the spitting feline from the room. Harry sees how thin and balding Scabbers is becoming, and thinks back to the shop-keeper at the magical Menagerie who told them that rats only live about three years. Harry knows that Scabbers, who does not seem to be at all magical, is already over 4 years old.

> It's a Rube Goldberg mousetrap...but have we caught ourselves a cat, mouse, or something else? That Sneakoscope sure seems to think there's a dirty rat some-where - so is it broken or not?

At Christmas dinner, Lupin is absent, however Professor Dumbledore is reassured that Snape has made some more potion for Lupin. Professor Trelawney shows up in a sequined green dress that makes her look like a glittering, oversized dragonfly. She predicts that Lupin will not be around very long, and points out that he "positively fled when I offered to crystal gaze for him – "

> Sick again? Lupin's already been ill 3 times this quarter - hopefully Lupin can stay well enough to make it through the whole year. We should consider if Snape is giving Lupin the potion before or after he is looking ill. We know Trelawney misinterprets, but she clearly sees danger for Lupin. This is not good. Now we're really depressed. ☹

When Harry and Ron return to Gryffindor from Christmas dinner, they find Sir Cadogan partying in his picture frame with some of the previous headmasters of Hogwarts.

> This jolly old knight in rusty armor is giving us some septology information. We know that the people in these portraits move around, can interact with the living, and even visit other portraits. We also realize that Dumbledore has to have spies and informants all over the castle. We now see that, in addition to the ghosts, these former headmasters are assuredly some of the ears and eyes for Dumbledore.

Professor McGonagall confiscates Harry's Firebolt to have it checked for jinxes, making Ron and Harry very upset at Hermione for reporting the broom to her.

Curiosities

✳ This is the second time that Professor Trelawney has been described as a glittering bug. According to Rule #1, that should mean something, but we have no clue what it could be.

Other Oddities

✳ According to Professor Trelawney, Harry and/or Ron will be the first to die of the Christmas dinner group.

✳ Staff that stayed over Christmas in Harry's third year:
Dumbledore, McGonagall, Snape, Sprout, Flitwick, Filch (Hagrid must have been spending Christmas dinner with Buckbeak)

Chapter 12 Analysis

Clues

This is Chapter 12.

There are not only a lot of references to the number 12 throughout the septology, but there are several mentions of "Chapter 12" in particular. Are all Chapter 12s somehow significant? We see gross (weighty) possibilities here.

Ron and Harry continue to be angry with Hermione, and they avoid her for the rest of the Christmas vacation. Oliver Wood can't imagine, either, how Black (with the whole country looking for him) could get to the shop and buy a Firebolt.

Hmmm...we're scratching our heads a little on this one, too. We are told more than once (Rule #1) that these brooms have registration numbers. That means that if nothing else, Harry could easily find out the shop that sold it, as well as at least some information about the sale transaction. When we had read this book the first time, we were sure that the registration would be used as a key clue because of the way J.K.R. was drawing attention to it. However, it's not a clue after all (at least not in this book).

Ron and Harry notice that Lupin isn't looking very good again, and while speculating what might be the matter with him, Hermione acts as if she knows. However, since they are feuding, they don't question her about it, and she stalks off, so they assume she really doesn't know but is just trying to get them to talk to her.

So much for holiday cheer. ☹ Notice this technique - even though Hermione does not divulge Lupin's secret (Rule #2), we are being told by J.K.R. that Hermione now has enough information to solve the Lupin mystery (that means we should have enough information to solve it). Glad she told us - now if HP Sleuths could only figure out where it's hiding (she's driving us loony).

Harry has his first anti-dementor lesson from Professor Lupin. Since it is not possible to practice on a real dementor, Lupin has captured another boggart as a substitute, which he found in Filch's filing cabinet. He teaches Harry the *Patronus Charm*, which produces a kind of silvery shield between the wizard and the dementor. It takes on a unique shape for each wizard. He advises Harry that it is very advanced magic, and that "many qualified wizards have difficulty with it." The incantation is *"Expecto Patronum!"* and the conjurer must be thinking extremely happy thoughts while summoning the Patronus.

Okay, so Lupin just happened to find this boggart in Filch's filing cabinet. Does he normally go looking for boggarts in filing cabinets? Not too likely. So what exactly was Lupin doing in Filch's filing cabinet - do we know of anything specific that he might be looking for? How many of you noticed this reference when you first read the book? Is J.K.R. sly or what?

Lupin opens the boggart case, the room goes icy cold, the lights go dark, and a dementor emerges. Harry fails on his first two attempts against the "dementors" (fainting as usual). On his third attempt, he is able to produce a frail Patronus shield and he stays on his feet - Lupin is happy with his progress. Harry probably would have done better except that he wanted to hear the sound of his mother's voice. He keeps trying to hear the sounds in his head:

"Not Harry! Not Harry! Please - I'll do anything -"

"Stand aside. Stand aside, girl."

"A man's voice, shouting, panicking -"

"Lily, take Harry and go! It's him! Go! Run! I'll hold him off-"

"The sounds of someone stumbling from a room - a door bursting open -
a cackle of high-pitched laughter -"

Finally! More information about the night of the murder - but as with all J.K.R. hints, they are partial clues with a lot of missing pieces. We are enlightened here by seeing that each time a "dementor" appears, the lights go out. Professor Lupin may have made wardrobes safe for us, but HP Sleuths should be alerted to cold, dark rooms.

When Harry tells Lupin he is hearing his mum's voice louder, Lupin looks "paler than usual." Harry then tells Lupin how he hears his dad's voice for the first time trying to hold off Voldemort so his mother could escape. "'You heard James?' said Lupin in a strange voice." Harry asks Lupin if he knew his dad (James) and Lupin said he had been friends with his dad. Harry also asks Lupin if he had known Black, and Lupin tenses at first, and then replies that he "thought he had."

If this sounds to you like Lupin may be one of the keys to Harry's past, you're right. The trouble is, though, Lupin seems to be as mysterious as everything else about Harry. Just **how close** was Lupin to Harry's dad? Yet another Lupin sep-tology clue – are HP Sleuths tracking these?

Slytherin just barely beats Ravenclaw in their Quidditch match, which means that if Gryffindor beats Ravenclaw, then Gryffindor would be in second place. The strain of work is clearly taking its toll on everyone. With Quidditch practice and anti-dementor lessons, Harry barely has time to complete Snape's essay on *Undetectable Poisons*.

Nasty stuff. If they're "undetectable," what do they do? How long before some-thing happens? Do you suddenly drop dead, or do parts of you fail? Think we'd better watch out for these – trouble is, without more information, we're not sure what we're supposed to watch for.

Hermione is especially stressed and irritable. Ron overhears her talking about her Arithmancy class with Professor Vector, and still can't understand how she supposedly has perfect attendance in so many classes that seem to have conflicting schedules.

So many classes, so little time...only Hermione would try a schedule like that. Too bad Ron doubts his own instincts - maybe that's why he is usually wrong with his analyses.

Professor McGonagall isn't happy when Harry asks her about the status of his broom for the 12th time. Harry also continues with his anti-dementor tutoring, although his Patronus remains indistinct. He asks Professor Lupin what is under a dementor's hood, and Lupin says that they only take their hoods off to administer the *dementor's kiss* to someone - sucking their souls out through their mouths. He also mentions that the Ministry has given permission to the dementors to perform the *kiss* on Black if they find him.

> Eeeew, yuck. But what if they make a mistake? Can it be reversed or is it permanent, like it sounds? That may also make a difference in the septology - if the dementors can regurgitate criminals back on the street, we could be in big trouble! Yet more twelves here in Chapter 12. Obviously they weren't foretelling anything major from when Harry was 12 - since he's now 13 and we're still getting dozens of hints.

Professor McGonagall finally returns Harry's Firebolt to him - telling him that there is nothing wrong with it, so Harry and Hermione are able to drop their feud and start talking again. At the entrance to their common room, Neville is arguing with Sir Cadogan to get in because Neville forgot the password (again), and has even lost the cheat sheet he made up of the week's passwords.

> Just like being on the Internet - what good are passwords if you can't remember them all without a list? At least most people would be able to remember the list. Is Neville's memory really that bad? This is not normal.

Ron is devastated to discover that Scabbers is missing - finding only blood and some cat hairs.

> Talk about bad omens - this is not a good sign with Chapter 13 just ahead....

Hermione and Ron are very angry with each-other (again).

Rowlinguistics

—✳— The witch who teaches Hermione's Arithmancy class is Professor **Vector**. A vector is a mathematics term used in trigonometry, calculus, science, and engineering.

Curiosities

—✳— The *Patronus Charm* is considered "well beyond" an O.W.L.

Clues

This is Chapter 13.

Welcome to *Whodunit13*. As HP Sleuths know, there are clues hiding wherever there is a superstitious number. J.K.R, therefore, could not resist the temptation to conceal the solution to each book's mystery within chapter 13. This is a trend that so far has held true through Book 4. The following are the key story-line events that take place in this chapter - we leave it up to HP Sleuths to decipher whodunit. Don't worry, if you can't solve it here, she always tells-all at the end of each book.☺

Ron is really upset about losing Scabbers. He feels Hermione is unreasonable and insensitive by suggesting that he just check under all the beds for Scabbers. Hermione is hurt that Ron has never given Crookshanks a chance. This causes a huge rift in their friendship.

Although Hermione might be a bit insensitive here, HP Sleuths know that she is rarely unreasonable. In fact, she is usually right about things. What if Scabbers is only injured and is in need of help? What if he is under a bed? Then again, what about Crookshanks' determination to get at Scabbers? He does not seem to be a normal cat.

Fred and George try to lighten Ron up by eulogizing the memory of Scabbers' "finest hour" (and only memorable deed) - biting Goyle's finger.

J.K.R. has now mentioned Goyle's damaged finger, Pettigrew's finger that was found at the scene, and even poor Scabbers' missing toe. All this finger stuff seems to be pointing to something...

Harry cheers Ron up by bringing him to the Quidditch pitch, where Ron rides the Firebolt. Madam Hooch drifts off to sleep while Ron tries out the broom. As it gets dark, Madam Hooch becomes alert, and hustles them back up toward the castle. On their way back, Harry sees what he thinks is the Grim. When Ron lights his wand, they see only Crookshanks in the bushes.

There's that bloody cat again ;o) If you think about it, we have learned that Harry doesn't usually just "see" things, so we should be suspicious whenever Harry thinks he is seeing something. Even now. Why did Madam Hooch fall asleep? Has she been keeping long or odd hours for some reason?

At breakfast before their Quidditch match with Ravenclaw, the Gryffindor team shows off Harry's new Firebolt, and everyone comes over to admire it. Even Percy's girlfriend, Penelope Clearwater from Ravenclaw, wants to handle it. As Percy is explaining how he has bet her 10 Galleons that Gryffindor will beat Ravenclaw, "Penny" calls over to him, and he runs off. The Slytherins are all huddled over at their table.

> We don't know much about Penelope (except, we worry about anyone who actually likes Percy!). We do learn some interesting things here. For some reason, Penelope wants to hold the Firebolt - is she interested in Quidditch brooms, or does she have a specific motive? She has bet 10 Galleons (a lot of money) on the match, which means she may have money to spare, or she may have inside information about something. It could be nothing, but in Book 2, she and Percy did choose to rendezvous right by Slytherin. Notice that when she calls to Percy, his controlling personality is easily controlled by her. We should mention that the name Penelope generally connotes faithfulness, but it also can mean deception - especially to suitors. Hmmmmm.

In the middle of the Quidditch match, three hooded "dementors" appear on the field. Without thinking, Harry pulls out his wand, performs the *Patronus Charm*, and then grabs the Golden Snitch to win the match for Gryffindor. Professor Lupin, who was "both shaken and pleased," comes over to congratulate Harry on his spectacular Patronus. Lupin shows him that those were not really dementors, but just Malfoy, his two Slytherin friends, and Marcus Flint, the Slytherin team captain - dressed-up as dementors.

> Penelope seems to be out 10 Galleons, but we never hear how she reacted. Now, HP Sleuths know that J.K.R. chooses her words very carefully, and Lupin is said to be a bit "shaken" when he comes over to see Harry. Lupin is not the type to be shaken up easily, so what about Harry's Patronus would have affected him so much? That's got us on the horns of a Lupin septology dilemma. It's also a story-line clue.

Fred and George bring up some great food for their Quidditch victory party. In a strangely high-pitched voice," Hermione reassures them that she saw the match, but is too frantic over her work to care about the party. Ron, who is still upset with Hermione, makes a snotty joke that she just thinks Scabbers has "gone on vacation or something" like that, but it's obvious it does affect her.

> Is Ron joking again? "On vacation" is a bit of a stretch, but he did say "or something," and we also know that we have to pay attention when Ron jokes. Stuff to ponder. Looks like one of the most important uses for a Marauder's Map (just like Invisibility Cloaks) is to obtain food.

After the Gryffindors have gone to bed, Harry dreams about something silvery-white that gallops away as Harry tries to chase it. Just as Harry is about to see what he is chasing, Ron suddenly wakes to see his curtains ripped and Sirius Black standing over him with a knife. He yells, the rest of the dorm wakes, and everyone gathers down in the common room, not sure whether to believe Ron or not. Professor McGonagall questions Sir Cadogan, who confirms that he let a man in who had a list of all the week's passwords.

> Okay, so Black got this list, but how did he get it? Is he hanging around the castle, or does he have spies? And what was Harry dreaming about? Rule #2, no doubt.

Professor McGonagall is incensed to find out that Neville had written down and then lost his passwords (that allowed Sirius entry).

Rowlinguistics

✳ In Greek mythology, **Penelope** was the wife of Odysseus (Ulysses). She is famous for holding off her suitors for 10 years – until Odysseus finally got back from the Trojan War and killed them all (Percy, that means dead).

Curiosities

✳ Harry's dreams are usually very significant.

✳ Ron's own brother, Percy, did not believe him when he said he was attacked by Black.

Other Oddities

✳ Marcus Flint was supposed to have graduated last year, but he doesn't seem to have done so. In an interview on Scholastic.com, J.K.R. explains that the reason is because he was held back a year. Sounds logical to us!

✳ According to Lee Jordon's commentary, the Firebolt has a "built in auto-brake." That could be handy. Wonder how that works – could we get a test-drive?

Chapter 14 Analysis

Clues

Black escapes unnoticed from the castle (again). The Fat Lady is back at her post, but has been given a bunch of security trolls as added protection. Poor Neville is not allowed to visit Hogsmeade anymore, cannot have the Gryffindor passwords, and gets a howler from his grandmother for losing the passwords that allowed Black to enter their dorm. Ron is quite elated that his encounter with Black has made him an instant "celebrity." Harry notices that no one is guarding or blocking the statue of the one-eyed witch, meaning that it is highly likely that Fred, George, Ron, Hermione, and himself are the only ones who know about that entrance.

> But they're **not** the only ones who know about that entrance... How about the authors of the map (or their descendents) - hope they're on our side!

Ron is confused as to why Black ran when he had no trouble blowing up a whole street of people. Harry figures he would never had gotten out of the castle if he had stuck around to finish the job. Hagrid tells Harry and Ron that Hermione (who they still are not talking to) is concerned about them. Hagrid explains that she is going through rough times herself - maybe taken on more work than she can handle. Plus, she has even been helping Hagrid with Buckbeak's case. Harry and Ron are guilty that they had not held up their promise to help as well.

> If you are following this story line for the first time, Ron asks a very good question. Why did Black run – was he afraid to stick around, was he confused when he didn't find his prey, or was there another reason?

Another Hogsmeade trip is announced. While trying to get to the secret passage, Harry encounters Neville who can't go to Hogsmeade either, so wants to work on Lupin's vampire essay together. As Harry is trying to pry himself away from Neville, Snape comes by and is exceedingly suspicious. Harry finally gets away from them both, puts on the Invisibility Cloak, and accompanies Ron around Hogsmeade. They go to see the Shrieking Shack, the most haunted dwelling in Britain. It is a boarded-up, creepy house on the edge of town that is even avoided by the Hogwarts' ghosts.

> There's that vampire essay again. And here's a potential septology hint. HP Sleuths should remember that this shack is shunned by everyone – **including the Hogwarts ghosts**. Since ghosts have the potential of being nasty spies, this place could be useful - that is, as long as you can survive whatever's in there....

All the entrances into the Shack are sealed shut, and Ron says that even Fred and George could not figure out how to get in. While Harry studies the house from under his Invisibility Cloak, Malfoy, Crabbe, and Goyle show up from the other side of the hill and start harassing Ron. As they all tussle, the Invisibility Cloak gets partially pulled off, exposing Harry's head. Malfoy knows he has something to report and runs off. Harry and

Ron realize that too, so Harry bolts back to the school as fast as he can run. Not daring to take a chance, Harry leaves the Invisibility Cloak in his bag down in the passageway. Harry makes it back and out of the statue, but Snape arrives just after he climbs out.

> Fred and George have a reputation for being able to break into (or out of) almost anything. We can therefore assume that there is very powerful magic sealing the Shrieking Shack. That means someone or something does not want anyone to get into there. Wonder why? Do we really wanna know?

Snape tries to get Harry to admit to being at Hogsmeade. Snape insults Harry's father, so Harry brings up how Dumbledore had told him that his father had saved Snape's life. On hearing that, "Snape's sallow skin had gone the color of sour milk," and his "uneven yellowish teeth were bared." He retorts that Harry's father saved him only because friends of his father tried to play a joke on Snape that could have killed him - which would have gotten them expelled.

> This is a bit confusing. Dumbledore is famous for not divulging all the details, but why would he omit that James rescued Snape only in order to save his own skin? Must be more to this story. Must be more to Snape (nice teeth).☹

Snape asks Harry to empty his pockets, and spots the old blank parchment (map). Snape knows it is important but he can't get it to function - it just writes out insults to him on the page. Frustrated, Snape takes some "glittering powder from a jar" and tosses it into the flames in his fireplace. He has conjured Lupin to his office. Lupin looks oddly at the old parchment, and says that from what he can tell, it is clearly a joke-shop prank that insults the reader. Snape says he thinks Harry got it "directly from the manufacturers."

> Snape conjured Lupin from inside Hogwarts? That's interesting. Does Snape know (or suspect) who the "manufacturers" might be? Probably. Is J.K.R. using Rule #2? Probably.

Ron bursts in saying that he's the one who got the stuff for Harry in Zonko's "ages ago," which settles the matter. Lupin tells Harry and Ron that he needs to have a "word about my vampire essay," and then quickly escorts them out of Snape's office.

> Is Lupin hinting at something when he mentions his vampire essay like that?

Lupin tells Ron and Harry that he happens to know that Filch confiscated that "map" years ago. Harry and Ron are amazed to hear that he knows it is a map. Lupin says they should have handed it in, and that he cannot let them have it back. He is sure that the "manufacturers" would want to lure Harry out of the school, and that he knows who they are.

> Everyone seems to know who the manufacturers are - so would somebody please tell us?! Well, at least we might have solved one small mystery: If Lupin knew that the map was taken away by Filch; and he happened to know that Filch kept his confiscated items in a filing cabinet; then maybe Lupin wasn't just looking for a boggart? Maybe he had tried looking in that filing cabinet for the map?

Why did Lupin go for that map? Was it to watch for Sirius, or were there other reasons? Imagine just how surprised he must have been to find that Harry had it all the time?

Hermione, who is waiting for Harry and Ron at the entrance to their common room, sadly shows them a letter saying that Hagrid had lost his case and that Buckbeak is to be executed.

Curiosities

✳ Was it significant that Malfoy and his sidekicks had been on "the other side of the hill" by the Shrieking Shack?

Other Oddities

✳ Filch has some actual talent – as he "expertly restored" the painting of the Fat Lady.

Chapter 15 Analysis

(The Quidditch Final)

Clues

Hagrid's tear-stained letter says that he is allowed to bring Buckbeak back to Hogwarts while they await the execution date. Ron is so upset with the news about poor Buckbeak that he and Hermione end their fight as he insists on helping her with the appeal. When Malfoy sees how unhappy Hagrid is about Buckbeak, he ridicules Hagrid – motivating Hermione to smack Malfoy across the face (to both Harry's and Ron's astonishment). As they enter their Charms class, Harry and Ron suddenly notice that Hermione is nowhere to be seen and she misses the class entirely. They find her back at the common room fast asleep.

> Hermione keeps doing that disappearing act. Is she becoming a scatter-brain from the stress or is she running off to other classes? This is a story-line clue begging to be solved.

Professor Trelawney has laid out crystal balls in Divination, saying that the "fates have informed her" that their examination will concern the Orb. However, Hermione is far from impressed, loudly commenting that it is Trelawney's own decision what goes into the exam, so it is hardly a "prediction." Hermione cannot stand it anymore and storms out of class. Lavender Brown is impressed that Trelawney had predicted at the beginning of the class that "Around Easter, one of our number will leave us forever."

> Trelawney may have some of the students (like Lavender) fooled, but HP Sleuths are not. Remember, when Trelawney sees a sign, we should heed it - but disregard her interpretation. Analyze what has been revealed to her with an open mind - your own interpretation will probably be closer!

Harry wakes from a nightmare in the middle of the night - thinking he had overslept from the match. He walks over to pour himself some water, and looks out at the weather conditions. He spots an animal prowling the grounds that he recognizes as Crookshanks, but then suddenly sees the huge, black, shaggy dog that he kept thinking was the Grim. Crookshanks clearly sees the dog too, and walks along with it back out of sight.

> What is this dog? For that matter, what is this cat?

At the Quidditch final, thanks to the speed of his Firebolt, Harry outruns Malfoy and snags the Snitch - winning the game and finally, the Quidditch Cup, for Wood and Gryffindor!

Curiosities

✳ Hermione is getting a LOT feistier. Seems that she is making a habit of putting what's right ahead of what's expected of them.

Other Oddities

✳ Warrington is the name of one of the Slytherin Quidditch players.

Clues

The school is near finals. Since he wants to get a job at the Ministry of Magic, Percy takes tests that are above O.W.L.s. – called N.E.W.T.s (Nastily Exhausting Wizarding Tests). Hermione, just like her class schedule, has an "impossible" exam schedule - multiple exams at the same time. She is definitely stressed.

> Hermione should have made it easier and just cloned herself. Can witches (other than on TV) do that?

Buckbeak's appeal is set for the last day of exams. Right before their final exam, Harry, Ron, and Hermione talk to Cornelius Fudge, who says that since he was visiting Hogwarts anyway, he will be a witness to the execution of a "mad hippogriff." Fudge does not seem to care about any appeal, and is accompanied by the executioner. It is clear they had already made up their minds, and Ron is especially upset.

> Fudge has fudged the facts just a bit. Even if the Ministry is concerned that Buckbeak may be dangerous, no one is truly convinced he is "mad." It is also interesting that Fudge happens to be conveniently available for the execution, and not at all concerned about justice. Obviously, Hagrid was right that Malfoy has control of this department - but does he also have control of Fudge? Note that Ron is being profiled as an animal lover.

Harry and Ron's last exam is Divination. Professor Trelawney is seeing students one-by-one to test them with the crystal ball. Harry is the last to be tested, so he waits while listening to a fly buzzing in the window. When Ron is done, he tells Harry that he hadn't seen anything in the orb, so just made something up. When Harry doesn't see anything either, he makes up the first thing that comes into his head - claiming he sees a hippogriff. This excites Professor Trelawney who jumps to the obvious conclusion (Buckbeak), but is then disappointed when Harry insists that his hippogriff does not lose its head.

> Now if you think that J.K.R. just happens to mention flies buzzing in windows for effect, "then your heads could do with filling." What is this bug – or maybe, **who** is this bug? We know that Professor Dumbledore is named after the olde English word for bumblebee, and that he was a transfiguration teacher. However, this is a fly, not a bee. This one is going to bug us throughout the septology!

As Harry picks up his bag to leave the Divination classroom, a strange, harsh voice says "It will happen tonight." Harry turns back to see Professor Trelawney in a spasmodic state - as if possessed. A "different" voice than her own is speaking. It says that the Dark Lord's servant: **"has been chained these twelve years. Tonight, before midnight...the servant will break free and set out to rejoin his master. The Dark Lord will rise again with his servant's aid, greater and more terrible than ever he was...."** Trelawney then seems to snap out of it, becoming herself again. She believes she had drifted off, and thinks Harry is imagining things - saying she would never predict such "nonsense."

> The WWP Sleuthoscope and HP Hintoscope both are creating a gross riot! Did she say twelve? Aha! Is this the twelve that has been fated for so long? So is this a true prediction? It looked very real – plus she has rejected it (a sure sign that it probably is real). If it is true, we should be very concerned about the threat of Voldemort's return. HP Sleuths should also be concerned about who or what possessed her. Was it alive or dead, and did it possibly have anything to do with that buzzing fly? With all these possibilities, this is much more difficult than a Muggle murder mystery.

Hagrid sends Harry, Ron, and Hermione an owl, telling them that Buckbeak lost his appeal and will be executed at sunset. Right after dinner, they go down to see Hagrid under the Invisibility Cloak. They quietly hide as they hear a pair of people run across the hall - slamming the door behind them.

> Who goes there? Who was that running across the hall? Remember this close encounter - J.K.R. is playing with us one more time.

Hagrid is so upset about Buckbeak that he drops a milk jug, which shatters loudly. Hermione finds another milk jug, but is shocked to discover Scabbers alive and hiding in it. Scabbers looks worse than ever, and struggles in Ron's grasp. Hagrid spies Fudge, Dumbledore, and the Committee members approaching his hut, so he sends the three kids out his back door.

> Well, it looks like Scabbers avoided being cat food after all ☺ That means Hermione was right again - maybe Ron should have looked under the beds! But Scabbers is acting weird - he doesn't even seem to ease up with Ron, or at least he is not the same sleepy, lump of a rat that we know. What is wrong with him?

As Harry, Ron, and Hermione walk back toward the castle under the Invisibility Cloak, they hear the swish and thud of the axe, and are in shock that an innocent creature has been executed.

Other Oddities

✴ Lupin's Defense Against the Dark Arts final is a really cool obstacle course of creatures that they have to negotiate - one of which is a boggart. Sure enough, Hermione's boggart turns into Professor McGonagall - who upsets Hermione by telling her that she has failed all her classes. Ron did joke about that in Chapter 7, didn't he? (Looks like Hermione needs to brush up on boggart charms....)

✴ The Astronomy final was held at midnight on the tallest tower (the Norbert tower from Book 1). We still have not seen any Astronomy class! Verrry mysterious (verrry definitely Rule #2).

Chapter 17 Analysis

(CAT, RAT, AND DOG)

Clues

On the way back up to the castle, Harry, Ron, and Hermione spot Crookshanks, as Scabbers leaps from Ron's grip, scampering off. Ron throws off the Invisibility Cloak and sprints after him, while Harry and Hermione have no choice but to run after them. Ron finally manages to rescue Scabbers and put him in his back pocket. Just then, a giant, pale-eyed black dog bounds out of the darkness, pushes Harry away, grabs Ron, and drags him off down through a large gap in the roots of the Whomping Willow. Ron has his leg wrapped around a root to keep from being pulled in, but the dog yanks him down, snapping Ron's leg, and he is carted off. Hermione is whimpering "help," so Crookshanks maneuvers between the branches and puts his paws on a knot on the side of the trunk - causing the tree to freeze.

> Doyou get the idea that the animals are in control here? They seem to know what is going on a whole lot better than the kids (or we) do. Did Crookshanks actually understand what Hermione was saying, and where did he learn how to freeze the Whomping Willow? Did you notice that the dog seems to have purposely attacked Ron? Why?

Harry and Hermione follow Crookshanks down under the Willow, along a tunnel, which leads directly into... the Shrieking Shack. The inside looks like *something* had torn the place apart, but Harry comments that ghosts would not have done that. They go upstairs, and enter a room where they see Ron on the floor and Crookshanks on the bed next to him. Ron blurts out that it is a trap.

> Harry's comment about ghosts is more confirmation that most ghosts cannot affect physical objects - at least not with much force. Obviously, Myrtle is not "most" ghosts... Ghostly abilities will most likely be an important septology issue.

The dog is really Sirius Black, an Animagus (a human transformed into an animal - like Professor McGonagall can do). Sirius instantly disarms Harry and Hermione, telling them that he has planned only one murder, and that he intends to carry it out. Harry is enraged, and with the element of surprise, jumps on top of Black while Hermione and Ron help. The weakly Black is overpowered and collapses on the floor. Harry grabs up his wand and stands over Black, with his wand pointed at Black's heart. But Crookshanks leaps onto Black's chest to protect him.

> So it wasn't a Grim - it was a big black Animagus dog. Too bad Harry didn't pay more attention in Professor McGonagall's class on their first day - maybe he would have realized what he was seeing. Professor Trelawney didn't realize what it was either. She did see the big black dog in Harry's cup, but, as usual, assumed it was the death omen. HP Sleuths keep your inner eye on Professor Trelawney!

Harry resolves to kill them both, but wavers, unable to do it, and loses the opportunity as Professor Lupin enters the room in a "shower of red sparks." Lupin disarms everyone again. Lupin then stares at Black as if trying to read his mind, and asks Black "...why hasn't he shown himself before now."

> We are being hit over the head again by J.K.R., but we are having trouble reading her mind. One possibility that comes to mind is that wizards who have creature blood in them (like Voldemort and snakes) may possess that ability. The most likely possibility is that characters who seem to be reading minds have some *inside information* and/or know each other better than we realize. Lupin is certainly hiding both story-line and septology secrets. What kind of wizard produces red sparks with his wand? Someone with ties to Gryffindor and/or phoenixes maybe? You guessed it – another Gryffindor/Lupin septology clue, of course.

Lupin is hit with a flash of insight. He exclaims to Black " - unless he was the one...unless you switched...without telling me?" Black nods, and Lupin helps Black to his feet, embracing him.

> This is not right – it is too weird. It's another J.K.R. twist ending (and it's not even the ending!)...and there's a lot of really suspicious things about Lupin.

This enrages Hermione who informs Ron and Harry that Lupin is a werewolf, and is now convinced he has been helping Black get into the castle.

> Lupin is a werewolf - wasn't that easy, HP Sleuths? No? Well, our first and primary clue was his name, Lupin. The word "lupine" means *wolfish*, it comes from the Latin word, *lupus* - meaning *wolf*. The next big clue was that he was getting ill about once a month. A more indistinguishable clue was that his boggart turned into a silvery-white globe because he fears the full moon. A fairly obscure clue was when Peeves sang "Loony Lupin" (the word "looney" is slang from the Latin word *luna* for *moon*). And don't forget Snape's essay on werewolves. (So what about Lupin's reference in Snape's office to an essay on vampires?) So, HP Sleuths, are you prepared to catch all the J.K.R. hints in Book 4?

Lupin explains that Hermione is only right with the werewolf part - that he has not been helping Sirius, and that "I certainly don't want Harry dead...." "An odd shiver passed over his face."

> Why would Lupin "shiver" when thinking about Harry being dead? We know he's a friend of James and would not want harm to come to Harry, but why would Harry's well being affect Lupin so personally? Unless... (You know, there's a really odd Lupin septology mystery going on here....)

Lupin calls Hermione the "cleverest witch of your age I've ever met." Nonetheless, he assures them that Dumbledore knew all about him when he was hired and had informed the rest of the staff.

> So if the rest of the staff knew, then Professor Trelawney would have known. Therefore, Lupin had no reason to escape from Trelawney's fortune telling except to avoid having to put up with her, right? Uhh... not so sure about that. It just confirms that Lupin is still holding a vital septology secret!

Lupin returns their wands, and asks them to listen. Lupin knew Sirius Black was on the grounds tonight because he saw him on the Marauder's Map, which he (Moony) helped to write. Lupin thought Harry, Ron, and Hermione might try to sneak down to see Hagrid under Harry's Invisibility Cloak, and figured he might see them on the map since they would still show up on it. Not only did he see them do that, he also saw a fourth person, an Animagus wizard by the name of Peter Pettigrew, with them.

> The HP Hintoscope is rustling over in the corner. Here is confirmation that the map even shows people under Invisibility Cloaks. That is a powerful map, which means that Lupin must be a powerful wizard. (We knew that.) But how did Lupin know Harry had his dad's Invisibility Cloak? Did he have something to do with that? How does he know so much about Harry?

Lupin asks Ron to hand-over Scabbers.

Rowlinguistics

✳ There is yet one final late clue that would have hinted that **Lupin** is a werewolf. At the beginning of the next chapter, Sirius will call Lupin by his first name, **Remus**. There is a classical myth that the city of Rome was said to have been founded by Romulus and Remus, twins who were raised by a she-wolf.

Curiosities

✳ Does Harry really know enough to kill Sirius with magic if he had decided to? Maybe at point-blank range to his heart, but that is not clear.

✳ A really subtle clue about werewolves (barely noticeable, and so typical of J.K.R.) is when Harry was staying at the Leaky Cauldron, he saw the lunascope – which gives the phases of the moon (extremely vital for werewolf planners). Harry also witnessed discussions on Transfiguration at the Leaky Cauldron. Don't ever say J.K.R. doesn't prep us. ☺

Other Oddities

✳ Didn't Gilderoy say (in Book 2) that he (or his poor victim) cured a werewolf with a *Homorphus Charm*? Is that possible?

Chapter 18 Analysis

Clues

Harry, Ron, and Hermione all think Lupin and Black are out of their minds - as Peter Pettigrew had died in front of witnesses. Lupin wants Sirius to explain everything to them since "there are parts of it even I don't understand," and Harry should hear the truth. Lupin also says that the Marauder's Map showed that Peter is here, and **"the Marauder's Map never lies."**

> Would Sirius Black escape from Azkaban and go through everything he's done just to nab Ron's pet rat? Hardly. Do Lupin and Sirius sound crazy to us? Hardly. Professor Lupin says "the Marauder's Map never lies." HP Sleuths, etch that in your brains - J.K.R. will be testing us on it in the future!

Hermione points out that all Animagi are registered with the Ministry of Magic, that there have only been seven Animagi this century (McGonagall is one), and Peter Pettigrew was not listed. Lupin says she is correct - that the ministry did not know about three unregistered Animagi at Hogwarts.

> This has very foreboding septology implications. Looks like the Ministry doesn't know everything, and we can't trust anything to be what it looks like. So who else was on that list of Animagi, besides Professor McGonagall, and what forms do they take? Who else may **not** be on the list? Did Hermione see Dumbledore (or anyone else we should know about) on it?

Sirius asks Remus (Lupin) to hurry up with the explanation since he has been waiting 12 years to get back at Pettigrew.

> We are now sure that even if "12 years" since the demise of Voldemort is not **the** 12, it is certainly an important 12 years that foretells danger. There is also some more potentially bad news here. Not only is Lupin's last name derived from the Latin word for wolf, but, according to the legend of Romulus and Remus, Remus (Lupin's first name) was murdered by his brother (or by his brother's followers). Does J.K.R.'s Remus somehow meet a similar fate? There is a lot more to learn about Lupin (like what does the "J" stand for in R. J. Lupin?).

The door to the room suddenly creaks open, but Lupin looks out and does not see anyone. He goes on to explain that by drinking the Wolfsbane Potion that Professor Snape has been giving him, he still transforms, but is not dangerous. When Dumbledore became headmaster, the Wolfsbane Potion was not available, yet Dumbledore allowed Lupin to attend Hogwarts by installing "precautions." The Whomping Willow was planted specifically for Lupin to cover the secret passageway, so that he could escape to the Shrieking Shack once a month, where he would howl and rip without injuring anyone.

When is a door not a door? When J.K.R. says it's a-jar... Why did the door creak?

Lupin had made three friends, Black, Pettigrew, and Potter, who learned how to become Animagi by their fifth year (they had to help Pettigrew do his). As Animagi, they were all able to keep Lupin company and keep him under control when he changed, plus he acknowledges "Highly exciting possibilities were open to us now that we could all transform." Harry is astounded to find out that his own father was an Animagus.

"Now that **we could** all transform"? Doesn't he mean, "now that they would transform with me"? Again, it seems picky, but J.K.R. is usually highly precise with her wording. James Potter and his friends managed this very complex *Animagus Spell* as fifth-year students. They were obviously exceptional wizards. That explains the wand James bought from Ollivanders - remember? Mr. Ollivander told Harry it was "excellent for transfiguration...."

Every month, Lupin and his friends would roam free, investigating Hogsmeade and the castle grounds. That is how they learned enough to write the map, signing it with their pseudonyms: Lupin was Moony, Sirius Padfoot, Potter Prongs, and Peter Wormtail. Harry starts to ask the kind of animal his father changed into, but is interrupted.

So if James was Prongs, that means Harry's own father was one of the authors of the Marauder's Map! Wicked. Guess Harry was doomed by his genes to be a rule-breaker. What is a *Prongs*? Notice how J.K.R. has Harry get cut-off just as we are about to receive this information? She's not fooling HP Sleuths this time - we know that's Rule #2 and we know it's important.

Lupin says that the reason why Snape doesn't trust Harry is because Black played a trick on Snape, and Snape thinks Harry's father was involved. The incident happened because Sirius was furious that Snape kept trying to get them expelled, so he told Snape how to get past the Whomping Willow (but omitted the part about the werewolf at the other end). Harry's father risked his own life to go in after Snape and pull him out before the werewolf got to them, but Snape had seen Lupin, and believed Potter saved him only to avoid being expelled.

So this is other side of the story - it was not James' fault that Snape was in there (meaning he would not have been accused), yet he still risked his own life for Snape as well as for his friends (who would have been expelled). Seems that Snape had it wrong and Dumbledore had it right. Wonder what Snape would say if he heard that...?

Snape is suddenly standing in the room as he whips off the Invisibility Cloak that Harry and Hermione had dropped when they chased Ron into the bottom of the Whomping Willow - Snape's wand is pointed at Lupin.

Rowlinguistics

✳ With a name like **Wormtail**, J.K.R. is giving us a big hint that he may be the prophesized servant of the Dark Lord - like *The Lord of the Rings* traitor, Wormtongue.

Curiosities

✳ Lupin must take the Wolfsbane Potion in the week preceding the full moon.

Chapter 19 Analysis

(The Servant of Lord Voldemort)

No one is happy that Snape showed up. Snape had gone to Lupin's office earlier in the evening to give him his monthly potion, and saw the map with the dot of Lupin running down the passageway. He is now convinced that Lupin had been helping his "friend" Black sneak into the castle.

> Guess Snape did get to hear their discussion, including that James was not personally responsible for the "trick" that almost took his life. Snape should be less antagonistic against Harry now, right? You would think so. If we review what was said from the moment the door creaked open, we realize that Snape now knows all about Peter being Wormtail and James being an Animagi too. So much for the "secret" map also. Snape now knows what it is - but does he know how to work it? If Lupin wasn't there to get his potion from Snape, then he didn't take any tonight. Wonder what happens if he misses a dose?

In spite of what he overheard, Snape is resolved to deliver both Black and Lupin to the dementors, and with a bang from his wand, magically ties-up Lupin. When Hermione tries to reason with Snape, he calls her a "Stupid Girl," and starts to bring them away. Harry blocks the door, and as Snape orders him to move, Harry, Ron, and Hermione all cast a *Disarming Spell* at the same time - blasting Snape into the wall and knocking him out.

> More banging sounds – putting our nerves on edge. Is Snape doing this for personal fame, or because of his grudge against Sirius? Either way, there are three rules to remember if you don't want trouble with Hermione: Don't call her a Mudblood; Don't insult her friends; and, Never...ever... call Hermione a "Stupid Girl"!

Ron wants to know how Sirius Black knew his rat was Peter. Black takes the *Daily Prophet* clipping of Ron's family out of his robe that he had been saving since Fudge had given it to him (to do the crossword puzzles during his last inspection of Azkaban). Lupin sees for himself Scabbers' missing toe (Peter's missing finger that he cut it off himself), which is visible in the picture.

> A whole handful of ironic "coincidences." Now we know the point J.K.R. was trying to make about fingers. Pettigrew may have faked his own death back then, and in Chapter 13, we saw that he could have done it again as Scabbers. But he could not escape the finger of fate...or will he? HP Sleuths listen up on this one too – we know from Chapter 4 that Scabbers also has a "tattered left ear" but we have not been able to find any more evidence about that as of Book 4. HP Sleuths may want to keep an ear out for it.

As a deception, Pettigrew had yelled out to the witnesses that Black had betrayed the Potters, and then, with his own wand behind his back, blew up the street behind him. Having transformed into a rat, he escaped down a sewer.

> WWP Sleuthoscope is flickering suspiciously.... This could be Rule #4. We know Pettigrew is still a coward, but is this the same Neville-like person McGonagall got teary-eyed over? The one who couldn't hold his own in a duel? Was that a great acting job back in school, or is this an indication that Dark magic can have a powerful influence on wizards? Or there are there still unanswered questions? If Sirius is telling the truth, then how did Peter beat Sirius? There is still something very cagey about this rat trap.

Ron is still not convinced that his pet rat is anything more than a rat - having been in the family for so long. Lupin confirms that Scabbers has been with the Weasleys for 12 years.

> Being with the Weasleys does not seem like "bondage" to us, but Professor Trelawney's prediction did say the Dark Lord's servant "has been chained these twelve years." We are starting to get a lot of 12 hints that may be related. Where **did** Percy get Scabbers? That is now a vital question. Does Percy have a soft spot for decrepit animals, or did someone he respect give it to him? As of Book 4, we still do not know, but we wish someone would start asking!

Black thinks that Crookshanks is "one of the most intelligent of his kind" - realizing that Black was not really a dog. Crookshanks also had seen through Peter's façade.

> Just what is Crookshanks' "kind"? Based on *Fantastic Beasts,* and an interview with J.K.R., Crookshanks is part Kneazle. That explains why Crookshanks was able to spot Peter as a rat.

Black conveyed to the cat that he wanted Peter, so Crookshanks tried to bring Peter to him. When that failed, Crookshanks stole Neville's password list from his bedside table. Crookshanks had even told Sirius that Peter put the blood on the sheets (faking his death).

> Being part Kneazle may explain how Crookshanks saw through Scabbers, but it does not explain how he knew enough to steal Neville's password list or managed to "tell" Sirius that Peter left some blood on the sheets. Is there something we should know about animal communications here?

Lupin explains that Peter had not tracked Sirius down, but it was Sirius who tracked Peter down. Although Sirius Black had been the Potters' Secret-Keeper, at the last minute he had switched with Peter - and no one else knew. Black thought it was a great decoy since no one would suspect they would have trusted a weak wizard (Pettigrew) with the information. Ron resignedly lets them have the rat. Lupin and Black remove the transfiguration charm, and a short (barely taller than Harry), balding Peter Pettigrew suddenly sprouts from what had been Scabbers.

So is this why the Sneakoscope went off in Ron's pocket when he tied it to Errol? Was Scabbers in his pocket then, or was it just because he was using Errol when he shouldn't? Notice how short Pettigrew is. Does he actually have rat blood in him or some other small creature ancestor? Here is interesting septology information. As of Book 4, we do not know anything about the spell to perform a transfiguration, but we now see that two wizards were able to remove it. Is that because they helped Pettigrew perform the spell in the first place, or is there a standard *Counter-Spell* that can force the restoration?

Pettigrew claims that Black was able to escape from Azkaban because 'He-Who-Must-Not-Be-Named' taught him some tricks. It amuses Black that Pettigrew (who can't even say Voldemort's name) would think that he needed to be taught anything by Voldemort.

More evidence that Black is a very powerful wizard. He is not even phased by Voldemort or his power, while Voldemort's own servant, Pettigrew, is in fear of just the name.

Black tells Hermione that the reason Peter had never hurt Harry at Hogwarts is because he wouldn't dare do it around Dumbledore – not unless Voldemort had returned to full power. Pettigrew couldn't act. He had messed-up by sending Voldemort to the Potters, so he has been hiding from Voldemort's followers these past 12 years. Sirius knows there are still many followers who claim to have reformed, but they are just waiting. Pettigrew needed to vindicate himself by delivering the "last Potter" to Voldemort.

The WWP Sleuthoscope and HP Hintoscope are again making a furious fuss!! What did Sirius say? The **"last Potter"**? He said it, and he should know. What is so special about the Potters? I guess if we knew that, we wouldn't be here trying to figure this all out, and you certainly wouldn't need a mystery guide (hehe). Maybe Wormtail didn't hurt Harry, but could he have been responsible for any unexplained activities? Who else is leading a double life?

As to how he escaped Azkaban, Black says he's not quite sure, himself. Black thinks it was because the dementors only feed off happy thoughts, and his brain was focused on his being wrongly accused - which was not a happy thought. That probably kept him sane, thus keeping his powers.

Black was able to fight off the dementors, so it **is** possible to do that. If a good wizard can do that, what about Dark wizards? Are they affected? Like Mr. Weasley questioned – just how safe is it to use dementors at Azkaban? Lots of very grim septology questions there.

Since dementors have no vision capability, Sirius could transform when needed into a dog, which, being an animal, had less complex emotions - fooling the dementors into thinking he was just losing his mind. When Sirius saw the picture of Ron's rat, he realized that Peter was at Hogwarts - just waiting for word of Voldemort. Sirius became obsessed with the desire to get out and go after him (a negative, yet empowering feeling that the dementors could not destroy). One night, as the dementors were delivering his food, Sirius slipped past them as an Animagus, swam to the mainland as a dog, and has been living in the forbidden forest.

> We won't ask what he has been living **on**...(ugh). So "he's at Hogwarts" did not mean Harry after all. Jumping to conclusions (especially through the help of her characters) is a big trap that J.K.R. craftily sets up for us to fall into blindly. Dementors can't see? That means they can be fooled (like Sirius did), and they can also make mistakes. Might that mean that Sirius wasn't the only escape from Azkaban after all?

Black and Lupin knew someone (Pettigrew) had been passing secrets to Voldemort for a whole year. Black emotionally implores to Harry that no matter what, he would not have betrayed his dearest friends (Harry's parents), and Harry then does believe him. Peter pleads with each of them for his life. Ron is revolted by the thought that he had Wormtail as a pet.

> We can see that Book 5 is going to be very rough on our sleuthing skills. There is considerable counterintelligence going on already, and it will be extremely difficult to sort out mystery from red herring, from spy, from transfigured wizard. HP Sleuths start sharpening your skills now - this is only the beginning....

Together, Black and Lupin raise their wands to exterminate Peter, but Harry suddenly stops them. Peter flings himself at Harry's knees, thanking him for saving his life, but Harry throws him off - saying that his father would not have wanted them to become killers to avenge his death. Harry judges that Azkaban would be a very appropriate punishment. Black and Lupin agree that it is Harry's choice.

> The dog wasn't the rat after all. The cat wasn't a rat either. Guess only the rat was a rat. We should have known that. Hopefully, Voldemort's followers who are in Azkaban will have a lot to say to Pettigrew.

They tie-up Peter, they splint Ron's leg, and then Black "conjures manacles from thin air," to shackle Peter to both Lupin and Ron (with a threat to kill him if he tries to transform).

> Wonder how difficult it is to conjure something (like manacles) out of thin air? Bet it's quite difficult. Bet that's more evidence of Sirius's wizarding powers. According to an interview with J.K.R. on SouthWestNews.com, things that are conjured "out of thin air" don't last. So, when ropes, manacles (or even camp beds) are conjured, they will go away after a bit. That means someone must cook actual food and send it up to the Great Hall, and wizards can't just conjure up money or jewels or whatever they fancy.

Lupin diagnoses that there is nothing wrong with Snape, then magically "strings him up" to pull him along (unconscious), as everyone heads back to the castle - Crookshanks in the lead.

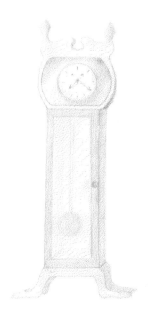

Curiosities

※ Peter Pettigrew is a rat and Piers Polkiss (Dudley's friend) has "a face like a rat" – just thought we'd mention that.

※ So, did somebody ever let Dumbledore or McGonagall know that Neville did **not** lose the list of passwords – they were stolen?

※ Sirius states that "Voldemort's been in hiding for 15 years..." Is Sirius just rounding the number, or had Voldemort gone into hiding a couple of years before his demise?

Clues

As Harry, Ron, Hermione, Black, Lupin, Pettigrew, Snape, and Crookshanks all awkwardly proceed along the passageway back to the castle, Black has a discussion with Harry. He mentions that he is Harry's godfather, and timidly inquires whether Harry might mind staying with him once his name is cleared. Harry agrees - exuberant that he could leave the Dursleys and move in with his father's best friend. They emerge from the Whomping Willow and start walking across the castle grounds, when suddenly they see the full moon come out from behind a cloud and Lupin is in trouble - he had not taken his potion that night. Black tells them to run, transforms to Padfoot, and fights to keep the werewolf Lupin under control and away from everyone else.

> This is an issue that has been a bit confusing to observant Sleuths. If Lupin does not turn into a werewolf until the moonlight hits him, then why can't he just stay indoors and not transform? Well, Lupin didn't have to be exposed to moonlight. According to an interview with J.K.R. on Scholastic.com, the moon just wasn't up earlier. That might need clarification - see the Curiosities at the end of this chapter.

In the commotion, Peter grabs Lupin's dropped wand, and with a couple of bangs out of the wand, knocks out Ron and Crookshanks. Even though Harry disarms him, Peter manages to transform, and scurry away.

> Are these the bangs for which we have been seeing all those clues? Could these be the tolling of doom, or just more loud noises?

Padfoot scampers after Lupin, but Harry and Hermione hear him yelp in pain, so they run toward the lake to help. They find Sirius as a human being, surrounded by a huge mass of dementors, that starts closing in on all of them. As Sirius and Hermione are overcome, Harry keeps trying to think happy thoughts about leaving the Dursleys, but he can only manage to conjure a thin, feeble Patronus that soon dissipates. One of the dementors nearest to Harry removes his hood, revealing empty eye sockets and a gaping mouth hole. It grabs Harry with strong, clammy hands, and starts to perform the *kiss* on Harry first - his mother's voice screaming in his head.

> The WWP Sleuthoscope is beaming an S.O.S.! Why is the dementor trying to get rid of Harry **first**? Possibly because he was trying to help Sirius? That is still not a reason for them to perform the *kiss* on him. This is a big gaping septology issue. Also, all that time in Azkaban, Sirius avoided being overcome by the dementors, but he is overcome here. Is that because he was happy again for once in his life, or were there just too many of them? We are left to mull over that in our own thoughts.

As Harry weakens, he notices a silvery light, and the dementor drops him back down to the ground and retreats. Harry sees a bright, shining animal (like a unicorn) circling Black, Hermione, and himself, driving the dementors away. It gallops to the other side of the lake where a strangely familiar figure welcomes it back.

Who was that familiar stranger? A story-line clue, of course. The shining animal is most likely some form of Patronus to be able to drive the dementors away like that. A very powerful Patronus.

Harry faints as he tries to make sense of what he saw.

Curiosities

✳ We assumed Crookshanks was okay since J.K.R. did not mention anything to indicate otherwise, but we will be biting our claws through another whole chapter before it is clear that he was not seriously hurt.

✳ Since, on the night of a full moon, it rises at sunset, there is more to the explanation of Lupin's transformation into a werewolf – probably having to do with the interpretation of the legend. A werewolf could be affected by either the **position** of the full moon, or the definition of a "full moon." Therefore, Lupin was about to change any way and the cloud just happened to part at that moment. Let's say Lupin (or any werewolf) does not transform until either (A) the moon reaches its apex (highest point it gets to in the sky), or (B) the moon is technically a full moon by astronomer *definition*. That means, if a werewolf changes only when the moon is exactly at apex, he would not transform until around midnight (could be up to a few hours before or after). The other option is a moon that has become *officially* a full moon can occur at any time of night or day within the month and that was the moment when it *officially* became full. We're not sure which one J.K.R. assumed. If you need to know more, just ask Professor Sinistra, or any Astronomy teacher.

Clues

Harry awakes in the Hospital to hear Fudge saying that it is a good thing that Snape was there to save everyone from Black, and that Snape should receive the Order of Merlin award for capturing Sirius Black. Fudge asks Snape what made the dementors retreat, but Snape says he doesn't know - as they were already headed away when he regained consciousness. Snape tells Fudge that Harry, Ron, and Hermione had been bewitched into thinking Black was innocent and they almost caused Black to get away, so suggests Harry be suspended. Fudge will not even consider it.

> What exactly is Snape's fixation with Harry getting expelled? Back in the Shrieking Shack, he overheard (while under the cloak) that James was not personally responsible for the trick, and how James had rescued him in good faith. Do Snape's grudges go that deep, or is there yet more to this story? A gnawing septology question.

Harry sees that Hermione is also awake. Madam Pomfrey tells them that Ron will be okay, that Black is being held, and that the dementors will be performing the kiss on Black at any moment. Harry and Hermione panic, jumping out of bed, which alerts Fudge and Snape. Harry and Hermione tell Fudge that they had seen Pettigrew as an Animagus that night, that he had faked his own death, and that Sirius was innocent. However, (with prodding from Snape) Fudge is sure the kids are confused.

> We are beginning to get a feel for the kind of stuff Fudge is made of. We saw earlier that he is not as concerned about justice as would be expected from the Minister of Magic. Here, we see that he has a very closed mind overall.

Dumbledore, who has just spoken with Black, enters the ward and asks to speak with Harry and Hermione alone. Fudge checks his large, gold pocket watch and goes to meet the dementors. After everyone else leaves, Dumbledore assures the kids that he believes them, but explains that it is their word (thirteen-year-old children), against a street full of eyewitnesses and his own testimony that Black had been the Secret-Keeper. He explains to Hermione that what they need is "more time." He instructs that Sirius is locked in Professor Flitwick's office, that according to the law, they "must not be seen," and that they may be able to "save more than one innocent life." Hermione understands (Harry doesn't). Dumbledore says, "three turns should do it."

> Is this what J.K.R. has been hinting about all this time? It's about time we had an answer. However, this is probably not the end of it. HP Sleuths keep alert! One thing about which WWP has not found any evidence as of Book 4, is how one *talks* with a dementor. We know Fudge does that a lot, but can they use their mouth for speech and how do they communicate with wizards? How do they communicate with each other? Do they work like a *collective* (a wireless brain network - like in *Star Trek*)?

Dumbledore tells Harry and Hermione that he is going to lock them in at five minutes to midnight. Hermione pulls out a tiny hourglass that was hanging on a chain around her neck - throws the chain over Harry's head too, and then turns over the hourglass three times. The ward fades away and they find themselves standing in the deserted castle entrance hall. Hermione grabs Harry and drags him quickly with her into a broom closet and *slams* the door shut. They listen as three pairs of footsteps go by. She explains that they have gone back in time three hours, and the footsteps that they hear pass them are their own as they go off to visit Hagrid earlier that day.

> They have materialized back at the identical scene from back in Chapter 16, where Harry, Ron, and Hermione are under the Invisibility Cloak trying to sneak out to be with Hagrid. Only this time, Harry and Hermione are the pair of footsteps that ran and slammed the door. Pretty weird - they have to run to avoid themselves, who were hiding from themselves. This is complex stuff. You can tell that J.K.R. loves this.

Hermione tells Harry how Professor McGonagall had given this *Time-Turner* to her so she could take all her simultaneous classes. McGonagall had to write many letters to the Ministry of Magic to get permission for Hermione to use it. Hermione was instructed that it is normally against wizarding law to use it, so she was not to use it for anything except her lessons, and was sworn to not tell anyone else about it.

> That means Hermione is not only breaking rules, she is breaking wizarding law. Wow! Of course, it was Dumbledore who asked her to, but this shows us that Hermione is willing to put morals in front of rules (unlike Fudge). Could Lupin have known about her Time-Turner? Is that possibly why he did not have her try the boggart in their first lesson?

Harry and Hermione try to figure out exactly what Dumbledore wants them to do. Harry deduces that by saving Buckbeak, they can then fly him up to Flitwick's window to save Sirius as well - thereby saving two innocent lives. Checking that the coast is clear, they dart out of the closet and out onto the lawns, where they sprint into the forest - heading toward Buckbeak and Hagrid's cabin. When they get down near Hagrid's house, they hide and watch an instant-replay of what had happened earlier in the day. Harry hears his own voice telling Hagrid that they have come to see him under their Invisibility Cloak, asking Hagrid to let them in.

> Time travel - one of the ultimate paradoxes in brain twisters. We have assuredly entered the realm of sci-fi here. J.K.R. never mentioned that she likes science fiction. Wonder if she's been holding back?

From inside the cabin, they hear a crash followed shortly by Hermione's shriek as she finds [found] Scabbers. Harry argues that they should go grab Scabbers now and get it over with - explaining that the only ones there to see them are "themselves" and Hagrid, but Hermione refuses. She points out that not only are they breaking a cardinal wizarding law already (no one is supposed to change time), but that it would be dangerous to themselves - as there are famous accounts of wizards having killed their past or future selves in confusion, thinking it to be Dark Magic. They "must not be seen."

> We are told that time travel is not only confusing, but potentially lethal. Sounds like it's perfect for Harry Potter! Now that we know time travel is not only possible, but not that difficult, HP Sleuths should watch for hints or inconsistencies that may indicate time travel has (or is) taken place. CONSTANT VIGILANCE!

Harry and Hermione watch themselves exit out Hagrid's back door, put on the Invisibility Cloak, and head back toward the castle as the Committee, accompanied by Fudge and Dumbledore, approach the cabin. The executioner looks out Hagrid's window and sees Buckbeak tied up in the pumpkin patch. As the witnesses sign "official" papers, Harry dashes into the pumpkin patch, bows to Buckbeak, unties him, and tries to lead him off. Buckbeak does not want to leave, and Harry struggles with him as he hears the people in the cabin start to walk toward the door. Dumbledore brings them back – with the explanation that the executioner forgot to sign the document. Harry just manages to get Buckbeak to the edge of the forest when the Committee emerges from the cabin and discovers Buckbeak is gone.

> When Dumbledore holds everyone up to go back and have the executioner sign, he seems to have some motivation - as if he might know that he needs to stall them. Does he have some way of knowing what is going on outside with Harry and Buckbeak? Does this sound like a septology clue?

There is a swish and thud of the axe as the executioner swings it into the fence in anger. Hagrid heaves great sobs in relief - believing that "Beaky" pulled himself free, but the executioner thinks someone has untied him, and wants the grounds searched. Dumbledore (who seems "amused") immediately points out that if someone stole a hippogriff, they would have escaped by air, and that the skies should be searched. He also requests to sit and have a drink.

> Ahhh – the paradox of how even dramatic changes of events in one space/time doesn't change anything in the general fabric of the universe. (In both time sequences, the axe swished and thudded, yet didn't cut anything after all; in both time sequences Hagrid sobbed, but we see here it was tears of joy). Dumbledore is apparently controlling the events here as he directs them to search the sky (away from Harry, Hermione, and Buckbeak's true location), plus stalls them by asking for a drink. How does **this** Dumbledore seem to know so much? He is unconcerned, not surprised, and even "amused" by all these events and twists on the events.

Harry and Hermione pull Buckbeak closer to the Whomping Willow so they can quietly keep watch for their next cue. They see it all just as it happened three hours ago: Ron chasing Scabbers followed by themselves, Padfoot knocking over Harry, dragging Ron into the Whomping Willow, Crookshanks disabling the tree, and then everyone disappearing down between the roots. Just as the tree starts to move again, they see Dumbledore and the Committee appear, heading back up to the castle.

Dumbledore has an impeccable sense of timing. Very interesting. Maybe he is used to playing with time? Dr. Who fans - can you envision him as a Time Lord?

Next comes Lupin, who is "haring toward the Willow." He uses a stick to freeze the Whomping Willow and slip down inside. Harry notices that the Invisibility Cloak is still sitting on the ground and insists on retrieving it before Snape can get to it. Thankfully, Hermione grabs and stops him just as Hagrid comes into view, headed for the castle. Snape then arrives, finds and puts on the cloak, uses the stick to stop the Willow, then heads into the passageway, triggering the next set of events.

As Dumbledore will elaborate on later, events in life are very complex, and the way one event is inter-woven with multiple others makes changing any one event highly risky. For instance, Snape came into the Shrieking Shack, heard some of the conversation, revealed himself, but then they stunned him. What if Harry were to have successfully retrieved the Invisibility Cloak now, and Snape entered without the Cloak and overpowered Sirius and Lupin before Harry, Ron, and Hermione heard the whole story or got to see Pettigrew with their own eyes? What if the information Snape heard in the Shack while under the Cloak did somehow (we're still looking) affect him positively? See how complex this time travel stuff is? It's better to let him have the Cloak. We will ponder another issue – does this mean the Marauder's Map cannot pick up both forms of Harry and Hermione, or were their future-selves just not moving when Lupin and Snape were looking at it?

While they wait, Harry tells Hermione all about the dementors and the bright, silvery animal, that must have been a very powerful Patronus to force them away. Hermione wants to know about the figure on the other side of the lake who conjured the Patronus. Harry explains that it looked just like his dad, but he knew that couldn't be. He wonders if since Moony, Padfoot, and Wormtail had been on the grounds that night, if somehow his dad had too...

WWP Sleuthoscope is shimmering intensely! HP Sleuths should consider if all four of them really did somehow make it onto the grounds that night – an ultimate J.K.R. *trick or treat*!! Could the wizard have been his father? Just how far can one travel in time, and can you travel forward (even past your own death?) If it helps you, WWP has **no** indication that travelling forward is possible (although this is J.K.R.'s own magical world - and she is revealing it to us as she wants). Have HP Sleuths figured out what a galloping Prongs would look like?

The leaves rustle in the breeze above Harry's head as he sits and waits with Hermione. Over an hour later, they see themselves emerge from the Willow, and Harry really wants to go nab Pettigrew, but Hermione is firm. However, Lupin is about to transform and charge into the forest - right where they are, so they hustle Buckbeak back to Hagrid's cabin.

> On the other hand, perhaps some messing with time and events might have been worth it with Pettigrew. In spite of all the dangers, nabbing that rat may have spared everyone (including our own Muggle world)... Wonder if any secrets ride those gentle breezes?

Although they are safer in the cabin, Harry can't see or hear what is going on, so he has to sneak outside. As Harry is leaving, Hermione reminds him that they came back to help Buckbeak and Sirius - nothing else. Harry runs behind a bush to watch from his side of the lake, knowing that the person who sent the Patronus should be there any moment. He keeps waiting, but no one appears; yet he sees the dementor has taken off his hood and is already starting to administer the *kiss* to his other self. Watching from his present vantage point, it suddenly occurs to Harry that the "great wizard" he had seen must have been "himself"!

> Dumbledore had said that Harry and Hermione would be saving "more than one innocent life," but he never even hinted that included their own! This is deep. Did Dumbledore know their own lives needed saving? Even more importantly, how did Harry go back and save his own life if he died the first time? You say he didn't die - that he came back from the future and saved himself? Well then, how did he get to the future so he could come back and save himself? Makes your brain hurt, doesn't it? If you think about it, this almost implies that Dumbledore (or someone?) might have had to save them the first time, and then have Harry and Hermione amend it (or are we getting too literal, J.K.R.?)

Desperate to save everyone, Harry jumps up and conjures a Patronus that takes on the form of a brilliant stag, which he finally understands is *Prongs*.

> James' Patronus and Animagus forms are both stags. According to a chat on aol.com, J.K.R. confirmed that the Animagus animal one turns into is significant. The stag is the symbol of Artemis, the ancient Greek goddess of the hunt and the moon. It is also rumored that Merlin the Great was famous for transforming into a stag. Is there a chance that James is somehow descended or linked to Merlin?

Hermione runs up with Buckbeak and is upset that Harry "interfered." They hide behind the bush while Harry recounts how he had to save everyone. Hermione is extremely impressed as a Patronus that strong is very advanced magic, but Harry reasons how he had the confidence to do it because he already had seen himself do it...(?)

> Did Harry say, he knew he could do it now because he had previously seen himself do it in the future? Huh? This is called recursive reasoning - otherwise known as the *chicken-and-egg theory*. In the *Terminator 2* movie, Kyle has an expression for this - he says "It messes with your brain." We agree.

Harry and Hermione watch Snape regain consciousness and lug everyone back to the castle. When they see the executioner run from the castle to bring the dementors, they realize it is time to rescue Sirius. Harry ties up Buckbeak's rope like a reins, and they fly off with Hermione hanging on in fear. They find Flitwick's window, which Hermione springs open; they pull Sirius onto Buckbeak, and soar up to the West Tower where Harry and Hermione dismount. As Harry and Hermione urge him to take off, Sirius inquires about Ron, and then admiringly tells Harry "You are truly your father's son."

> Sirius has no idea - if only he had seen that Patronus! And Sirius must truly be a dear friend – as his first concern was about Ron's welfare. Wonder what septology secrets Sirius is holding about Harry's past?

They watch as Black flies out of sight on the powerful wings of Buckbeak.

Curiosities

—✶— Those of you who may not be familiar with the *chicken-and-egg theory* - the philosophical question is asked: "Which came first...the chicken, or the egg? (and how do you know?)."

—✶— Fudge asks Snape about what made the dementors retreat. He was very interested to know.

—✶— When they go back in time, how do they know where (in what location) they will end up (or do they)? Hermione seemed to have it down fairly well, but it may be difficult to be precise.

Other Oddities

—✶— We got to see more of the West Tower here – we now know the exact location of Flitwick's office ("seventh floor... thirteenth window from the right of the West Tower").

—✶— That hour-glass turning over and the ward dissolving into an earlier scene reminds us of one of the movie productions of Charles Dickens's *A Christmas Carol*. Could J.K.R. be influenced by any other concepts from that novel?

Clues

Hermione informs Harry that they have exactly ten minutes to get back down to the hospital wing without anybody seeing them. At the bottom of a staircase, they have to pause out of sight when they hear Snape and Fudge go by. At another point, they have to duck into a classroom to wait while Peeves passes, leaving only three minutes to go. They sprint to the ward, and then creep up to the door where they see Dumbledore backing out, as he is issuing the instructions they received three hours earlier, saying that he is locking them in. Dumbledore pulls out his wand to lock the door, and on seeing that, they panic and run up to him.

> It's déjà vu all over again (hee-hee). Time travel is so weird. Here's one to think about: Since the Harry and Hermione who have just come back have already fixed everything, where are the Harry and Hermione that are about to leave going and what are they going to find? Actually, we believe that J.K.R. is assuming that the two timelines converge again when a full cycle is completed, but that still gets pretty profound.

Harry and Hermione tell Dumbledore that Sirius has escaped on Buckbeak. Checking to make sure their past selves have already evaporated from the room, Dumbledore lets them into the hospital room and locks the door as they slip back into bed. Just a moment later, Madam Pomfrey comes out of her office as she hears the headmaster lock up, and administers chocolate to them.

> Due to Harry and Hermione's perfect timing, there has been virtually no discontinuity between past and present events along the primary time-line - it is as if Harry and Hermione never left.

Harry and Hermione sit in their beds tensely waiting and listening. They suddenly hear loud, angry voices above them, and then as the voices come nearer, they hear Snape saying that since no one can Apparate or Disapparate inside the castle, it "has something to do with Potter."

> We keep hearing that no one can Apparate or Disapparate inside the castle - it has become a running bit. However, this is one of those issues where J.K.R. is using the running bit to overshadow the clues. We already know that Dobby and Fawkes can do something-or-other inside the castle, even if it's not Apparating, so why not others? This appears to be a septology enigma.

As they burst into the room, Fudge is upset, Snape is furious, but Dumbledore's eyes are "twinkling behind his glasses." He seems quite amused.

> Where have we seen this "amused" or Cheshire Cat-like look on Dumbledore's face before? Was it earlier in this book, in Hagrid's hut, when Buckbeak got

free? How about in Book 2 when Fawkes brought Harry, Ron, and Ginny (we won't mention Lockhart) back up from the Chamber of Secrets? Remember how Dumbledore contentedly "beamed" while everyone else is in shock just to see them alive? There is something about his eyes. This impish look tends to coincide with Dumbledore having prior knowledge of the events (or maybe even a hand in them?). Therefore, whenever Dumbledore has an amused expression, HP Sleuths should be suspicious that he is (was?) (will be?) up to something.

Snape accuses Harry and Hermione of helping Black escape, but Dumbledore comments that unless Snape is saying that Harry can be "in two places at once," he could not have done anything. Madam Pomfrey and Fudge are dumbfounded at Snape's accusations, while Fudge even questions his sanity.

HP Sleuths – you are getting a rare and valuable lesson here! We get to see exactly how Dumbledore's brain (a.k.a. J.K.R.'s own brain) works. This time we have the advantage of knowing what Dumbledore knows, so we can observe how he plays with people. Notice how Dumbledore actually tells Fudge and Snape how it happened (Harry in two places at once), but in such a way that they have to dismiss it? He keeps doing that, too. And he (J.K.R.) will do it again to others (and us) in the future - when we don't know all the facts. CONSTANT VIGILANCE!

Fudge is worried that if people find out the hippogriff also got away, his reputation may suffer. He assures Dumbledore he will have the dementors removed from the school grounds - as he is aghast that they would have tried to administer the *kiss* on an innocent student. He suggests maybe putting dragons at the school entrance. Dumbledore replies that "Hagrid would like that." Dumbledore escorts Fudge and Snape out of the hospital wing. They are happy to see Ron wake up, and Hermione tells him the whole Time-Turner story.

Were the dementors working on orders, or simply looking for a tasty snack? Since they can't see, did they know they were attacking Harry, or did they think he was someone else? This really reveals Fudge's priorities here. He is far more concerned about his reputation than he is about the welfare of innocent beings. Dumbledore's comment implies that he might have somehow observed or found out about Norbert. Just more mystery type stuff.

By the next day, Snape had coincidentally "let slip" to all of Slytherin that Professor Lupin is a werewolf, so Lupin has resigned. As Lupin packs, he tells Harry that although Dumbledore convinced Fudge that Lupin had been trying to save Harry, the parents will not want a werewolf teaching at the school. Harry bemoans that Lupin was the best Defense Against the Dark Arts teacher they ever had, but Lupin says he does not want to endanger the students. Lupin asks about Harry's Patronus, and Harry wants to know how he knew about that. Lupin says it had to be a Patronus that drove the dementors away, and verifies that Harry's father did, indeed, transform into a stag, which is why he was called "Prongs."

Oops! There goes another Defense Against the Dark Arts teacher... Are we convinced that Lupin really just assumed Harry had cast a Patronus to disperse the dementors, or did he have some *inside* information? Why was Harry's Patronus in the form of his father's Animagus animal? Is that strictly because of the influence of his father in Harry's subconscious, or is there more meaning to it?

Lupin gives Harry back his Invisibility Cloak and Marauder's Map, commenting that he has "no hesitation" in saying that Harry's father would have been disappointed if Harry had never found any secret passages. He assures Harry that they "will meet again." Dumbledore comes in and says goodbye to Lupin who leaves quickly.

Lupin is so confident about what Harry's father would think. That is another hint in our Lupin septology mystery. So, does it qualify as a coincidence or just ironic that Harry ended up with the Marauder's Map? Clearly, the Marauder's Map and the Invisibility Cloak (which we now know both came from Harry's father), are being used exceptionally well...

Harry tells Dumbledore about Professor Trelawney's prediction - that the Dark Lord's servant would attempt to return (before midnight) to help him come back to power. Dumbledore is interested, saying that might be her second accurate prediction ever. Dumbledore explains that (as proved by all of Professor Trelawney's erroneous predictions) the complexity of peoples' actions on others around them makes "*predicting*" the future extremely difficult.

You mean Trelawney actually had another accurate prediction? If her first accurate prediction was anything like this one, the first must have been a real whopper. Wonder what it was? Most likely an important septology clue, of course (Rule #2). HP Sleuths don't need an orb to see how all the characters are working hard to convince us that Professor Trelawney is a fraud. Dumbledore is rightfully as skeptical of Professor Trelawney's forecasting talents as the rest of the school. However, notice that he only questions her capability to interpret the outcome of events, and not her knowledge of those events. He is giving credence to her ability to really see the signs. HP Sleuths are anxiously waiting her next *mis*-interpretation.

Harry is upset that because he stopped Sirius and Lupin from killing Pettigrew, it would be his own fault if Voldemort comes back into power. Dumbledore tells Harry that he should have learned from the Time-Turner that fate is highly complex, with too many options to make assumptions about any one action. He also informs Harry that when one wizard saves another's life, it creates a unique bond.

J.K.R. is doing it again - giving us only pieces of information. What kind of bond is created? Is there a magical connection as well? Does this mean that Peter would be obligated to save Harry from Voldemort in return, or how does this "bond" thing work? We need to know more!

Dumbledore explains that Voldemort would not like his servant to be in the debt of Harry Potter. He advises that there may come a "time" when it will benefit Harry that he did so.

Now **that** is a leading statement...

Harry tells Dumbledore how he thought the person he saw cast the Patronus was his father. Dumbledore is not surprised, as everyone thinks it uncanny how much Harry resembles his father - except for his....

...Yes ...his eyes - which Dumbledore reinforces are his mother's. Dumbledore is relentlessly beating into us that Harry is his father's son (Gryffindor?) - except for those (Slytherin??) green eyes from his mother. What is so special about Harry's eyes?

Dumbledore also emphasizes to Harry that it was Harry's father's influence in him that produced that particular Patronus - that last night, "Prongs rode again." Sirius had revealed to Dumbledore (when they talked last night) about how they had all become Animagi, which Dumbledore considered to be an "extraordinary achievement" (especially keeping it secret from him).

Here is another example of how J.K.R. so cleverly integrates plot elements with the previous events. We find out that all 3 Animagi kept their secret from Dumbledore. Why was that so difficult? Because we learned in Book 2 that Dumbledore was their Transfiguration teacher. (Wonder how well they did on their exams? tee-hee) If they kept that from Dumbledore, what else might they have kept from him?? (Sounds like a potential monster of a Lupin septology clue that gives us goose bumps and makes us head for Ogden's Old Firewhiskey when we think about it!)

All of Harry's class is depressed about losing Professor Lupin. They speculate about who could be hired to replace him, and Dean Thomas hopes it will be a vampire.

Did anyone ever tell Dean to be careful about what he wishes for - since it might come true (in not quite the way he expected)? Wonder if there is a potion to counteract the effects of vampirism similar to Wolfsbane potion? No matter, according to Percy, Snape is always interested in the job. (hehe) Wonder if he'll get it next year?

As the school year is coming to a close, Harry becomes more depressed thinking about whether Pettigrew has returned to Voldemort and about his own return to the Dursleys. Having thought for even a short time (half-hour) that he was definitely free of the Dursleys, makes the reality of going back to them far worse.

The first half of Professor Trelawney's prediction did come true exactly as foretold. HP Sleuths should not doubt that the second half could come to pass. The events have been set into motion, and the Voldemort time bomb is ticking...

Harry, Ron, and Hermione pass all their exams, yet Harry suspects that Snape had been coerced by Dumbledore to let him pass Potions. Percy receives top-grade N.E.W.T.s, Fred and George get a few O.W.L.s, and Gryffindor wins the House Cup for the third year in a row. Hermione decides to regain some sanity by dropping her Muggle studies course (along with Divination) and gives up the Time-Turner.

> Hermione has discovered the odd contradiction that by giving up all that time, she ends up with more time. ☺ If HP Sleuths recall, J.K.R. gave us a big hint that Hermione was up to something with this year's class schedule all the way back in Book 2 (Chapter 14). When everyone was trying to decide between all the different classes, J.K.R. told us that Hermione "signed up for everything." Of course, it looked like a figure of speech, and we were intended to interpret it as such, but she had meant it literally. Gotta watch those figures of speech...

On the Hogwarts Express, a very tiny gray owl that can barely carry a letter appears outside the train window. Harry retrieves it. The bitty owl is acting very pleased with itself for making the delivery.

> This bitty owl may be a young owl, a burrowing owl, or (as mentioned in Chapter 14) a *Scops* owl, which is described as handling local deliveries only. Although this owl seems even smaller than a Scops, it can obviously handle (and is excited to do so) much farther deliveries. HP Sleuths should keep an eagle eye on owls since we have seen that the breed of owl in the Harry Potter septology is highly significant.

The letter is from Sirius - he says he is in hiding, but dares not mention where. He was concerned about whether the teeny owl could make it, but realized it was very eager to try. He also lets Harry know that he was the one who sent Harry the Firebolt. ("Ha!" says Hermione.)

> Yes - Hermione was right even about the Firebolt. We are fairly confident that we can trust her judgement, so that is why we have added a corollary to our 4 Rules of Constant Vigilance (HP Sleuths keep in mind, however, that when emotions are involved, rules can be broken...).

Sirius explains that Crookshanks took the order to the Owl Office, using Harry's name, but deducting the gold from Sirius' own Gringotts vault.

> We know that wizards use owl-order. Do they also have Gringotts debit cards? How does that deducting money thing work? Also, how is it that no one noticed any activity on the account of an escaped convict? Is Gringotts sort of like a Swiss bank account - where their transactions are all private? There is also the question as to how Sirius got so much money himself? What is his background and who/where are his relatives?

To Harry's delight, Sirius has enclosed a signed statement (as Harry's Godfather) giving Harry permission to visit Hogsmeade on weekends during the next year.

> HP Sleuths - we seem to already have a clue for Book 4. How did Sirius know that Harry needed permission to visit Hogsmeade? He obviously has already been in communication with **someone** (Dumbledore?) from his hideout.

If Harry ever needs him, Sirius says that Hedwig will find him. On the back side of the letter, Sirius has a P.S. saying that it was his fault Ron no longer has his rat, so Ron should keep the little owl. Ron holds the owl up for Crookshanks' inspection, and upon receiving a purr, Ron accepts. Harry keeps re-reading his letter from Sirius, and it is still in his hand when Uncle Vernon spots him, asking if it is another form to sign. Harry replies that it is from his Godfather - his parent's best friend - who is a convicted murderer and has broken out of wizard prison.

> Now, we know Hedwig is highly intelligent, and we know she can find Harry wherever he ends up, but how does she find a convicted murderer in hiding when no one else can find him? There is definitely some interesting magic or communication process going on with owl deliveries or animal communications that has yet to be explained.

Harry explains to a horrified Uncle Vernon that his Godfather likes to stay in touch and make sure Harry is happy....

Curiosities

★ Sirius hasn't been spending much money in Azkaban, and he must have enough Galleons to be able to afford a Firebolt. Wonder if his source of gold is related to the mystery?

✳ You could make a case that there had been other hints about Lupin being a werewolf from a number of moon-type references in this book (such as Magnolia Crescent), but they were so masterfully subtle that they did not make for strong evidence. If HP Sleuths want a challenge, they can go back and find a number of them (one, in paticular, seems to be a continuity error).

✳ Well, Harry's miniature Sneakoscope seems to have been functioning normally after all. However, were there other instances (besides tying it to Errol's leg) when there could have been more than one deception going on at a time? Highly possible.

——————✳——————

Key Rememberit Clues from Book 3

(HARRY POTTER AND THE PRISONER OF AZKABAN)

Book 3 Mysteries Not Yet Solved

- Why did the dementors try to get rid of Harry first?
- How do dementors communicate?
- Where do dementors come from, and to whom will they be loyal?
- Could anyone else have escaped from Azkaban?
- Can Sirius or other wizards "talk" to animals?
- What is the magic behind Owl Post and Owls?
- Is there something going on with flies and bugs?
- Where did Percy get Scabbers? (And why was Ron allowed to take him to school?)
- What kind of bond is there now between Harry and Wormtail, and how does that work?
- Could the prediction of Voldemort's return after 12 years be the destiny of 12?
- Did Prof. Trelawney make a true prediction (is the rest going to happen)?
- Why did (does) Voldemort want to kill Harry?
- What happened the night Harry's parents died, and why was the house destroyed?
- Was the male voice, in Harry's flashback, his father?
- Voldemort says he killed Harry's father first – Voldemort's a liar, do we believe him?
- How did everyone all know about and communicate the events that took place the night Voldemort attacked the Potters?
- How did Dumbledore get James' Invisibility Cloak, and how did Hagrid get the key to the Potter's vault?
- Who are Harry's ancestors on *both* sides?
- What happened to Neville's parents?
- What is the septology mystery around Lupin?
- Who is keeping track of Harry and how?
- Is Dumbledore in control of events?
- Who are Dumbledore's sources that are keeping track of Voldemort, and how?
- Who is Dumbledore, what does he know, and what is his past.

- Who was on the list of registered Animagi (was Dumbledore?), and what forms do they take?

- If you can't Apparate or Disapparate in Hogwarts, then what is it that Dobby and Fawkes do to appear and disappear?

- What are *Switching Spells* and how do they work?

- Does the victim of a *Shrinking Solution* keep his/it's memory?

- Do the people who seem like they can read minds have *inside* information?

- Why does Snape hate Harry so much?

- Is Cornelius Fudge a fair, honest Minister?

- Can Penelope be trusted?

- How much control does Lucius Malfoy (and his money) have over the Ministry?

- What happened during the goblin rebellions, and who won?

- How did Nick get (nearly) beheaded, and who (nearly) did it?

- Do ghosts show up on the Marauders Map?

- Do you have to be moving to show up on Marauders Map?

- Why haven't we seen an Astronomy class or the tallest tower?

- Who/What drives Hogwarts Express and what did Lupin "discuss" with him/it?

 # BOOK 4 MYSTERIES

About Book 4

Statistics

Book 4 Title - *Harry Potter and the Goblet of Fire* - by J. K. Rowling

Working Titles: *Harry Potter and the Doomspell Tournament*
Harry Potter and the Triwizard Tournament
by J. K. Rowling

Facts & Statistics:
- First United Kingdom printing, Bloomsbury Publishing - July 8, 2000
- Simultaneous First United States printing, Scholastic Inc. - July 8, 2000
- Initial U.K Print Run of 1.5 million copies
- Initial U.S. Print run of 3.8 million copies
- Almost 3 million copies sold in the first week
- Fastest selling book in history
- Many U.S. bookstores were open at midnight to sell to the waiting crowds

Awards:
- Scottish Arts Council Book Award, 2001
- Children's Book Award 9-11 category, 2001
- Audio Book Grammy Award - Best Spoken Word Album for Children, February 2001
  Jim Dale, reader
  Random House Audio Publishing Group

Key Mystery Characters

STUDENTS

Lavender Brown (Gryffindor)
Cho Chang (Ravenclaw)
Penelope Clearwater (Ravenclaw)
Colin Creevey (Gryffindor)
Dennis Creevey (Gryffindor)
Crabbe (Slytherin)
Fleur Delacour (Beauxbatons)
Cedric Diggory (Hufflepuff)
Seamus Finnegan (Gryffindor)
Marcus Flint (Slytherin)
Goyle (Slytherin)
Hermione Granger (Gryffindor)
Lee Jordan (Gryffindor)
Viktor Krum (Durmstrang)
Neville Longbottom (Gryffindor)
Draco Malfoy (Slytherin)
Parvati Patil (Gryffindor)
Padma Patil (Ravenclaw)
Harry Potter (Gryffindor)
Dean Thomas (Gryffindor)
Fred Weasley (Gryffindor)
George Weasley (Gryffindor)
Ginny Weasley (Gryffindor)
Percy Weasley (Gryffindor)
Ron Weasley (Gryffindor)
Oliver Wood (Gryffindor)

RELATIVES

Mr. Crabbe
Crouch's Wife & Son
Amos Diggory
Cousin Dudley Dursley
Aunt Marge (Miss Marjorie) Dursley
Aunt Petunia Dursley
Uncle Vernon Dursley
The Fawcetts
Gabrielle
Mr. & Mrs. Granger
Mr. Goyle
Longbottom Relative - Neville's Gran
Lucius Malfoy
Mr. Nott
James Potter
Lily Potter
Mr. Arthur Weasley
Bill Weasley
Charlie Weasley
Mrs. Molly Weasley

TEACHERS & STAFF

Prof. Binns (History of Magic)
Prof. Albus Dumbledore (Headmaster)
Argus Filch (Caretaker)
Prof. Flitwick (Charms)
Rubeus Hagrid (Groundskeeper and Keeper of the Keys)
Professor Karkaroff (Headmaster of Durmstrang)
Mme. Olympe Maxime (Headmistress of Beauxbatons)
Prof. Minerva McGonagall (Deputy Headmistress/Transfiguration)
Prof. Mad-Eye Moody (Defense against the Dark Arts)
Madam Irma Pince (Librarian)
Madam Pomfrey (Nurse)
Prof. Sinistra (Astronomy)
Prof. Severus Snape (Potions Master)
Prof. Sprout (Herbology)
Prof. Sibyll Trelawney (Divination)
Prof. Vector (Arithmancy)

Key Mystery Characters (continued)

OTHER HUMANS

Ludo Bagman
Sirius Black
Frank Bryce
Barty Crouch
Arabella Figg
Mundungus Fletcher
Florence
Cornelius Fudge
Bertha Jorkins
Lestranges
Macnair
Mr. Ollivander
Warlock Perkins
Peter Pettigrew
Rita Skeeter
Lord Voldemort ("You-Know-Who")

CREATURES & ENTITIES

Bloody Baron (Slytherin Ghost)
Buckbeak (Beaky)
Crookshanks the cat/Kneazle dementors
Dobby
Fang the boarhound
Fat Lady Portrait
Fawkes (the phoenix)
Hedwig the owl
Hogwarts Lake Squid
Merchieftainess Murcus
Sir Nicolas de Mimsy-Porpington
Moaning Myrtle
Nearly-Headless Nick (Gryffindor Ghost)
Mrs. Norris the cat
Peeves the Poltergeist
Pigwidgeon the owl
Padfoot (Sirius Black dog Animagus)
Scabbers the rat   (former Pettigrew Animagus)
Snuffles (Nickname of Padfoot)
Winky
Wormtail (Peter Pettigrew – rat Animagus)

Bits and Rememberits

These are clues and unsolved mysteries from previous books that HP Sleuths should keep in mind as they read Book 2. Keep alert for more evidence....

Rememberits

Running Bits That May Be Clues

Body Parts
- Noses
- Eyes
- Ears
- Feet
- Heart
- Stomach
- Hands and Fingers
- Untidy and/or long Hair

Creatures
- Slugs
- Spiders
- Beetles, Cockroaches, and Scarabs
- Flies and Bugs in general

Numbers
- The number 12 and Chapter 12s
- The number 13 and Chapter 13s

Woolies
- Socks
- Mrs. Weasley's Sweaters

Wonderland
- Watches and Clocks
- Hares and Rabbits

Miscellaneous
- Ogden's Old Firewhiskey
- Orphans
- Banging noises

Questions Still Bugging Us...

- Where do dementors come from, and to whom will they be loyal?
- Could anyone else have escaped from Azkaban?
- What is the magic behind Owl Post and Owls?
- Is there something going on with flies and bugs?
- What kind of bond is there now between Harry and Wormtail, and how does that work?
- Could the prediction of Voldemort's return after 12 years be the destiny of 12?
- Did Prof. Trelawney make a true prediction (is the rest going to happen)?
- Why did (does) Voldemort want to kill Harry?
- What happened the night Harry's parents died, and why was the house destroyed?
- Was the male voice, in Harry's flashback, his father?
- Voldemort says he killed Harry's father first – Voldemort's a liar, do we believe him?
- How did everyone all know about and communicate the events that took place the night Voldemort attacked the Potters?
- Is there a reason that Mrs. Figg's house smells just like an Apothecary?
- Who is keeping track of Harry and how?

- Is Dumbledore in control of events?
- Who are Dumbledore's sources that are keeping track of Voldemort, and how?
- Who was on the list of registered Animagi (was Dumbledore?), and what forms do they take?
- Who is Dumbledore, what does he know, and what is his past.
- What is the significance of long fingers?
- Can Dumbledore see through Invisibility Cloaks?
- If you can't Apparate or Disapparate in Hogwarts, then what is it that Dobby and Fawkes do to appear and disappear?
- What are *Switching Spells* and how do they work?
- Do the people who seem like they can read minds have *inside* information?
- Why does Snape hate Harry so much?
- Is Cornelius Fudge a fair, honest Minister?
- How much control does Lucius Malfoy (and his money) have over the Ministry?
- Why did Lucius Malfoy call Harry's parents "meddlesome fools" - what did they find out?
- Why are house-elves subservient to wizards – how did that happen?
- How powerful are house-elves?
- What happened during the goblin rebellions, and who won?
- What happened to Neville's parents?
- Why did the Sorting Hat take so long with Seamus and Neville?
- What is the background of the Bloody Baron and what is he up to?
- Why is Peeves allowed to remain at Hogwarts?
- Are Myrtle's special water skills unique for a ghost?
- Why haven't we seen an Astronomy class or the tallest tower?
- Will Gilderoy get his memory back?
- Remember *Memory Charms*

    Don't forget *Memory Charms*

    "*Obliviate!*"

    Memory Charms????

—— *Interesting Tidbits* ——

Some Background on Book 4:

- As many fans will recall, the *working title* for Book 4 was *Harry Potter and the Doomspell Tournament.* J.K.R. explains in an interview with *Entertainment Weekly* that she actually had considered another potential title, "*Harry Potter and the TriWizard Tournament*" before choosing "*Goblet of Fire.*" She decided on *Goblet of Fire* because goblets convey an image of "destiny."

   ☞ During an interview with *SouthWestNews.com*, J.K.R. says that she had already written what she thought was half the book, when she discovered a fatal flaw. She ended up having to go back and delete a character and re-write a large part of it (as if it wasn't big enough). According to the interview with the BBC, J.K.R revealed that the character was a cousin of Ron Weasley's, but her presence blew the plot. Hmmmm....

Tidbits:

   ☞ WWP's First Edition Book 4 (for which we stood in line at midnight on the night they released it) did not survive.☹ It now consists of several "pamphlets," since the binding could not stand up to all the bending, highlighting, folding, and scribbling we did to it (plus, we estimate we read all 700 pages about 7 times!). You might say it's our super-annotated version. It's also our favorite copy of the book.

What HP Sleuths Have to Notice in Book 4

   ☞ Book 4 ends an era of Harry's life. That is what J.K.R. has specified in an interview with *CBC Newsworld*. She said that Harry will not be as protected after this. (Shiver)

WWP's Rules of CONSTANT VIGILANCE!

Never let your guard down with J.K.R. These are The Rules to remember (unless your memory is as bad as Neville's). Rules for HP Sleuths:

1) **If she reinforces it, she means it (and wants us to remember it).**
2) **If she suddenly interrupts something, she's hiding a key clue!**
3) **There's no such thing as a coincidence.**
4) **Don't take a character's word for it.**
        Corollaries
        4a) Hermione is usually right (except when she gets emotional)
        4b) Ron is usually wrong (except when he makes a joke about it)

(see WWP Help Desk FAQs for full explanation)

Chapter 1 Analysis

Clues

In the village of Little Hangleton is "the Riddle House." It had been owned by the "rich, snobbish, and rude" Riddle family (consisting of mother, father, and grown-up son, Tom – who was even more rude than his parents). One morning, about fifty years ago, all three Riddles had been found dead by their maid. Their gardener, Frank Bryce, who lived in a cottage on the grounds, was suspected and questioned, although they didn't believe him when he described a dark-haired, pale teenager who he saw there that day. Frank was acquitted by a medical inquest, as there was astonishingly no evidence whatsoever of any physical injuries. Their deaths remained a mystery.

People may debate over whether this book is a children's fantasy or not, but there is no doubt from this chapter that this book is a mystery. Why were these people killed? How were these people killed? Why were there no marks at all on their bodies? Who is this current wealthy owner? HP Sleuths are correct to assume from Chapter 17 in Book 2, that the grown-up Tom Riddle is Tom Senior, father of Voldemort. He must have gone back to live with his own parents after supposedly abandoning his wife - Voldemort's mother. Of course, the dark-haired pale teenager who Frank saw would have been Tom Riddle Junior (Voldemort), fresh out of Hogwarts, as he came to commit the murders. We conclude from this that Voldemort murdered his own grandparents as well (Riddle managed to forget to mention that part to Harry).

The Riddles were buried in the Little Hangleton churchyard, and Frank returned to his duties as gardener. The current "wealthy" owner does not reside there, but pays Frank to keep up the grounds.

"Wealthy" owner? We do know someone who fits that description. It could be Lucius Malfoy, or Voldemort, himself. This will haunt us for a while.

It is an August night of the present time, and Frank sees light glimmering in the upper windows, so goes up to the house to investigate. Thinking it to be intruders, he creeps up the stairs and listens through a partially open door. He hears a man called "Wormtail" talk to his "master," who is seated in a chair with its back to the door, about "milking Nagini" for feeding. They discuss staying here a week (maybe longer), and about a plan that must wait until after the "Quidditch World Cup."

As we know from Book 3, Wormtail is an alias for Peter Pettigrew, formerly known as Scabbers (but his best friends just call him rat). We now know that Wormtail has, indeed, returned to his master, which means that the final part of Professor Trelawney's prediction has been set in motion. (shiver)

The "master" is clearly Voldemort. Wormtail is uncertain about their plan, and questions that "if he murders..." but he is cut-off and told that "if he follows the plan, the Ministry need never know that anyone else besides Bertha Jorkins has died." Voldemort tells Wormtail to do it "quietly and without fuss...one more death and our path to Harry Potter is clear."

> WWP Hintoscope is wobbling perilously! Someone **else** will die? Someone besides Bertha Jorkins? Voldemort says this other person will die as a means to get to Harry. Wouldn't you know it, just as Wormtail is about to mention who, he is cut-off by Voldemort. Once again, we are denied evidence (Rule #2) - meaning this is a critical clue. HP Sleuths should be aware that this was never completely clarified as of the end of this book, so is it still a mystery?! HP Sleuths – watch for evidence.

The plan involves information they retrieved from Bertha (who worked for the Ministry), before killing her. Voldemort says that *Memory Charms* are able to be broken by powerful wizards "as I proved when I questioned her," and that Bertha was "fit for nothing after my questioning."

> The HP Hintoscope is making a big rumbling sound.... HP Sleuths should try to remember what Voldemort says about *Memory Charms* – like the one Bertha had done to her. It doesn't sound as if breaking memory charms is very safe.

Frank hears Voldemort talk about a plot with "his faithful servant at Hogwarts" to murder a boy named Harry Potter.

> Now, whom do we know is mean and nasty, knows Dark magic, has it in for Harry, and is at Hogwarts? We could guess Snape, but that is exactly what J.K.R. probably wants us to do. On the other hand, who else could be a servant of Voldemort? There are still a few teachers we know nothing about, but none of them have ever tried to do anything to Harry (let alone attack another wizard). This story-line clue could be a red herring, but keep your fishing poles handy....

Wormtail defends his loyalty - having kidnapped Bertha and brought her to Voldemort, but Voldemort knows it's a lie. Voldemort asserts that Wormtail got stuck with Bertha and is only here because he has no where else to go, plus is thinking about deserting again.

> Here is reinforcement that Voldemort can truly sense when someone is lying. We saw it before in Chapter 17 of Book 1, when Voldemort told Quirrell that Harry was lying about the Stone, and, in fact, knew it was in Harry's pocket. This confirms that was not due to some special spell or incident that is unique to Book 1, since we now see Voldemort using that *instinct* here again.

Voldemort says he has a task for Wormtail that "many of my followers would give their right hands to perform." Voldemort asserts that Wormtail's task will be as essential and "useful" as Bertha Jorkins'. He reassures Wormtail that he's not implying that Wormtail will also be killed.

So would those of you who have already read this book like to comment on J.K.R.'s sense of humor? Or should we just say that Voldemort is serious about loyalty?

Voldemort calls a 12-foot long snake that slithers right past Frank into the room. The snake, Nagini, notifies Voldemort about the Muggle that is right outside listening to them. Voldemort has Wormtail "invite" him in. Frank claims that his wife will soon be looking for him, but Voldemort says not to lie - he can always tell.

Even if we don't believe everything Voldemort says (we have seen him lie several times), we now have seen enough evidence to believe that Voldemort probably does have the capability of knowing if people are lying to him.

Frank demands that the Dark "Lord" turn his chair to face him. Upon seeing Voldemort, the man shrieks in terror, and the Dark Lord slays him with a wave of his wand.

Gulp! Voldemort can wave a wand? HP Sleuths - it's time to go to *red alert*. Unless something happens to stop him, it looks as if, with the help of his servant, Voldemort will return as predicted.

At that moment, Harry Potter (who is 200 miles away at Privet Drive) jolts awake from a nightmare.

Curiosities

In an interview with SouthWestNews.com, J.K.R. has specifically stated that Harry is, *by instinct*, becoming very talented in the Defense Against Dark Arts. From what we can see in this chapter, he's going to need it.....

Chapter 2 Analysis

Clues

Harry, who has just awakened from a nightmare, feels a sharp burning sensation from the scar on his forehead. He checks it in the mirror, but it looks normal otherwise.

> Harry's own personal built-in Dark detector! And Voldemort does not have to be nearby (we are told 200 miles away) to activate it. J.K.R. is showing us that Harry is also tied to Voldemort through "dreams."

Harry can remember the dream about Voldemort and Wormtail, but cannot remember the name of the person they supposedly had killed, and did not recognize the old man. Harry does remember that they now were plotting to kill him.

> Unfortunately, Harry did not remember the detail about Voldemort holding a wand, so is not alerted and is not able to able to let anyone else know that.

Harry peers outside his window, but does not see anything - not even a cat.

> This obviously implies that there are usually cats hanging around - even in the middle of the night. Is their lack of presence significant, or are they just off chasing a rat?

Harry is concerned, since the last time his scar had hurt, Voldemort had been close by. In his room at Privet Drive, Harry cannot conceive of Voldemort, the most powerful Dark Wizard in a century, sneaking around this Muggle neighborhood. He listens for a creaking stair or the sound of a cloak swishing, but Dudley's snore is the only sound.

> We have already been told (Rule #1) that one of the Dursley's stairs creaks. We should not rule out a visit by someone unexpected (and uninvited). HP Sleuths need to keep on their toes.

Harry contemplates whom he might be able to ask about the scar pain, and when he thinks about Dumbledore, he realizes that he has no idea where Dumbledore spends the summer.

> Okay, we got the hint - J.K.R. must want us to start thinking about where Dumbledore is during the summer. We're thinking about it.... We're still thinking about it.... Now that we've thought about it... we can confidently say... we have no clue. During the summer, Dumbledore could visit Harry's neighborhood (in disguise), he could be working with Nicolas Flamel, he could be doing vital wizarding projects, or any number of our other theories. The problem is, we seem to lacking something here - evidence. HP Sleuths just keep on thinking....

It finally occurs to Harry to write to Sirius (who is still in hiding in a sunny location), but Harry does not mention the dream, as he does not want it to appear that he is too worried.

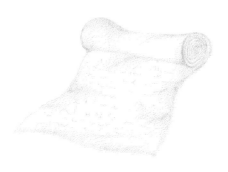

──────────── Other Oddities ────────────

✳ J.K.R. describes how, as the sun began to rise, "Harry's lamp seemed to grow dimmer as cold gray light that proceeds sunrise slowly crept in." Talk about observant – now that's a description for both artist and scientist. ☺

✳ Again, we are reminded (Rule #1) that Voldemort is the most powerful wizard in a century. Why is it so important to know this? And who was his predecessor?

✳ Although Harry stands in front of his mirror twice, we are specifically told that he only looks at his reflection once. It is probably nothing, but just in case....

Chapter 3 Analysis

Clues

Harry's Cousin, Dudley, has had a bad summer. Back at his boarding school, Smeltings, Dudley has been getting bad marks, bullying other students, and worst of all, the school outfitters do not stock knickerbockers big enough to fit him anymore. Aunt Petunia requires the whole family to go on a diet as a support group for Dudley. They eat what Uncle Vernon calls "rabbit food," and for breakfast, they each get a single grapefruit quarter. In desperation, skinny Harry writes to his friends for food that he secretly stashes under the loose floorboards in his room. They have also sent him cakes for his birthday - which he carefully rations over the next couple of weeks.

> More rabbit references - does anyone know what happened to Rabbit in J.K.R.'s very first book? Did he run off to Hogsmeade or nibble on some cake in Wonderland?

Mrs. Weasley sends a letter (plastered in stamps) via Muggle postman, to formally ask Uncle Vernon's permission to bring Harry to the Quidditch World Cup match. They offer to have Harry stay for the rest of the summer and to get him back to school when it is time. Harry tells Uncle Vernon that if he can't go to the World Cup, he will just go up and finish his letter to Sirius, his convicted murderer godfather. Harry explains that he hasn't written to him in a while, so if he doesn't do so soon, his godfather may think Harry is being "mistreated." After pondering that predicament, Uncle Vernon decides to let Harry go to the Weasleys and the World Cup.

> It is unclear whether Harry has told the Dursleys that his "convicted murderer" godfather is the one and only Black they saw on TV. We don't think so, since Sirius is still officially on the run, and the house does not seem to have bars on all the windows.

Harry sends his letter with Hedwig to Sirius, asking about the scar and letting Sirius know that he will be attending the World Cup with the Weasleys.

Curiosities

✳ We are being led to assume that Hedwig can definitely find Sirius.

Chapter 4 Analysis

(BACK TO THE BURROW)

Clues

While waiting for the Weasleys to pick up Harry, the Dursleys hear voices from behind their boarded-up electric fireplace. The Weasleys have arrived, but are trapped. Mr. Weasley blasts through the wall, saying that he will repair it before they leave - but that does not make the Dursleys any less outraged. Mr. Weasley tries to explain that he had temporarily hooked up their fireplace to the Floo Network so they could easily stop by for Harry, but did not know it had been converted. Fred and George go up to Harry's room to get his stuff, and in the process, get a good look at the infamous Dudley. On their way back out with Harry's trunk, Fred drops some candies out of his pocket and scrambles to pick them back up.

> Makes sense – the ultimate Muggles rejecting anything natural. No proper appreciation of fireplaces. Something to keep in mind here - any fireplace can be connected to the Floo Network at any time. Have you inspected your fireplace lately?

Harry says "goodbye," and turns to go, but when the Dursleys do not reply, Mr. Weasley insists that they show Harry some courtesy. Suddenly Dudley starts gagging and they are aghast to see his tongue has grown a foot long, where he lies on the floor next to one of Fred's candy wrappers.

> We do not have to be told that Fred and George are pranksters, but in Book 4, their escapades have been elevated to *professional* level. As much as we love Fred and George, we are learning not to trust them - especially if it's food.

Mr. Weasley attempts to calm the Dursleys, but they are hysterical, so Harry leaves - letting Mr. Weasley deal with them.

Curiosities

✳ We have still not been told how to tell Fred and George apart (if there is any way).

✳ So what did Mr. Weasley have to do in order to placate the Dursleys?

Chapter 5 Analysis

Clues

Harry arrives at *the Burrow*, where Fred is ecstatic to hear that Dudley had fallen for the Ton-Tongue Toffee bait (which he and George had invented). Previously, they had invented Weasley's Wizard Wheezes for a joke shop they wanted to open up, but Mrs. Weasley burned the order forms. She was upset with them for only getting a few O.W.L.s, and afraid they will get into trouble with the Improper Use of Magic Office. She also is frustrated by their booby-trapped items (such as fake wands) that they leave around.

> Hmmm - *Fred and George's Fine Wands since 2000* (hehehee) We don't know if we even **want** to know what "Weasley's Wizard Wheezes" do. We are being warned not to trust anything from Fred and George - not even wands. Wonder if anyone's told the bad guys? So why aren't Fred and George getting pelted with owls for breaking the *Decree for the Reasonable Restriction of Underage Sorcery*? (The department probably just gave up on them... after too many owls dropped dead from exhaustion – hee-hee).

Harry finally meets the two oldest Weasley brothers - Charlie, who works with dragons in Rumania, and Bill, who works in Egypt for Gringotts Bank. Harry had presumed Bill would be an older version of the bossy, stiff-collared Percy, but instead, Bill has a pony tail, a fang-tooth earring, and wears dragon-hide boots (Ginny thinks he's cool). Hermione Granger is already there, too.

> Watch out Indiana Jones - here comes Bill Weasley! A true treasure hunter, and a hunk at that ☺ There's a big role in a movie hiding in here somewhere. We can see it now - *Bill Weasley and the Temple of Doomspell (co-starring Harry Potter)*. (hehehee) Were those boots a present from Charlie?

Percy stays to himself in his room - working on a project for his new job in the Department of International Magical Cooperation at the Ministry of Magic. Ron says Percy is obsessed with his work, and reveres his boss, Mr. Crouch.

> Percy is so impressionable (translated *gullible*). Is that how he ended up with that rat for a pet?

Ron's owl, who he is calling "Pig," was named by Ginny, and is short for *Pigwidgeon*.

> The name Pigwidgeon is a variation on the name Pigwiggen, used by Michael Drayton in his poems from the 1600s. Pigwiggen is a tiny, fiendish fairy. As of Book 4, Ron's Pig has, thankfully, shown no signs of deviant behavior (we hope not - we like Pig).

After a bout of "table boxing" with Charlie, Bill repairs damage to one of the table legs and conjures a tablecloth out of mid-air with a "flick of the wand." Everyone sits down for dinner.

> Now doesn't Bill make sorcery look so easy? More indication that conjuring things out of mid-air is a sign of a powerful wizard. Still wondering how long *conjured* items last?

Percy and Mr. Weasley discuss Ludo Bagman, head of the Department of Magical Games and Sports, who secured the World Cup tickets for the Weasleys. Mr. Weasley had done a favor for Ludo - helped his brother Otto, who had gotten into trouble on account of a lawnmower with unnatural powers.

> Ludo Bagman sounds like a real friendly type of guy, although J.K.R. hasn't given him a very friendly last name. A "bagman" is sort of like a *bookie* - not totally appropriate for someone working in Games and Sports. Otto is not important to the story line but, just in case, HP Sleuths might make a note that Ludo has a brother that messes with Muggle things.

They also discuss how a member of Ludo's department, Bertha Jorkins, has been missing for over a month and Ludo has yet to send anyone to search for her. She has gone to Albania on holiday and never returned – no one has heard from her since. Mr. Weasley comments that Bertha is notorious for getting herself lost.

> Yes, we know from Book 2 who's supposed to be hiding in Albania. Even though Harry has forgotten that Bertha was the woman Voldemort killed in his dream, *we* have not. Why hasn't Ludo sent anyone to find her? Is he that inept? Possibly. Possibly not. Is Bertha really that inept? Possibly. Possibly not. Tons of story line and septology clues.

Percy says that Mr. Crouch seems to be personally concerned for her. Based on Crouch's behavior, it is Percy's opinion that Mr. Crouch is even "quite fond of her."

> That seems like more than just concern about an employee. Is that a Percy interpretation or is this relationship more than just business? If it were a positive relationship, it would seem that Mr. Crouch would have been on the case, with or without Bagman. So what's wrong with this picture?

Mrs. Weasley tells Harry to leave his school list with her so she can buy his supplies at Diagon Alley while they are all at the match.

Rowlinguistics

✳ The character of **Pigwiggen** is also related to Queen Mab and King Oberon (as appeared in Shakespeare's *A Midsummer Night's Dream*). Oberon is associated there with puckish pranks as well.

Curiosities

✳ Mr. Weasley Apparates with a "faint popping noise."

✳ Mrs. Weasley complains that Bill's hair is too long, but Ginny points out that it's not nearly as long as Dumbledore's. The most powerful wizard has extremely long hair, and a very powerful one has quite long hair. This is beginning to sound like a guy we read about called Samson. If anyone notices someone by the name of Delilah, please warn us immediately.

Clues

Since the kids are underage and do not know how to Apparate (de-materialize from one place and then re-materialize at another), Mr. Weasley will use a "Portkey" to transport them to the World Cup. The Portkeys must be placed and set up in advance, so they use items (punctured footballs, empty drink cans, or other litter) that can be left in plain sight. Percy (who is showing off his new ability) will be Apparating directly to the World Cup around midday with Bill and Charlie. Mrs. Weasley catches Fred and George trying to smuggle some Ton-Tongue Toffees to the World Cup. She is infuriated with them as she uses a *Summoning Charm* to retrieve the candies from all the places where the twins had stashed them.

> The purpose of this whole section is a wizarding lesson. We learn about Apparating, Portkeys, *Summoning Charms*, and that Fred and George are serious about their venture. Hopefully, HP Sleuths were good students and your heads aren't still filled with "dead flies"....

They get to Stoatshead Hill where their Portkey, a moldy-looking old boot, is located. Amos Diggory and his son, Cedric, greet them as they arrive. Mr. Diggory works in the Department for the Regulation and Control of Magical Creatures. Cedric is the Hufflepuff team Captain (and Seeker) who unintentionally beat Gryffindor last year, when Harry fainted from the dementors and fell off his broom. They determine that the Lovegoods are already at the site, and the Fawcetts could not get tickets, so everyone is present for the Portkey. When it is time for their Portkey to activate, they all gather around, holding onto it.

> The Lovegoods and Fawcetts have not been important, however, we should be aware of them. We do know that the Fawcetts currently have a child attending Hogwarts (S. Fawcett), who is a Ravenclaw and is interested in Quidditch (we will let HP Sleuths try to figure out how we know about the Quidditch part☺). We are told here that both of those families are in the general Weasley neighborhood, along with the Diggorys.

The Portkey activates with a lurch, and upon arriving at their destination, they land hard, most everyone falling over when they hit the ground.

Other Oddities

* For some reason, Charlie had to take the Apparating test twice.

* Fred and George were asleep at the foot of Harry's mattress in the morning – when and how did they get there? (What were they up to last night – maybe some candy stuffing?)

* Mr. Weasley and the kids stumble into rabbit holes as they are climbing Stoatshead Hill. Nonetheless, they don't see any white rabbits.

Chapter 7 Analysis

(Bagman and Crouch)

Clues

Mr. Weasley and the kids walk over to the field where they are renting camping space from a Muggle landowner. When the Muggle gets suspicious from watching them have trouble counting Muggle money, a wizard suddenly Apparates and performs a memory charm to "modify" his memory.

> HP Sleuths need to remember what they learn here about memory charms. Did someone say "Obliviate!"?

Although the tents around them were supposed to look Muggle-like, many had been "altered" by the addition of chimneys, multiple floors, and other unnatural features. Harry and Hermione erect a pair of Muggle-style two-man tents that hardly look big enough for them, however, when Harry steps inside, it opens into a three-room flat.

> Note the Dr. Who TARDIS-style enhancements of the tents, which is similar to the spatial *adjustments* Mr. Weasley had done on his Ford Anglia. For those HP Sleuths who are not as familiar with the Dr. Who series, the Doctor uses a police box (called a "TARDIS") as a time machine. It is a tiny little booth on the outside, but has multiple spacious rooms on the inside. The explanation is that the part we see on the outside is in our own time/space, however, the inside opens into a different time, so it occupies the larger space in that other time. Could J.K.R. be giving us *yet* more hints about time travel?

Mr. Weasley had borrowed the tents from his employee, Perkins. Harry found it interesting that it was furnished in "exactly the same sort of style as Mrs. Figg's house," and even has a smell of cats.

> Now the WWP Sleuthoscope is running in circles! Is there something special about Mrs. Figg's house? Why would Perkins have a tent decorated in Mrs. Figg's tastes? Remember - Mrs. Figg's house smells like cabbage (Polyjuice Potion?) and Perkin was the first name of the British imposter, Perkin Warbeck. There's something strange going on here.

Mr. Weasley has Fred, George, and Ginny help search for firewood, while sending Ron, Harry, and Hermione off for water. As they pass through the tents, Harry sees a strange assortment of witches and wizards from all over the world. Ron explains that the Bulgarian Seeker, Krum, is only about eighteen years-old and a "genius" at Quidditch.

> We already know that Fred and George can be a bit slippery, but HP Sleuths need to watch them really carefully as they search for firewood here. Are you watching? (Don't blink.)

On the way back from the water tap, Harry and Ron come across Oliver Wood, who introduces Harry to his parents and tells them that he has just been signed to the Puddlemere United reserve team. They also see a group of students from one of the other wizarding schools, and Harry is amazed to find out that there are a number of wizarding schools like Hogwarts in existence.

> Now, let's think - what do we know about Puddlemere United? If we consult our *Quidditch Through the Ages* reference, we see some potentially scary information. (If you don't have yours, get your e-Owl Order in now!) The team anthem is sung by Celestina Warbeck. Wow! There's the more hostile half of that imposter's name again (Perkin Warbeck) - what do we know about Celestina? It says she was raising funds for "St. Mungo's Hospital for Magical Maladies and Injuries." We have reason to believe that St. Mungo's is not the upstanding institution it claims to be (more on that shortly). So, Wood may have stepped into a hotbed.

Harry, Ron, and Hermione get back with the water and are greeted by George with the comment "You've been ages."

> WWP Sleuthoscope is spinning out of control! **Who's** been "ages"? Look who's talking! Seems to us Fred and George are the ones who might have spent a little extra time gathering that wood. Were they in the forest? Did anyone keep track of them? We now know that they are highly skilled wizards - even if they do use their talents mostly on practical jokes. We also know that *little* things (like rules and laws) never stopped them from getting into mischief. So, what trouble did they get into this time?

Mr. Weasley points out a number of the Ministry of Magic members as they go by. He mentions Cuthbert Mockridge, Head of the Goblin Liaison Office, Gilbert Wimple, with the Committee on Experimental Charms, Arnold Peasegood, an Obliviator, and Bode and Croaker - top secret agents ("unspeakables").

> A Who's Who of the Ministry. These names are both appropriate and interesting, but as of the end of this book, we have not encountered any of them again. Knowing J.K.R., that doesn't mean a thing. HP Sleuths – keep your quills sharp and just keep careful notes....

Ludo Bagman stops by and Harry gets to meet him. Bagman was a Beater on England's Quidditch team (the Wimbourne Wasps), but he is now out of shape, and has a broken nose that Harry figures was broken by a Bludger. He is dressed in his black and yellow Quidditch robes. Bagman is giddy with excitement about the match. While all the wizards around him are practically worn out from doing crowd control, Bagman comments that there isn't much for him to do.

> Broken and injured noses are running bits and may have similar intrigue as the fingers and hands we saw in Book 3. Hope HP Sleuths are remembering Rule #4 - we're not totally buying that Bagman's broken nose was caused by a Bludger,

especially because that does not make sense. We know that in the magical world, broken bones can be mended in minutes, and there is immediate medical coverage at these matches. The only reason a broken bone would probably not be able to be fixed is either that the injury involved some spell that prevented fixing, or that he wasn't able to get to a mediwizard in time. Wonder what he was up to?

Ludo is collecting bets on the match. Although Mr. Weasley does not approve, Fred and George go ahead and bet him 37 Galleons, 15 Sickles, and 3 Knuts (their life savings), that the Bulgarian Seeker, Viktor Krum, catches the Snitch but Ireland wins anyway.

The poverty-stricken Weasley twins are betting their life savings on a whim? We don't think that's too likely. So, how would they have gotten the inside scoop? Seen any firewood lately? And of course, our Mr. Bagman (surprise, surprise) appears to be a bagman.

Fred and George also show Bagman one of their fake wands. It impresses Bagman so much he gives them 5 more Galleons credit.

We can picture it now – a face off of Harry vs. Voldemort...a horrible moment...Voldemort grabs a wand, and...casts a deadly spell, and...out bursts...a bouquet of flowers! (tee-hee) These wands must be really good. Thanks to Fred and George, even sorcery can have a magical twist. If Fred and George are around, watch for fake *anythings*....

Bagman also mentions he is having trouble communicating with his Bulgarian counterpart who does not appear to understand English very well. Bagman has been looking for Mr. Crouch, who speaks 200 languages, to help him out.

Wow! Mr. Crouch is extremely talented with language - it's not surprising he's in an International Department. Wonder where/how he learned all those languages, or if it just runs in the family?

Crouch does show up at the Weasley tents. When Percy asks his boss if he would like some tea, Crouch accepts, calling him "Weatherby," putting Fred and George into smothered hysterics. Crouch talks to Arthur Weasley about Ali Bashir who is upset that they won't lift their embargo on flying carpets so he can sell to Britain.

Percy must have been doing *extremely important* work for his boss, as Crouch (who speaks 200 languages) can't even remember Percy's name.

Ron buys a miniature souvenir of Viktor Krum, whom he idolizes. Harry buys all three of them Omnioculars (binoculars that do slow-motion and instant replay), but has to promise Ron and Hermione that those are in place of Christmas gifts.

Yea! Harry gives great presents!

They all head off to the beginning of the match.

Rowlinguistics

✳ **Celestina Warbeck** – you might say that name sounds like a *heavenly imposter* (or one who hides treachery behind good deeds)

Crouch reminisces that his grandfather had an **Axeminster** flying carpet. That is a well-known, real brand of Muggle carpeting.

Curiosities

✳ Harry thinks about how the Dursleys never took him on a holiday – always left him with Mrs. Figg. (Did Mrs. Figg encourage that?)

✳ Bagman quips that Bertha's got a memory "like a leaky cauldron," Percy's job is to regulate cauldron thickness to prevent leaks, and the entrance to Diagon Alley is through the *Leaky Cauldron*. We're not sure if there's any correlation, but we do find it funny.

Clues

They have seats in the Top Box, where Harry watches advertisements flashing in gold letters across a big black scoreboard. One of the ads pitches "Mrs. Skowers All-purpose Magical Mess Remover," and another mentions a clothing store located in Paris.

> We know about the Leaky Cauldron and Diagon Alley in London. Wonder what they have in other cities, like Paris? Maybe Le Chaudron Qui Rit? (cheesy joke)

Harry notices a house-elf behind him hiding her head. Her name is Winky, and she knows Dobby! Harry asks how Dobby is getting along, and Winky laments that the freedom Harry gave Dobby has changed him - that he now wants to get paid for his work - which she says is unnatural. She is fearful of heights and does not like the Top Box, but her master has sent her to hold a seat for him. She continues to hide her frightened eyes when she has finished talking to them. Fudge remarks that he sees Crouch's house elf is saving him a seat.

> Getting paid is *unnatural?* We still don't know how house-elves ended up with this oppressive arrangement. Looks like Winky is not going to see much of the match. Wonder what else she might miss? And why is Crouch missing? Clearly a story-line clue.

The Minister of Magic, Cornelius Fudge, introduces Lucius Malfoy and his wife, Narcissa, as his personal guests. He indicates that Lucius has made a "very generous contribution" to St Mungo's Hospital for Magical Maladies and Injuries.

> Not good.... The WWP Sleuthoscope just started hyperventilating! Is this evidence that there may be some *mal* practice going on at St Mungo's? We know from Book 3 that Malfoy uses his money and influence to control some of the Ministry. Now we see that even the wizarding hospital may be under his control. So, anyone he doesn't like could end up not recovering, or worse... ☹ What about people Malfoy does like? Are they given special *treatments?* So, this is where Lockhart is getting his therapy? Hmmmm.

Each team brings their mascots to perform for the spectators. The Bulgarians have brought "veela," beautiful woman-like creatures, who draw men to them like Sirens. The Irish team has Leprechauns cast gold coins into the stands from a shamrock hovering overhead. Everyone scrambles to collect handfuls of coins - Ron gives Harry all of his coins as payment for the Omnioculars.

> By the way, Leprechauns can be very crafty creatures. There's also something in existing legends about leprechaun gold....

Bagman is the announcer for the tournament. When the teams take to the air, Harry sees the famous Krum, who he thinks looks like "an overgrown bird of prey." It is a very brutal, dirty, game as they execute a number of very clever but dangerous moves - like when Krum performs a diving Wronski Feint. The Irish Chasers easily get past the Bulgarians, scoring constantly. At one point, a riot breaks out between the mascots, and Harry watches as the veela assume their true form - heads like birds and scaly wings on their backs. The Irish are up 170 to 10 when Viktor's nose is broken by a Bludger.

> There seems to be an odd epidemic of **broken** noses in this book. We detect Rule #3. We also suspect that J.K.R. wants us to notice what happens when a nose gets broken by a Bludger. We will see how badly this messes up Viktor's appearance.

At that moment, Lynch, the Irish Seeker, dives for the Snitch, but in spite of the blood flowing on his face, Krum races him for it and nabs it first - the game is over. Unbelievably, the Bulgarians have caught the Snitch, but the Irish win the Cup.

> Who would ever have thought of such a crazy ending? Only a crazy person. Do we know any crazies like that? Fred and George do qualify, but how could they have been tipped off? CONSTANT VIGILANCE!

Harry watches Krum come up to the Box as the spectators applaud. Harry notices that Krum walks very awkwardly - a bit duck-footed and round-shouldered. When they announce Krum's name, the crowd goes wild - he is clearly a favorite with the fans.

> Here is a potential septology clue. We know that wizards can mate with trolls and other creatures. We are never told why Krum would be duck-footed or round-shouldered, but we do know that he flies like a bird! Wonder what might be in Krum's lineage?

When Bagman finishes his announcing, Fred and George come over and collect the winnings from their wager with Bagman.

Rowlinguistics

✳ **Narcissa** Malfoy's name comes from the Greek legend about Narcissus. Narcissus had fallen so in love with his own reflection, that he couldn't stop looking at himself and was pining away. The gods took pity on him and turned him into a flower that would sit by the water. We can assume that Narcissa Malfoy is vain.

✳ **"Winkies"** are servant slaves of the Wicked Witch of the West in *The Wizard of Oz* story. They are freed by Dorothy after she melts the witch. Will the house-elf Winky experience a similar fate?

✳ **St Mungo** is the real patron saint of Glasgow, Scotland, and rumored to be a relative of King Arthur. Mungo may mean, *my dear heart* or *my hound.*

Other Oddities

✳ Known Members of the World Cup Teams:
   - Bulgarian National Quidditch Team consisted of: Dimitrov (Chaser), Ivanova (Chaser), Zograf (Keeper), Levski (Chaser), Vulchanov (Beater), Volkov (Beater), and Viktor Krum (Seeker).
   - Irish National Quidditch Team consisted of: Connolly (Beater), Ryan (Keeper), Troy (Chaser), Mullet (female Chaser), Moran (female Chaser), Quigley (Beater), and Aidan Lynch (Seeker).

✳ Did HP Sleuths notice that Ireland has two female chasers? We really like that professional Quidditch is a coed sport. ☺

Clues

Fred and George tell their father that they have "big plans" for their spoils - about which *no one* wants Mrs. Weasley to find out. They go to sleep while listening to "the odd echoing bang" and other sounds of celebrating in the distance.

> Hmmm... More odd banging. Well, Fred and George are serious about investing this money. Is it true they want to start a joke shop, or is it something even more demented?

Mr. Weasley wakes everyone up suddenly in the middle of the night, ordering them to get outside right away. Wizards are screaming and running every direction, while hooded figures are terrorizing the campers - setting fires and torturing Muggles. Mr. Weasley tells the kids to go into the woods and stay together while he takes Bill, Charlie, and Percy to help the Ministry officials. Fred pulls Ginny on ahead while everyone else follows, with George in the rear. Ron trips and falls to the ground, so Harry and Hermione stop to help him as he explains that a tree root got him. In the confusion, they have now lost sight of Fred, George, and Ginny.

> The WWP Sleuthoscope is flickering eerily! What really happened here? According to Rule #4, it is just as likely that something (purposely) hit Ron's foot, as it is that his foot hit a root. Simple and effective way to separate them all. So Fred and George went suddenly missing - now where could they be? Could they be wrapping up their mission that revealed the final score in advance? (Translation: time traveling?) Firewood may not the only thing they went looking for earlier in the day. The most dangerous part of Fred and George going to meet up with a past Fred and George is that since no one can handle the two of them - imagine if there are four of them? Actually, as they are twins, it was not necessary for both of them to go back - one of them could have done it. As of the end of this book, there is no proof that any time travel occurred here, however, we present the evidence and the motive. As an HP Sleuth, what do you think? HP Sleuths should also note that Ginny was with them both times. Poor little Ginny would not have been involved - would she?

Harry, Ron, and Hermione run into Draco Malfoy, who is not at all embarrassed to imply that his father might be one of the hooded wizards. He says they're after Mudbloods, and taunts Hermione, claiming that they have ways of recognizing/identifying half-bloods.

> What? They have ways of recognizing or identifying half-bloods? How? (The ones who are not snobs?) Do we believe Draco? We do believe that his father could be in the hood.

They leave Draco as the situation becomes more dangerous, and decide to pull out their wands, but Harry discovers that his is missing. While looking around, they notice Winky, the house-elf, struggling as if "someone invisible were trying to hold her back."

> Is that a figure of speech? Knowing J.K.R. - what do you think? Was someone or something important attempting to hold Winky back?

Harry, Ron, and Hermione pass by some Goblins who are cackling over a sack of gold. The goblins are not in the least concerned about anything else going on around them.

> We already knew that money motivates goblins, but this is proof that not even a riot can distract them from their gold. Goblins don't care about wizard affairs - the whole focus of their existence is money. We can also conclude (as a septology clue) that it is not wise to get between a goblin and his gold....

They observe a crowd of adolescent wizards (including Stan Shunpike from the Knight Bus) mesmerized by some veelas, but as Harry turns to make a comment to Ron, he finds Ron captivated as well. Harry and Hermione have to break him away.

> We know Harry was affected by the veelas when they first came onto the field, so why is he apparently immune here? Or why is Ron so infatuated? There has not been any explanation about this specifically, but it may be a clue.

Harry, Ron, and Hermione eventually work their way into the heart of the wood where it is quieter and they are able to hear anyone approaching. Ludo Bagman wanders in and seems to be unaware of the events at the campsite. When they tell him about the rioting, he exclaims "damn them!" and Disapparates. Hermione comments that he is "not exactly on top of things."

> Maybe Hermione is starting to sound like Percy - but Bagman does seem quite distracted. Could he have won a bunch of money and still been celebrating, or been off somewhere finishing his bookie rounds? Since his department was in charge of the event, you would think he would be more alert.

They hear another sound of footsteps, but cannot see the person who is in the dark, just on the edge of the trees. The person whispers an incantation, and then a big green sparkling skull with a snake in its mouth rises into the air. Hermione urgently tries to get Harry and Ron to leave the area, explaining that the skull is the "Dark Mark" of Voldemort, but before they can escape, a whole bunch of wizards Apparate on the spot and attack. Harry throws the three of them to the ground, narrowly avoiding being blasted. One of the wizards, Mr. Weasley, recognizes his son and halts the attack.

> Not visible, Apparating, and Disapparating people seem to be in fashion here. It's hard to keep track of everyone.

Mr. Crouch is insistent that one of the kids must have cast the mark, but a witch in a long woolen dressing gown points out they are only kids. The other wizards don't even consider them suspects. When Hermione points to where they heard the spell uttered,

Amos Diggory searches and returns with Winky, unconscious in his arms. None of the wizards can believe Winky could have done it, since she would need a wand, and "no non-human creature is permitted to carry or use a wand." Amos informs them that she had a wand - as he had found one gripped in her hand.

> A witch in a long woolen dressing gown? Do we know anyone else (like an old headmaster) who runs around in one of those? (If it were not for Rule #3, we wouldn't even mention it.) We noticed that humans have established a well-orchestrated monopoly on magic in this world. Do elves have any rights? Did Professor Binns cover this when everyone was dozing?

Mr. Crouch does not seem to accept what has happened. He immediately takes off and searches the woods himself, but does not seem to find anything. He comes back very pale, his hands and moustache twitching.

> Even though Crouch did not find anyone, you can't be too sure someone else wasn't there with all the people popping in and out all over the place. Mr. Crouch is acting especially nervous here, but it must be because his elf is being implicated, isn't it?

Ludo Bagman suddenly Apparates among them and asks why Crouch was not at the match - as his house elf had been saving a spot for him. Mr. Crouch replies that he "was busy." Mr. Diggory brings Winky to consciousness, and as he holds up the wand to ask her about it, Harry recognizes it and calls out that it is his. Amos is suspicious, but Harry explains that he noticed it was gone at the edge of the forest, where Winky admits to picking it up (but insists she did not use it).

> So, where/how did Harry lose his wand? And what about Crouch? What exactly does "busy" mean? Bet you anything it means Rule #2! Talk about people popping in and out - **now** where has Bagman been? The last time we saw Bagman, we were sure he was going back to lead the cavalry. So when he said "damn them" back there, who was the "them" he talking about, and where has he been? He's not the Dark Mark type, but he isn't leading the charge against evil either. HP Sleuths had better put a homing device on this guy.

Hermione interrupts the debate to let everyone know that it could not have been Winky who cast the Mark since the voice they heard was human, and both Harry and Ron agree. Mr. Diggory checks to see the previous spell that the wand performed (*"Prior Incantato!"*), and they all see that it was, indeed, the wand used to conjure the Dark Mark. Mr. Weasley wants to know how Winky could have learned to cast the Dark Mark since *"Morsmordre!"* is not a well-known spell, but Mr. Crouch is insulted by the implication that it could have come from him. He is, in fact, almost maniacal as he insists that he detests the Dark Arts and "those who practice them."

> This is both a story-line and septology clue. If the Dark Mark is not a well-known spell, then that implicates whoever uses it of being either a Voldemort supporter or being taught by a Voldemort supporter. Then there's Mr. Crouch, who is

rather scary in his own way. He sounds quite extremist, which means he could be covering up for something, or a dangerous reactionary (even if he is a Ministry wizard).

They determine that Winky probably picked up the wand just after the incantation, and they realize that she must have been right next to whoever did it. Diggory asks her if she saw anyone, and she "trembles worse than ever." She answers "I is seeing no one."

> How is it that on this night, no one seems to be able to see anyone? It is true that Winky had to be extremely close to whoever did it. For being such powerful creatures, elves are easily intimidated by humans - are they always this fearful?

Mr. Crouch asks Amos if, instead of taking Winky for questioning, he could just take her home and handle it himself. Mr. Diggory does not like the idea, but does not see how he could refuse such a high-ranking member of the Ministry. Mr. Crouch says he will punish her - telling her that "this means clothes," and she sobs uncontrollably. Hermione is upset about the way Winky is being treated, but Mr. Weasley says that although he agrees with Hermione, they cannot discuss elf rights at that moment.

> Question Winky privately? We don't like that idea much either. What is Mr. Crouch up to? He is awfully nervous himself - he is not acting as if he is completely innocent. We also want to know why Mr. Crouch did not show up for the Quidditch Match. Does he have information? It's as if he is covering up something.

When the kids and Mr. Weasley get back to the tents, they find everyone else has made it back safely, although Bill had a gash in his arm and Percy did end up with a bloody nose.

> Yet another battered nose? We all know that if you poke your nose in places where it doesn't belong.... So now we're even more interested in knowing where Bagman has been sticking *his* nose.

Mr. Weasley discusses with them the way the Dark Mark was cast whenever Voldemort or his followers killed someone, and this is the first time it's been seen in thirteen years. The older wizards explain to the kids that the hooded wizards are Voldemort's supporters, called "Death Eaters," - that the ones they saw this night have avoided Azkaban by denouncing Voldemort. They used to torture and kill Muggles just for sport.

> Thirteen years - a foreboding number. We now understand that Voldemort's rule was a rule of terror. We see how the bigotry against "Mudbloods" was used as ammunition in Voldemort's campaigns. J.K.R. parallels the horrors of Nazism in this description, and we will see other similar references to that in this book.

The Death Eaters had Disapparated when the Dark Mark was cast, so the Ministry was not able to get near enough to unmask any of them. As the Death Eaters had also been spooked by the skull, everyone in the tent debates whether the skull was conjured in support of the Death Eaters or to scare them into thinking that the Dark Lord might be nearby looking for them. Either way, Mr. Weasley is sure that the person who conjured up the skull had to have been a Death Eater at one time - even if not one now.

HP Sleuths - this could be a crucial issue in the septology. Mr. Weasley is not always right, but he is very open-minded and very observant... and we still do not know for sure if the person who cast the Dark Mark here was a Death Eater or not. CONSTANT VIGILANCE!

Harry remembers that only three days earlier his scar had hurt, and now all the Dark events happen tonight.

Harry seems to be learning Rule #3.

Harry wonders if Sirius had gotten his letter and/or sent a reply, and as he tries to fall asleep, Harry ponders what it all means.

Curiosities

─✳─ Bagman Disapparates with a small pop.

Other Oddities

─✳─ The foreign female who asks, "Où est Madam Maxime? Nous l'avons perdue" is French, and she is saying, "*Where is Madam Maxime? We have lost her.*" (Zut! Ce n'est pas facile!)

✳

Chapter 10 Analysis

Clues

Everyone packs up and goes to find a Portkey, where they see Mr. Roberts is a bit dazed. Mr. Weasley explains that people can get slightly disoriented when their memories are modified. He also emphasizes that in this case, Mr. Roberts might be a bit more disoriented as they had to make him forget a LOT.

> SEPTOLOGY ALERT! The WWP Sleuthoscope is spinning dizzily and the Rememberit Quill is scrawling furiously so we don't forget! Except for the murder of Harry's parents, this is possibly the most important clue in the Harry Potter mystery. We must watch for signs of memory altering - it is more common than we had realized....

Mrs. Weasley is frantically waiting for them at the Burrow with a copy of the *Daily Prophet* in her hand. Mr. Weasley takes a shot of Ogden's Old Firewhiskey as he reads an article that states the Ministry had bungled the affair - calling it a "national disgrace." The reporter is Rita Skeeter, who stirs up trouble even where there isn't any. Percy shows his indignation by quoting regulations, but is shut up by Bill. Mr. Weasley and Percy hurry off to the Ministry to try to conduct damage control.

> The word "Skeeter" means *mosquito* - how appropriate for someone who is always bugging people and out for blood. Even Bill is not willing to listen to Percy's dribble about rules and regulations. Notice how Bill can shut down Percy - he doesn't hear another word. Now **that's** a powerful wizard (tee-hee).

Hedwig still hasn't returned, and Harry finally gets to tell Ron and Hermione about his having had a dream about Voldemort plotting to kill someone (he doesn't mention it was himself), his scar hurting, and his letter to Sirius. Mr. Weasley and Percy spend most of their time at the Ministry, which is in an uproar as Rita Skeeter (who is "ferreting around") continues to create scandals. She has now dug up the story that Bertha Jorkins is missing (although she has not found out about Winky). The Ministry is also inundated with property claims - such as Mundungus Fletcher, who said he lost a luxury tent at the World Cup, whereas they knew he had been sleeping under a cloak propped on sticks.

> They have wizard insurance? Do they need special clauses for dragon and troll damage? Mundungus Fletcher is a real character. He is also interesting from a septology perspective. Remember, in Book 2, he supposedly "tried to put a hex on Mr. Weasley when his back was turned"? HP Sleuths make special note of Mundungus - it's hard to believe, but rumor has it he's on our side.

Hermione and Percy have an argument over house-elves, as Hermione continues to fret over their welfare.

One thing we learned about Hermione in Book 3 - she is stubborn. When she is convinced she is right, there is no stopping her. Thus, HP Sleuths can probably tell already, when it comes to the plight of house-elves, Hermione will be equally unstoppable.

The weather has turned very bad – it is windy and raining, and the ghoul in the attic is howling. Mr. Weasley finally makes it home from work.

A lot of darkness and storminess lately in the wizarding world. Hope that ghoul appreciates the Weasleys' warm, dry (we hope) roof over his head.

Mrs. Weasley has bought Harry stylish dress robes, but Ron's "new" dress robes (from a second-hand store) are very old-fashioned and edged with lace - Ron is furious.

Curiosities

* How did Mrs. Weasley get Harry's money out of Gringotts Bank to buy his school supplies and dress robes for him? What is the process of someone getting money from another's vault?

* We were wondering why the Weasleys' Clock did not display for Mrs. Weasley that Mr. Weasley and the kids were okay? (Here in the Muggle world we just don't understand how those wizard clocks work.)

* Ferrets are clever critters. HP Sleuths better keep an eye out for them.

* In a interview with the BBC, J.K.R. revealed that a journalist, like Rita, was initially planned for Book 1. She was to appear in the Leaky Cauldron scene (chapter 5), but J.K.R. decided that she would work better in Book 4, where Harry has to deal with the ramifications of his fame.

Clues

The morning that they are to leave for Hogwarts, Mr. Weasley receives an emergency communication from the Ministry. Harry sees Amos Diggory's head suspended in the kitchen flames, telling Mr. Weasley that Mad-Eye Moody had thought (once again) that he heard an intruder, and had set off self-propelling dustbins (*garbage cans* to U.S. Sleuths). Moody is starting his new job today, so Mr. Weasley needs to smooth it over immediately, and goes off to do damage control.

> Amos gives us the *heads-up* on Mad-Eye Moody. Although we don't know what it is yet, Moody's new job must be fairly important since the Ministry seemed to be quite concerned about it. Wonder what kind of job a Mad-Eye would do?

George says he heard Mad-Eye is a "nutter," but Bill explains that Moody had been a great wizard. Moody was responsible for capturing about half of the Dark wizards that are now in Azkaban, so had made a lot of enemies in the process (mainly their family members) who seek vengeance.

> After what we've already seen of what one wizard can do to another, if we had wizards with grudges looking for us, you might call us a bit paranoid too. We know he's called "Mad-Eye," and people think he's a "nutter," but he may only be a bit overzealous (Rule #4).

Since Mr. Weasley is busy at the Ministry, Mrs. Weasley calls for Muggle taxis to get them to the King's Cross train station. In the train compartment next to theirs, Harry, Ron, and Hermione hear Malfoy telling people that his father would have preferred if he had attended Durmstrang, where they actually *teach* Dark Arts (instead of just the defenses), but his mother did not want him to go to school that far away. When Ron and Harry ponder where that school is located, Hermione isn't sure, but thinks that Durmstrang is probably in the far north where it is cold, since their standard uniforms call for fur capes.

> Malfoy's father supposedly wanted him to learn the Dark Arts - so what else is new? We don't find out where Durmstrang is located, so we will consider Hermione's usually reliable evidence as a strong possibility.

Hermione explains that no one knows for sure where Durmstrang is because, just like Hogwarts, it is hidden and disguised. To a Muggle, Hogwarts would look like a dilapidated ruin with a sign on the entrance saying "Danger, Do Not Enter, Unsafe," while Durmstrang and Beauxbatons could be using "Muggle-repelling charms" like they did for the World Cup, or enchanted buildings so they are "unplottable" on maps.

> We know J.K.R. never wastes words or descriptions. Maybe this was so we Muggles would understand better why we haven't stumbled across a sprawling

seven-story (or more) castle (or the Leaky Cauldron), but maybe it will also impact the plot in a later book.

The Hogwarts Express arrives at Hogsmeade station, and they disembark into a gale-force thunderstorm.

Other Oddities

✳ How do Muggle taxis find the Burrow – is it normally *findable* to Muggles?

✳ Mr. Diggory vanishes with a "small pop."

Curiosities

✳ Fred says "Dumbledore's not normal – he's a genius." Percy had said the same thing in Book 1. HP Sleuths probably don't need Rule #1 to be convinced that Dumbledore is surely a genius.

Chapter 12 Analysis

(THE TRIWIZARD TOURNAMENT)

Clues

This is Chapter 12

> The hints about 12 have continued through Book 4. We are still thinking it might relate to Trelawney's predictions in Book 3, as we have the second part of that prediction yet to fulfill....

The students pass through the gates of Hogwarts in a driving thunderstorm. On either side of the gates are statues of winged boars.

> Statues are inanimate objects, right? This is an epic fantasy, right? Thought we'd mention it, just in case.

In the Great Hall, Dumbledore gazes at the black and purple clouds and flashes of lightning on the enchanted ceiling while resting his chin on his long, thin fingers. Harry thinks it looks stormier than he had ever seen it.

> There's Dumbledore's long, thin fingers again. There's Rule #1 again. This storm looks very foreboding - it sure has Dumbledore's attention. Remember, there is a second half of a prediction yet to be fulfilled.

At the sorting ceremony, the Sorting Hat sings this year's new song to describe the houses and the purpose of the Sorting Hat. The Hat sings about it's own creation over 1,000 years ago and that it has "never yet been wrong".

> Straight from the Hat's mouth - it's never been wrong yet. Are we getting a reminder, or a red herring? Don't ask us - we don't look a gift hat in the mouth....

Dennis Creevey, Colin's pipsqueak brother, is a first year and ends up in Gryffindor. He excitedly tells Colin how he had fallen into the lake and how something in the water pushed him back into the boat. Colin thinks it was probably the giant squid. The two of them think it was a great, fun adventure.

> Is this bravery, or is danger just not in the Creeveys' dictionary? Clearly, the Sorting Hat sees it as brave and chivalrous. What we see is Dennis as a potential hero. Watch that little squirt. J.K.R is giving him the spotlight for a reason. We already thought the squid might be friendly – we just don't have any proof yet. So if it wasn't the squid, what pushed Dennis back into the boat?

As they eat their feast, Nearly Headless Nick tells them that it is lucky there is a feast, as Peeves had caused trouble in the kitchens. Nick tells them that they had held a ghost's council in which the Bloody Baron and Fat Friar debated about Peeves because he had torn the kitchens apart - terrifying the house-elves. Hermione is outraged to hear that there are over 100 house-elves "enslaved" at Hogwarts and refuses to touch her food. She is so indignant, she eats nothing at the feast.

> If there is a Ministry of Magic, then a ghost council probably shouldn't be much of a surprise. Wonder who the members are and what kinds of control they can have? We are likely to find out more later in the septology.

While Dumbledore is making his announcements, they hear a loud thunderclap and the doors to the Great Hall "bang" open. A bolt of lightning illuminates a stranger limping on a clawed wooden leg, who goes up to Dumbledore at the head table. His face is heavily scarred, part of his nose is missing, and one of his eyes is an oversized eyeball that rotates independently in all directions - including the back of his head. After a couple of words with Dumbledore, he sits down, drinking from a flask, and Dumbledore introduces him as Professor Moody, the new Defense Against the Dark Arts teacher. Harry, Ron, and Hermione realize this is *Mad-Eye* Moody.

> Awesome! Now that's an entrance... and **that's** a Dark Arts Defender. Another bang and yet another broken nose? We can only imagine what kinds of places a true Dark Arts fighter might have been sticking his nose! Wonder what kind of spell can remove part of the nose? On second thought, never mind. The one thing that's really creepy was his entrance. Was that thunder and lightning effect a coincidence or a story line clue? (If you're not sure, check Rule #3).

Dumbledore announces that there won't be any Inter-House Quidditch Cup this year due to the Triwizard Tournament that will be taking place at Hogwarts (this news gets an interesting reaction from the students). He explains (for those who don't know) that the Triwizard Tournament was established about 700 years ago as a friendly competition to cultivate good relationships between Hogwarts, Beauxbatons, and Durmstrang, the three largest wizarding schools in Europe. A champion is selected to represent each school and they compete in three magical tasks to decide the winner. It used to be held every five years, rotating hosting between the schools, but the death toll became too high and they discontinued it.

> The death toll became too high? Does he have a different meaning for the word "friendly"? If this was meant to put us on alert, it succeeded.

This year, through the work of the Ministry's Department of International Cooperation and Department of Magical Games and Sports, they have been able to mediate an agreement with all the schools in which the rules have been amended to protect students against mortal injuries. The winner will be awarded the Triwizard Cup for their school and a thousand Galleons in personal prize money.

> A thousand Galleons? Well, on second thought, maybe we can be persuaded that it's friendlier this year (we could check first to see if Professor Trelawney has seen any death omens lately).

Dumbledore lets them know that the other schools will arrive with their finalists in October, and on Halloween, "an impartial judge" will decide who the three champions (one from each school) will be. There is an age restriction this year, which requires the participants to be at least 17 years-old as part of the safety precautions (eliminating the Weasley twins by only a couple of weeks). Dumbledore warns that no spells or tricks will be able to get past the age screening.

> We are being given a story-line hint that Harry, himself, is out of danger this year. Is that for reel? We are also being given a bit of Rule #2. Since Fred and George don't even get to put their names in, we don't get to find out if either of them would have qualified. In spite of their goofing around, they seem to be very talented wizards.

The Gryffindors all talk about the tournament as they head back to their tower. On the way, Neville, whose memory "was notoriously poor," forgets about the trick stair and has to be pulled out by Harry and Ron.

> EEEEK!! All the HP Sleuth detectors are going off at once! Could it be? We have been reading all about the effects of *Memory Charms*. We saw what it did to Lockhart. We saw what it did to Mr. Roberts at the World Cup. We heard about what it did to Bertha. We know that Neville's memory is far worse than *normal*. Even the Sorting Hat took forever to dig into his mind. Is there a chance that someone tried to alter Neville's memory? Why would anyone have done that? This is a septology clue that may be as big and as important as the mystery behind Harry's attempted murder. Then again, anyone (even Harry) could forget about a trick stair, right? HP Sleuths - stay on top of this assignment!

The new Gryffindor password is "balderdash."

> Balderdash is a drink that combines uncomplimentary ingredients to create a disgusting taste. We have learned that the passwords are significant, so, why are we being told about yucky drinks?

Everyone goes off to bed dreaming of being the Triwizard champion, except Hermione who is muttering to herself about "slave labor."

Other Oddities

✳ We are informed that wizard siblings do not always end up in the same house at Hogwarts - for example, one of the Patil Twins is in Gryffindor and the other is in Ravenclaw.

✳ Dumbledore announces that Filch has a list of 437 objects that are banned at Hogwarts – we want to know how many of those Fred and George are personally responsible for?!

✳ This is the first Sorting Ceremony we have seen since Book 1. Just for reference, the new students that we saw sorted this year are:

Stewart Ackerley	Ravenclaw
Malcolm Baddock	Slytherin
Eleanor Branstone	Hufflepuff
Owen Cauldwell	Hufflepuff
Dennis Creevey	Gryffindor
Emma Dobbs	(House not given)
Laura Madley	Hufflepuff
Natalie McDonald	Gryffindor
Graham Prichard	Slytherin
Orla Quirke	Ravenclaw
Kevin Whitby	Hufflepuff

Chapter 13 Analysis

Clues

This is chapter 13.

Welcome to *Whodunit13*. As HP Sleuths know, there are clues hiding wherever there is a superstitious number. J.K.R., therefore, could not resist the temptation to conceal the solution to each book's mystery within chapter 13. This is a trend that so far has held true through Book 4. The following are the key story-line events that take place in this chapter - we leave it up to HP sleuths to decipher whodunit. Don't worry, if you can't solve it here, she always *tells all* at the end of each book.☺

Harry is in the Great Hall eating breakfast when the owls arrive, but there is no white owl among them (Harry worries about Sirius). Draco's eagle owl alights on Draco's shoulder carrying his regular stash of treats from home.

The HP Sleuths who have been keeping detailed notes will remember that J.K.R. places significance on the species of owl. The school owls that are available to everyone are typically barn owls and the large package delivery-type owls tend to be screech owls, however, we still don't know about any other white owls besides Harry's. We have already seen that the owl of choice for Malfoy is an eagle owl. HP Sleuths should watch this like a hawk.

Harry, Ron, and Hermione's first class is Herbology where they need to wear their drag-on-hide gloves as they drain some disgusting bubotubers. These plants produce a petrol-like yellowish-green fluid that is used to cure acne, but undiluted, will cause painful welts. In their Care of Magical Creatures class, Hagrid has them caring for baby Blast-Ended Skrewts. These (charming) beasts look and feel like shelled lobsters, but the males' antennae are stingers, the females have suckers on their undersides, and they all eject blasts of sparks and fire out their ends. Hermione postulates that they could grow to be six feet.

Is it too much to hope Hermione got this one wrong? Probably. Hagrid does have this thing for exotic beasts. For some reason, Newt Scamander does not list Skrewts of any kind in *Fantastic Beasts and Where to Find Them*. Hmmm ... wonder where Hagrid got them? Very curious. Also, if there is ever a smell of petrol in the air, be on your guard - it could be bubotuber pus.

During Divination, Professor Trelawney makes one of her typical predictions to Harry - saying that she can see "past his brave face," and that the thing he dreads will come to pass, maybe sooner than he thinks. He is irritated, but ponders her previous year's trance that Dumbledore had thought to be genuine (and has partially come true already). Trelawney then wrongfully assumes that Harry was born in mid-winter.

This **is** Chapter 13 - so are we being warned about the second half of her prediction? We were already convinced by the end of Book 3 that it is probably real, but just how accurate is it? Will Voldemort rise to be more terrible than before, and how soon are we talking? (Too soon, if we believe Trelawney.) Trelawney is up to her fortune-telling tricks again - trying to deduce Harry's birthday. She was totally off (wasn't she?). Uhhh, we think so. How **did** Petunia and Vernon know when Harry's birthday was? Did Dumbledore happen to put it in the letter with the baby Harry? Oh, this is dumb. J.K.R. would not mess with Harry's birthday - it's the same as her own. Forget it.

In the corridor between classes, Draco Malfoy insults Ron's mother, so Harry counters with an insult to Malfoy's own mother, then turns to leave. Malfoy curses Harry behind his back, just grazing him. Before anyone else can react, there is a bang. Professor Moody has changed Draco into a white ferret.

Geez! Guess we don't wanna make Mad-Eye mad. We really didn't need convincing, but we have witnessed that Moody is a very powerful (and quick) wizard. We know that is obvious, but HP Sleuths should write it down for later reference. Humor us - just do it.

Moody sees Crabbe behind him reaching for the ferret and shouts at him to leave it alone. It is apparent that Moody's magical eye can see out the back of his head. Moody then bounces the ferret (Draco) off the floor (for emphasis), while saying that he doesn't like anyone who attacks people from behind.

This seems to be a personal vendetta of Moody's. He is quite sensitive to this. More Rememberit Quill notes.

Professor McGonagall is appalled, restores Draco with a loud snapping noise, and tells Moody that Transfiguration is not to be used as a punishment on students. Moody regards Draco with disdain and brings him off to see Snape instead. Draco starts muttering about his father, and Moody says he knows his father well, and that Snape is an "old friend" too, with whom he has been wanting to "chat."

The disdain that Moody has for Malfoy and Snape just oozes from him. He is not acting - we can see that it somehow is personal. Wonder what it's all about? We know that Aurors despise Dark Wizards, so is that the reason? Is that the only reason?

Fred and George tell everyone how Moody's class is the best. They describe that he has actually been out there seeing and fighting the Dark Arts.

Another real Dark Arts teacher. Like Lupin, he probably holds some crucial Chapter 13 story-line clues. Like Lupin also, we assume he may hold key septology clues.

Hermione is on some personal mission, and after another quick dinner, splits for the library.

Curiosities

* They discuss how Eloise Midgen recently tried to curse her acne off, but blew it – she ended up needing to have Madam Pomfrey put her nose back on - yes, another zapped nose reference.

* Draco is transfigured with a bang, and restored with a loud snapping noise.

Chapter 14 Analysis

Clues

When Neville melts his cauldron in Potions (the sixth one), Snape cruelly makes him disembowel horned toads for detention. Snape is especially mean this year, and the kids discuss how "it is common knowledge" that he wants the Defense Against the Dark Arts position, but has missed out on it again. However, unlike his reaction to the other teachers, Snape does not show open hostility to Professor Moody.

> Poor Neville.☹ This was probably especially hard on him. We think he may have brought Trevor (his toad) to school not because he's a nerd, but because Neville's bloodline may be aquatic. As to it being "common knowledge" that Snape wants the Defense Against the Dark Arts position, we still think we are being duped into Rule #4.

Moody and Snape are chatting, but Snape seems to be avoiding either of Moody's eyes. Snape even appears to be somewhat afraid of him.

> Moody's giving Snape the *evil eye* (snicker). Nice to see Snape on the defensive for once. Although we cannot be sure that Snape fears Moody, he sure seems to be on his best behavior around him.☺ Count that as a story-line clue.

In their Defense Against the Dark Arts class, Moody starts to say that he has "only one year" to teach them about Curses... When questioned, he pauses and tells them that he is only there for one year - as a favor to Dumbledore - and follows with a harsh laugh as he mentions that he will then be returning to his "quiet retirement."

> Was this supposed to be a slip? Does Moody or Dumbledore know something that they can't say, or did Dumbledore decide to foil the Defense Against the Dark Arts jinx rumors by purposely making it a one-year stint? Whatever it may be, it sure feels suspicious.

While Moody is talking, he interrupts himself to stop Lavender and Parvati from looking over a horoscope that they were holding out of his view under the desk. They now realize that he can even see through solid wood.

> We only question one decision that the Sorting Hat has made - the placement of Lavender and Parvati in Gryffindor. We have already seen bravery in Neville, but these two freak out if they break a fingernail! And it doesn't get any better through Book 4. We assume that eventually we will understand why these duffers are in Gryffindor.

Moody tells the class that, according to the Ministry of Magic, he is not supposed to actually show them the *Unforgivable Curses* until they are in their sixth year - only the counter-curses. However, he says that Dumbledore agrees with him that if the students do not know or see the actual curse, that they will not know what they are fighting and will not be able to recognize that it is being used.

> We know Dumbledore and Moody both have their own way of doing things. Back at the "bouncing ferret" incident, we saw that although Moody had already been told not to use transfiguration as punishment, he took it upon himself to administer it anyway. Is he showing that streak of independence here, or has he truly discussed it with Dumbledore? Is it possible that Dumbledore is preparing Harry and his class for the worst (which means Dumbledore is worried)? The Rememberit Quill's is trembling as it writes.

Moody brings out three spiders in a jar to demonstrate the three *Unforgivable Curses* to the students. He tells them that using one on another human being draws a life sentence in Azkaban. He takes one spider out and performs an *Imperius Curse* (*"Imperio!"*) on it, taking total control of the spider. He can force it to do anything he wants - including harm itself. This curse was used a lot during Voldemort's time, and the Ministry had a rough time trying to figure out who was being controlled and who was acting of their own free will.

> We have learned that memories can be altered, and that a person can be completely controlled by another. This is beginning to sound both dangerous and complex. Do wizards have a mind of their own? This will be a real detective challenge in the upcoming books.

Moody asks if the students can name any of the other curses that carry the highest penalties for use. Harry is surprised to see that Neville knows one called the *Cruciatus Curse*. Moody pulls out the second spider, which sits immobile on the desk - "apparently too scared to move." On that second spider, Moody first enlarges it for better effect (makes a big effect on Ron) and then performs Neville's *Cruciatus Curse* (*"Crucio!"*). The spider is in silent agony, and as the pain is amplified, Hermione makes him stop as she sees Neville clutching at his desk in horror.

> Either Neville had no idea what was coming, or he is as petrified of this curse as Ron is of the spider. Poor Neville, it hit him really hard - that is significant. Which is more scary for him – Snape or this curse?

For the third spider, Moody zaps it with the *Killing Curse* (*"Avada Kadavra!"*). With a flash of blinding green light, there is a "rushing sound as though a vast, invisible something was soaring through the air," and the spider is instantly killed - leaving no mark on it's body. Moody informs the class there is no counter-curse for that one, and that *the only person who has ever survived it is Harry Potter*, himself.

> There it is... the green light ... And WHAT??? ... NO MARK ON THE BODY??? The WWP Sleuthoscope is blinding us with it's flashing and the Rememberit Quill already needs another roll of parchment! Okay, we can assume it was *The Killing Curse* that killed the Riddle family and Frank Bryce (in the first chapter of this book). There was no mark on their bodies either. Moody tells us straight out that Voldemort used *The Killing Curse* on Harry and that blinding green light

seems to fit, so what's with this scar? How could it have left a mark? And why was the whole house destroyed by that deadly, yet "**undetectable**" curse?? Moody says there is no counter-curse. What about Harry? Was it only his mother's spell that saved him, or does Harry carry immunity? If so, where did he get it? The implications are stupefying. HP Sleuths Review Rule #4 - are we sure that Harry is the only person to survive it? J.K.R is spinning a web of intrigue.

Harry now sees exactly how his parents had died. Moody goes on to tell them that there is a lot more magic behind the curse than just the words - that if all of the students were to point their wands at him and say the words, that he probably wouldn't "get so much as a nosebleed." Even though there is no counter-curse, he emphasizes that the reason he has shown them this one is so that they can be wary of it. Moody yells "**CONSTANT VIGILANCE!**" and the students jump.

This hits Harry pretty hard since, even though Harry had been the recipient of the curse, he had never actually seen this curse performed before. The memory of it is so traumatic, however, that the green light has haunted him for 13 years.

After the lesson, Professor Moody has the traumatized Neville come to his office. Moody compliments Neville on his herbology skills, and then to make Neville feel better, lends him a book on magical water plants.

That is really nice of Moody. We already know that something in Neville's heritage makes him get along with water-type things anyway (remember Great Uncle Algie, who gave Neville his toad?). Neville also seems to do better with inanimate objects. So far, we have not seen much about anything magical in the water except for grindylows, some Kelpies, and the Giant Squid. Not everything seems to be real friendly either. There are probably a lot of very unusual magical plants hiding in the underwater world. Story-line clues are swimming all around us.

Harry and Ron are totally stumped on their Divination homework, and in exasperation, decide to make up a bunch of ominous predictions as Professor Trelawney seems to thrive on them. As they devise preposterous disasters, Crookshanks gives them an inscrutable (Hermione-type) look.

That's probably the Kneazle coming out of Crookshanks. (We assume that HP Sleuths have now read-up on Kneazles in *Fantastic Beasts*). Harry and Ron do border on suspicious here, so they deserve what they get.

Hermione shows Harry and Ron the project she has been working on. She has made up badges and formed an organization called the "Society for the Promotion of Elfish Welfare" (S.P.E.W.). Her goals are to get "fair wages" for house-elves, and to try to get elf representation in the Department for the Regulation and Control of Magical Creatures. Ron tries to tell her that house-elves "like" being enslaved, but she thinks he is being ignorant. The three of them do not agree on this issue.

Although we agree with Hermione, that's still a pukey name. Plus, we need to get the elves' opinion on this whole issue. (It could have been worse - she could have named it:

Wizards for Elf Independence, Rights, and Dignity) ☺

Hedwig finally returns with an answer from Sirius. His letter says that Harry's scar is just one of several rumors indicating that something is going on - including news that Dumbledore has brought Mad-Eye out of retirement (meaning that Dumbledore must know something as well). Sirius instructs Harry to go straight to Dumbledore if his scar hurts again. Sirius also says he is now heading back up north immediately.

Wow, Sirius thinks this is serious. So there is something going on with Voldemort. CONSTANT VIGILANCE!

Harry is upset that he even mentioned the scar and has trouble falling asleep - fearing if Sirius comes back and gets caught, it will be Harry's fault.

Curiosities

✳ We know that giant spiders can talk, but how is it that Moody's little ones seem to have understood what was happening to them? We have not learned anything more about it after this lesson, so we are not even sure it's a clue, but we do remember that Harry's cupboard was full of the little guys!

Other Oddities

✳ It was mentioned that Neville was not snoring, which means he also had trouble falling asleep because something was affecting him badly as well. The *Cruciatus Curse* really got to him – wonder why?

Clues

Before breakfast, Harry writes back to try to change Sirius's mind - saying that he was half-asleep when he wrote last time, that the scar did not really hurt, and there is no need for Sirius to return. In their Defense Against the Dark Arts class, Professor Moody tells the students that Dumbledore wants them taught what the *Imperius Curse* feels like. Hermione doesn't understand how he can do that if they're illegal. He actually teaches them how to resist the (Unforgivable) *Imperius Curse* by performing it on each one of them and having them attempt to resist it. As Harry struggles with it, Moody instructs the class to watch Harry's eyes - that they can see the effects there.

> Now Dumbledore supposedly wants them taught what an *Unforgivable Curse* **feels** like? Is that true or is Mad-Eye getting carried away? If it's true, Dumbledore must think the danger is close. Hope HP Sleuths are also paying attention in Moody's class – and watch those eyes!

Harry is the only one in the class that has any luck resisting the curse initially, and Moody performs it with Harry three more times until he can completely combat it.

> It's probably nothing, but we see that Harry has resisted veelas, *Imperius Curses*, and even *Killing Curses*. Is there something more we should know about Harry?

Ron, Harry, and Hermione are working harder than ever on their studies as all the teachers have given the fourth years extra work. Professor Binns, of course, continues to drone on about 18th century goblin rebellions.

> Here we find out about goblin rebellions of the 18th century, and we knew about the one in 1612 (17th century). How many Rebellions were there, and have they all actually been resolved? How long do goblins live? Could the same ones that rebelled centuries ago (or their descendents) still be alive? For that matter – who *won* the goblin rebellions?

Professor McGonagall is upset with Neville for not being able to "perform a simple *Switching Spell*" in which he "accidentally transplanted his own ears onto a cactus." Fred and George, who seem unusually intense, are huddled, saying something about having to send someone a letter since "he" is avoiding talking to them.

> So we have just a bit more information about *Switching Spells*, but now we're confused. How are they supposed to work, and what are they primarily used for? In Book 1, Professor McGonagall described Transfiguration as "complex" magic... so is a "simple *switching spell*" really simple, and what is the difference between transfiguration, switching, Animagi, etc.? (We need more Red *Lesson Cards*.) Fred and George are up to something. That's not unusual, but it's the

intensity of what they are doing that raises suspicion. HP Sleuths are doubly suspicious about this story-line clue.

Hermione still is not finding much support for her S.P.E.W. campaign. Fred and George, who have been down in the kitchens and met the elves, think they are not only happy, but honored to be working at Hogwarts. However Hermione claims it is because they are uneducated and brainwashed.

We've heard Fred and George's eye-witness interpretation of house-elf conditions. Sounds like the elves are, indeed, quite happy. We would still like to hear directly from the elves on the issue.

Sirius' reply to Harry's last Owl is "Nice try, Harry" - he does not fall for Harry's ploy to pretend his scar didn't hurt. Sirius also warns Harry to switch owls each time, so it is not easy to track their correspondence. Hermione makes the comment that snowy owls are not native birds.

Hermione is sort of stating the obvious here since it is not really difficult to notice a single bright white owl among a hundred brown ones. What do we know about Hedwig's heritage? Presumably, she is from a northern (snowy) climate, but otherwise, we know nothing as of Book 4. As with everything in the Harry Potter series, there will probably be a good tale behind her.

It is time to initiate the Triwizard Tournament. The students are all led out onto the lawns to await the arrival of Beauxbatons and Durmstrang. Harry sees Dennis Creevey "shivering with anticipation."

Dennis does not seem *normal* (guess that's why we like him ☺). He is not phased by anything, and is happily excited about everything that comes at him - good or bad. We also find him much more intriguing than his brother, Colin.

The students have not been told how the other visiting schools will be traveling to Hogwarts, so they speculate about their modes of transportation. Ron hypothesizes a Portkey. They all wait … looking, … watching, … and then Dumbledore announces the approach of Beauxbatons. A sixth year spots something in the sky; one of the first-years fears it is a dragon. Dennis Creevey tells her not to be stupid - that it's a "flying house." Actually, the Beauxbatons students are traveling by air in a gigantic blue carriage, the size of a house.

You can't Apparate at Hogwarts, but Ron asks a good question – could they have used a Portkey? (Notice no one disputes him.) Although it was more like a monstrous carriage, Dennis was basically correct. He is just a first year with a Muggle family, but he is highly perceptive. It may be a no-brainer that it was not a dragon to him, but he was the first one to realize what he was seeing - and flying houses are not common objects. We assume he may be quite intelligent.

The Beauxbatons carriage is decorated with a coat of arms showing two crossed wands radiating three stars each, and is pulled by twelve giant, winged Palomino horses. The chaperon for Beauxbatons is Madame Maxime, a huge woman whose immense physique reminds Harry of Hagrid.

> We now see that other large wizards exist. Where does Hagrid come from? We do not know anything about his background before Hogwarts. Are large wizards common or rare? Could they have some other blood, or are they aberrations like Squibs?

They then await Durmstrang.... Lee Jordan is the first to announce that there is a whirlpool jet from the center of the lake.

> Lee Jordan is really cool with his Quidditch play-by-plays, a funny guy, and a good friend of the Weasley twins. We see here that he is also an observant wizard in general.

The Durmstrang students arrive by ship from out of a swirling whirlpool in the Hogwarts lake. It docks at the edge of the water. The headmaster for Durmstrang (the school that teaches Dark Arts) is Professor Karkaroff, a tall, thin, man with gray hair and a goatee, who is wearing unique, sleek, silver furs - similar to his hair. His students are wearing cloaks of some kind of shaggy, matted fur.

> The name "Durmstrang" is a permutation of the term *Sturm und Drang*, an artistic movement in Germany (Deutschland) from the late 1700s. One of the most famous pieces from that era was the play *Faust* - the story about a pact with the devil. We're not surprised this school teaches Dark magic. Out of J.K.R.'s Durmstrang comes the mystery man, Professor Karkaroff, in his strange silver furs. HP Sleuths should keep a penetrating eye on him - all of him. We can assure you that Mad-Eye will be doing just that.

As Harry and Ron watch, Professor Karkaroff brings a student with a prominent, curved nose out of the ship - they are astounded to see that it is Viktor Krum, the Bulgarian Seeker.

Rowlinguistics

✳ The phrase "**beaux batons**" is French for *beautiful sticks* (or *fine wands*) - thus the emblem of the two crossed wands.

Curiosities

✳ Hedwig is a clever owl – notice that even when she is coming from a long distance, she tries to time her deliveries for the Great Hall so she can get a treat.☺

✳ The swirling water with the mystery ship rising out of it conjures images of the legend of the Flying Duchman. That legend tells of a Captain and his ship that sank in a swirling storm around the 17th century. It cursed to roam the seas as a death omen for those who encounter the phantom ship.

Chapter 16 Analysis

Clues

Harry and Ron, along with all the other students, can hardly believe that Viktor Krum is there in person.

> The most prominent thing here, HP Sleuths, is Krum's nose. Not the shape of his nose - but the fact that it is **not broken**. As we discussed earlier, the mediwizards at the Quidditch matches, just like Madam Pomfrey, can fix broken bones properly if attended to in time. Therefore, Bagman's broken nose most likely occurred when he wasn't near to any mediwizard (or any Bludger), but instead was too close to some spell or business that got him (and his nose) into trouble.

At dinner, the Beauxbatons students sit at the Ravenclaw table. Krum and the other Durmstrang students join the Slytherins, which Malfoy flaunts.

> The seating arrangements tell us about the personalities of these other schools. Just as Malfoy had mentioned on the train, Durmstrang is the Slytherin type.

One of the female Beauxbatons students, who has a very seductive appearance (and a strange affect on Ron), appears to be a veela. Hermione gets emotional and insists that no one else is affected by that student except Ron, but she (somehow) managed to miss that Harry and other boys are also distracted.

> Ooouh...Do we notice a hint of jealousy? Hermione is getting emotional, so she may not be right (for once). The heritage of this Beauxbaton student is a small, yet intriguing story line mystery. *Bet* we don't have to ask the guys to watch this one closely...

Dumbledore announces that Ludo Bagman, Mr. Crouch, Professor Karkaroff, Madame Maxime, and himself will comprise the panel that will judge the Triwizard Tournament champions. Filch delivers a jeweled, wooden chest to Dumbledore's table. Tiny Dennis Creevey has to stand on his chair just to see, as the others all stand up in excitement.

> Okay, J.K.R. is making sure we notice that Dennis is verrry shrimpy. He also might have some non-human blood in him. We know that Professor Flitwick is tiny, and we already speculated that he may have some of that powerful elf heritage. Could the demi-Creevey also be part elf (or something like that) somewhere back in his lineage? J.K.R. has not given us anything else to imply that, but according to Rule #1, his size is a big hint – we're just not yet sure how big.

Dumbledore proclaims that there will be three tasks spaced throughout the school year which will test the champions for various skills: magical prowess, daring, powers of deduction, and ability to cope with danger. They will be marked on performance for each task, and the champion with the highest total at the end of all three tasks will win the Cup.

This sounds really exciting – too bad it's so lethal.

The impartial selection of the champions will be made using the "Goblet of Fire." Dumbledore opens the chest and lifts out a "large, roughly-hewn wooden cup," that is filled with "dancing blue-white flames." He tells the students that in order to submit a name for consideration as champion, they must write their name and school on a piece of parchment and drop it into the Goblet. On the following night (Halloween), exactly 24 hours later, the Goblet will dispatch the names it has chosen to be most worthy as champions. Dumbledore will erect an "Age Line" around the Goblet, which will prevent any under-age wizard from submitting their name.

HP Sleuths take note that the only required elements to enter are "name" and "school." That gives Fred and George precisely 24 hours to figure out how to fool the Age Line. We can be sure this is a challenge they can't pass up.

Dumbledore impresses on them the seriousness of submitting an entry – that once entered and chosen, they are bound (by magical contract) to finish the tasks.

And what if they don't finish? What would be the consequences? Do they magically find themselves plopped back into the middle of a task? Are they sent to Azkaban, tortured, or stripped of their magic? Maybe we are left to imagine the gory details…. Suffice it to say, based on what we know about the tournament's history, it probably would not be pleasant.

As everyone is leaving the Great Hall, Harry, Ron, and Hermione walk by Professor Karkaroff and the Durmstrang students. When Karkaroff sees Harry's scar, he stares at Harry "as if he can't believe his eyes." Professor Karkaroff then sees Moody, and his face expresses both fear and fury. Moody returns an especially loathsome look.

First Malfoy, then Snape, now Karkaroff? They all "know" Moody "personally?" Mad-Eye sure gets around. We are also beginning to understand why he is so paranoid – as none of these people seem to be happy to see him. What would they have done to have had a run-in with an Auror? HP Sleuths will have to keep an eye on all of them. CONSTANT VIGILANCE!

The next morning, they find the Goblet of Fire sitting on the Sorting Hat's stool in the center of the Entrance Hall, with a golden circle, ten feet in diameter, surrounding it. Since Fred and George are barely underage, they take a single drop of aging potion and try to cross the Age Line. It doesn't fool the Line – they are hurled out and sprout beards, giving Dumbledore a chuckle. He tells them that two other students, Miss Fawcett (Ravenclaw) and Mr. Summers (Hufflepuff), have also sprouted beards in their attempt.

There's Fawcett again. Not only did Dumbledore's Age Line work, but he seems to have added a little extra hairy bonus. Now that's the Dumbledore sense of humor.

Harry, Ron, and Hermione go down to visit Hagrid and see that the Beauxbatons carriage is parked not too far away. They are amused to see that Hagrid has made an awkward attempt to groom himself and even put on a suit. When he encounters Madame Maxime descending from her carriage, he becomes "misty-eyed," and followers her – forgetting completely about the kids.

> Aw...Gee, Hagrid seems to be an adult after all. J.K.R. still has not told us about the heritage of large wizards, so it must be another story-line clue.

At the Halloween feast, everyone is especially tense. That is, except Mr. Crouch, who is looking "quite uninterested, almost bored."

> We like Crouch better this way. Can we get Percy to act like this too? Unfortunately, it's not normal for Crouch to be like this, so something is wrong with him. HP Sleuths get ready – this is just the beginning of a very complex story line mystery that is about to evolve.

When it is time, the Goblet of Fire turns red, and ejects the first name – it is Viktor Krum for Durmstrang. The second parchment ejected from the Goblet declares that Fleur Delacour (the veela-like student) will represent Beauxbatons. The Goblet names the Hogwarts champion to be Cedric Diggory. As Dumbledore is calling for support for the three chosen champions, he suddenly stops as he notices that the fire in the Goblet has turned red again, and yet another parchment is ejected from the Goblet of Fire. There are now **four** champions.

> How did this happen? This was **not** a simple matter of stuffing another name into the Goblet. Back when Dumbledore gave the instructions, he told everyone that they had to write down their name and school to qualify. Since there are only three schools and only one champion per school, how can there be four champions?

After a very tense pause, Dumbledore reads the fourth name: "Harry Potter."

Rowlinguistics

✦ J.K.R. has verified that **Fleur Delacour**'s name is translated *as fleur de la cour* or *Flower of the Court (a Noblewoman)*. However, since J.K.R. has been known to alter spellings slightly just to throw us off-guard, we had initially thought that it was a play on *coeur*, which means heart. Don't feel bad Narri, we were fooled too! (Re: AOL chat with J.K.R.)

Curiosities

✦ The Goblet of Fire, an extremely valuable goblet, is apparently hand-made of wood. We can't help seeing a similarity to the Holy Grail.

Chapter 17 Analysis

(THE FOUR CHAMPIONS)

Clues

Dumbledore calls Harry up to the Head Table and then ushers him through a door into a room where the other three champions are waiting. There is much confusion and Dumbledore tries to sort it out. Harry denies putting his own name in, nor asking an older student to put it in for him. Moody feels it would have needed an exceptionally strong *Confundus Charm* to trick the Goblet into thinking that a 4th school existed so that Harry could be eligible.

> That was pretty smart of Moody figuring out how it was done, wasn't it? Notice that Dumbledore did not read off a school name for Harry. So, was there any school name written on there or not? We are not told (sigh). Maybe it didn't need a school name if it thought Harry was the only one eligible (?).

Mr. Crouch is looking a bit eerie - standing back from the group with his face partially hidden in the shadows, giving him a "skull-like appearance." He recites the rules, which state that whatever names come out of the goblet are bound by magical contract. This is good enough for Bagman, who is clearly excited to have Harry as a champion.

> Why is Bagman so jubilantly happy to have Harry in the competition? (Maybe Krum's odds just went up?) Then there's Crouch, who is not feeling himself at all. Wish we could get a better look at him - he may be ill. Things are already getting weird - it is imperative that HP Sleuths keep in control of this mystery.

While everyone else is furious about the rules, Moody points out that they might want to be a bit concerned about Harry, since his life could actually be in danger. Karkaroff reminds everyone that Moody has a reputation for being paranoid, to which Moody replies about Karkaroff "remembering" that he knows how Dark wizards think...

> The daggers are flying! Karkaroff seems to want us to think Moody is a bit "mad," while Moody is almost implicating Karkaroff with his own little reminder. Is Moody overly paranoid, or incredibly observant? Is there something about Karkaroff that could be a threat to Harry? HP Sleuths will have to sort this out.

Dumbledore asks if anyone can suggest an alternative to accepting Potter's eligibility; but as no one can, he makes the selections "official." Crouch delivers the first task - telling the students that the purpose of it is to test their daring, so they will not be told anything in advance except that they will have only their wands. Also, the participants will be exempt from their end-of-year exams. Harry notices that Mr. Crouch has dark shadows under his eyes and appears to be ill, then Dumbledore vocalizes his own concern to Crouch as well, but Crouch just says that things (including Percy) have been difficult at the Ministry

Of course! Why didn't we think of that - he has to deal with Percy...That would make anyone sick! (Hehehee - only kidding... sort of.) Obviously, Dumbledore did notice a problem, so we need to get control of this quickly.

Harry worries about why someone had put his name into the tournament. No one else may know, but Harry is aware that somewhere, someone (Voldemort) is, indeed, plotting his murder. He cannot see how, but wonders if the two are connected.

Nice try, J.K.R.. HP Sleuths also know Rule #3. We also haven't forgotten Rule #4 - Harry is **not** the only one who knows about the murder plot. We readers know about it, and HP Sleuths know from Chapter 1, that Voldemort's faithful servant knows about it and is supposed to be at Hogwarts. We also know that Dumbledore just happened (coincidentally?) to think it important to have the Auror, Moody, at the school this year - so he at least suspects something. But how could the Triwizard Tournament possibly relate to that?

To Harry's shock and dismay, Ron does not believe that Harry hadn't submitted his own name, and is upset with Harry for again getting all the attention.

Curiosities

* When Cedric leaves to go celebrate with his house, he instead heads for a door to the right of the marble staircase, down the stone steps behind it. That's an odd detour.

* We meet Violet (a gossipy portrait from behind the Great Hall). She dashes 7 staircases to get to the Fat Lady. This is a verification (Rule #1) that Gryffindor House is on the 7th floor.

Chapter 18 Analysis

Clues

Hermione knows that Harry had not entered himself into the tournament - as she had seen the stupefied look on his face when his name was called. She does not believe a *student* could have done it to him either, since the magic needed to trick the Goblet would most likely be too far advanced. She tells him how Ron is so upset because he is always in Harry's shadow, and this was once too many. She also recommends he write and tell Sirius about it all right away.

> This is why we all love Hermione - she is so analytical. (Remind us we said that the next time she is such a know-it-all.)

During Care of Magical Creatures class, Hagrid talks to Harry alone and tells Harry that if he says he didn't do it, he believes him, and that Dumbledore believes him too. However, everyone else in the school seems to think that Harry entered himself just to get more attention. The Slytherins have made up "Potter Stinks" badges, and Malfoy provokes Harry into a duel. Their spells collide in mid-air - causing Malfoy's *"Densaugeo!" Hex* to hit Hermione instead, making her already-elongated teeth grow, and she runs off to the hospital. Snape gives Harry and Ron detentions. During Potions, Snape is in the process of hinting that he will be poisoning someone to test the students' antidotes (he looks at Harry), when Colin Creevey conveniently walks in. Snape stares down at Colin, whose eager smile disappears as he explains that he has to take Harry away for publicity photos (embarrassment city for Harry).

> Nothing normally phases the Creevey brothers, but we are shown that Snape can even affect their enthusiasm. Harry may be embarrassed to death, but at least he's not poisoned to death. That was a lucky coincidence that the photo session prevented Snape from trying it, wasn't it? Did we mention the "C" word? Hmmm. J.K.R. has that habit of interrupting important clues (guess that includes poisonings). Was there something we might have found out if Snape had a chance to go through with it? Possibly, but there was also a chance that Harry could have been in mortal danger, so we'll just pass on that clue.

The publicity event is actually a "wand weighing ceremony" conducted by Mr. Ollivander, the wand-maker from Diagon Alley. Bagman gives Rita Skeeter permission to interview Harry for the *Daily Prophet*. Harry is introduced to a reporter with "curiously rigid curls," a "heavy-jawed face," holding a large handbag with her "thick fingers." She smiles at Harry, exposing three gold teeth, grabs him with a "surprisingly strong grip," and brings him into a broom cupboard to privately talk with him. She pulls out an acid-green "Quick Quotes Quill," puts the tip to her mouth, sucks on it with "apparent relish," and sets it on the parchment where it starts writing all by itself. Harry sees that it is writing words he has not even spoken. Dumbledore finds and rescues Harry from Rita, who extends one of her large mannish hands in greeting.

This is a really strange "lady." A number of things bother us. Could it be her "heavily jawed face," her "surprisingly strong grip," or maybe those "large, mannish hands and thick fingers?" HP Sleuths - does this sound like a *lady* to you? Is this some kind of J.K.R. bait-and-switch? What about those "curiously rigid curls" - almost as if it's a wig, maybe? HP Sleuths might also want to savor that sucking action on her quill. This is not a normal character (even by magical standards). We are being told to take note of Poison-Pen Skeeter's appearance (all the way to her three gold teeth). J.K.R. didn't even spend this much time on her description of Harry!

Mr. Ollivander inspects each wand and comments about its core and its characteristics. When Harry hears that Fleur's wand has a veela hair from her grandmother as its core, it confirms that she is part veela. Mr. Ollivander relates to them how he had a near miss with the horn of the unicorn from which he got the hair for Cedric's wand.

There is no doubt that Mr. Ollivander not only makes his own wands, but obtains the cores from living specimens (who may fight back)!

Sirius writes back to Harry - scheduling a meeting with him in the Gryffindor common room at 1:00 AM.

Curiosities

Fleur's wand produces pink and gold sparks, has a veela hair from her grandmother as the core, and Ollivander considers it "temperamental." Maybe this is what Ollivander was referring to when he told Harry that "you never get as good results with another wizard's wand" (Book 1) – maybe Fleur's wand would be unpredictable for another wizard?

Other Oddities

* These are the wands we know about as of Book 4:

Harry: 11" - Holly with Phoenix feather core, "nice and supple"

Voldemort: 13 1/2" - Yew with Phoenix feather core, "powerful"

James: 11" - Mahogany, "pliable, a little more power, excellent for transfiguration"

Lily: 10 1/4" - Willow, "swishy, nice wand for charm work"

Ron (new) 14" - Willow with 1 unicorn tail hair

Fleur: Rosewood with hair of veela (her grandmother's hair) – "inflexible" (length and wandmaker, unknown)

Viktor: 10 1/4" - Hornbeam with dragon heartstring, "quite rigid, thicker than one usually sees" Made by Gregorovitch.

Cedric: 12 1/4" – Ash with tale of male unicorn, "pleasantly springy"

Hagrid: 16" – Oak, "rather bendy" (Now in pieces. Will he get a new one?)

J.K.R.   Mahogany with phoenix feather core (Chat on BBC Online)

(All wands made by Mr. Ollivander unless noted)

Rita Skeeter had turned her "tournament" article into a story on Harry Potter, that just happened to mention the tournament in a few places - omitting Cedric's name completely. Additionally, she claims Harry is having a relationship with Hermione. Everyone is giving Harry a hard time, and Harry is still not talking to Ron, so is spending more time in the library with Hermione. They notice that Viktor Krum spends a lot of time there too (along with a clique of female admirers).

> Either Krum is a bookworm like Hermione, or he is up to something. He can't be up to very much in a library, but he doesn't seem the bookworm type either. Therefore, HP Sleuths have yet another suspect to watch. (Groan)

On the Saturday before the First Task, Harry goes into Hogsmeade with Hermione, but insists on wearing the Invisibility Cloak to avoid harassment from all the taunting students. He contemplates how the town is frequented by some less desirable magical creatures, such as hags, who are less adept at disguising themselves.

> Hags appear to be less magical or weaker power. In fantasy, they are generally considered bad or even evil, and most likely sided with Voldemort. It seems that a lot of darker creatures hang out in Hogsmeade - a truly rough crowd.

As Hermione sits drinking butterbeers with Invisible Harry in the Three Broomsticks, they see Moody sitting at a table sipping from his flask, while talking with Hagrid. Moody had told Harry's class that he never eats or drinks anything that someone else has prepared, as it is too easy for Dark Wizards to poison someone's drink.

> Now that's a pleasant thought - it's easy to poison a drink.☹ Guess Snape isn't the only one Harry should be worried about - hope he paid attention to the antidote lesson (he was there for that part of the lesson, wasn't he?). Wonder if Mad-Eye ever spikes his flask with anything strong? (tee-hee)

Hagrid and Moody come over to Hermione, but Moody sort of leans over toward Harry and lets him know that his eye can see through Invisibility Cloaks. Hagrid then bends down and tells Harry to meet him at his cabin at midnight wearing his Invisibility Cloak.

> Wow, so where do we get one of these eyes? You think he might lend us that eye for a quick walk by Slytherin house?

Back at the Gryffindor common room, Dennis and Colin are trying very hard (based on with their limited magical knowledge) to alter the Potter Stinks buttons. Near midnight, with the help of Hermione, Harry exits under his Invisibility Cloak. He follows Hagrid, who picks up Madame Maxime for a stroll to the far side of the grounds.

Dennis and Colin may be just a bit overly enthusiastic (okay, maybe a **lot** over-ly enthusiastic), therefore it may not occur to Harry, but the Creeveys would be extremely loyal to him if he ever needed them. Also, Dennis has not been like his brother - he has not shadowed Harry or tried to impose on Harry's activities (and is very observant). J.K.R. appears to like Dennis, and we do too. So where does Hagrid go for a midnight stroll?

On the far side of the castle grounds, Hagrid leads them to four huge dragons. Charlie Weasley is there, and tells Hagrid that they have brought one dragon for each of the champions, and that he thinks what they have to do is to get past the dragon. The most vicious of the four is a Hungarian Horntail – that has spikes all along its tail. As Harry is hurrying back to the castle, he (literally) runs into Karkaroff who is sneaking off to get a look at the dragons as well. Harry is now aware that all of the champions will be tipped-off about the dragons, except Cedric.

Hope you HP Sleuths saw this! This exposes a big septology clue. We know it's dark, but Karkaroff is not that small - especially with that big silver fur cloak of his. It's very clear how Karkaroff missed seeing invisible Harry, but how did Harry miss seeing him? Was Harry really that lost in thought? Possibly...Not. The reason Harry most likely missed seeing Karkaroff can be found by reviewing *Fantastic Beasts and Where to Find Them* (not our fault if you haven't got yours by now - we did tell you it was recommended reading). Look under Demiguise - Karkaroff seems to have run across that animal somewhere.

At the appointed time, Sirius' head appears in the flames of the Gryffindor common room fireplace, and Harry is there alone to greet him. When Sirius asks him how he is doing, Harry gushes out all of the events up to the most recent encounter with the drag-ons, in which he is sure he will be toast.

Do dragons prefer their wizards rare, medium, well done, or extra-crispy? So, wizards can use fireplaces to communicate at Hogwarts. Is Hogwarts also on the Floo Net?

Sirius informs Harry that Karkaroff used to be a Death Eater, and Moody was the Auror that caught him and put him into Azkaban. However, Karkaroff got out of Azkaban by turning-in a bunch of other wizards, and from what Sirius heard in Azkaban, Karkaroff now has a lot of enemies. That is probably why Dumbledore has an Auror at the school this year.

Not a surprise to HP Sleuths. Karkaroff sounds like a real role model - just the kind you want to be teaching your kids (ahem). Moody put him in Azkaban? That would certainly explain why Karkaroff and Moody get along so well together (snigger). Could Karkaroff be back in Voldemort's good graces? He sounds fickle enough to go either way. CONSTANT VIGILANCE!

Sirius tells Harry that from what he has been reading in the *Daily Prophet*, there are a number of seemingly unrelated events that may be related. He believes that Moody's "false alarm" on the night before he came to teach might have been an attempt to stop him from getting to Hogwarts. He also says that Bertha Jorkins (who was at Hogwarts when Sirius was there) would have known about the Tournament since she worked at the Ministry. She disappeared in Albania - one of the last places where Voldemort was supposedly seen.

> Amazing! Is Sirius good or what? (Not as good as Hermione, but he's really good.) So is Voldemort still hanging out in Albania? Not according to Harry's dream in Chapter 1. Wonder where Voldemort is now? He could be anywhere - as he said he was only staying at the Riddle house a week or so. HP Sleuths are starting to experience information overload....

Sirius thinks that getting Harry entered into the Triwizard Tournament would be an easy way to kill him while making it look like an accident. Sirius is worried about all these things. Before Sirius can name the simple spell to get past the dragons, Harry hears footsteps coming down into the common room, and tells Sirius to ditch. Harry has to turn away, but knows Sirius has disappeared when he hears a "tiny *pop!*"

> The good news is that Harry wasn't just imagining things with his scar...The bad news is that Harry wasn't just imagining things. The worse part is that Sirius never finished telling him how to survive a dragon. If HP Sleuths unroll their parchment back to Book 2, they might be able to think what kind of spell. Of course, WWP figured out from Book 1 the easiest way of all to fight a dragon. It's simple – just call Charlie Weasley.☺

It is only Ron coming downstairs, and after throwing insults at each-other, Harry (who now has no idea how to get past the dragon) goes to bed fuming.

Curiosities

✳ The popping sounds of wizards and other things that appear and disappear are obviously audible. Unless you're expecting guests to pop in, beware of popping and cracking sounds. (Although, you may recall from book 1 that Dumbledore makes no sound at all....)

Other Oddities

✳ Ernie and Hanna from Hufflepuff collect FW&W cards. Have they studied them?

✳ Dragons can shoot fire at a range of 20 feet, and the Hungarian Horntail can reach 40 feet.

✳

Chapter 20 Analysis

(The First Task)

Clues

Harry and Hermione search the library for simple spells that might be useful on a dragon, but the only information they find states that dragons are difficult to slay since their hide is protected by ancient magic - penetrated by only the most powerful spells. Hermione looks at *Switching Spells*, but doesn't think those would help "unless you swapped its fangs for wine-gums," but Harry wouldn't be able to cast anything through the dragon hide.

> More information trickling in about *Switching Spells*. We now know you can switch human ears onto cactus plants and fangs for wine gums on dragons. Just how much can be changed by switching? Can you go so far as to change your mind?

On their way back from breakfast, Harry follows Cedric up toward the Charms corridor, and splits open Cedric's book bag with a well-timed spell. As Cedric stays behind to pick up all his books, Harry is able to quickly tell him about the dragons. Moody shows up and takes Harry to his office, where he tells Potter that what he did for Cedric "was a very decent thing."

> Actually, Harry just thought it was unfair that Cedric wasn't having nightmares like the rest of them (hehehe). Was that good luck or bad luck that Moody just happened to show up? We'd say that is Rule #3.

Moody has some strange objects in his office, which he calls "Dark Detectors." One of them is a large, cracked Sneakoscope that he laments had to be disabled due to the fact that it is "extra sensitive"; another is a "Secrecy Sensor," which is supposed to pick up concealment and lies, but he says it has been humming since his arrival due to all the "interference" from the students; and then he has what looks like a mirror on his wall that he calls a Foe-Glass where he can watch his enemies coming. Moody says that if he sees one coming, then he goes to his trunk (he utters a harsh laugh). As Harry is about to ask what's in the trunk, Moody brings the subject back to dragons.

> Grrrr.... Moody changes the subject. An aggravating habit of J.K.R.'s – also known as Rule #2. It makes sense that Moody would have the state-of-the-art in Dark Detection. We're not surprised that the "Secrecy Sensor" doesn't work at Hogwarts (Harry would probably be setting it off worse than anyone), but it's odd how those Sneakoscopes keep getting a bum rap. And what's the private joke Moody is telling himself concerning that trunk? Since Harry is trying to avoid being murdered, he should have asked to borrow Moody's Foe Glass (although it would look dumb carrying it around)...
> CONSTANT VIGILANCE!

289

Moody says that he is not going to tell Harry outright how to get around the dragons - but gives him some general advice to "play to his strengths." Moody confides that the other schools will be giving their students all the help they can (you might call it cheating) - hoping to beat Dumbledore so they can "prove he's only human" (he gives a sharp laugh). Harry figures out that he just might get past a dragon on his broom, but needs a *Summoning Charm* to get the broom to him. He asks Hermione to teach him how to do a proper *Summoning Charm.*

Something must be pretty funny, but Moody's not going to let us in on it (of course). This short laugh of Moody's happens whenever he is telling himself a private joke. We saw it when he mentioned in class that he was only going to be teaching one year, and we see it here when he comments about his trunk and then about Dumbledore being human. Yes, we know that's a hint, and we've already investigated Dumbledore's possible ancestry in our analysis of Book 1, Chapter 12. Moody will be telling more private jokes, so we might want to set up a Joke Detector!

Hermione drills Harry all day between classes – every chance they get. During boring divination, Harry practices summoning small objects and even a fly (which he is not sure if he summoned it or it was just dumb enough to fly into his hand).

Another fly? Who, (ahem)...that is...What is this? Is it just a fly again? Professor Trelawney didn't go into a trance this time, nonetheless, things are really buzzing up in the North Tower.

On the day of the First Task, the champions are called to a tent by the Quidditch Field. Bagman holds up a purple silk sack, and they all drawn out a small model of the specific "thing" they will be facing. Bagman tells them that their task will be to "collect the golden egg." Cedric goes first with a bluish-gray Swedish Short-Snout, Fleur Delacour is second with a Welsh Green, Krum is third with a scarlet Chinese Fireball, and Harry ends up last against the dreaded black Hungarian Horntail. Harry sees by everyone's expressions that they all, indeed, knew about the dragons in advance. Before going off to call the play-by-play, Bagman surprises Harry by taking him aside and offering him help.

This is both a story line and septology clue. Bagman seems to have no scruples when it comes to competition or winning. Why is he willing to risk so much to help Harry?

The three other champions are able to accomplish the task, but not without terrifying near-misses. It is then Harry's turn. Harry walks out to face the Horntail, which is crouched over her eggs looking very mean. He casts a successful *Summoning Charm*, gets onto his broom, and suddenly feels confident - imagining he is in a Quidditch match. He draws the dragon up off her eggs, and although grazed by its tail, dives and retrieves the golden egg. Bagman is exceedingly impressed - commenting that it will "shorten the odds" on Harry. Ron is clearly shaken from watching Harry face the wizard killer. Ron admits that it is obvious that whoever put Harry's name in the Goblet wants him hurt. That ends their feud.

There's Mr. Bagman sounding like the bagman again. He really gets into that betting stuff. Wonder what Fred and George are doing with the money they won from him at the World Cup?

Ron tells Harry that Cedric transfigured a stone into a dog - causing a diversion which would have worked flawlessly had the dragon not decided at the last minute to forget the dog and go for Cedric instead. Fleur used a trance that put hers to sleep, but when it snored, it caught her robe on fire. Krum used a spell to blind his, but it trampled some of her own eggs, so he had points taken off. As Madam Pomfrey treats all the wounds, her comment is: "Last year dementors, this year dragons, what are they going to bring into this school next?"

Oh no...She had to ask! Do HP Sleuths have any guesses? What about the Lethifold? (The one in *Fantastic Beasts*) J.K.R. says that it's one of the nastiest, and we won't argue!

Bagman announces that the second task will not take place until February, but in the meantime, the golden eggs they have retrieved are hinged and hold their clue to the next task.

Other Oddities

✳ Professor Trelawney tells her class that the positions of Mars and Saturn foretell that people born in July are "in great danger of sudden, violent deaths." If that's what the planets are saying (if she is not misinterpreting), Harry could be in grave danger (as usual).

✳ When Harry splits open Cedric's bag, one of the books that falls out is a text on Advanced Transfiguration. We now know Cedric's quite good at transfiguration. Bet he knows a lot about *Switching Spells*.

Chapter 21 Analysis

Clues

Harry tells Ron about all the information Sirius discussed with him. Ron reminds Harry that, on the train, Draco had been talking about his dad being friends with Karkaroff.

> Oh, we are so surprised (smirk). We also assume this is telling us that there is probably a direct connection between Malfoy and the Death Eaters. We will just have to wait to see how chummy he is with them.

There is a celebration in the Gryffindor common room. Dean Thomas, who is good at drawing, had created some banners, while Fred and George are selling some "Canary Creams" they had invented (temporarily turns the victim into a giant yellow canary, complete with feathers). The twins talk Neville into eating one. They also instruct Hermione how to get into the Hogwarts kitchens.

> We now have references in at least three books that Dean Thomas is good at drawing. Those are not in there just for color. What is J.K.R. trying to hint at? We already know Dean offered to forge Uncle Vernon's signature. Is that the kind of thing J.K.R. has in mind, or something even more deceptive? HP Sleuths can draw your own conclusions.

The Gryffindors egg Harry into opening the clue to see what's inside. The golden egg emits a horrible screeching wail, and Harry immediately closes it. Seamus hypothesizes that it has something to do with a Banshee, while Neville is petrified - saying it sounds like someone being tortured by the *Cruciatus Curse*.

> The wailing that egg makes must be awfully gruesome. We know that Neville was terrified to witness the *Cruciatus Curse* in Moody's class, while the thing Seamus fears most (according to Book 3) is a Banshee. There is something sinister about that egg, or for some reason we are being reminded of Neville's and Seamus's grave fears. (Which reminds us of Rule #1.)

There are only ten Skrewts left, they have increased to about six feet in length, and have grown a thick, gray armor. As Harry, Ron, Hermione, and a few other students help Hagrid corral the fire-spewing beasts, Rita Skeeter shows up. Hagrid comments that he thought Dumbledore said she isn't allowed at the school anymore, but she re-directs the conversation to scheduling an interview with Hagrid.

> We seem to recall that (back in Chapter 13) Hermione did mention something about the Skrewts growing to six feet. It's not that we doubted her, but we were hoping it was at least an exaggeration. It's not like Dumbledore to ban people from the school, so he must consider Rita to be truly dangerous. Wonder why?

In their Divination class, Professor Trelawney tells them about an image of death she had viewed in her crystal, circling lower and lower over the castle.

> Even though we know Trelawney is probably right about some of this, we can't stop yawning either. The trouble is trying to separate her interpretations from her actual visions.

On their way back from the Divination class, Harry and Ron pass the Bloody Baron, his eyes staring "sinisterly."

> Here's a quiz - what do Professor Trelawney and the Bloody Baron have in common? Answer - we have no idea...but either he is hanging out with Trelawney or with someone in her tower. Whatever he's doing, he's obviously up to no good. Wonder if his "sinisterly" eyes are a J.K.R. hint to link them to Professor Sinistra? It's another septology clue that is driving us bloody well crazy.

Hermione drags Harry and Ron down to the Hogwarts kitchens, which they enter through a painting of a giant fruit bowl (by tickling the pear). Dobby is there and is excited to see Harry. He has no shirt, but is wearing a horseshoe patterned tie, soccer shorts, a tea cozy for a hat, and two different socks - one of which was the sock that Harry had used to set him free. The rest of the elves are all wearing stylish, monogrammed tea towels. Dobby explains that he could not find paid work for two years, but that Dumbledore, who he likes very much, is paying him to work at Hogwarts. Dobby now admits that the Malfoys were Dark wizards. He could not say that before because, as part of the house-elf's enslavement, they keep the family's secrets and uphold their honor (never speaking ill of them).

> With the Malfoys, isn't it more like upholding the family's **dishonor**? Dobby was not happy to be working for a Dark Wizard - would other house-elves feel the same - or is Dobby more moral?

To their surprise, Winky is there too, but although Crouch has let her go, she feels disgraced, refuses to accept paid work from Dumbledore, and is in tears the whole time. Winky says that Bagman is a bad wizard. Crouch does not like him, and has told her "things" about Bagman. She insists her "master" is in dire need of her help, and she refuses to divulge Crouch's secrets.

> Why does Crouch dislike Bagman so much? We're not ready to suspect him as Voldemort's faithful servant - at least not with Karkaroff and Snape lurking around. (Obviously, Winky could tell us, but we see that's not going to happen.) We knew Crouch might be sick, but this sounds as if he is totally inundated with things. What kind of things? He obviously has something secret going on since Winky is telling us so. This is a huge story-line clue, but J.K.R. just does her stealth attack (Rule #2).

Dobby asks Harry if he can visit him sometime up at the school, which Harry gladly says is fine, while Ron promises to give Dobby his mom's Christmas sweater.

Curiosities

✳ Winky says she has been looking after the Crouches all her life – her mother before her, and her grandmother before then.

Other Oddities

✳ Even independent Dobby cannot overcome the upbringing of a house elf. When Dumbledore made him a work offer, Dobby insisted on **lower** wages.

Chapter 22 Analysis

Clues

McGonagall and Moody keep the students working right up to the holidays, while Professor Binns continues to bore them with bloody, vicious, and monotonous goblin rebellions. Professor McGonagall has her class turning guinea fowl into guinea pigs, and gives them an assignment to "Describe...the ways in which *Transforming Spells* must be adapted when performing cross-species Switches." After class, she instructs Harry that as a champion, he must have a dance partner for the traditional Yule Ball that accompanies the Triwizard Tournament.

> Cross-species switches? We overheard these instructions for a reason – hope no one's thinking of changing into a man-eating manticore. How do *Transformation Spells* differ from other *Transfiguration spells*? We're getting confused between switching, transforming, and transfiguring. We need a lesson, J.K.R.!

Hagrid informs Harry, Ron, and Hermione that when Rita interviewed him, she was not interested in his creatures after all. She spent the whole interview trying to get Hagrid to say bad things about Harry. Of course, Hagrid had nothing bad to tell her.

> Oh no – bad news. Poison-Pen Skeeter is starting a negative campaign against Harry. We will see how the power of the Press can undermine an innocent 14-year old.

Harry and Ron try to get up the courage to ask someone to the Ball, but they are frustrated and confused by the observation that females giggle a lot and always seem to travel in packs. Harry eventually does ask his first choice, Cho Chang, but by then she has already committed to going with Cedric (although she sincerely tells Harry that she is sorry). Ron starts to make fun of Neville, but Ginny stops him. It turns out that Ginny is going as Neville's partner. Hermione has already been asked, but is secretive about her partner.

> ...And we thought we were the only ones to notice the shrill noises and flocking tendencies, which comprise the social habits of females. What we are interested to know is do Ginny and Neville have a good time? They are both somewhat mystery characters since Harry does not interact with them much. What do they talk about? What do they know about each other that we have yet to discover? They are both most likely holding keys to some surprising septology clues.

As they are running out of candidates, Harry and Ron end up going with the Patil twins (Harry with Parvati from Gryffindor and Ron with Padma from Ravenclaw).

Other Oddities

✳ J.K.R. says that "Snape would no sooner let them play games in class than adopt Harry" - she's joking, right?

✳ In Snape's class, Harry forgets to add the bezoar. HP Sleuths, of course, know how crucial that ingredient is... (you should have it in your notes).

✳ More boring goblin rebellions (Rule #1). Although, these sound worse than we had heard before – being described as "bloody and vicious goblin riots"

✳ Fred tells Ron to keep his "nose out" of their letter-writing affairs.

Chapter 23 Analysis

Clues

Gryffindors have learned not to accept food of any kind from the Weasley practical jokers. George confides in Harry that he and Fred are in the process of developing something else really big.

> Fred and George still haven't said anything about the money they won from Bagman - wonder if that is what they are working at? Whatever it is, hope it's not edible. (If it is, we're not eating it.)

Harry and Ron notice that they hadn't noticed Hermione's oversized teeth are no longer oversized. Hermione explains that when Madam Pomfrey shrunk them after the duel, she just let them shrink a bit extra.

> Hermione never did tell us how her (dentist) parents reacted to this.

Sirius sends an owl to Harry congratulating him on getting past the dragon. Sirius divulges that a dragon's weakest point are its eyes, so that's what he was about to tell Harry when they talked the other night. He reinforces that Harry should write immediately if he sees *anything* unusual.

> The weakest part are it's eyes – did HP Sleuths remember? We've seen it before with the Basilisk from Book 2. We might see it again. HP Sleuths need to keep this information visible.

On Christmas Day, Harry is startled awake to find himself face to face with Dobby. Dobby has brought a present for Harry - they are a pair of red and green socks (one sock of each color) with a Quidditch pattern. Dobby tells Harry how he had knit them himself - buying the wool with money from his own wages. Harry grabs the pair of Uncle Vernon's old, mustard-yellow socks out of his trunk, removing the Pocket Sneakoscope. He gives them to Dobby with the excuse that he forgot to wrap them.

> The WWP Sleuthoscope is blinking like a Christmas tree! Harry gets woolen socks for Christmas but Dumbledore doesn't? (Awww.) What is there about woolen socks for Christmas that is so special? We know Dobby really likes Harry, so there is a possibility that Dobby put something extra-special into these socks (he is a very powerful little elf).

Ron gives Dobby more socks plus his mother's "famous Weasley Sweater" that he had promised to him. Dobby proclaims that Ron is a great wizard, being noble and generous. Sirius has sent Harry a pocketknife that will unlock or untie anything.

> Those images of Dr. Who keep popping into our brain. We can't help it - J.K.R. keeps doing that to us. First we have TARDIS-like tents, and now we have an

unlocking tool (an indispensable prop of the fourth Doctor). That should be very useful - hope Harry keeps it with him.

At the Yule Ball, Harry sees Krum enter with a "pretty girl in blue robes Harry didn't know." As Harry lines up next to Krum and his partner, he is dumbfounded to see that the "pretty girl in blue" is Hermione. Krum has trouble with her name (her-my-oh-nee) - first calling her "Hermy-own," and then his best is "Herm-own-ninny." Krum also discusses how Durmstrang only lights fires to do magic and only has 4 floors.

Don't lie now - how many of you made the same kind of mistakes as Krum when you first tried to pronounce Hermione's name? We're guilty too. This dialogue was here to either help those who had not yet heard the name spoken in a movie, audio book, or by J.K.R., and to make us laugh as we see someone else try it. We also got some *inside* information about Durmstrang (sounds depressing). HP Sleuths should be taking notes since this may help us if we ever take any *field trips* to Durmstrang (or need to storm the gates). Although Durmstrang sounds small, there are probably secret rooms, hidden passageways, and plenty of underground chambers, just like Hogwarts.

Harry and Parvati sit down at the head table next to Percy, who is there representing Mr. Crouch. Percy proudly informs them that he has been recently promoted as Mr. Crouch's "personal assistant." He tells Harry that Mr. Crouch isn't feeling well, and hasn't been well since the World Cup - mostly on account of "that Skeeter woman buzzing around" the Ministry.

HP Hintoscope is humming loudly! What's that Percy is saying about Poison Pen Skeeter? What exactly is she up to with all this buzzing around? Does she know something? Maybe it's not what she knows, but *who* she knows there? This is a huge story-line hint. If you think she's been bugging people too much already, just wait 'til you see how much she can really interfere. We can only imagine the kind of damage she could cause - it could be of septology proportions.

Percy also mentions that they had some trouble with Ali Bashir. Ali was trying to smuggle a "consignment of flying carpets into the country."

Ah, the subtlety of J.K.R. For our readers who have not yet encountered the word "consignment," it means being a *middle man* to buy or sell for someone else. Therefore, the question is, who was Ali buying or selling for? We don't know yet, so HP Sleuths will have to ride this one out.

The famous music group, the Weird Sisters (heard on the WWN - Wizarding Wireless Network), is the entertainment at the Ball.

We already know that Celestina Warbeck probably uses her media influence for her "causes." While people in the U.S. do not relate to this as well, HP Sleuths in the U.K. know that the media can be an incredibly powerful weapon. Therefore, it could be crucial to know more about who runs the WWN. HP Sleuths - stay tuned to the WWN!

Moody "dances" with Professor Sinistra, who is attempting to avoid being tromped by his wooden leg. As Moody dances past Harry and Parvati, Moody makes the comment "Nice socks, Potter." Harry replies that Dobby knitted them for him.

> We are still a bit suspicious of the elusive Professor Sinistra. There is nothing wrong that we can see, but we will remember that this is another rare sighting of the Astronomy Professor. Guess we are not supposed to forget about those socks from Dobby (see Rule #1).

While everyone else is dancing, Harry and Ron spend time talking to each-other, much to the frustration of the Patil twins - who give up and socialize with some boys from Beauxbatons. Ron spends most of the evening glaring at Hermione and Krum, while Harry refuses to look at Cho and Cedric.

> The big mystery here is how Harry and Ron managed to get themselves into this predicament.

Ron and Harry head out to a grotto that has been conjured in front of the castle, complete with a rose garden and fairy lights. They walk by Snape and Karkaroff who is saying that they can't pretend something isn't "happening," since for months "it" has been getting clearer. Snape advises Karkaroff to flee - telling Karkaroff that he will cover for him, but that he (Snape) will remain at Hogwarts.

> Right chummy of Snape. He won't even give Harry a slight break, but he is willing to cover for Karkaroff - a Death Eater? We know Dumbledore has been trusting of Snape, but it's hard for us to do so. What exactly has been getting clearer? Just like Sirius and Dumbledore, Karkaroff must be getting some signs too. We can spot that something nasty is brewing.

Ron and Harry pause in the bushes, trying to figure out how to avoid everyone else. They hear the voices of Hagrid and Madame Maxime, who are seated nearby. Trying not to listen in, Harry concentrates his attention on a crawling beetle, but when they hear Hagrid start talking about his parents and childhood, Harry stops watching and listens more intently. Hagrid tells Madame Maxime about his normal-sized wizard father, who died shortly after he started school, so Dumbledore had looked after him. Hagrid admits to being part giant on his mother's side.

> We don't blame Harry - there isn't much interesting about a beetle that can possibly distract from such an intriguing conversation. So that's it.... Hagrid is part giant. This is obviously what J.K.R. has been leading up to with all those hints about people looking like they have troll or veela in them. Hagrid is not completely human after all - maybe that's why he is so nice? (smirk)

Madame Maxime is upset, however, with Hagrid's inferences about her own bloodline, insisting that she does not have any giant in her. She leaves in a huff. Ron is astounded that Hagrid is part giant, and explains that giants are dangerous by nature, and, like trolls, seem to kill just because they like it.

> HP Sleuths - this is a gigantic story line clue (well, maybe not quite that big). Just like in C. S. Lewis's *The Chronicles of Narnia*, J.K.R. portrays giants as man-killers. However, also like Narnia, J.K.R has created nice giants. Hagrid's bloodline must come from a nice lineage. Wonder where his relatives are?

As the students leave the Ball to return to their dorms, Cedric calls Harry over to talk to him privately. He tells Harry that he "owes him one" for the tip-off about the dragons, and then says to "take a bath, and...take the egg with you." He encourages Harry to use the Prefect bathroom - giving him the password (pinefresh).

> "Go take a bath"? At least he didn't tell Harry to go jump in a lake. Was this meant to help Harry, or to zap him?

When Harry returns to the Gryffindor common room, Ron and Hermione are in the middle of an argument that seems quite a bit like jealousy.

Curiosities

✳ We can't see any significance yet, but just in case... Harry's socks from Dobby are a red one with broomsticks for the left foot, and a green one with snitches for the right foot. Does that mean the socks are custom-knit like that? This might be confusing to sailors, pilots, and engineers who learned that *right is red*.

Other Oddities

✳ Fawcett (a Ravenclaw female) who apparently lives near Ron (Chapter 6) attended the Yule Ball with Stebbins from Hufflepuff.

Chapter 24 Analysis

Clues

When Harry, Ron, and Hermione arrive at their Care of Magical Creatures lesson, instead of Hagrid, they find an aged witch, by the name of Professor Grubbly-Plank, in front of his cabin door. She informs them that she is their "temporary" teacher, giving no information about Hagrid's whereabouts. The Professor has brought a unicorn for their lesson, and allows the girls to approach (while holding the males back), explaining that unicorns "prefer the woman's touch."

> Have you ever wondered why almost **all** females seem to be attracted to unicorns? According to J.K.R., it's because of their special preference for females. (Does make you wonder....)

While the girls inspect the unicorn, Malfoy shows the boys the latest Rita Skeeter article, in which she tries to undermine Dumbledore's authority by questioning his appointments of Moody and Hagrid as teachers. Harry is so furious with Rita's story that he is not able to concentrate on the unicorn lesson. The article quotes Malfoy who talks about "multiple" injuries to students from Hagrid's classes. It reveals that Hagrid is half giant by his mother, Fridwulfa, whose whereabouts are unknown.

> Yet another orphan. That sucks. But it's not that uncommon in fantasy – even Frodo Baggins from *The Lord of the Rings* was an orphan. Being a wizard seems like a high-risk gene. Now, what is Poison Pen Skeeter up to? She is trying to discredit everyone – even Dumbledore.

Rita's article recounts how giants had sided with the Dark Lord, that they had a reputation for mass murders of Muggles, and that there are still giant communities in foreign mountain ranges. She then ties-in Harry's friendship with Hagrid.

> So the giants sided with Voldemort. Well, Rita is definitely not open-minded, and she's certainly no help for the good guys if she is willing to hurt Hagrid that badly just for an article. Why would she do that? Is she really that cold-blooded? Is there something more we don't know about Rita? Based on J.K.R.'s description of her, we have to question not only her personality, but her identity.

Hermione thinks Rita had to have overheard Hagrid in the rose garden, but Ron is emphatic that they'd have seen her if she had been there. Harry thinks Rita couldn't coerce Hagrid to say anything bad about Harry, so she went after Hagrid instead. Ron and Hermione are intent on trying to figure out how Rita ever found out about Hagrid.

> How Rita found out really bugs Ron and Hermione. Ron's been insistent before, but that's when he's got the right idea, but the wrong answer. Knowing Hermione's track record (Rule #4) – we'd better listen to her too. So, then how could Rita have been there, and be seen but not have been seen? Uhhh... we'll

have to concentrate on this one. However, with sources like Malfoy, Rita probably could find out enough material to fill a weekly magazine. We'll have to keep
track of where Malfoy is hovering.

In the middle of January, Harry, Ron, and Hermione take advantage of a Hogsmeade
weekend. As they are leaving the castle grounds, they observe Krum dive off the deck of
his ship into the frigid lake and swim around.

If Hagrid is part giant, does that mean Krum is part penguin? (We're only half
kidding.)

In Hogsmeade, they run into Bagman who is being shadowed by a gaggle of menacing
goblins. Bagman privately tells Harry that Barty Crouch is not ill - that they do not really know where Crouch is, and that although they were able to determine that Bertha
Jorkins did make it to Albania, everyone lost track of her when she went to visit her Aunt
one day. Bagman also asks Harry, once again, if there is anything he can do to help
Harry with the Tournament. Harry, of course, refuses, but is even more skeptical of
Bagman's intentions.

Bagman is up to something - otherwise, once he had seen that Harry did alright
in the first task, he wouldn't still be trying to help him so badly again. What's
his angle? What's he got his nose into this time? The information about Crouch
is disconcerting and confusing. If Crouch is ill, why is he trying to hide his illness? We know what happened to Bertha, so that is not a mystery to us, but it
doesn't help solve the other issues (or does it?).

When Fred and George come over and ask Bagman to join them in a drink, Bagman
leaves with the goblins. Hermione explains that goblins, unlike house-elves, are clever
and "capable of dealing with wizards."

Are Fred and George still making bets? Bagman doesn't want to spend much
time with them - could they have won yet more money from him? Speaking of
money, there's more Goblins. Yes, they are exceedingly self-sufficient (they do
run the bank).

Rita Skeeter comes into the Three Broomsticks, trying to dig up more dirt – this time on
Bagman. Harry and Hermione accuse her in public of trying to ruin the lives of Bagman
and Hagrid. Rita replies, calling Hermione a "silly little girl."

Rita shouldn't have done that!! HP Sleuths know from Book 3 that there are
three rules to remember about Hermione: Don't call her a Mudblood; Don't
insult her friends; and Never...ever... call Hermione a Silly Girl! (or anything
remotely like that....)

Rita says that she "knows things" (bad things) about Bagman. Ron warns Hermione
that Rita will probably try to get back at her.

Bagman may not be so innocent (we somehow figured that). Even Winky says he's a bad guy. However, he still doesn't seem likely to be the servant of Lord Voldemort. Plus, we've got too many better suspects, anyway.

Harry, Ron, and Hermione go straight back to Hagrid's hut. They find Dumbledore is also there paying him a visit because Hagrid has asked to resign due to that Rita article. They all convince Hagrid that most people want him to stay. Dumbledore tells Hagrid that he does not accept his resignation, and leaves them to talk among themselves. Hagrid shows the kids a picture of his wizard father seated on Hagrid's seven-foot-tall shoulder the year he entered Hogwarts (at the age of eleven). His father had been so proud of him, but died during Hagrid's second year - thankfully never saw him expelled. Since Hagrid had no mother or father, Dumbledore had taken him under his wing.

So Dumbledore has been Hagrid's guardian since he was 12 years old! That explains Hagrid's loyalty to Dumbledore. ☺

Just as everyone else has done, Hagrid asks Harry how he is doing with his egg, and just as he has done with everyone else, Harry lies. But it makes him feel guilty enough, that he is finally motivated to take Cedric's advice about the bath.

Curiosities

✳ If what Harry missed in the unicorn lesson applies to Rule #2, at least Hermione was there and listening.

Other Oddities

✳ Dumbledore claims that his brother, Aberforth, was "prosecuted for practicing inappropriate charms on a goat." (We can't take Dumbledore **completely** seriously.)

✳ Rita's article reveals that Hagrid's Blast-Ended Skrewts are a new breed of creature that Hagrid created – being a cross between manticores and fire-crabs. If HP Sleuths have any questions about how dangerous that could be, just consult your well-worn *Fantastic Beasts and Where to Find Them* textbook!

✳ Harry says Rita went "ferreting around" for information about Hagrid. Let's see, Mortlake had some odd ferrets (Book 2), Malfoy impersonated one, and again now, Rita is acting like one for the second time (see Chapter 10). Could there be some kind of link between Rita and Mortlake? The Rememberit Quill has just drawn us a ferret cage to hold all of these.

Chapter 25 Analysis

(THE EGG AND THE EYE)

Clues

Taking the egg, the Marauder's Map, and his Invisibility Cloak, Harry heads up to the Prefect's bathroom, as Cedric instructed. Harry fills the luxurious, swimming pool-sized bathtub with bubbles and oils, and gets in under a painting of a sleeping mermaid. Harry opens the egg, only to find that it still wails away. He immediately clamps it back up (thinking that Cedric might have been intending for him to be caught in there by Filch). He freaks as Moaning Myrtle unexpectedly addresses him.

> Why it's the bubbly Moaning Myrtle, come to sulk with Harry. HP Sleuths note - Myrtle is away from her toilet. Intriguing.

Myrtle instructs Harry to open the egg (like she saw Cedric do) and listen to it under water. Harry tries it and hears a song instead of screeching. Myrtle *likes* feeling as if she knows more than Harry and enjoys telling him how to work the egg. Myrtle informs Harry that "all sorts" of creatures live in the lake, and with the painting of the mermaid facing him, Harry guesses that there are merpeople down there. The song tells him that he will have one hour to look under water for something of his that the merpeople will have taken from him. Unfortunately, Harry barely knows how to swim, let alone breathe underwater.

> Guess there's nothing bad about the egg after all. It just sounds bad. All sorts of creatures live in the lake? We did see Krum dive in once. He didn't seem to be holding the egg, but he could have been practicing swimming underwater. Wonder if the creatures are generally friendly, and if they tend to stay in the lake? Bet there's even some red herring swimming around in there too....

Myrtle tells Harry how sometimes she is flushed into the lake if she is caught off-guard. She also carries on about how she had been haunting Olive Hornby everywhere until the Ministry of Magic made her stop and live in her toilet. She is quite pleased that Olive did not forget about it 'til the day she died.

> WWP Sleuthoscope is splashing around madly. Did Myrtle say that flushing water can actually push her? Did she also say that she was following Olive around at other locations? Myrtle always appeared a bit more "dense," but this is not your average spirit. Moaning Myrtle may not be very social, but she is a very versatile ghost. Wonder what might have happened to Olive - is she resting peacefully?

On the way back from the Prefect's bathroom, Harry sees on his map that there is a dot moving in a room in the "bottom left-hand corner" of the parchment. To his amazement, not only is Barty Crouch at Hogwarts but he is in Snape's office. It just doesn't make sense to Harry that the Percy-like Crouch would be sneaking around Hogwarts at night. Instead of returning to his dorm, Harry heads toward Snape's office, staring at the map, not believing what he is seeing.

The HP Hintoscope just broke the sound barrier! Now we know that Crouch's illness/ disappearance has a critical link to the story line, and this is a key event. J.K.R. seems to have caught us - hook, line, and sinker. HP Sleuths also pay close attention now to that "bottom left-hand corner" there.

Harry is so engrossed, that he forgets about the "trick" stair. He falls right into it - dropping the egg and map. The egg clatters down the stairs and then bursts open, sending its wailing through the corridors. Harry is stuck with his leg jammed in the stair, cannot reach the map, and quickly covers himself with his cloak. Filch comes running with Mrs. Norris, yelling Peeves', name (who he thinks has stolen the egg and is causing the racket).

(Okay, so even Harry can forget about that step.) We see a slightly different side of Filch in this scene. Although out to get Peeves (as usual), he appears to be genuinely concerned about the property of the student champions.

Snape arrives - complaining that someone had broken into his office. Snape is sure it could not have been Peeves because his office is sealed with a spell that can only be broken by a wizard.

Only a wizard can break into Snape's office? We'll have to keep that in mind. Knowing Snape, we wouldn't be surprised if it's even booby-trapped.

Then Moody shows up and challenges Snape, saying if there might have been something in his office to take.

Something else in Snape's office? Like what?? As of the end of this book, J.K.R. has not told us about anything that Dark Wizards would have in their possession that would link them to Voldemort. What's that all about? Is that a septology clue? We think so, but those red herrings are in mating season right now...

Moody claims that searching the office was "Auror's privilege," but Snape cannot believe that Dumbledore would order it, as he trusts Snape. Moody counters by saying that Dumbledore may believe in "second chances," but Moody thinks "there are spots that don't come off." At these words, for some reason, Snape grabs his own left forearm with his right hand.

J.K.R. made it easy to spot this story-line clue. That was no nervous twitch. Seems that something somehow might have left it's mark on Snape. Was that a battle wound of some kind? Whatever, Moody made it clear that Snape is on a "second chance."

Because of his magical eye, Moody can also see Harry in his awkward situation but almost ruins everything as he mistakenly alerts Snape to the map. However, Harry signals wildly from under his Cloak, and Moody summons the map before Snape can nab it. Moody convinces Snape and Filch to leave, mutters "close shave," and pulls Harry up from the trick stair. He asks if Harry had happened to see who broke into Snape's office "on this map, I mean." Harry lets him know it was Mr. Crouch, which alarms Moody who does not seem to be able to locate Crouch anywhere on it now.

> Moody is obviously quite captivated by Harry's map. He also looked over the map quite carefully and apparently does not see Crouch on it at the moment. Where could Crouch have gone?

Harry asks Moody if he might have an idea why Barty Crouch was in Snape's office in the middle of the night.

> HP Sleuths - if this feels like the million-dollar question, then you are right on the money. However, don't go trying to figure this one out unless you happen to be the ultimate HP Super Sleuth. We have (sort of) been given enough information to come up with the solution, but to solve it you would have to blow away a bunch of assumptions, make some new ones, and do a few leaps of faith. Not worth it. Let's just say that this is a case of "the Marauder's Map never lies...."

Moody confirms Harry's thoughts that there have been some "funny rumors flying around" - which he says have been "helped along by Rita Skeeter, of course."

> The WWP Sleuthoscope is airborne. Yes, indeed, those rumors certainly have been "helped" along by Rita. Our suspicions of Rita grow stronger with every reference....

Moody comments that if people say "Mad-Eye" is obsessed with catching Dark wizards, he's "nothing compared to Barty Crouch."

> We thought Crouch may be extreme, but that's a strange comment from a guy that looks as if every Dark Wizard has taken a piece out of him already. So is Crouch that obsessed or does Moody have personal information on him too?

As Moody's eye spotted the left-hand corner of the map, he mutters about one thing he hates is "a Death Eater who walked free...."

> The HP Hintoscope is whispering excitedly. Moody is again oozing disdain, and not at all hiding his contempt for the Death Eaters who did not end up in Azkaban - you can tell he truly hates them. Are HP Sleuths catching that he is looking in the left-hand corner of the map when he says this? In the left-hand *top corner* is Dumbledore's office, but that doesn't make sense. In the left-hand *bottom corner* is Snape's office, so he most probably means Snape. Are we supposed to take this as evidence that Snape was a Death Eater? We might have been less sure except that J.K.R. cut off the conversation at that moment (Rule #2). Yup, a sure sign.

Moody is entranced with the map and asks Harry if he can borrow it, which Harry thinks is only fair after what Moody did to get him out of that tight situation.

> Moody wants another toy. Wonder what he's going to use it for? Wonder if he is looking for someone in particular?

Harry contemplates why a very ill Crouch would turn up in the middle of the night at Hogwarts, and what he thought Snape might have in his office.

Curiosities

✳ What might Snape have in his office? People keep asking that, and we keep thinking of Rule #1.

Other Oddities

✳ Since there is a statue of *Boris the Bewildered*, he must have been important for some reason. He is described as a "lost-looking wizard with his gloves on the wrong hands." Wonder if we was a victim of a *Memory Charm*, or if the gloves were actually correct, but the hands were on the wrong arms due to a bad *Switching Spell*? Did we say, "*Switching Spell*"?

✳ The wand and map issue seems like an oversight, so we will overlook it.

Clues

This is Chapter 26.

Is Chapter 26 (double 13) a Whodunit chapter also? Is this second task part two of Chapter 13?

During class, while practicing *Banishing Charms* on cushions (and occasionally on Professor Flitwick), Harry tells Ron and Hermione about the egg and what happened on his way back. They wonder what Snape did that caused him to need a "second chance." Harry also sends a letter to Sirius, telling him all about it. They go off to Hagrid's class, where he has some unicorn foals to show them. These baby unicorns are pure gold and more trusting, thus the males can approach them more easily.

So was Snape a Death Eater? How many HP Sleuths vote "No"? Ahem, do any HP Sleuths vote "No"? Well, even if we really, really, don't like him, it doesn't mean he's a Death Eater, does it?

It is the night before the second task and Harry still has not found a spell he can do himself that will allow him to stay underwater. Ron and Hermione do everything they can to help Harry that evening, but while they are in the library, Fred and George come down to get Ron and Hermione because Professor McGonagall wants to see them in her office. Harry continues to pour over the references in panic, and then returns to the library after midnight under his Invisibility Cloak.

Harry's getting a hard lesson in procrastination. He needs a life saver – or at least a water expert. Wonder if Great Uncle Algie could have helped? Neville was doing some reading a while ago on water type things. Wonder if he noticed anything?

Harry finds himself being prodded awake - he had fallen asleep in the library. He realizes his Invisibility Cloak must have slipped off his head, and now Dobby is in front of him, urging that there are only ten minutes left until the start of the second task. Harry is sure he has now failed this task, but Dobby has brought him gillyweed (that the house-elf overheard McGonagall and Moody discussing). Dobby says that Harry must eat the gillyweed right before he goes in, so he can breathe underwater in order to save his "Wheezy" (Weasley) from the merpeople. When Harry realizes that it is a human who has been taken, he is now panicking since, according to the riddle, if he does not succeed, Ron is lost!

Did the Invisibility Cloak really slip off Harry's head on its own? Are we sure that's how Dobby found him? Dobby's a great guy - guess that makes up (a bit) for almost getting Harry killed in Book 2. What a lucky coincidence that Dobby ended up overhearing Moody and McGonagall, wasn't it? Wasn't it? Okay, so we can't fool HP Sleuths - probably not a coincidence - maybe Moody came through for Harry again.

Harry takes the gillyweed and races down to the lake, barely in time for the start of the Tournament. He gets scolded by Percy (who is substituting for Crouch on this task). Bagman signals the beginning of the second task, and Harry begins eating his gillyweed as he enters the icy water. Harry shivers as he feels "a cruel breeze lifting his hair." Gills have formed on his neck; his hands and feet have become webbed as he dives for a breath of water. His eyes now have clear underwater visibility - allowing him to move quickly and easily through the deep lake.

Harry's not the only one who is looking a bit fishy. Where is Crouch this time?

While searching the murky waters for his hostage, Harry comes across interesting sights – including an underwater plain "littered with dull, shimmering stones." He passes directly over some weeds out of which a grindylow suddenly grabs Harry around the ankles. Harry uses his wand to cast a "Relashio!" Spell, which sends jets of boiling water at them, and manages to kick one of them senseless, so they leave him alone. Moaning Myrtle comes floating by and points him in the right direction.

Moaning Myrtle has been extremely helpful. You know, HP Sleuths, Myrtle could be quite valuable. Even if her personality were to prevent her from volunteering help, we bet she would come to Harry's aid if needed.☺ Wonder what house she was in?

Harry hears mersong and follows it to an underwater village where he finds Ron, Hermione, Cho Chang, and Fleur's 8-year-old sister tied down, and surrounded by a group of merpeople with spears. The merpeople have grayish skin, dark green hair, yellow eyes, and look quite intimidating. Harry tries to borrow a spear from one of them to cut the hostages loose, but they are insistent that they are not allowed to help.

Cool! An entire underwater village of merpeople. There's a lot going on in the Hogwarts lake - it's a whole world down there, of which we have only seen a small bit. Do HP Sleuths recall from Book 1 and Book 2 that the lower levels of the castle may extend under the lake? Also, could the lake continue on somewhere as an underground lake? We were told in Book 1 that there is a lake below Gringotts - could this one either be connected or part of a vast network of underground tunnels and lakes?

Sirius's handy present of the penknife is sitting back in Harry's room, so Harry has to use a jagged rock to cut Ron loose. Harry then starts to cut the others loose as well, but is restrained by the merpeople, who laugh as they tell him that he is to leave with only his own hostage. Concerned about time, Harry checks his watch, but it has stopped.

Whoa! The WWP Sleuthoscope is going faster than the speed of light! It's that time.... This Chapter 26 does seem to hold a key to one of the themes of the whole Harry Potter mystery - the time references. Harry's watch has stopped. That just might mean the time has come for the destined event to occur....

Cedric eventually arrives, using an air bubble around his head, and cuts Cho loose. He is followed by Krum - who has partially transformed his upper body into a shark-head to rescue Hermione. When it appears that Fleur is not going to make it, Harry pulls out his wand, chases off the merpeople, and rescues Fleur's sister along with Ron.

> Was this what Krum was doing when Harry, Ron, and Hermione saw him diving into the lake on their way to Hogsmeade? Probably – but since no mention was made of him having an egg or a wand, it still could have been a refreshing January swim (...for a penguin or otter, that is).

As Harry gets to shore, Ron opens his eyes and is exasperated that Harry took the song literally and rescued the others. Dumbledore would not have let them drown - it was just to reinforce their time limit. Nonetheless, Fleur, who was stopped by the Grindylows, had taken the song seriously too, and is on the bank, hysterical over her sister, Gabrielle. Krum and Hermione are wrapped-up in thick blankets - where she is brushing a water beetle out of her hair.

> Another beetle? Hogwarts seems to be infested with these bugs. Fleur is very attached to her sister – wonder if it's just that she was entrusted with her care, or if there are other family-related reasons?

The female chief of the merpeople, Merchieftainess Murcus, comes up and has a conversation in mermish with Dumbledore. Dumbledore then calls for a discussion with the judges before awarding the scores.

> This confirms that the merpeople were in on the whole task, and it seems that Dumbledore may be friends with them. So, the merpeople can exist out of water as well. Good allies. Was it one of them, or something else, that rescued Dennis Creevey when he fell into the lake? Wonder how many of the merpeople can speak a human language? Wonder how many other languages Dumbledore can speak? Is there a chance that Neville can communicate with any water-type creatures? Just more septology gobbledygook.

Fleur is exceedingly impressed that Harry saved her sister even though she was not his hostage. Fleur kisses Harry and Ron in appreciation while Hermione looks on, fuming.

> It is not a mystery that Ron and Hermione really like each-other - even if they haven't admitted it to themselves. Yet, the question is, are they right for each-other? We also like Hermione and Krum, and it might be quite interesting to see Ron and Fleur if she would ever consider it (maybe Harry could put in a good word now, heehee).

Bagman announces the scores. Although Harry returned last and long after the time limit, the Merchieftainess let them know that Harry actually arrived first, but was delayed because he persisted in insuring that all hostages were rescued. For that, Harry receives almost full marks, and is now tied for first place with Cedric.

Harry had help for this task from Cedric, Moody, Dobby, and Myrtle. This proves that even in the wizarding world, you're only as strong as your advisors. Obviously Dumbledore already knew that. Harry now seems to be gaining an understanding for the importance of a reliable network.

The third task is to take place at dusk on June 24th, and they will be given instructions one month before that.

Rowlinguistics

✳ The spell Harry uses on the grindylows is **"*Relashio!*"** It probably comes from the French word *relacher*. Although spelled differently, both words are pronounced the same because the ch = sh when spoken. It means to *loosen, relax,* or *cease activity*.

Curiosities

✳ For some reason, when fighting the grindylows, Harry did not use Lupin's advice to break the grip of their brittle fingers.

✳ Hagrid tells us that unicorn foals are pure gold, turning silver around two years old, and pure white when completely grown (around seven). They don't get a horn until about four years-old. Even unicorn foals are not thrilled about males, so if a wizard ever needs to approach a unicorn, it's best to remember not to send a guy in to do a woman's job....

✳ The merpeople, Mrs. Norris, Basilisks, and Madam Hooch all have yellow eyes.

Other Oddities

✳ Harry is under the impression that the merpeople "knew no more magic than the giant squid." Should we be asking how much magic the giant squid knows?

314

Chapter 27 Analysis

(PADFOOT RETURNS)

Clues

Ron receives a lot of attention due to his adventure as a hostage, which he thoroughly enjoys (and embellishes on). Sirius sends a letter telling Harry, Ron, and Hermione to meet him at Hogsmeade and to bring food - they can't believe he has returned to Hogsmeade. In Potions class, the Slytherins are eager to point out that Rita Skeeter has struck again. She goes after Hermione in her latest article, saying that Hermione created a lover's triangle due to her personal relationships with Harry and Krum. It mentions that Krum had asked her to visit him in Bulgaria. At first, Hermione ignores the whole issue as she crushes beetles for a wit-sharpening potion. However, it suddenly bugs her when she realizes that although the information was accurate, there is no way Rita Skeeter should have known. The information does have an interesting effect on Ron, however.

> Skeeter is starting to drive everyone buggy. Not only does she attack Hermione, she drags Krum and Harry into it. It's almost as if she has ulterior motives. We are now convinced she does.

Snape gets Harry alone during his class and threatens that if Harry breaks into his office again, he might use Veritaserum on him (a truth serum so powerful its use is controlled by the Ministry of Magic). Snape had found gillyweed and boomslang skin (for Polyjuice Potion) missing - he knew Harry used the gillyweed and that Harry had been out of bed that night. Although Harry knew Hermione had ripped-off some boomslang skin in their second year for the Polyjuice Potion, Harry is truthfully insistent that he did not break in. Harry contemplates drinking from a hip flask, like Moody, to avoid Snape's truth serum.

> WWP Sleuthoscope is hovering in stealth mode. So is this where Dobby got the gillyweed? The implications are staggering. If Dobby did get the gillyweed from Snape's office, how did he get in there? Does he have some special house-elf's privilege of even getting into Snape's office, or can he get past Snape's security spells? If Dobby did not get the gillyweed from Snape's office, then who did? The same thing with the boomslang skin - was that taken by Hermione two years ago and it took this long for Snape to discover the theft, or did someone else need it? There's a lot brewing in this cauldron.

Karkaroff comes in during Snape's class, accusing Snape of avoiding him, and waits until class is over to talk to him. Pretending he is cleaning up a spill of armadillo bile, Harry watches as Karkaroff shows Snape his left inner forearm. Karkaroff is saying that it has never been this clear, and that Snape must have also noticed.

> Snape had grabbed his left arm when Moody talked about "spots," and now Karkaroff is showing Snape his left arm. We won't even suggest this might only be a coincidence - we know better. So, what is getting clearer, and is it contagious?

315

Harry, Ron, and Hermione go to meet Padfoot along the road heading out of Hogsmeade. He leads them up into the mountains and through a narrow fissure that opens into a cave. Buckbeak is there with him. Sirius devours the chicken that Harry has brought him - telling Harry that he has been mostly living off of rats. Buckbeak happily chews on the bones, while Harry and Ron look at old newspaper articles that Sirius had scavenged. There's one on Crouch, which reports he has not been seen by anyone lately (although St Mungo's Hospital declined comment).

> Why would St Mungo's decline comment? The only reason to decline comment is if you are covering up or protecting information. If Crouch is not a patient, then that is all they have to say. So does that mean they have seen Crouch, or are leading us to believe they have seen him? That place cannot be trusted. Hope no one we care about ends up in St Mungo's Hospital.

Sirius asks Harry if he had checked his pocket for the wand before he left the Top Box, and Harry realizes he had not. They try to remember who else might have been in the Top Box that day. While going over the details, Hermione keeps insisting that the elf (Winky) is innocent, and was mistreated by Crouch. Sirius supports her - saying that the way to "know what a man's like," is to see "how he treats his inferiors, not his equals." Sirius says it is not like Crouch to not show-up for things.

> Everyone imaginable was up there in the Top Box – everyone, that is, except Crouch. So he's the only one we can be sure didn't take Harry's wand, right? Guess with J.K.R., you can't be too sure of anything. So where was Crouch and why did no one see him?

Sirius reveals that as former Head of the Department of Magical Law Enforcement, Crouch was the one who sent Sirius to Azkaban with no trial. Barty Crouch became so obsessed with capturing and destroying Dark wizards, that he gave his Aurors orders to start killing and throwing people (like Sirius) into Azkaban without trials. However, before Crouch could rise to head the Ministry, his own son was caught in the company of some Death Eaters who were trying to find and revive Voldemort. Sirius isn't sure if Crouch's son was guilty or not (he might have been in the wrong place at the wrong time, like Winky).

> As in Sirius's case, it seems that there may have been other innocent people who ended up going to Azkaban. What if Crouch's son was innocent? What does that say about Crouch?

Due to the panic in the community at the time, Crouch's actions were supported. However, Moody always tried to deliver his people alive - never killed if he could help it.

> Moody avoided killing if at all possible? This is good to hear - and probably very important to the septology to remember. We already knew we liked Moody - yep, we can recognize a good guy when we see one, can't we?

Sirius describes how Crouch's son was screaming for his mother in Azkaban, and went quiet after only a few days. He then died only about a year after they brought him in.

He went quiet after only a few days? We think we need some more information about what happens in Azkaban. Can the prisoners easily talk to one-another? If Crouch's son was innocent, what affect would the other prisoners have had on him? Could there be another reason why he went quiet so quickly?

On account of his Ministry position, Crouch and his wife were allowed to visit his son right before he died, and Sirius had seen Crouch supporting his weak wife, who also died shortly after the visit. Sirius tells Harry, Ron, and Hermione that he watched the dementors bury the boy on the Azkaban grounds as Crouch never even came for the body. They all discuss Crouch's odd behavior thoroughly, but Sirius cannot figure out why Crouch would not be on the school grounds for the Tournament, but then come to search Snape's office.

Hmmm... We really hate to bring this up with such a tragedy, but there's that coincidence thing again with Crouch's son and wife both dying about the same time. Crouch does not seem to be very friendly or humane either. All these story-line clues make you start imagining things.

Ron still doesn't trust Snape, and thinks a really clever Dark wizard (like Snape) could fool even Dumbledore. Hermione insists that Dumbledore wouldn't trust Snape if he wasn't absolutely sure.

Could a really clever Dark wizard fool Dumbledore? How clever is Snape? What do HP Sleuths think?

Sirius cannot understand why Dumbledore hired Snape. The Snape he remembers arrived at Hogwarts already knowing more curses than "half the kids in the seventh year." He hung out with a Slytherin gang that included the Lestranges, Avery, plus Rosier and Wilkes (who were killed), of whom almost all became Death Eaters. Harry tells Sirius that Snape seems to know Karkaroff, and how Karkaroff had showed Snape something on his arm. However, Sirius did not know what that would be about. Sirius still can't believe Dumbledore would have Snape teaching if he ever worked for Voldemort.

Sirius doesn't know and can't believe that Snape would have been a Death Eater, but Moody (who seems to know) was definitely implying it. Both of these characters are highly reliable, so who is right? J.K.R. is not making this easy.

Even though Percy and Bagman have already made comments about Crouch, Sirius thinks it is a good idea for Ron to send an owl to Percy for more specific information about Crouch's whereabouts. Sirius recalls that the Bertha Jorkins he knew had a great memory. Although she was a nasty busybody, he can't figure out why she has a reputation for a bad memory. Sirius thinks she could have been a liability to the Ministry, and that may explain why Bagman took so long to look for her. Sirius instructs Harry not to leave Hogwarts without permission and to call him "Snuffles" as a code word when discussing him.

Oh wow! The HP Hintoscope and WWP Sleuthoscope are making a huge racket. Bertha had a great memory? What is it that Voldemort had said back in Chapter 1 about "*Memory Charms* can be broken by a powerful wizard, as I proved when I questioned her"? Was her memory problem due to a strong *Memory Charm*? Who (or should we ask, "how many people") would have put one on her and why? Was she such a liability that maybe neither Bagman nor Crouch really wanted to find her? How many other people might not have wanted her to return?

Hermione can't believe what Crouch did to his own son, and doesn't believe Percy could ever be that much like Crouch. Ron isn't completely sure Percy wouldn't act the same way if one of his family stood in the way of his career....

This is a crucial issue for the septology. Could Percy be persuaded to turn-in any-one in his family? If anyone in his family has to play double-agent, or investigate the Ministry, would Percy turn them in without knowing all the facts, if it appeared they were doing something wrong? What if someone were to *force* Percy to do something against his family – would we know the difference? J.K.R. is doing her famous smokescreen, and we are having trouble separating facts from fish.

Ron marvels how Snuffles must really like Harry if he is willing to live off rats for him.

Curiosities

✳ Snape says that Veritaserum is controlled by **very strict** Ministry guidelines.

✳ We're not surprised Snape used to be in with the Lestranges and Avery. Friendly folk. (Not)

✳ The law-abiding Crouch authorized the use of *Unforgivable Curses* on suspects? Not very nice... not very legal.

Chapter 28 Analysis

Clues

Harry, Ron, and Hermione go down to the kitchens to give Dobby a present of several pairs of socks for helping Harry with the gillyweed. They see that Winky is worse than ever - drinking butterbeer all day and barely comprehensible - still persistent that Mr. Crouch is her master. When Harry mentions that Mr. Crouch is not showing up at the Tournament anymore, Winky is upset - saying that he needs her help with very secret business, but then passes out. Hermione tries to encourage the other elves to help her, but Winky is a disgrace and they are offended. Harry gets some extra food to send to Sirius, as the elves escort the three of them out of the kitchen.

> Crouch's Secret business? It's so secret, that even Crouch's boss doesn't know where he is! Winky does know something, but thanks to Rule #2, she's not saying a word.... With all those elves around Hogwarts, they must know a lot about what goes on. Great source for Dumbledore - glad they're so loyal to him.

After Harry sends the food package off to Sirius, he watches from the Owlery as an eagle owl soars past Hagrid's cabin, toward the castle. He notices Hagrid is in front of his cabin doing some digging.

> It's not the Great Hall mail delivery, so whose owl is this? What important message is being sent right now? We know that eagle owls do not typically deliver good news. What bad deed is being planned? Are HP Sleuths keeping an eagle eye on this?

Hermione has taken out a subscription to the *Daily Prophet* so they won't be blind-sided anymore by news. Unfortunately, Hermione starts getting hate mail from people who had read Rita's article about her. One of the pieces of mail spills pus on her hands, growing painful boils all over them. Pansy Parkinson seems to take particular delight in hearing about it.

> Hermione has found that no news is good news. We are being led to believe that Pansy Parkinson may have been responsible for the pus. Seems likely to us (we're easily convinced).

For Care of Magical Creatures class, Hagrid has created a game in which he has buried gold coins in the ground, and has brought some Nifflers (little black furry creatures with spade-like front paws) to dig out the coins. Nifflers will ruin anything just to get at sparkly things or treasure, and are mostly found digging through mines. The student whose niffler digs up the most gold coins wins a prize. As Goyle is pocketing the coins, Hagrid lets him know that he used leprechaun gold - so it would vanish in only a few hours anyway.

> Blarney, that leprechaun gold sure is tricky stuff. Would Bill Weasley use Nifflers for his work? Could Nifflers also have been doing something interesting

under the ground in front of Hagrid's cabin, or elsewhere? We have no clue what, but it might be worth digging into.

Hermione continues to be frustrated - trying to figure out how Rita Skeeter is listening in on private conversations if she is banned from the school. Hermione asks Moody for help (in case Rita used an Invisibility Cloak), but his magical eye did not see Rita "anywhere near the judge's table"..."or anywhere near the lake" during the second task. Harry suggests that maybe Rita had somehow bugged Hermione with an electronic listening device. Ron had never heard of Muggle bugging devices, but jokes as he envisions it like putting "fleas on someone or something...." Hermione lets them know, however, that electronics don't work around Hogwarts due to all the magic surrounding it.

Okay, Hermione's usually right, and when Ron jokes, he's usually right. So can they both be right? And was that meant to be a complete, or partial answer? Let's just say that this is crawling with story line clues.

Hedwig does not come back with Percy's response about Crouch until after the Easter holidays. Percy has written back to Ron with a very curt letter, telling him nothing new, and insisting that Ron not "bother" him "unless it's important."

This sounds exactly like Percy. On the other hand, it sort of resembles a robot carrying out directions. Also, why did it take so long for him to answer? If it was anyone else but Percy, we'd be worried...

The champions meet down on the Quidditch field to receive their instructions for the final task. On the way, Cedric tells Harry that Fleur thinks the task will have something to do with underground tunnels and finding treasure.

No Fleur, that's probably Book 5 you're thinking of... Does Fleur think it has to do with that because Mme Maxime saw Hagrid with the nifflers, or is there something else we should know about?

When they get to the field, they find a huge maze of hedges has been grown over it, and the Triwizard Cup is to be in the center of the maze. The champion who navigates the maze (including "obstacles") and touches the cup first, will win. As the champions head back to the castle, Krum escorts Harry over by Hagrid's cabin to ask if what Rita printed about Harry's relationship with Hermione is true. Harry assures Krum that he and Hermione are just friends, and Krum compliments Harry on his flying.

The third task is going to be quite amazing. Krum seems like a nice guy - he even compliments Harry's flying ability.

Harry suddenly spots Mr. Crouch. Mr. Crouch's robes are torn and bloody, he is unshaven, and he appears to be hallucinating - talking to a tree as if it were Percy (Weatherby). He also acts as if his wife and son were still alive – commenting about the 12 O.W.L.s his son received. In-between incoherent babble about 12 students per visiting school, Crouch attempts, with great effort, to communicate that he needs to talk to

Dumbledore. He is raving that he has done something "stupid," someone "escaped," that Bertha is dead, something about "his fault...his son," that he must warn Dumbledore, and the Dark Lord is stronger.

> We get some information, and then Crouch cuts himself off...we get some more information, then he cuts himself off again, etc. - this is like Rule #2 stuck on an endless loop! J.K.R. is showing no mercy (and yes, bunches of twelves). We may be close to the destiny of 12. These are vital story-line clues - and the only new information we seem to get from this is that someone escaped (from where?), that Crouch did something stupid (which thing?), and that this high-ranking official from the Ministry is verifying that Voldemort is getting stronger (we already suspected that). Just call this story a mystery for masochists (yes, that's a synonym for HP Sleuths).

Harry cannot drag Crouch up to the castle, so he leaves Krum there and runs up himself to get Dumbledore. Harry no longer has the password to Dumbledore's office, and when Snape comes by, he does not help Harry (he just stalls him more). Dumbledore suddenly emerges, however, and accompanies Harry outside. They find Krum lying on the ground, stunned, and Crouch is missing.

> This was obvious - as soon as Harry left the scene, we knew that at least one of the two would have ended up dead or missing. At least J.K.R. didn't disappoint us (hehe). We did notice that Dumbledore somehow knew that Harry needed him. Did one of the ghosts, portraits or other inanimate objects help, or did Dumbledore have a way of seeing what was happening? We do have a clue that this whole event happened because of something with that eagle owl. So who sent it to whom?

Dumbledore sends up a silvery "flare" for Hagrid that streaks "through the trees like a ghostly bird." Hagrid comes running over immediately, crossbow in hand.

> The WWP Sleuthoscope is twirling and glittering. That bird-like signal is very interesting. A Batman fan might relate to it like the shining of the bat image in the sky to call Batman. Hagrid obviously dropped everything to run to Dumbledore immediately. It's as if he were part of a secret (or not so secret) society where when one member needs another, they send out this birdlike symbol. Could that birdlike symbol be in the shape of a phoenix? Could this be the special emergency signal for members of the "Order of the Phoenix"? (Remember - Book 5 is to be called *Harry Potter and the Order of the Phoenix*.) Hmmm, we don't know, but this sure is a clue....

Moody, who says he heard what happened from Snape, arrives and then searches the forest for a sign of Crouch. When they revive Krum, he tells them that he thinks Crouch attacked him from behind. Dumbledore tells Harry to go up to the dorm and not leave it – not even to send an owl. Harry wonders how Dumbledore could have known what he was thinking.

Suffice it to say that in this case, Dumbledore is not reading minds - he is just very well informed. No wonder Moody was such a good Auror - he seems to always be on top of everything, always around whenever there's trouble. It's a little creepy, but if you're not doing something bad, it's comforting to know he's poking his nose in everywhere.

Hagrid, who is fuming over Mme. Maxime's efforts to extract information from him about the third task, escorts Harry back up to the castle.

Curiosities

━✸━ Crouch mutters constantly about twelves. We have been wondering about the second half of Trelawney's prophecy. So, is this related? Is this why we are being buried in twelves, or will these twelves continue through Book 5?

━✸━ Crouch's son must have been a talented wizard if he got 12 O.W.L.s.

Clues

While Harry, Ron, and Hermione are in the Owlery sending a letter to Snuffles, they hear Fred and George coming up the stairs talking about how to communicate something to someone without it being considered blackmail. Hermione thinks Ron should report them to Percy, but Ron is convinced Percy would turn them in. Ron mentions to Harry how he feels Fred and George are obsessed with making money and are really serious about starting up a joke shop.

> We know this is a story line clue, but it's not the main mystery, so we won't strain our brains here. Fred and George are up to something, as usual, and it comes as no surprise that they are serious about selling their inventions. We still are wondering what they did with their winnings from the World Cup - but we know better than to worry about that too.

Harry, Ron, and Hermione try to figure out what happened to Crouch and Krum. Hermione reasons that either Crouch zapped Krum, or someone else attacked both of them. Ron figures it must have been Crouch, but Harry thought he was too weak to do much. Crouch was talking as if his wife and son were still alive, but was most coherent when referring to Voldemort.

> If HP Sleuths abide by the rules, we know that Hermione is usually right and Ron is usually wrong (except when he's joking), so we at least know it was either Crouch or someone else who knocked out Krum. What if Hermione was completely right (could it have been both - someone else and Crouch)? But Crouch was hallucinating, right? His wife and son are dead and the tree was not really Percy. Uhhh, on second thought, Percy might make a good tree - so maybe we should find out more about his son and wife.

Hermione is sure that Crouch could not have Disapparated. She reminds them that no one can Apparate or Disapparate on the Hogwarts grounds.

> But...but...what about phoenixes and house-elves? Somehow, there are exceptions.

Ron wonders if Snape could have beaten them to Krum. However, Harry is sure that was impossible - unless he can "turn himself into a bat or something," to which Ron jokes that he "wouldn't put it past him."

> Ahem, Ron is joking again.

They visit Moody who informs them he did not find Crouch. Hermione asks him if there might be other ways to disappear from the Hogwarts grounds, beside Disapparating, and Moody is impressed – complementing her. However, he does not know specifically what happened to Crouch, so the mystery continues.

So there **are** other ways of appearing and disappearing (had to be). How **many** other ways? We still don't know how Dobby and Fawkes do it, but HP Sleuths might know of one, and didn't Ron have some ideas?

Snuffles sends back a letter scolding Harry for taking a chance by walking near the forest after dark with Krum. Snuffles is sure the person who prevented Crouch from getting to Dumbledore had to be right nearby while Harry and Krum were talking. Snuffles also tells Harry to practice Stunning and to learn some hexes for the third task. During Divination, Professor Trelawney describes the fascinating relationship between Mars and Neptune. She uses a crystal miniature of the solar system to demonstrate it.

In astrology, Neptune represents the Underworld, secrets, and questionable activity. Mars is drive and momentum. Mars would cause the activities of Neptune to surface quickly. This would indicate that something very Dark and foreboding is about to emerge very soon. For some reason, Professor Trelawney doesn't proclaim an explanation for this disastrous event, or she is invoking Rule #2.

Trelawney's classroom is so warm that Harry opens a window. He feels a soft breeze on his face, cooling him off. It doesn't keep him awake, though, as he ends up dozing off while listening to a buzzing insect in the window.

The HP Hintoscope is whirring away. We are suspicious of insects around Hogwarts, but we find out very shortly here that Dumbledore is busy in his office with company, so it couldn't be Dumbledore. Still, it is annoying.

Harry has a dream in which he is flying on the back of an eagle owl up to a mansion and into a dark room, where he then dismounts. Nagini and Wormtail are seated on the floor.

There's another eagle owl - got to be bad news. Just as J.K.R. has been equating the evil tactics of the Death Eaters to Nazism, their preference for eagle owls is reminiscent of the name of Hitler's infamous stronghold - the *Eagle's Nest*.

The eagle owl lands in a chair and then Harry hears a voice say that Wormtail's blunder has not ruined everything since "he" is dead. The voice, which belongs to Voldemort, talks about needing to teach Wormtail a lesson, and a wand appears as the voice casts the horrible *Cruciatus Curse* on Wormtail.

Who is dead? Are we to assume this relates to Crouch? Was the eagle owl that Harry just rode a **return post**? Is the servant of Lord Voldemort communicating with Voldemort from Hogwarts? Voldemort seems to be doing awfully well with that wand. Numerous possibilities - none of them good.

As Wormtail writhes and screams, Harry's scar burns on his head. He yells from his own pain and awakes to find himself lying on the floor of Professor Trelawney's classroom. Even though Professor Trelawney guesses that it is being caused by his scar - Harry insists that it is a migraine, and says he has to go to the hospital wing to get something for his headache.

When it comes to Voldemort, Harry really knows how to use his head (groan). This is further proof that Harry is linked to Voldemort through his scar. Not only does it work as a Voldemort detector, but Harry can witness real events.

Following Sirius' orders about his scar, Harry heads straight for Dumbledore's office. Through trial and error (and some knowledge of Dumbledore's personality), Harry figures out that the password to Dumbledore's office is now "Cockroach Cluster." As Harry gets to the top of Dumbledore's spiral stairs, he hears the voice of Cornelius Fudge stating emphatically that there is no evidence that Bertha Jorkins' disappearance and Barty Crouch's strange circumstances are linked, and suggests that Mme. Maxime could have been responsible for Crouch. Dumbledore tells Fudge he is prejudiced.

Another cockroach? We still do not know why Lupin's boggart (Book 3, Chapter 7) became a cockroach when he dispelled it. He could be thinking of Cockroach Clusters - but they don't crawl around. Just musing here - it's really bugging us.

Moody informs Dumbledore and Fudge that he can see Harry waiting outside the door.

Curiosities

* It looks like Voldemort is back at the Riddle House, but we can't be positive. Where else has he been all this time?

* Moody definitely was able to see right through Dumbledore's door.

Chapter 30 Analysis

(THE PENSIEVE)

Clues

Harry enters and lets Dumbledore know that he needs to talk with him, but Dumbledore must accompany Fudge outside, so he tells Harry to wait in his office. While waiting, Harry greets Fawkes on his perch, and then notices a shimmering light emanating from a stone basin. When he pokes his wand at it, the contents start swirling. He looks deeper into it, sees a room, and as his nose touches the surface, Harry is pulled down into the room. He finds himself sitting on a bench next to Dumbledore, but just like the Riddle Diary, Dumbledore is a phantom in someone's memory.

> Harry is definitely daring. With what little we already know about J.K.R.'s magical world, we wouldn't go poking our wands or noses (did we say noses again?) into anything that looked unusual.

The scene is a dungeon. While Dumbledore looks the same as he does presently, a much younger Karkaroff is being escorted by two dementors into the room and seated in a chair where chains clamp themselves around his arms. Harry listens as Karkaroff offers to expose other Death Eaters to (a younger-looking) Mr. Crouch, in exchange for his freedom. When Karkaroff names Evan Rosier (who has already been killed), a much younger Moody (no magical eye) complains to Dumbledore that it took him six months to capture Karkaroff, and now Crouch is about to let him go.

> And we thought Moody and Wormtail had a lot of people after them. Looks like Karkaroff may be at the top of the rat list. No wonder he's so twitchy.

Karkaroff claims that the Death Eaters never knew the identities of *all* Voldemort's followers. Karkaroff names:
- ꙮ Antonin Dolohov (tortured Muggles)
- ꙮ Evan Rosier (died while disfiguring Moody's nose)
- ꙮ Travers (helped murder the McKinnons)
- ꙮ Mulciber (specialized in the *Imperius Curse*)
- ꙮ Augustus Rookwood of the Department of Mysteries (a spy)

> From the way that Karkaroff was so eager to supply names in return for his freedom, we assume that he would not hold back if he could help it. Therefore, when he tells Crouch that the Death Eaters did not know all the identities of Voldemort's followers, we think that is probably true. If so, that does make it much more difficult to monitor and/or capture them all, of course.

Karkaroff explains how Rookwood had placed a network of spies within the Ministry of Magic. Crouch finds this disclosure to be valuable.

Did he say network of spies in the Ministry? Not good. We cannot be sure that they were all accounted for, so HP Sleuths shouldn't trust *anyone*. CONSTANT VIGILANCE!

Then Karkaroff names Severus Snape. Crouch tells him that Snape has been cleared, but Karkaroff insists that Snape is for real. Dumbledore stands and announces that he had already given testimony that Snape had been a Death Eater but had returned before the fall of Voldemort and become a spy "at great personal risk." (Moody seems to be skeptical).

We knew it - Snape hates Harry, he's mean, and he was even a Death Eater. However, we also again see that Dumbledore has exonerated him. There's something definitive that makes Dumbledore support him, so we keep trying to do so too, but it's really difficult to like a cruel, close-minded bully.

That memory dissolves, and Harry is sitting in the same room, different seat. A young Rita Skeeter, with short blond hair, is sucking on her acid-green quill. Ludovic Bagman (physically fit and nose unbroken) is on trial for passing information to Rookwood. Bagman explains that the Rookwood family had been friends with his and he thought he was helping "our side." They let him go, to the delight of the attendees, but Crouch comments that the day Ludo Bagman joins the Ministry will be "a sad day indeed."

Guess Rita changed her hair style (although nothing else seems to have changed about her). And look, Bagman's nose was not broken back during his Quidditch years. HP Sleuths - is Bagman completely innocent? Maybe he did make a mistake then, but now he is still doing questionable things - like offering to help Harry cheat. This is not a trustworthy person. You would think a famous, popular guy like him would not do that. Who, or what, has Bagman gotten mixed-up with?

A new scene appears in which four people are brought in front of Crouch, who is seated next to a frail witch. They are accused of capturing an Auror (Frank Longbottom) and his wife and torturing them with the *Cruciatus Curse*. One of the prisoners is a young, blond-haired boy. Next to him are a thickset man, a nervous-looking man, and a woman with heavy eyelids and thick, dark hair. The boy addresses Crouch and the frail witch and as "Father" and "Mother," pleading that he is innocent. The witch next to Crouch whimpers as she rocks back and forth.

So this is Crouch's son? Like Sirius said, he could have been in the wrong place at the wrong time - he does sort of act like Winky did. Strangely, his mother sort of acts like Dobby did.

The dark witch declares that when the Dark Lord rises again, he will "reward us beyond any of his other supporters! We alone were faithful! We alone tried to find him!" As Harry watches this, the *real* Dumbledore appears at his side and escorts him back up to his office.

Talk about loyalty… We fear we will see more of that Dark witch (and possibly the thickset man and/or nervous-looking one too). We suspect she is one of the Lestranges.

Dumbledore explains that what Harry saw is called a "Pensieve." It contains Dumbledore's own thoughts - which he can place inside it and organize them so as to look for patterns and links. Harry can't relate to having so many thoughts that that they have to be organized, so only says "Er….," as he tries to think of an appropriate response. Harry watches as Dumbledore places his long hands on the Pensieve, puts his wand to his head, draws a silvery thread of memory from it, and adds it to the basin.

The WWP Sleuthoscope didn't even bother to budge (we have been hit with so many references to long fingers). Dumbledore has them, Voldemort has them, Mr. Ollivander has them, and house-elves have them. Maybe it's just a… (cough) coincidence? Okay, okay, then what is it? We still can't put our finger on it, so we're sticking to our theories of either power or ancestry until we receive further evidence.

As Dumbledore swirls the glistening contents, Harry sees Snape saying "it's coming back…Karkaroff's too…stronger and clearer than ever…." Dumbledore comments that he should have made that connection. Harry watches him stir up another memory from years before at Hogwarts. Bertha Jorkins is telling Dumbledore that "he" put a hex on me just because I said I had seen him kissing Florence.

This is not a random thought - especially since Dumbledore put it in his Pensieve. Who was kissing Florence, and do we care who Florence is? It may be just a (shhh!) coincidence, but the name "Florence" is "Firenze" in Italian (remember the Centaur from Book 1?). Since J.K.R. purposely denied us hearing the boy's name (Rule #2), we know the "he" is someone important and we probably know him. We also know that Bertha was at school about the same time as Sirius, James, Lupin, Wormtail, and Snape. Who of that list might have put a hex on Bertha (and what kind of hex)? It could have been Snape. Can we picture Snape kissing a girl? Then again, can we picture a girl kissing Snape? Uck. Maybe he needed feeding? (Only joking.)

Harry tells Dumbledore how he drifted off during Divination and about the dream and his scar. Dumbledore asks Harry if his scar had hurt any other time except over the summer, which surprises Harry to find out that Sirius and Dumbledore have been communicating. In fact, it was Dumbledore who recommended that Sirius hide in the mountainside cave.

Now we understand how Dumbledore knew Harry might have tried to send an owl the night that Krum was attacked.

Dumbledore hypothesizes that Harry's scar (from the failed curse) links him to Voldemort and that it hurts when Voldemort is feeling strong hatred. Dumbledore feels that the dream probably really did happen. They discuss that if the dream happened, then it is apparent that Voldemort is able to hold a wand. Dumbledore recounts to Harry how the last time Voldemort rose to power, there were unexplained disappearances then as well. Dumbledore tells Harry that not only have Bertha and Crouch now disappeared, but also a Muggle who lived in the village where Voldemort's father grew up. He believes these current disappearances are linked and that it is a possible sign that it is all happening again.

> We knew all that. Yeah, but J.K.R. wants the characters to know it, and to reinforce it to us, so we can be sure that's exactly what is going on (Dumbledore sure knows Rule #3). Harry's scar is, indeed, some sort of Voldemort detector, and he does have telepathic "dreams." Dumbledore and Sirius have seen the signs that Voldemort may be coming back, and Voldemort is now able to hold a wand. (Shudder).

Harry asks if Dumbledore thinks he may be "getting stronger." Dumbledore replies "Voldemort?", and gives Harry one of his famous piercing looks as he asks the question.

> You mean that Dumbledore has to ask **who**? Who else? Is Dumbledore worried about someone else, or is he maybe nursing someone back to health? Too many possibilities. Eeeeek... We need our own Pensieve!

Harry asks Dumbledore about the trial he observed involving Neville's parents, and Dumbledore is perplexed to hear that Neville has never mentioned his parents to other kids (although Harry feels guilty that he had never even asked). He confirms that Neville's father was an Auror just like Moody.

> Neville's father was an Auror? Wicked! Tortured with the *Cruciatus Curse*? Poor Neville. How ironic - now Moody is teaching their son. Is this maybe why Moody felt so sorry for Neville...?

Dumbledore explains that, after Voldemort's downfall, when everyone was thinking they were safe, some of Voldemort's followers tortured the Longbottoms with the *Cruciatus Curse* - trying to find out what had happened to Voldemort. Neville's parents are still alive, but so insane that they don't even recognize Neville.

> Wow! This is it, HP Sleuths - a MOTIVATION for the cause of Neville's poor memory! Based on the clues that J.K.R. has been giving us, there is solid evidence now that Neville is not only the victim of a *Memory Charm*, but a key to the whole Harry Potter mystery! Did Neville see something incriminating? If Harry was a year old when Voldemort attacked him, and can remember some of it, then Neville would also have been one or two years-old by the time his parents were tortured. A *Memory Charm* might have been a bit too strong for an infant. Who would have wanted Neville's memory altered? Could someone have done it to cover identities? Neville's past is easily as tragic as Harry's, and the mystery behind it possibly just as consequential to the whole septology!

Dumbledore bitterly recounts to Harry how, during holidays, Neville visits his parents at St Mungo's Hospital for Magical Maladies and Injuries. The Longbottoms had been popular and people were adamant about revenge, however, as the evidence given by the mentally-damaged Longbottoms was questionable, it is unclear as to whether the people who were accused were all truly guilty.

> WWP Sleuthoscope is going into cardiac arrest (but is declining treatment)! Oh no! Not at St Mungo's! This is even worse.☹ If people want something covered up enough to put a *Memory Charm* on an infant, then they certainly wouldn't want the parents to recover and be able to tell what they saw. Considering St Mungo's may be under the influence of Dark Wizards, it seems likely that someone there could be making **sure** Neville's parents do not recover! Who did his parents see? Bet it was someone from the Ministry. This is very bad. How is it that the more we learn, the more involved this mystery gets?

Dumbledore lets Harry know that Ludo Bagman had not been accused of any Dark conduct since then.

> Did HP Sleuths notice how J.K.R. did that? Not being accused is not the same thing as not being suspected. We aren't necessarily saying that Bagman is presently engaged in Dark activities, but you'll notice that Dumbledore did not necessarily say that he was innocent. We're not sure. We have already seen that Bagman has a habit of getting himself (and his nose) into the wrong situations a lot, and although it may not be intentional, Bagman is not highly ethical (he *is* a bookie, remember).

Dumbledore also assures Harry that Snape has definitely stopped supporting Voldemort, but will not divulge the reason for his certainty.

> Hey, Dumbledore - how 'bout a hint? Did Voldemort curse Snape or spurn him? Did Voldemort kill his woman? It's driving us crazy, and we *don't* want to get committed to St Mungo's. (Arrgh!)

Dumbledore asks Harry not to mention Neville's parents to anyone else - leaving it to Neville's discretion to do so when he is ready.

Curiosities

* J.K.R. had said in an interview that Dumbledore is 150 years old, so that is why the others in the Pensieve looked younger, while he looked the same. Nonetheless, she has also reiterated in this chapter (Rule #1) how Harry has a hard time thinking of Dumbledore as being "old."

* Crouch thinks Bagman would be a detriment to the Ministry. Is that because he has no faith in Bagman's abilities, or is it because he is concerned about Bagman's scruples?

* By using Alan Rickman in the Harry Potter movies, Snape actually becomes appealing. We had not envisioned Snape to be a hunk like that – but we *do* think the image works well (you just have to get past his greasy hair, uneven teeth, and foul personality).

Chapter 31 Analysis

Clues

Harry tells Ron and Hermione about the Pensieve and his discussion with Dumbledore. Ron doesn't think that Bagman would have been involved on purpose, but Hermione just shrugs.

> We know by now that Ron is usually wrong, and even always-right Hermione can't say if Bagman may have been guilty or not. Do we think J.K.R. may be hinting at something? (Do we think Bludgers hurt?)

Harry is feeling fairly confident about the third task as they keep practicing in Professor McGonagall's empty classroom during lunch. Harry masters the *Impediment Curse* which slows down the attacker, the *Reductor Curse* which blasts objects out of the way, and the *Four-Point Spell* which Hermione thought would help him keep his bearings in the maze. However, he has trouble with the *Shield Charm* (a protective wall against any minor curse).

> Harry may need some of these for the maze, but there's also the reality that he can only escape Dark Wizards so many times before he will need to know something about defending himself with real magic. Hope he's been paying attention in Moody's class.

From a window, Harry, Ron, and Hermione watch Malfoy outside holding his hand up to his ear, then to his mouth and speaking into it. To Harry, it looks just like Malfoy's using a walkie-talkie, but Hermione reminds him again, that electronic devices do not work within the castle grounds.

> The HP Hintoscope is crackling with story-line information! Here's solid evidence that the place is swarming with Malfoy's antics. We can't quite explain how yet, but we know he is the instigator.

Rita Skeeter runs a scathing story in which she now attacks Harry. She claims that Harry regularly collapses in class complaining about his scar hurting. She quotes top experts at St Mungo's Hospital for Magical Maladies and Injuries as saying that his brain could have been affected by the attack, and it either reflects a mental disorder or that he is just pretending and looking for attention.

> WWP Sleuthoscope is throbbing with light! So this is what Poison-Pen Skeeter is up to! Does this mean that Voldemort may have already taken control of the wizarding print media? (Gulp!) Rita is not *just* a scandal reporter - she is purposely trying to discredit Harry and all the others who may be a threat to Voldemort. Add to that, we're fairly certain this isn't even Rita. This is the scariest thing we have seen yet in the Harry Potter series!! It implies that Voldemort may be attempting an internal take-over of the Ministry of Magic and a number of other key organizations - and Rita's articles are destroying the credibility of those who

could thwart it. When you don't even know what the truth is, it is hard to fight for it. We can see how Voldemort may become even more fearful than last time.

Rita reveals to the world that Harry can speak Parseltongue, and quotes a member of the Dark Force Defense League as saying that Harry's friendship with werewolves (Lupin) and giants (Hagrid) can be attributed to a violent personality.

The WWP Sleuthoscope is pulsing rapidly. Where do they find these experts anyway? Do we know anyone on the Dark Force Defense League? The only one we can think of is just an honorary member, and that guy had lost his memory. (Then again, maybe Gilderoy's got it back?) J.K.R. said in an interview with the BBC that she can't promise anything, but if Gilderoy Lockhart is at St Mungo's, he may even be under the control of someone else or back for revenge! (Gulp)

Harry cannot believe Rita had heard about the scar incident, because Divination (and the window he opened in class) are at the top of the North Tower. He asks Hermione if she has found anything in her research on "magical methods of bugging." Hermione ponders it again as she runs her hand through her hair in frustration, which gives her an idea - and she takes off for the library.

That's Hermione - when in doubt, go to the library. Seems to work so far. We could say that bugging Harry up there under the roof is eavesdropping for sure. (groan)

Bill and Mrs. Weasley come to watch Harry compete in the final task. They reminisce about Apollyon Pringle, the old caretaker, and Ogg, the gamekeeper before Hagrid. Mrs. Weasley admits to Bill that Arthur Weasley still has "the marks" from having been caught out of the dorm one night by Apollyon Pringle, the caretaker back then.

Does that mean scars? Looks like Harry and Dumbledore aren't the only ones with distinctive marks.

They tell Harry that Percy is having a terrible time at the Ministry where they want Crouch's disappearance hushed-up, and they are interrogating Percy heavily about the instructions that Crouch mails in. They are suspicious that Crouch may not be writing them himself.

Awww, poor Weatherby. And Crouch was finally starting to get your name right.... Are the instructions being forged? We hope those interrogations of Percy are not too invasive. This does not sound good.☹

Percy is not being allowed to sub for Crouch this time. Cornelius Fudge is taking Crouch's place for the third task, himself.

Mr. Always-in-the-Spotlight Fudge is conveniently subbing for Crouch in the most important task of the highly popular Tournament. Is this political only, or does he have other motives?

When Ron's mum asks him how he did in his exam, he tells her that he couldn't remember the names of all the goblin rebels so he made some up.

> Ron may be sorry he didn't study harder if the goblins rebel again or take sides in a conflict.... We can't be sure if the rebels, or their direct descendents, aren't still around.

The champions go down to the maze to start the third task. If they want to be rescued, they are to send up red sparks and someone will get them. Harry and Cedric, who are tied for the lead, enter first together while Krum and Fleur wait for their signal. Harry enters the maze, and using his wand as a compass, works his way toward the center of the maze. He is alert for danger, yet finds his path to be a bit too clear, which feels ominously wrong.

> Harry's got great instincts – his path is a bit too clear....

Harry finally encounters a dementor that stumbles from his Patronus, alerting Harry that it really is a boggart and the *"Riddikulus!" Spell* annihilates it.

> Wasn't that easy? Maybe dementors are getting almost too easy for him? HP Sleuths beware! Harry does not seem to fear dementors as he once did, so what will be the shape of his next boggart? (The next boggart you see may not be recognizable as a boggart.)

Harry comes across a golden, twinkling, mist, floating in mid air. He is trying to decide what to do, when he hears Fleur scream. He tries to run through the mist, but it twirls him around and even inverts the sky and ground. Harry is now hanging from his feet, while gravity is pulling him toward the emptiness of space. He is afraid to move as he dangles precariously from a "sky" of grass, ready to fall away from the earth. Since he knows of no spells to help him, he just closes his eyes and pulls his foot away from the grass. He gets flipped back around and falls harmlessly back to a right-side-up world. However, he was not able to get to Fleur (and she has been eliminated).

> WWP recognizes this mist, but can't remember where we saw it before. Do any HP Sleuths or Animé fans remember who else encountered a similar mist?

Harry comes upon a ten-foot long Blast-Ended Skrewt. The *Impediment Charm* simply bounces off its armor, but when Harry falls over, he is able to stop it by zapping its unprotected underside. As Harry tries to find another way past the skrewt, he hears Cedric yelling, so he blasts a hole through the wall of the maze to find Krum casting the *Cruciatus Curse* on Cedric. Harry hits Krum with a spell ("*Stupefy!*"), knocking him out. When Cedric recovers, he and Harry shoot red sparks over Krum's stunned body and continue on their own - the final two contestants.

> Is this really Krum's personality? It doesn't seem likely that he could have faked it that convincingly all through the story and suddenly been a completely different person could it? Okay, so Quirrell did that in Book 1, but we know Krum so much better than Quirrell - at least Hermione does. Yes, we know she liked Lockhart too, but she was only 12 - now she's so much more mature and experienced at 14 (tee-hee).

Harry next encounters a Sphinx, solves her riddle, and is allowed to take the short path to the Cup. He checks his wand compass, sees that he is "bang on course," and makes a run for it.

> All this banging with no explanation is definitely giving us a headache. Unfortunately, it's beginning to have a familiar ring. It is so reminiscent of the "doom, boom" booming of Moria in J.R.R. Tolkien's *The Fellowship of the Ring*. That booming preceded a "death." Maybe it's a different kind of banging....

As Harry approaches the Cup, Cedric spurts into the path ahead, unaware that a huge spider is coming toward him from the side. Harry warns Cedric and tries to stun it, but the spider is "so large or so magical" that instead of being slowed down, it just grabs Harry and lifts him up.

> Now, does this lifting action seem like a mean spider intent on harming Harry? It would not make sense, that after running across the maze to get to Cedric and Harry, this giant spider would then gently lift Harry up just to look at him. Why would it not be already tearing off a quick snack? One reason Harry is probably not being harmed is because it, presumably, would not be allowed by the new tournament rules anyway. Just as Aragog agreed to not harm humans for Hagrid, this one might also be a particularly good friend to Hagrid and could have agreed to help in the maze (maybe even a favor for almost killing his friends last time).

Harry squirms in its grip, kicking the spider's pincers. It squeezes Harry's leg, injuring it. Harry uses the *Disarming Spell*, and the spider drops him from twelve feet up - right onto his bad leg. From the ground, he stuns the spider at the same time that Cedric utters a spell, and the spider is finally knocked out.

> Ouch! If you were kicked in the mouth by a squirmy human that you were holding, you might suddenly squeeze its leg too. We suspect this spider did not intend to hurt Harry's leg. But now that Harry has hurt the spider, does it resent him for it? What would happen if they ever met up again - would it want revenge? Harry might be able to recognize this spider if he left a scar where he hit it in the pincers. We have no indication that Harry will ever see this Acromantula again, but if he does, we hope it is the understanding type.

Harry notices that he has some sort of gluey secretion on his torn robes from the spider's pincers. He also has an open wound and tries to wipe up his bloody leg with his torn robe.

> Is this secretion a kind of blood? Possibly, but if we check our reference (*Fantastic Beasts* is always handy), it says that one of the Acromantula's distinctive features includes "a poisonous secretion." A WHAT? The WWP Sleuthoscope just went ballistic! If this is poisonous, and it is not only around the wound, but Harry goes and wipes his own wound with it, then how come Harry isn't poisoned? There can only be two reasons. One is that this is a different secretion

than the poison described (hardly). The other is that there is something very strange about Harry (we knew that) beyond his ability to deflect *Killing Curses*. We would have assumed that this protection was in him all along - except that he was almost killed in Book 2 by the poison from the Basilisk fang. Of course, Snape has told us that antidotes do not work on all poisons (ref Book 1), so since Basilisks are so rare, maybe that poison was an exception (or maybe Fawkes somehow made him immune?). If Snape had tried to poison Harry in class, would it have inadvertently revealed that Harry cannot be poisoned? Maybe that was the reason for Colin's coincidental arrival...?

As he can barely walk, Harry encourages Cedric to go ahead and claim the Cup. Cedric refuses. They argue - each insisting the other deserves it more until they both agree to grab it simultaneously.

Cedric is a great guy, a great competitor, and a great Hufflepuff! We **really** like Cedric a lot, after all, don't we?☺

As their hands touch the Cup, the *Portkey* transports them away from the maze....

Curiosities

✶ Bill Weasley says he hasn't seen the school in about 5 years. In Book 1 (Chapter-9), Fred says that Gryffindor hadn't won the Quidditch cup since Charlie left and we are later told that Slytherin had won the Quidditch Cup seven years in a row. We figure Bill and Charlie have been out of school for about 7 years, so why was Bill visiting 5 years ago (or was this writer's license)?

✶ A screech owl regularly delivers Hermione's *Daily Prophet*.

✶ Fleur liked what she saw of Bill Weasley (great taste).

The complete solution to the Sphinx's Riddle is:

1st part: Person who lives in disguise = **Spy**

2nd part: The "middle" of the word *middle* = **dd**
           or "the end" of the phrase *the end* = **d(d)**

3rd part: Sound a (British or French) person makes when trying to think
           of a word = **er**

Put them all together and you have: **Spy+d(d)+er** = *Spider*

Chapter 32 Analysis

(FLESH, BLOOD, AND BONE)

Clues

Cedric helps Harry stand up and they look around. They can see that they are in a graveyard next to a small church, overlooked by a house on a hill. Cedric wants to know if anyone had mentioned that the Cup was a Portkey, and Harry wants to know if this was part of the task; but neither of them know anything.

> Obviously, this is what Professor Moody was referring to when Hermione asked if there are other ways to disappear from the Hogwarts grounds. It is now clear that Portkeys work differently from Apparating and Disapparating. But what about house elves and phoenixes? They don't use Portkeys – so how do they do it?

Harry and Cedric see a hooded figure walking toward them carrying a bundle in its arms. As it comes up to Harry, his scar sears in pain, and he collapses to the ground, unable to move. Harry hears a "high, cold voice" say "kill the spare," and another voice screeches *"Avada Kadavra!"* and Cedric hits the ground, dead – not a mark on his body. Harry is pulled by a short man over to the gravestone of Tom Riddle Senior, then tied securely to it, and gagged with a rag. The man hits him, and Harry sees a missing finger by which he recognizes Wormtail.

> Cedric! (*Sob....*) We never had a chance to get to like you as much as we now realize we would have.☹ Again, no mark – not even a scar (we've got to think about this a lot more...). The high voice we know is Voldemort's, so therefore the second voice that cast the *Killing Curse* on yet another innocent victim had to have been Wormtail's. If there was any question in anyone's mind about whether to feel sorry for Wormtail, we hope this sets that straight - we definitely do not like Wormtail. No we do not. No, no, no.

Wormtail then drags a stone basin over to the foot of the grave where he conjures up a fire and stirs the cauldron, as a huge snake slithers around the headstone. He then opens the bundle to reveal a dark, reddish, scaly thing the size of a child, with the face of a snake.

> Harry may be able to talk to snakes, but he sure hasn't had much luck with them lately. If Voldemort hasn't read Rita's article, he may not yet know that Harry is a Parselmouth. Wish Harry could have at least tried here, but right now he isn't able to talk at all with that gag in his mouth. This snake didn't seem too talkative anyway.

Wormtail conjures "bone of the father" from the grave. He then amputates his own right hand to drop in the "flesh of the servant." Lastly Wormtail cuts into Harry's right arm with a silver knife - capturing a dribble of "blood of the enemy" in a glass vial, the final ingredient, which he pours into the cauldron.

Eeeww gros! Good thing Dean Thomas wasn't here to see that hand fall off - this wasn't just a boggart. Wait a minute - didn't Voldemort tell Wormtail in Chapter 1 that he had an important role, which many of his followers "would give their right hands to perform"? Voldemort is a very sick person (not to mention evil).

From the hissing and sparking cauldron, Lord Voldemort rises again.

Curiosities

※ Guess the destiny of 12 could not be avoided (we'll know for sure by Book 5). Looks like Professor Trelawney now has 2 accurate predictions!

※ It's probably nothing important, but since we have been told that wizard cauldrons are typically made of pewter, and J.K.R. was careful to mention that the cauldron Voldemort used was a stone cauldron, we felt it was worth noting.

※ There is a large Yew tree in the graveyard. This is not surprising since legends say that yew trees feed off corpses, and are symbolic of *death* and *regeneration*. By the way, they also happen to contain a poison. J.K.R has said told us in a chat on Barnes&Noble.com, that one of her favorite books is *The Little White Horse*, by Elizabeth Goudge. In that story, Yew trees were ominous symbols of wrongdoing that took on "sinister" shapes. Observant HP Sleuths will also remember that Voldemort's and was made of Yew wood.

Clues

Voldemort's red, slitted eyes inspect his new body. With his "unnaturally" long fingers, he pulls out his wand from deep inside a pocket in his robes. He tries out his powers by blasting Wormtail into the headstone.

> Nice guy - like the way he thanks Wormtail for all his trouble. Note that Voldemort's wand was in his robes – deep inside a pocket (how did it get there?). Long fingers...long fingers...Hmmm...where have we seen those before? These are now "unnaturally" long. Hope we're wrong that longer means stronger.

Voldemort examines Wormtail's left arm, which has a red image on it in the shape of the Dark Mark. Voldemort presses his finger on Wormtail's mark, causing Wormtail to cry out in pain as the mark turns "jet black," and Harry's scar throbs in pain. Numerous cloaked and hooded Death Eaters start Apparating into the graveyard, having been summoned by the Mark.

> Now that's service. So this is the mysterious "spot" on Snape's and Karkaroff's arms - it's a Voldemort pager system. HP Sleuths should have noted that the Mark turns bright red when strongest and jet black when the Death Eaters are being called to him.

The Death Eaters fall into a circle - leaving gaps for missing wizards. Voldemort tells them he can smell their guilt. He wonders why they are healthy and have not searched for him - especially knowing the extent of his precautions against mortal death. Voldemort reminds them that he had shown them proof that he was "mightier than any living wizard."

> Do HP Sleuths sense a hint here? Since this guy is practically a snake, bet his sense of smell (olfactory system - for you scientists out there) is at least as good as a reptile and apparently better. Could that be why he may not only "smell" guilt, but even catch the aroma of a lie?

Because Wormtail returned to him out of fear rather than loyalty, the Dark Lord's verdict is that Wormtail deserves pain, yet since Wormtail has been helping him, Voldemort will reward him. Voldemort conjures a silvery new hand onto Wormtail's wrist. Wormtail tests it by crushing a twig into powder - he is delighted with his new hand. Voldemort warns Wormtail his loyalty had better not waver in the future.

> The WWP Sleuthoscope is quivering in the corner. Uhhh, we hate to mention this, Wormtail, but we saw a movie from the 1950s, and you would not believe what happened to this guy's hand....

Voldemort makes his way along the circle of Death Eaters, passing by some of them but identifying others. He addresses Lucius Malfoy, and Macnair (who he promises to supply with "victims"). He asks Crabbe, Goyle, and Nott to all "do better this time."

> We know that there is a T. Nott at Hogwarts who is in the same year as Harry, but we don't know yet which house the student belongs to, or even if the child is male or female. If Crabbe and Goyle's parents are as intelligent as their offspring, then it may be to Dumbledore's advantage to have Mr. Crabbe and Mr. Goyle working for Voldemort!

In addition to personally acknowledging some of the Death Eaters, Voldemort addresses the empty spaces. He announces that three of the Death Eaters are dead, two are in Azkaban, another is too cowardly to return (and will pay), there is another who he believes has left him forever (so will be killed), and his most faithful servant is presently at Hogwarts. It is his faithful servant at Hogwarts who has delivered Harry to Voldemort's "rebirthing party."

> If any HP Sleuths did not expect to see these particular wizards here, you are to go back to Book 1 and start over (hee-hee). So, who are: the "faithful servant" at Hogwarts, the cowardly one, and the one who is to be killed? We know that Snape and Karkaroff both have those dark spots on their arms, so who did Voldemort mean? Dumbledore has vouched for Snape. Yet the cowardly Karkaroff (who Harry overheard to be in fear of his life) does not seem the loyal type. Is there someone else? Is Snape or Karkaroff here under a hood? How about Bagman or one of the other teachers? Is there anyone else? This is a tough one....

The two faithful Death Eaters in Azkaban, the Lestranges will be "honored beyond their dreams." They will rejoin Voldemort when Azkaban has been broken open, along with the dementors who are his "natural allies."

> Wasn't that just like what the dark witch from the Pensieve said? She was probably one of the Lestranges. She was clearly faithful (fanatical would even be accurate). But there were two men with her in the Pensieve, and Voldemort says there are only two people (total) of his in Azkaban. What happened to the other male – did he die, was he actually innocent, was he released, or has he also managed to escape like Sirius? Why are the dementors Voldemort's natural allies? No matter what, according to Voldemort, it appears that Azkaban will certainly be under Voldemort's control very soon.

See Diagram of Death Eater Circle at end of Clues section.

Voldemort plans on recalling the banished giants, and an "army" of fearful creatures to his side.

> This is beginning to sound like a war, isn't it? Like an epic war that will force all creatures to take sides one way or another. How far will it go before it ends? How many more valiant Wizards will die? Can anyone stop it? Wonder what will happen to half-bloods like Hagrid and Mme Maxime? (Yes, we are just as sure as Hagrid that Mme Maxime is half-giant.)

Voldemort explains to his followers that, in dying, as a means to save her son, Harry's mother had used old magic that Voldemort had not counted on, and therefore he could not touch Harry. Voldemort then touches Harry's cheek as he shows them that it is no longer true, while Harry's scar burns in pain.

> Get your #@!#!! hand off Harry! Drat, Harry is no longer protected from Voldemort's touch (but now Voldemort can use a wand anyway). So what had happened to Voldemort the night he attacked Harry? And we still wanna know why everyone is so confident that it was his mother's spell that saved Harry?

The rebounded curse from the infant Harry had ripped Voldemort from his body, but he stayed alive – proving that his precautions against death had clearly worked. He was trapped, however, because any of the spells he needed to return required a wand. He possessed other animals, but was wary of doing so around people, as Aurors were on the lookout. He used mostly snakes, but without arms, he could not perform magic, plus possession of an animal body shortened its life-span.

> Yes, Voldemort **is** going to be very difficult to defeat if he cannot die. He has no remorse about killing others, so if he cannot be killed, that puts the good guys at a terrible disadvantage. So, Voldemort's possession of the animals shortened their life span - wonder what the animals thought about that? Bet they weren't too pleased.

Four years ago, a gullible teacher from Hogwarts (Quirrell) came upon him in the forest, and Voldemort took over Quirrell's body. Voldemort recounts how he had tried to get the Sorcerer's Stone, but tells how Harry stopped him again, and how Quirrell died when Voldemort left his body.

> You might say that Quirrell's life span was a bit shorter than Quirrell had anticipated. Then again, what exactly **did** happen that caused Quirrell to die?

Wormtail had heard from other rats about a place in the Albanian forest where small animals had been killed by a dark shadow that possessed them. On his way there, Wormtail made the mistake of running into Bertha Jorkins from the Ministry, though managed to bring her to Voldemort. Voldemort extracted information from her about a faithful Death Eater and about the Triwizard Tournament. The *Memory Charm* that someone had put on her had been so strong, that in breaking it, he damaged her mentally and physically, so she could not be possessed and he finished her off when he was done.

Note that Voldemort didn't actually come out and say to the Death Eaters here that Wormtail is an (unregistered) Animagus. Do they all know? So it's true Bertha had an ultra-strong *Memory Charm* put on her. Who would have wanted to do that? It couldn't have been Lockhart - he was still trying to remember what a wand was for (wasn't he?). It could have been anyone at the Ministry - we heard Bertha was a liability there. Maybe it was even caused by multiple people who didn't realize the other guy had already done one! (hehehe)

Voldemort explains that he used various spells, including some he invented himself, to provide himself a frail body until he could perform the one spell that would bring his old body back. He ultimately wants to give himself an immortal existence, but will settle right now for a human form. He felt that if he were to rise more powerful than before, he had to insist on using blood from Harry Potter - as Harry's mother's protection would then reside in him as well.

So, was the protection the only thing to be transferred from Harry to Voldemort, or do other things transfer as well? Also, does the process of taking blood from Harry create any other special bonds for Harry or Voldemort? We have already seen that getting scarred by Voldemort links Harry to him. Wonder what other unexpected "gifts" they might give one-another? Voldemort might want to hope Harry wasn't coming down with a virus or something.... J.K.R. could have a lot of fun with this one....

Voldemort explains that Harry is protected even better than Harry, himself, might realize - whereby Dumbledore used some old magic that protects Harry against even Voldemort while Harry is in his relation's care. However, Harry is unprotected here, and Voldemort wants to demonstrate to his audience that Harry is not stronger than he is - that Harry only survived by a lucky chance. Voldemort performs the *Cruciatus Curse* on Harry.

The WWP Sleuthoscope just went dark and is slipping out of sight.... So THAT'S the reason! Now we have proof why Harry has to keep going back to Privet Drive (his privé/*private life*) every summer. Not only are people assuredly looking out for him, but there is strong magic protecting him there. Does Voldemort mean the *Fidelius Charm*, or even more than that? No matter what, it looks like Harry doesn't get out of that Dursley situation anytime soon (assuming he can get out of his current situation, that is).

Voldemort has Wormtail untie Harry and give him back his wand, so Voldemort can kill him in front of witnesses, proving that Harry is not really more powerful than he is.

CIRCLE OF DEATH EATERS

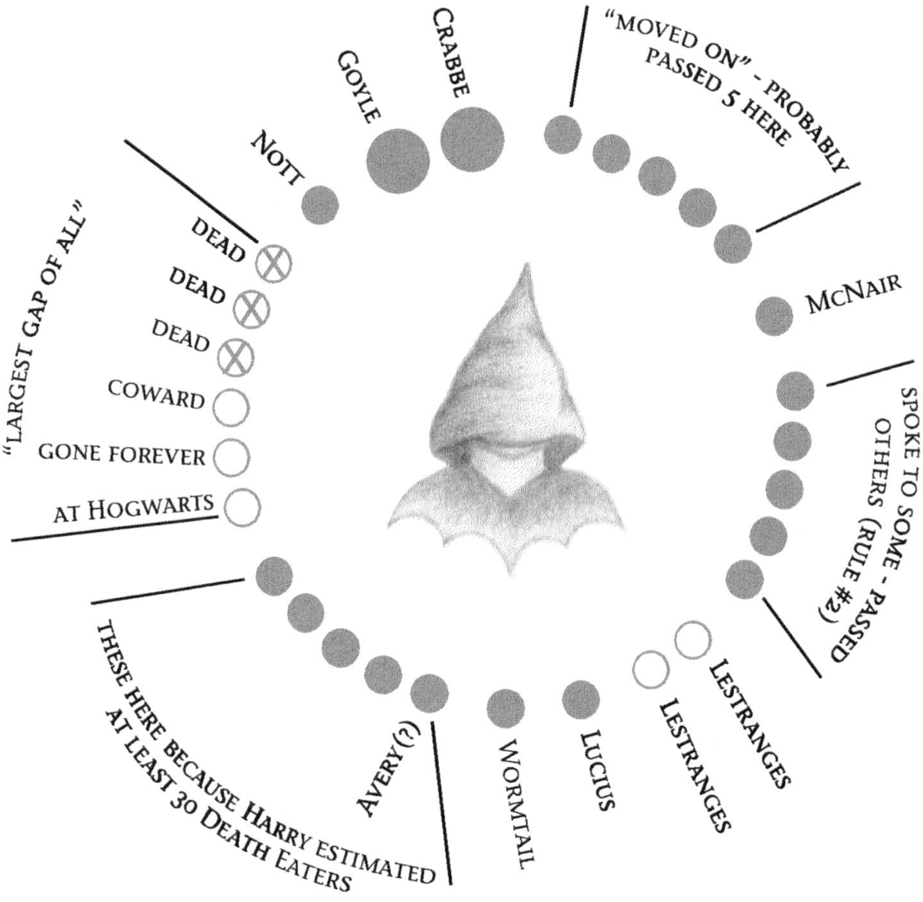
CRABBE
GOYLE
NOTT
"MOVED ON" - PROBABLY PASSED 5 HERE
MCNAIR
SPOKE TO SOME - PASSED OTHERS (RULE #2)
LESTRANGES
LESTRANGES
LUCIUS
WORMTAIL
AVERY(?)
THESE HERE BECAUSE HARRY ESTIMATED AT LEAST 30 DEATH EATERS
"LARGEST GAP OF ALL"
DEAD
DEAD
DEAD
COWARD
GONE FOREVER
AT HOGWARTS

Curiosities

- Wormtail's Dark Mark is also on his left arm. Seems like they are on the left arm for everyone (but we won't rule out exceptions - especially if someone is trying to hide their Mark).

Chapter 34 Analysis

Clues

Avoiding eye contact, Wormtail hands Harry back his wand, and then joins the circle of at least 30 Death Eaters who have closed-in on them. Voldemort wants Harry to duel with him. He taunts Harry and then tries to force Harry to reply by using the *Imperius Spell,* but Harry fights it and refuses.

> Seems that Moody was right to teach them how to resist that curse after all, right? Why did Wormtail avoid eye contact? Is it just uneasy, or is it more than that? We can see from this that Voldemort's power over people is as much mental as it is physical. It is a true reign of terror in which Voldemort attacks his enemies psychologically, using bullying and cult-style tactics to rally his followers. HP Sleuths note that we are told there are about 30 Death Eaters present at this "party."

Whereas Voldemort is now eager to get it over with, Harry refuses to die at Voldemort's feet, so as Voldemort casts the *Killing Curse,* Harry simultaneously casts the *Disarming Spell.* When the two beams meet, both wands start vibrating uncontrollably. As Harry hangs on, he and Voldemort are lifted into the air, then land in an area away from the graves, entwined in a golden dome-shaped web. Harry sees Voldemort struggling to break the connection, making Harry instinctively hold on even tighter. Harry is heartened when he hears the web vibrating with the song of the phoenix, encouraging him to hold on.

> Can you feel that phoenix power? Is that because both wands have a phoenix core? Each time that Harry has been empowered in a dangerous situation, it is the phoenix song that has given him strength, which we learn from *Fantastic Beasts* also instills fear in the "impure." We are more intrigued than ever to find out all about the "Order of the Phoenix" in Book 5.

Beads of light start moving toward Harry along the thread, making his wand fiery hot and vibrating worse the closer they get. Seeing that, Harry concentrates as hard as he can to move the beads of light toward Voldemort

> Is this heat related to the warmth Harry feels from Fawkes? Look how well Harry can focus himself. Harry was able to mentally overpower Voldemort in this confrontation. Was it the phoenix song preventing Voldemort from being at full mental capacity, or is Harry somehow actually superior to Voldemort?

One of the beads connects with Voldemort's wand, and as Voldemort yells in pain, the previous victims of his wand emerge from its end, in reverse order. First Cedric's shadow appears out of the wand telling Harry to hold on, then the old man (Frank Bryce) from Harry's dream.

> Voldemort's wand is a bit puzzling to us – but not the same issues that are discussed on the Internet. Our greatest confusion is from the most recent use of the

wand at the gravesite. We did not see Wormtail put a wand into the pocket of Voldemort's robes, and we did not see if Wormtail has a wand of his own at all. Yet, we know that Wormtail killed Cedric, we know that Wormtail conjured fire and ropes, and we know he extracted bone dust from the grave of Tom Riddle Sr. Did Wormtail put the wand back into the robes before amputating his hand? We were not told if he did, but Voldemort pulled his wand from "a deep pocket" inside his robes. We also know that since Cedric came out of Voldemort's wand, that it was the same wand that was used to murder Cedric. For that matter, what about any wand work Voldemort might have done at any of their hide-outs? Voldemort was "torn from his body" when he attacked Harry 13 years ago, so wouldn't the wand have been left in the rubble at the Potter's house? Well, then, where did Wormtail find Voldemort's wand after all these years? Where was it (or who had it)?

Bertha comes out of the wand next, and says, "Harry – don't let go!" All the figures circle around Harry and Voldemort - encouraging Harry and uttering things (Harry could not hear) to Voldemort, who is clearly fearful and caught off-guard by this as well.

How did Bertha know Harry's name? What are we to infer from that?

Harry then sees his Father and Mother spill out of the end of the wand. His father says to him "your mother's coming...she wants to see you...."

Many discussions have taken place about the apparent wand order "error" in which Harry's father comes out first and announces that his mother is following. WWP was never bothered by that at all since, if we accept the already strange concept that these shadows knew of each-other and were able to communicate between themselves **before** they both emerged from the wand, we figured it was easily possible for them to switch places **intentionally** before coming out. If Harry's father can say "Your mother's coming ..." then he can also have come out first of his own accord. Why is that all he says to Harry, anyway? That is, itself, a clue! Nonetheless, it was changed in later editions. Therefore, it you are reading a newer edition, it is Harry's mother who comes out first – then his father, who whispers in his ear and tells him about the Portkey (see below). So, is this writers license, a legitimate capability of these shadows, or unanswered mysteries?? Just more fun - See Restricted Area for more...

Voldemort watches in fear as all of his victims parade around, muttering nasties to him.

Is there anything Voldemort is afraid of, if he doesn't even fear death? How about being surrounded by the shadows of those he has murdered? Is it possible that Voldemort ultimately could be defeated by the shadows of his slain victims? Voldemort seems to fear these shadows, so they could hold the key to his demise. There is no other evidence, but we now have found at least one thing that puts fear into Voldemort.

Harry's mother [father] quietly tells Harry that when the connection is broken, the shadows will linger and shield Harry from Voldemort for enough time to get back to the Portkey. Cedric's shadow asks him if he will take his body back to his parents and Harry promises to do so. Harry wrenches his wand upward and breaks the connection.

> So how did the shadows know that the Portkey is set to travel back to Hogwarts and how did it get set to do that? These shadows are not just images - any more than the Fat Lady or Sir Cadogan are just pictures - they have personality, memory, and awareness.

Harry runs wildly on his painful leg through the gravesite, dodging spells, casting his own back over his shoulder, and as he seizes Cedric's body, he summons the Cup to him and is transported away as Voldemort screams in frustration.

Curiosities

＊ The beads of light may remind *The Prisoner* TV Series fans of a scene where he tries to prevent some projected shapes from sliding along a thin line into his head by concentrating very hard. It's a mind-control technique.

＊ Wormtail certainly had no remorse about tying Harry up and helping Voldemort. So what happened to the "bond" from when Harry spared Pettigrew's (Wormtail's) life? Does that only count if Wormtail is doing the killing, or does Harry have to ask to be spared?

＊ If HP Sleuths care to lookup the different versions, the passage is on page 579 of the U. K. hardcover printing, and on page 667 of the U.S. hardcover printing.

Clues

Harry hits the ground as he lands back at Hogwarts, next to the maze, and remains facedown trying to recover - his scar burning dully. Dumbledore is telling Harry to release Cedric, as Fudge (whose face looks white) is attempting to get Dumbledore to talk to Cedric's parents. Someone tells Dumbledore that he will take Harry, but Dumbledore replies that he prefers not - and then tells Harry to stay. But in the confusion, Moody carts Harry off to the hospital wing, as Harry's scar pounds so badly he wants to throw up.

> HP Hintoscope is pounding relentlessly! What is going on here? Why is Fudge trying to drag Dumbledore away from a serious situation - even if it *is* to talk to Cedric's parents? Why is it that Moody did not realize that Harry was to stay there? Why is it that Harry's scar, which had gone to a dull ache, is now pounding so badly? Is Voldemort zapping people back at the gravesite or is it something else? What is going on?

Moody, who Harry thought looked "as white as Fudge had looked," brings Harry to his office (not the hospital), where he gives Harry some burning peppery drink that stops the pain from his scar. Moody wants to know the exact details, and Harry tells him all about Voldemort's potion and the return of the Death Eaters. Harry realizes that he had forgotten to tell Dumbledore, back at the maze, that there is a Death Eater at Hogwarts.

> So Moody was able to stop Harry's scar from hurting so badly. That was helpful. Was it just Pepperup potion, or was it more like the burning potion that the Orcs gave to Frodo in Lord of the Rings to clear his head? Hope Harry remembers that potion if he needs it again. Interesting coincidence how Fudge and Moody looked so similarly off-color. Oh, did we say the "C" word? Well, almost everyone is looking quite pale right now, aren't they? This obviously is affecting Fudge and Moody the same way....

Moody tells Harry that he already knows about the Death Eater at Hogwarts, and when Harry assumes it is Karkaroff, Moody scoffs, saying that Karkaroff fled but won't get far - as Voldemort "has ways of tracking his enemies."

> You know, this Voldemort guy just seems to grow on people, doesn't he? This must be Voldemort's idea of keeping in touch. We hope Karkaroff is still wearing his furs - looks like he may need them.

Moody discloses to a confused Harry that he (Moody) is the Dark Lord's servant who cast the Dark Mark at the World Cup and put Harry's name into the Goblet. He wants to hear that "Voldemort" had tortured the Death Eaters for not being loyal, and that the Dark Lord had told them all that he was the faithful one. Moody repeats that the one thing he hates most is "a Death Eater who walked free."

Moody used the name "Voldemort"? Was that intended? Moody is overly obsessed with finding out that Voldemort tortured the other Death Eaters who did not go looking for him. Moody is quite vexed that Voldemort was not more angry and ruthless with those who had not shown extreme faith. Obviously, this man has somehow fooled everyone - including Dumbledore. (*Very* scary)

Moody explains how he had protected and helped Harry by encouraging Hagrid to show Harry the dragons, by giving Cedric the clue to the egg, by making sure that Neville had the book about gillyweed right in his dorm (even though Harry would not ask Neville for help). To get around that snag, Moody summoned Dobby to collect some clothes while loudly discussing gillyweed in front of him, so Dobby went to Snape's office and nabbed the gillyweed for Harry.

So Dobby *did* steal the gillyweed from Snape's office. How did Dobby get through Snape's spells? Did Moody need to help him get in, do house-elves have special privileges, or can Dobby somehow get past those spells? How did Moody know that Dobby could? This is important.

Moody also lets Harry know that in the maze, he cursed obstacles out of his way, he stunned Fleur, and he put the *Imperius Curse* on Krum to make him attack Cedric.

HP Sleuths - we have now seen Krum attack due to the *Imperius Curse*. We now know how difficult it is to distinguish between someone acting on their own free will and someone under that spell. Could anyone else be acting under the *Imperius Curse*?

Moody is pointing his wand directly at Harry as he recounts to Harry how similar his own life is to that of Voldemort - how they both were named after their fathers and both killed their own fathers. He exclaims that if he delivers Harry to the Dark Lord, that he will be honored above all others as Voldemort's "closest supporter...closer than a son."

Oedipus Rex has competition here! It strikes us as really odd to hear Moody talking about his father. He somehow seemed much more confident in himself, and not the type where his actions are based on the approval of his parents - especially after all he's been through. Notice that Harry's "scar alarm" was going off after he got back. Could it even react to some Death Eaters, or was Voldemort busy doing something to set it off?

It seems that Moody had helped Harry all the way through the tasks so Harry would get to the Triwizard Cup first. Moody describes how he was watching Harry "all the time...all those hours in the library."

He was watching Harry that much? Parvati is right – Moody's eye is really creepy.

Harry sees some shapes appearing in the Foe Glass behind Moody. Suddenly Dumbledore, McGonagall, and Snape blast through the door, knocking Moody out. The three enter the room as Snape sees their faces reflected in the Foe Glass.

> The Foe Glass has just given us proof that Snape is an enemy of this Death Eater! (That's a good sign...)

Dumbledore explains that this is not Alastor Moody, as Moody would never have removed Harry from his sight against his request. Dumbledore unlocks all seven key-locks in series on Moody's trunk – ultimately revealing an underground room where they discover the "real" Moody lying semi-conscious on the floor.

> Oh, well, HP Sleuths knew it all along, didn't we? Uh, uh ... um ... maybe at least for the last couple of minutes we figured something was terribly wrong. Well ... uh ... Dumbledore didn't even suspect anything. So see - it probably was really tough to figure this one out. Guess there were enough clues by the end to maybe get this one, but we weren't looking in the right place - you can't trust anyone, can you? Ron was right about a Dark Wizard fooling Dumbledore, but (as usual) he guessed the wrong wizard. We better start boning up for Book 5 now....

Dumbledore sends Professor McGonagall to lead Padfoot to his office, and Snape to get Winky. He then empties out the imposter's hip flask (that the true Moody had always used for normal nourishment), but Polyjuice Potion pours from it now, which Dumbledore finds ingenious. As they sit and watch, the imposter's features eventually return to "normal," and they see Barty Crouch **Junior** lying before them.

> You would think that with all this Polyjuice stuff floating around that we might have gotten a taste of what was happening. It's the "bouncing ferret" that did it. J.K.R. is a genius - Moody won our trust, and demonstrated contempt for people who do not play fair, so we assumed he played fair and was trustworthy. We could tell Crouch Junior's disdain for Snape, Malfoy, and Karkaroff was very real, but that was not because he thought they were evil. It was because he was very upset that they were *walking around free and had not tried to find Voldemort.*

Snape has brought Winky into the room, and Dumbledore administers Snape's Veritaserum truth serum to Crouch Junior. Crouch Junior discloses the truth of the whole intricate deception:

◆ His mother saved him from dying in Azkaban - she was dying also, so she convinced his father to swap them. When his parents came to visit him, he and his mother each took Polyjuice Potion with the other's hair, and they changed identity. As the dementors are blind, they sensed one healthy and one dying person entering and then leaving - not aware that the two dying ones had switched places. She continued to take the potion and was buried with her son's appearance.

> There have now been two confirmed escapes from Azkaban!

- Crouch Senior staged his wife's death with a "private" funeral, but the grave is empty. The house-elf (Winky) nursed young Crouch back to health, but then his father had to use the *Imperius Curse* so he would not return to Voldemort, and he was forced to wear an Invisibility Cloak all the time.

  > Barty Crouch Senior used the *Imperius Curse* on another human being... on his own son...?

- When Bertha Jorkins had stopped by one day, Winky was talking to young Crouch in the kitchen. Bertha heard enough to figure it all out. When Crouch Senior got home, she confronted him, and he put such a powerful *Memory Charm* on her that it damaged her memory.

  > Her memory was **permanently** damaged - like Neville's?

- Winky had talked his father into letting him go to the World Cup. Crouch Junior was actually sitting with her in the Top Box under his Invisibility Cloak, but he had been getting stronger and was starting to be able to fight the *Imperius Curse*. When Winky was hiding her eyes in fright, he saw the wand sticking out of Harry's pocket, and stole it. He saw the Death Eaters (who were still free) reveling after the game, so in his anger, had tried to go after them. However, Winky used "her own brand of magic" to restrain and drag him away from them into the forest, but he was able to release the *Dark Mark* from there.

  > So there really was "someone invisible" dragging on Winky that night, and she (truthfully?) said she was "seeing no one" (even though he was there with her).

- When the Ministry wizards shot their stun spells, he was zapped. Crouch's father had searched the area and felt him there, then returned later to retrieve him. His father dismissed Winky for allowing him a wand and almost allowing him to escape.

  > Crouch Senior does seem every bit as ruthless as he has been portrayed.

- One night, Wormtail had arrived at their house carrying Voldemort, who performed the *Imperius Curse* on Crouch's father. Crouch Senior was then forced to continue working under Voldemort's control.

  > Back in October, Crouch Senior was certainly looking very odd, but we had no idea Voldemort was a "house guest."

- Voldemort told Crouch Junior that he needed a servant who was willing to risk all. Crouch Junior was ecstatic to be chosen to serve Voldemort and prove that he was faithful.

  > Just for the record, this does not sound like a long-term follower – Junior acts more like a recent convert or an eager newbie.

- Crouch Junior and Wormtail had gone to Moody's house. The real Moody put up a struggle, but they were able to subdue him and stuff him into his own trunk before

Arthur Weasley arrived. Crouch Junior kept Moody alive in the trunk in order to retrieve hairs and question him about his past and his habits in order to fool Dumbledore.

> The real Moody presumably saw Pettigrew that day, while McGonagall and Snape now witness Crouch Junior finger Wormtail – all proof of Pettigrew's faked death (and Sirius's innocence).

◆ Wormtail watched over Crouch Senior in their house, but when his father started being able to fight the *Curse*, Voldemort decided it was too dangerous, and that Crouch Senior should say he was ill and mail-in his instructions. However, his father escaped from Wormtail, so Voldemort sent Crouch Junior word to stop his father at all costs.

> The eagle owl (Chapter 28) was carrying that order from Voldemort.

◆ The map, which Crouch Junior remarks almost ruined everything when Harry saw "Barty Crouch" on it, saved the situation. Crouch Junior saw his father appear on it the night Harry found him on the grounds, so he put on his Invisibility Cloak, and went out to get his father. Dumbledore asks, "what map?" and Crouch Junior explains that it was Harry's map.

> ("What map?") – Something else Dumbledore didn't know about Mooney, Padfoot, and Prongs....

◆ Since his Master needed Harry, Crouch Junior let Potter go, but he stunned Krum and then killed his own father. He had turned his father's body into a bone and buried it in the freshly-dug earth in front of Hagrid's cabin.

> Do boarhounds like bones? (Nifflers probably don't.)

◆ Crouch Junior offered to carry the Triwizard Cup into the maze where he turned it into a Portkey.

> Too bad no one answered Ron's question about the Portkey.

Crouch Junior claims he will be rewarded beyond belief. He slumps back into unconsciousness.

> If you think the mystery's solved, think again...
>
> ☾ When Moody stated that he does not like people who attack when their back is turned, and does not like Death Eaters who walked free – it was not an act, he really meant it! Why would Crouch Junior, a Voldemort supporter, be so concerned about anyone being attacked from behind?
>
> ☾ We saw from the white ferret incident that Crouch Junior is a very quick and powerful wizard. We would think most wizards couldn't have performed an instant transfiguration on a human. He was still a young wizard

when he ws sent to Azkaban, so how did Crouch Junior get that powerful? Is this due to Dark Magic, or was he already powerful? Who taught him the Dark Arts? Where did Crouch Junior learn the *Killing Curse*? Is this evidence that he has been a Dark wizard all along? It seems unlikely, but what do we know about his mother? Or about his father, who used the Unforgivable *Imperious Curse* on him? How about the Lestranges?

- Was Crouch Junior guilty or not at the time he was convicted by his father? Could the Lestranges have converted Crouch Junior to the Dark side while in prison? If Neville's *Memory Charm* relates to this, would it clear or implicate Crouch Junior?

- Sirius said Crouch Junior "went quiet" after a few weeks. Maybe he was innocent after all but (with help from other prisoners) now became focused on revenge through Voldemort (mostly toward his father)? Just like with Sirius - none of those would have been happy thoughts.

- He was an impressionable kid who had been let down by his own father. Could he be seeing Voldemort as a substitute role model? Remember, he specifically desired that Voldemort would consider him "closer than a son."

- Why would Crouch Junior teach Harry to resist the *Imperious Curse* – since this would help him resist Voldemort as well as all Dark Wizards? Was that because of Crouch Junior's own personal disdain for that curse?

- Winky would probably know the answer to most of these questions but is she going to be willing to divulge her "Master's secrets" to anyone?

- So if Moody was still alive, who was Voldemort referring to when he told Wormtail "one more death" in Chapter 1? Was Crouch Junior unable to kill anyone besides his own father, or was there another murder we haven't yet read about?

J.K.R. is getting even better at answering a question with a new question!

Winky is in tears - her Master's secret out, along with some unexpected twists.

─────────────────────── *Curiosities* ───────────────────────

✳ Crouch Junior says he kept Moody alive. Was this originally part of the plan? If *not*, then maybe that's what Voldemort meant when he said "one more death" in chapter 1. However, if it *was* part of the plan, then *who else has died?*

✳ When Crouch/Moody is standing there looking at Harry's map is chapter 25, he could have been lying about not seeing a Crouch "dot" on it. Yet, looking at J.K.R.'s careful wording, it is almost certain that the Crouch dot really wasn't there at that moment. Since Crouch was standing there talking to Harry, that's further evidence that they have to be moving in order to show up on the Marauder's Map.

✳ We are not sure if Voldemort will be happy now if anyone else kills Harry for him. Since Harry has now slipped through Voldemort's fingers three times (not counting the one as a shadow in his diary), Voldemort may need to prove that he can kill Harry himself. Otherwise he couldn't claim to be the "greatest wizard alive."

✳ The underground room in the trunk is, of course, another TARDIS-like effect (space/time warp).

✳ So, does Polyjuice hold the alternate person's identity if the drinker dies while looking like that other person? How long did Mrs. Crouch continue to look like her son? Also, how long did Crouch Senior continue to look like a bone?

✳ We know about Edmond's plight on the L'ile d'If in *The Count of Monte-Cristo*, by Alexandre Dumas, so why didn't that occur to us here? Did one of you HP Super Sleuths get this one?

─────────── ✳ ───────────

Chapter 36 Analysis

Clues

Dumbledore binds up Crouch, leaving McGonagall standing guard, and sends Snape to find Cornelius Fudge to further question Crouch Junior. Dumbledore brings Harry to his office where Sirius is waiting. Dumbledore reinforces that Harry has shown exceptional bravery. With the help of a single soft phoenix note that warms and strengthens him, Harry recounts the night's events as he strokes Fawkes. When Harry mentions that Wormtail took his blood, Sirius and Dumbledore jump up in alarm and inspect his arm. Yet Harry thought he noticed a brief look of triumph in Dumbledore's eyes before saying that now, unfortunately, Voldemort has overcome "that particular barrier."

A look of triumph? What devious scheme could Dumbledore have devised? Could he have somehow implanted something sinister in Harry's blood? Maybe it gives Voldemort a weakness or a means of being tracked? Remember Snape's lesson in undetectable poisons? There is definitely something weird about Harry and poisons. HP Sleuths should monitor all vital signs. If Dumbledore went through all that trouble, they obviously knew Voldemort was not dead and would try to come after Harry again (which is yet more evidence that there is something very significant about Harry). And what does Dumbledore mean by "that *particular* barrier"? How many "barriers" have they set up, how, and why? Voldemort could be in for some rude surprises! (snicker)

Harry mentions how the wands connected, and Dumbledore reveals that both Harry's and Voldemort's wands contain a feather from the same phoenix - Fawkes. Two wands that are "brothers" will not work against each-other - one will force the other to regurgitate its spells in reverse. The dead people that Harry saw had not come back to life, so what he encountered were just their shadows (or echoes of their id). As Harry finds himself overcome while speaking of Cedric, Fawkes cries on his leg, healing the spider's wound.

Seems that Harry's and Voldemort's wands are *just birds of a feather*. (ahem) Was Harry pre-destined for that wand, or is it because of his link to Voldemort? Did Dumbledore "help" with that *coincidence*? We already knew that Fawkes is no ordinary bird since he is a domesticated phoenix, however, the more we learn, the more we realize that he may be extremely special. He again heals one of Harry's wounds, which again may have been poisonous. Our brains are getting fuzzy from all these potent clues - has J.K.R. affected our senses?

Dumbledore leads Harry and Sirius down to the hospital wing where Ron, Hermione, Bill, and Mrs. Weasley are anxiously waiting. Madam Pomfrey gives Harry a potion for dreamless sleep, but Harry only dozes for awhile before waking to the sound of arguing. Fudge comes, in loudly demanding to talk to Dumbledore, so Mrs. Weasley angrily tries to quiet him. Dumbledore arrives almost immediately – asking what is wrong.

Yeah, Mrs. W! Look at her stand up to the Minister of Magic! Guess after dealing with Fred and George, a Minister is trivial (tee-hee). Now, where was Dumbledore and how did he know to get back so fast? We keep seeing that he is always somehow quickly alerted to trouble.

McGonagall complains to Dumbledore that Fudge had brought a dementor when he went to talk to Crouch Junior, saying he was concerned about his personal safety. McGonagall is infuriated because Fudge had the dementor perform the kiss on Crouch Junior.

Uck! Kissed by a dementor - that's **much** worse than getting kissed by Moaning Myrtle.☹ So what exactly is the status of Crouch Junior? Is his body still alive? If so, where is it and who has custody of it? Is there a possibility that the dementors can regurgitate Crouch's soul, or is the kiss permanent? If it's not permanent, then we could end up seeing Crouch Junior again. If we do, will he still be faithful to Voldemort after what happened to him here? If there is a chance that Crouch Junior could be restored, we should consider if he was, himself, a victim. If he was a victim, his experience at Hogwarts as a teacher might have affected him positively. At Hogwarts, he had the trust and respect of many people (something he never received from his father), and he watched as other victimized kids struggled with their own family problems (including Neville). Crouch Junior teaching Neville is either very ironic or very scary – considering we still don't know whether Crouch Junior was actually innocent of torturing the Longbottoms or not. Crouch Junior is complex.

Dumbledore is **extremely** upset with Fudge, as now Crouch Junior cannot give testimony.

The WWP Sleuthoscope is gyrating in a mad spin! Was Fudge maybe afraid that Crouch Junior might spill-the-beans on **other** things? What is Fudge doing?

1. First, Fudge refuses to investigate the links between the disappearances
2. We already know Fudge seems to like dealing with the dementors
3. Fudge appointed himself as judge for the tournament
4. Fudge then pulls Dumbledore away from Harry so Moody/Crouch can take Harry
5. Fudge has the same (pale) expression as Moody/Crouch upon hearing that Voldemort has returned (and we now know why Moody/Crouch looked that way)
6. And now Fudge destroys evidence about Voldemort's return - not to mention no trial for Crouch Junior.

Sounds like he's covering up for **someone**. If not, he may have a **lot** of explaining to do to Voldemort. We can't be sure whether this is a fishing trip or a hunting trip, but either way, Fudge is the prey. HP Sleuths, don't let your guards down.... CONSTANT VIGILANCE!

Dumbledore explains to Fudge that Harry's scar acts as a warning signal for Voldemort's activities, but Fudge insists that Harry is deranged and untrustworthy (supported by the evidence in Rita's article)... and declares Dumbledore a madman. He refuses to believe that Voldemort has risen, and when Harry mentions the names of the Death Eaters (omitting Snape), Fudge is affronted that Lucius Malfoy is named - saying he was cleared, and had made important donations.

> Looks like Poison Pen Skeeter has succeeded in her mission - she has destroyed Harry's credibility with the Minister of Magic, plus who knows how many others. When Harry lists the names of the Death Eaters, he may have gained some respect from Snape by not mentioning him. Lucius Malfoy certainly does seem to "donate" a lot of money - wonder who's on his "charity" list besides St Mungo's?

Dumbledore asks Fudge to extend diplomacy to the giants and remove the dementors from Azkaban before Voldemort tries to take control again, but Fudge refuses. Dumbledore feels that Fudge has always put too much emphasis on purity of blood, and that if Fudge shuts his eyes to what is happening, they will have a "parting of the ways."

> Fudge's bigoted opinion sounds a bit too much like Malfoy. Is he already in Malfoy's pocket(book)? Malfoy can wield a lot of power with his money. (Wonder how he gets along with goblins?) Dumbledore is convinced that the dementors would side with Voldemort, so there is no question about what happens with Azkaban if Voldemort takes over. This is looking bad all around. HP Sleuths should be prepared – Dumbledore's position at Hogwarts may not survive a political confrontation with the Minister of Magic.

Dumbledore pleads with Fudge that they need to work together against Voldemort. As further evidence of Voldemort's return, Snape shows Fudge his arm, where the Dark Mark is less pronounced but still very black. Fudge is appalled, unwilling to listen, and only states he will be in touch with Dumbledore the next day concerning the way he runs his school. Fudge dumps the thousand Galleons that were supposed to be Harry's winnings on the table next to him and storms out.

> This does not sound good. Not at all. Fudge is now questioning the way Dumbledore is running the school, and we know that it was specifically because of Dumbledore that Voldemort could not take over the school last time. Not only do we want Dumbledore at Hogwarts, we *need* Dumbledore at Hogwarts! Did Fudge understand what was on Snape's arm? Did Fudge know about that mark? How many people know about the mark? Is Fudge a wimp, or a traitor?

As soon as Fudge leaves, Dumbledore starts to organize a strategy. Bill volunteers to go immediately to contact Arthur Weasley and have him notify everyone in the Ministry (who is open to hear it) that Voldemort has risen again. Dumbledore warns Bill to be discrete so that Fudge won't think they are undermining him.

Yea!! We can't wait to see Bill in action.☺ Okay HP Sleuths, just how discrete will Bill need to be? Is he going to tell Percy? If he *does*, he runs the risk of Percy giving him a difficult time by thinking that Bill is exaggerating, or worse still, inadvertently leaking it to "probing" members. If Bill *doesn't* tell Percy, he runs the risk of having Percy suspect that his father (or other family member) is up to something, and then Percy might turn them in (as Ron fears). It would hurt Percy later if he were to find out he wasn't trusted. **What do HP Sleuths think?** We can only hope that the Sorting Hat was correct when it put Percy in Gryffindor (and was not simply blinded by the red hair).

Dumbledore has McGonagall go down to request that Hagrid (and Mme Maxime, if willing), meet him in his office. He sends Madam Pomfrey to retrieve Winky and bring her down to Dobby in the kitchens.

This could be tricky - Winky was not very strong to begin with. Doubt there's enough Butterbeer in the castle to drown out this disaster. Will she tell Dobby and/or the other house-elves everything? How will Dobby or the other house-elves react if she tells them all about Voldemort coming back? What would happen with the house-elves if Voldemort took over or tried to take over Hogwarts?

When the others have left, Dumbledore has Padfoot transform back into Sirius in front of Harry, Ron, Hermione, Snape, Bill, and Mrs. Weasley (who has to be reassured that Sirius is safe). Dumbledore is adamant that he trusts both Sirius and Snape, and that they now must work together (with each other) as they are on the same side (they reluctantly agree). Dumbledore explains that Fudge's attitude will make everything harder.

This one has our curiosity. Did Dumbledore purposely send McGonagall away before having Sirius expose himself, or was he in too much of a hurry to have her wait and see? Maybe he had already informed her, and it was not necessary for her to be there? This is more like a brain tickler.

Dumbledore sends Sirius off to contact Lupin, Arabella Figg, Mundungus Fletcher, and the rest of the "old crowd."

The WWP Sleuthoscope is glowing brightly! J.K.R. has verified in an interview on Scholastic.com, that Arabella is, indeed, **the** Mrs. Figg from the Privet Drive neighborhood. Therefore, we have proof that Mrs. Figg is a witch; but is she more than that? Could she have a vital secret of her own? What is her relationship to Perkins and that cabbage smell? So, *this* is the "old crowd".... Sounds like a fun bunch (smirk) - can't wait to see what J.K.R. has in store for them!

Dumbledore tells Sirius to inconspicuously stay with Lupin, where Dumbledore will contact him. Harry is very sad to see Sirius leaving again.

Where does Lupin (a werewolf) live? What will Sirius and Lupin discuss while they are together? What will be revealed? What will these old mischief makers plot?

Dumbledore cryptically says that Snape knows what he has to do, asking Snape if he is prepared to do it. Snape says he is, and leaves silently. Dumbledore watches him go with a look of "apprehension."

> Whatever it is that Snape is doing, it must be highly secretive and/or dangerous since Dumbledore looks concerned and does not divulge it to anyone there. Guess we'll have to try to like Snape as much as Dumbledore likes him. (We agree with Sirius - we'll just shake hands and leave it at that.) After all he's done to Harry, Snape will have to earn our respect.

The part that had been gnawing at Harry all night finally floods his thoughts - his guilt that it is his fault that Cedric touched the Portkey and is dead. He tells Mrs. Weasley how it was his idea that Cedric touch the Cup with him, but she insists that it was not his fault, while she holds him like a mother. Hermione slams something on the window with her hand - holding it tight, apologizing to everyone for the noise.

> We've been seeing a lot of banging, but we are specifically told here that Hermione "slammed". Hmm... What has Hermione got now?

Harry drinks more of the dreamless-sleep potion and finally goes to sleep for the night.

Other Oddities

— Dumbledore pointed out that (having killed his father) Crouch Junior was the "last remaining member of a pure-blood family."

— No spell can re-awake the dead – Dumbledore (and J.K.R.) are firm on this. If the fans and J.K.R. want a deceased character to reappear, then J.K.R. would have to be creative about it... but that's what she is – extremely creative!

— Ollivander had written to Dumbledore as soon as Harry had bought the brother wand to Voldemort's. They were clearly expecting something "interesting" with that wand.

Chapter 37 Analysis

Clues

Harry meets with the Diggorys the next morning, which is one of the most painful experiences of all. They do not blame him for what happened, and even thank him for returning Cedric's body to them. Harry tries to give them the prize gold, but Mrs. Diggory refuses, saying it is his, and that she couldn't take it.

> Hopefully, the Diggorys are well-off because the Tournament Rules stated that whoever touched the cup first was the winner - not who got back alive from an unofficial encounter with Voldemort. Hopefully, the Diggorys will remember Harry's generosity and good intentions.

Harry, Ron, and Hermione wait for any word about what might be happening with events in the outside world. Ron says that his mother has asked if Harry can stay with the Weasleys over the summer, but Dumbledore had reasons for wanting Harry to go back to the Dursleys - at least at first.

> Dumbledore's reasons wouldn't relate to what Voldemort said about Harry being protected there, would they? (hint, hint) This could be a very odd summer. Hope Harry is safe if he visits the Weasleys; hope the Weasleys are safe if he visits the Weasleys!

Harry, Ron, and Hermione talk to Hagrid, who had been having a cup of tea with Olympe (Madame Olympe Maxime). Dumbledore has given Hagrid and Olympe a job over the summer (which is a secret).

> Gee, this one seems difficult. Hagrid is related to the giants. Mme Maxime is surely related to the giants. Voldemort said he is expecting support from the giants. Dumbledore told Fudge that the giants needed to be contacted and offered reconciliation immediately. Wonder what Hagrid's and Olympe's "secret mission" might be? Hmmm. Knowing J.K.R., it is probably more complex than that, but we can be reasonably sure that it has something to do with gaining the allegiance of the giants.

Hagrid says he always presumed that Voldemort would come back some day - as he knew Voldemort was out there trying. Hagrid also comments that as long as they have Dumbledore, he's not too worried.

> Oh no...Oh no! Did he really have to go and say that? The WWP Sleuthoscope just flew into orbit!

At the Leaving Feast, the Great Hall is covered in black in memory of Cedric. The real Moody sits at the staff table, still a nervous wreck from his ordeal.

Remember that storm which accompanied the fake Moody's entrance at the beginning of the year? It was truly a foreboding of what was to come. We are unfortunately going to see stormier times ahead. Another Hogwarts student has died – is this "the end of Hogwarts"? Is this what Professor McGonagall was starting to say in Book 2?

At the head table, Hagrid is there, sitting next to Mme Maxime. Snape is also there, sitting next to McGonagall, with his typical sneer. But when his eyes meet Harry's, they hold an expression that Harry cannot interpret. Harry ponders why Dumbledore trusts him and what task Snape had been given by Dumbledore. Harry remembers that Dumbledore told him how Snape had turned spy against Voldemort "at great personal risk," and wonders if he will be continuing that role.

We see that Snape's back from whatever he did, or from getting ready for his task. Has he made up some special potion for the occasion? Is Snape going to masquerade as a Death Eater? Does he have a network of "friends" he has put on alert? Maybe he is an animagus or something? There is so little evidence on which to base a theory. Guess we'll just have to wait for at least another book....

Dumbledore makes the announcement to the students that Voldemort murdered Cedric. Dumbledore explains that the Ministry of Magic did not want him to tell the students, and that some of their parents will be "horrified" since they either refuse to believe it or think the kids are too young to hear it. He is resolute that it would be an insult to the memory of Cedric if they were to be told that he died because of an accident or due to a mistake he had made.

Uh oh.☹ It is almost as if Dumbledore already has signs that people are trying to hush up the whole incident. Wonder what was said when Dumbledore and Fudge had their little talk about how the school is being run?

Dumbledore leads the students in toasting Cedric and Harry. Harry sees that certain Slytherins are showing disrespect, but realizes that Dumbledore cannot see them without a "magical eye" (like Moody's). Dumbledore reminds all the students that the spirit of the Triwizard Tournament (creating bonds among different wizarding cultures) is more crucial than ever under threat of Voldemort's return. He tells his foreign guests that they are welcome back any time if they wish to return. He says he is aware that many of them have already been hurt by Voldemort, and emphasizes that they all have to be united against Voldemort, for it is Voldemort's ability to feed off discord that gives him the power to control them.

Just like famous non-wizard tyrants (we won't grace them all by giving them names, but everyone knows who they are), Voldemort uses bigotry, intolerance, and social discord to keep everyone under his control. Dumbledore's invitation to the foreign guests is a crucial statement. Hogwarts could be a safe refuge for many wizards during a war (hope they can keep Voldemort out). *Could Dumbledore have a magical eye?* Even though he may not, Moody *does*, and he is right there. Hopefully, one of them noticed.

Fleur comes over to tell Harry that she hopes to see him again, and that she is trying to get a job in Britain to improve her English. Ron comments that her English is already very good, to which she smiles at him (while Hermione scowls).

> J.K.R. has indicated in interviews that there will be a female Defense Against the Dark Arts teacher. There are theories growing on the Internet that Fleur will be taking the job. However, Fleur seems a bit young and inexperienced to us (unless she has some power and/or experience we don't yet know about). There are also more sinister possibilities, but we have no evidence to support any of them. Suffice it to say that the position of Defense Against the Dark Arts is, once again, open (strange how this keeps happening...).

Ron ponders how the Durmstrang students will get back without Karkaroff to steer the ship, but Krum informs him that Karkaroff had the students do the steering. Krum says that Cedric was always nice to him *even though he was one of Karkaroff's students* (he "scowls" as he mentions this). Krum asks Hermione to talk with him alone, and Ron does not take his eyes off them.

> Krum is not happy, possibly even embarrassed about Karkaroff. Would most of the Durmstrang students feel the same way, or are most of them like Malfoy? Hey... Maybe we could work out a trade – Krum for Draco?

On the train back, Hermione pulls out a *Daily Prophet* and sees that there is nothing in the paper at all about the Triwizard events - not even a mention about Cedric. There had been only a small mention that Harry won the tournament and nothing since. It appears Fudge is keeping things hushed-up. Hermione informs Harry and Ron that Rita won't be writing anything nasty for at least a year unless she wants Hermione to tell everyone what she knows about Rita. Hermione pulls a glass jar from her bag - showing them a beetle. It is Rita. Rita is an unregistered Animagus, and she **really** *was* "bugging" them. Hermione caught her on the hospital windowsill. They remember that there was a beetle present at all times that Rita had scooped a story:

- the beetle in the Rose Garden with Hagrid
- the beetle in Hermione's hair by the lake with Krum
- the buzzing insect in the Divination window with Harry

> Beetles are sort of like cockroaches. Is this possibly related to the cockroach hints, or is that something else?

Hermione tells them that she will let Rita go once they are back in London.

> The WWP Sleuthoscope is up to warp 10. Oh no! No, Hermione! Don't do that! That's a bad person and it's probably not Rita! You've managed to capture her (him?) and now you're gonna let her fly off (we're gonna be sick).☹

Draco, Crabbe, and Goyle stop by to gloat about the Dark Lord's return. Draco insults poor Cedric, so Harry, Ron, Hermione, (plus Fred and George, who had come over to investigate), all cast spells simultaneously, knocking out the three Slytherins. Fred and George step **on** the Slytherins as they join the others in the compartment. Fred and George comment that the mixture of spells seem to have caused some unusual growths on the Slytherins.

> Aww, Ickle Slytherins look all icky. Harry had been itching to do this ever since he witnessed their disrespect at the Leaving Feast. We are not as convinced as Harry, however, that Dumbledore could not have seen them. He could have other ways.

Fred and George explain that the person they were concerned about **not** "blackmailing," was Ludo Bagman, who had paid them in leprechaun gold for their World Cup bet. At first they figured it was a mistake and had written to him, but he had ignored their letters. Then they tried talking to him at the Tournament, but he kept getting away until finally he ended up telling them they were too young to be betting. They eventually gave up and just asked for their money back - but he refused. They then found out that Bagman has big gambling debts. He owes money to many people (including Lee Jordan's dad). Worst of all, he is in debt to the goblins! He had tried to pay them back by betting on Harry, the underdog, for the Tournament, but since Harry did not win outright, he lost the bet. Bagman had to flee from the goblins.

> In debt to the goblins - isn't that a synonym for *this is going to hurt?* Wonder if it is possible to hide from goblins? We don't think so. This is how Bagman probably got his nose permanently broken. What will Bagman do? Check out the RESTRICTED AREA at the end of this book if you are willing to explore the most likely possibilities.

Harry privately confronts Fred and George - threatening them with his wand to take the sack of prize Galleons for their joke shop venture.

> Considering how valuable their Marauder's Map has been to Harry, the 1,000 Galleons is probably a fair exchange. Come to think of it, where is that map now? It could become priceless.

As the students greet Mrs. Weasley at King's Cross Station, she hugs Harry while whispering to him that Dumbledore might let him come and stay at the Burrow later in the summer, so he should stay in touch.

Rowlinguistics

---

* Madame Maxim's first name is **Olympe**. As with many of the names, Olympe comes from Greek mythology. The Greek gods lived on Mount Olympus, and are descendents of a race of Titans (Giants). Guess that's a big J.K.R. hint that Mme Maxime probably does have giant blood in her.

Curiosities

---

* According to Book 2 (Chapter 14), the 12 governors would have to vote Dumbledore out of the school – Fudge can't do it alone (however, we already know that the governors can be influenced).

* Lee Jordon's dad also had trouble collecting his money from Bagman – so he knows of Bagman's problems.

* Since Harry and Cedric touched the Cup at the same time, Fudge should have split it in half and offered it to them both that way. However, since a teacher sabotaged Fleur and Krum, and helped Harry during a task, maybe **all** (or **no one**) should have won - each contestant receiving 1/4 of the prize (250 Galleons) for all of their agony (which is still a **lot** of Galleons). Nonetheless, we're really glad Fred and George ended up with the loot. ☺

* The *Daily Prophet* reported that Harry won the Triwizard Tournament and that Harry got the prize money – guess that's not good enough for goblins. Seems that Hagrid was quite right about goblins.

Key Rememberit Clues from Book 4

(HARRY POTTER AND THE GOBLET OF FIRE)

Book 4 Mysteries Not Yet Solved

Godric's Hollow Cliffhangers

- ☾ What happened the night Harry's parents died, and why was the house destroyed?
- ☾ Voldemort says he killed Harry's father first – Voldemort's a liar, do we believe him?
- ☾ Why was the order of the shadows, that emerged form Voldemort's wand, changed in the later editions of the book?
- ☾ How do they know it was Harry's mother's spell that protected him from Voldemort's *Killing Curse*?
- ☾ How did everyone all know about and communicate the events that took place the night Voldemort attacked the Potters?
- ☾ How did Voldemort get his wand back, where was it, and who had it all this time?

Privet Drive Cliffhangers

- ☾ What/who protects Harry at Privet Drive, and how?
- ☾ Are Mrs. Figg's cats (or any others creatures in Harry's neighborhood) magical?
- ☾ What is the relationship between Arabella Figg and Perkins?

Dumbledore Cliffhangers

- ☾ Is Dumbledore in control of events?
- ☾ Who are the other members of the "old crowd" and what are Dumbledore's other sources that are keeping track of Voldemort, and how?
- ☾ What other "barriers" has Dumbledore set up to thwart Voldemort?
- ☾ Who else did Dumbledore think was "getting stronger"?
- ☾ Where does Dumbledore go during the summer?

Voldemort and Death Eater Cliffhangers

- ☾ Does Voldemort's return after 12 years fulfill the destiny of 12?
- ☾ What kind of bond is there now between Harry and Wormtail, and how does that work?
- ☾ In what way(s) is Harry linked to Voldemort (dreams, etc)?
- ☾ Did anything else from Harry's blood transfer to Voldemort, besides his protection from Voldemort's touch?

- Why did (does) Voldemort want to kill Harry?

- Did Voldemort kill someone else ("one more death" in Chapter 1)?

- Where did Karkaroff go?

- What happened to the other male who was accused with the Lestranges in the Pensieve?

- Who are the cowardly Death Eater and the one that has left Voldemort forever?

- What would Snape (or any Death Eater) be hiding in his office that would link him to Voldemort?

- Was Barty Crouch Junior guilty when they put him in Azkaban?

- How did Barty Crouch Junior get to be such a powerful wizard?

- Whose decision was it to teach Harry how to fight the *Imperius Curse*, and why?

- What has happened to Barty Crouch Junior's body, and what condition is it in?

- Why did Harry's scar start hurting again when he got back to Hogwarts – does it react to Death Eaters as well as Voldemort himself?

- Can anyone really recognize a half-blood wizard or Muggle (and if so, how)?

- Who is the "wealthy owner" of the Riddle House?

Hogwarts Cliffhangers

- How can house-elves (and Phoenixes) appear and disappear on Hogwarts grounds?

- Why haven't we seen an Astronomy class or the tallest tower?

- As Madam Pomfrey asked – what terrible thing are they going to have at school next year?

- Why does Snape hate Harry so much?

- What did Snape do to earn Dumbledore's trust?

- What is Snape's dangerous task?

- What is Hagrid's and Olympe's mission?

- Why did Fridwulfa leave Hagrid's dad and where is she now?

- Is Neville's memory problem due to a *Memory Charm*, and if so, who did he see?

- Who was Florence, who was kissing her, and who put the hex on her?

Weasley Cliffhangers

- How did Fred and George know, in advance, the final outcome of the world cup?

- What are Fred and George going to do with the money Harry gave them?

- Is Percy in any danger and would he recognize it if he is?
- Would Percy turn-in a member of his own family?

Organizations and Ministry of Magic Cliffhangers

- Is Cornelius Fudge a fair, honest Minister?
- What happened when Dumbledore and Fudge discussed Dumbledore's running of the school?
- How much control does Lucius Malfoy (and his money) have over the Ministry?
- Who are Voldemort's spies in the Ministry?
- Was Bagman actually guilty?
- Where did Bagman go?
- Who's side is Rita Skeeter on?
- Is Rita Skeeter a female, and is "she" really Rita?
- Is St Mungo's under the influence of Lucius Malfoy?
- Where do dementors come from, and to whom will they be loyal?
- Could anyone else have escaped from Azkaban?

Ghost and Creature Cliffhangers

- What is the magic behind Owl Post and Owls?
- What are Hedwig's heritage and magical abilities?
- How powerful are house-elves?
- How did Dobby get into Snape's spell-protected office?
- Why are house-elves subservient to wizards – how did that happen?
- Will Winky tell any of the other house-elves, and if so, how will they react?
- What happened during the goblin rebellions, and who won?
- What is the background of the Bloody Baron and what is he up to?
- Why is Peeves allowed to remain at Hogwarts?
- Are Myrtle's special water skills unique for a ghost, and what other capabilities might she have?

Spells and Potions Cliffhangers

- What are *Switching Spells* and how do they work?
- If the *Killing Curse* doesn't leave any marks, why does Harry have a scar?

- How did the shadows from Voldemort's wand know that the Portkey is set to travel back to Hogwarts and how did it get set to do that?

- What's going on with Harry and poisons (or any other immunities)?

- Do you have to be moving to show up on Marauders Map?

- Do ghosts show up on the Marauders Map?

- Where is the Marauders Map now?

Miscellaneous Cliffhangers

- What are all those "banging" noises?

- What is the significance of long fingers?

- Do the people who seem like they can read minds have *inside* information?

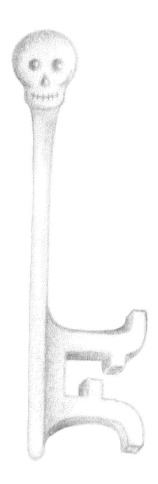

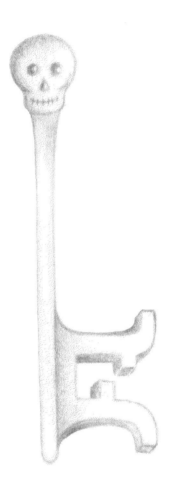

BOOK 5 AND BEYOND
(WHAT IS FORETOLD)

BEWARE!

The WWP Super Sleuths have read the stars...

The following information contains a few staggering revelations that J.K.R. has hidden in the books, which we have not yet mentioned.

The RESTRICTED AREA also holds facts about what will happen - according to what J.K.R. has actually divulged in media interviews.

Additionally, there are forward-looking predictions by WWP Super Sleuths - based on the clues in the books, combined with J.K.R.'s interviews.

A little knowledge can be dangerous, but a little more knowledge can make you crazy! Even though we have sleuthed vital secrets about the characters and plots, it is an unfinished mystery and a J.K.R. puzzle – a game she invented that we are now playing. We are now even more anxious to read Harry Potter and the Order of the Phoenix to find out if we got it right and how it all comes about!!

READ ON AT YOUR OWN RISK!

RESTRICTED AREA

—It's Not Where You Come From, It's the Choices You Make—

J.K.R. has warned us in an interview on CBC Newsworld: *"the worst is coming...."*

Hagrid was right – the Centaurs know things. In Book 1, they saw the rise of Voldemort and predicted the deaths of innocents. Mars, the war planet, has been getting brighter as the possibility of war draws closer.

Are we, indeed, headed for a war? Epic fantasies, such as *The Lord of the Rings*, by J.R.R. Tolkien, traditionally have included an epic war between good and evil, and the Harry Potter series seems to be following in that tradition. As HP Sleuths review each book, all characters should be evaluated to determine which side they would take if the war breaks out.

We already see wizards caught in moral and social conflicts similar to George Orwell's 1984, and are aware that if a war does happen, it will be fought on both a physical and psychological front. In a BBC interview, J.K.R. specifically compared it to Hitler's regime. Voldemort is already infiltrating the Wizarding Community, taking control of people, creating rifts between wizards, and making it difficult to know who is friend or foe. During Hitler's take-over, despite there being no *Imperius Curse*, it was also very difficult to know whose side anyone was on – as even children turned-in their own parents.

J.K.R. explained that she wants a bad guy who we get to know personally and whose motives are explored. She describes Voldemort as a "bully" who, like Hitler, uses his own half-breed (part "Mudblood") status as a model for creating an enemy. J.K.R. says that in Book 4, Harry must deal with choices and how different choices make us what we are – no matter what our background. Harry sees how Voldemort's wrong choices have affected him and what he has become.

In an interview with *Entertainment Weekly*, J.K.R. is emphatic that the thing she detests most is bigotry and intolerance. Her stories are making significant social statements. She is concerned about the way oppressed groups deal with their situation – by arguing among themselves and splintering into bickering sub-factions, instead of uniting against their oppressor. Obviously wizards are not any better.

J.K.R. is presenting the philosophy that differences between people are a positive and a strength. She (Dumbledore) is right, but are her magical and Muggle worlds ready to believe and accept that? Just like our own real world, probably not without a fight, and probably not before devastating tragedies. Who will make what choices in Book 5? Will they remember Cedric Diggory...?

RESTRICTED AREA

Voldemort's War Strategy

The reason we are convinced there will be a war is because J.K.R. has already stated that Voldemort is looking to do the conquer-the-world thing.

Voldemort's Battle Plan

In a chat on Scholastic.com, J.K.R. said that although Voldemort will affect everyone, his plan (like Hitler's) is to take over Europe first. Otherwise, we are not sure how much influence he is exerting in the Middle East or elsewhere.

WWN (Wizarding Wireless Network)

Voldemort's strategy is to work on everyone psychologically – so they do not know who is good and who is evil. As part of that strategy, he is apparently taking control of the media. He seems to already have the famous singer, Celestina Warbeck, infiltrating the wireless media. We are nervously waiting to see what role Celestina will play in Book 5. We also know that Kirley McCormack, a son of the famous Pride of Portree Chaser,* is lead guitarist with the Weird Sisters band – can we trust a Weird Sister? (Hope so.)

Rita & the Press
(Daily/Evening Prophet & Witch Monthly)

Because of Rita Skeeter, Harry Potter is no longer the knight in shining armor and unquestionable hero of good wizards. Rita has publicly cast doubt as to whether he somehow used evil magic to defeat Voldemort and escape from him so many times. She has also profiled him with a "dangerous" personality – giving as evidence his friendship with werewolves (Lupin) and giants (Hagrid). By presenting it that way, she also directs people to assume a negative opinion of Lupin and Hagrid as well. Her other attacks have included Headmaster Dumbledore, Arthur Weasley, Hermione Granger, and anyone who is a known friend of Harry's, or is a half-blood, or is sympathetic to Muggles. Rita has purposely opened the door for suspicion and mistrust – even Mrs. Weasley was tricked when she read that Hermione was two-timing Harry! What damage has Rita done? She was in the hospital room at the end of Book 4 – how much did she hear? If she really is Rita Skeeter, will she reconsider what she has done, or will she promote evil?

Recognizing and Identifying Half-bloods (and Muggles)

According to Draco Malfoy, the Death Eaters can identify half-bloods. We have not yet had confirmation if that is true, but if it is, that would make half-bloods easy targets from anyone. It would cause them to have to go into hiding or surround themselves with pureblood friends who are willing to fight for them if needed.

Annihilating the Potters

For some reason (in fact, the primary plot of the mystery), Voldemort wants to (or needs to) destroy all Potter family members. We know that, 1000 years ago, Godric Gryffindor was Salazar Slytherin's nemesis. Based on all the clues, the Potters are probably direct descendents of Godric. That alone would be incentive for Voldemort, however, there could also be some prophecy or information that predicts Voldemort will be stopped by Godric's heir.

*HP Sleuths should have read about Pride of Portree in *Quidditch Through the Ages*

People to Watch If There Is a War

Ludovic (Ludo) Bagman

Winky and Crouch Senior described him a "bad." His huge financial debt will cloud his judgement. He will be in fear for his life (and/or limbs) and will succumb to the same temptations that almost landed him in Azkaban the first time. He will most likely go to rich Malfoy for help and we anticipate him turning traitor. His only way out of that mistake, then, would be as a double agent – which could prove to be lethal.

Penelope Clearwater

How did she and Hermione *both* get petrified using that one little mirror? We still think that one was suspicious. We don't know if we can trust her (after the Trojan War, Odysseus's wife, Penelope, was cleverly deceptive to her enemies). However, based on her name, she is most likely going to be deceiving **someone** (we're just not sure *who*). Does she really like Percy, or does she consider him only a "suitor"? If something happens to Percy, she may even turn out to be the only one faithful to him.

Barty Crouch, Junior

Is he gone for good? Remember, the dementor's kiss does not kill – it only sucks out the soul from the body. So, where is his "body"? Can someone take control of it? If that happens, what side will he be on? WWP thinks that he might have been in total despair in Azkaban, and being vulnerable, the Lestranges "recruited" him. The link to the Lestranges is strong when we hear him talking about how Voldemort will reward him. If it wasn't the Lestranges, **someone** (his Mother of Father?) *had* to have taught him the Dark Arts. It is doubtful that Voldemort could have made him that powerful in only a couple of weeks. Nonetheless, Voldemort did not punish the infidels and all Crouch Junior got for his loyal work was a little "kiss." Therefore, if the dementors can regurgitate his soul, he may be on our side this time. If Crouch Junior wasn't guilty of the Longbottoms' torture, then was he framed to cover-up for someone? Clever way to get back at Crouch Senior.

Fleur Delacour

During WWII, the French people were famous for their bravery and ingenuity as resistance fighters. They had one of the most extensive "underground networks" that was used for both spying and saving innocent lives. As part Veela, Fleur could probably be very effective at getting information from the enemy.

Dumbledore

Everyone says Dumbledore is the only one Voldemort fears. They also say they're not worried *"as long as we've got Dumbledore...."* (ahem!)

Death Eaters

Who are the *unnamed* Death Eaters? When walking around the circle of Death Eaters, Voldemort passed by some people who he did not identify. During the trial that Harry witnessed in the Pensieve, Karkaroff claims that Voldemort never divulges the identities of all his followers – even to the Death Eaters, themselves. Therefore, only Voldemort knows for sure who answers to him – which gives him psychological control over even the Death Eaters, as well as a strategic counter-intelligence advantage. Do all the Death Eaters have the Dark Mark, and is the Dark Mark always on the left forearm? We doubt it.

Uncle Vernon Dursley & (Mad-dog) Marge Dursley

They're tough and they'd fight any wizard! Since Harry is such an important target in Voldemort's battle plan, the Dursleys will most likely be paid a visit by the bad guys. Just remember to listen for "the swish of a cloak" (and that the bottom stair creaks!).

Cornelius Fudge

Is Fudge just bungling and naive, or corrupt and a puppet of Lucius Malfoy? Either way, he appears to be expendable to both sides. (People like that don't live very long.)

Hogwarts Portraits including the Old Headmasters

Dumbledore is always alert and immediately aware of anything that happens anywhere in Hogwarts. It is likely that the portraits of people, especially old headmasters, may play a key role in his surveillance network. They will most likely also be a key asset to thwart spies and intruders.

Igor Karkaroff

Is Karkaroff the Death Eater Voldemort was referring to as the one who is too cowardly to return, or the one who has left him forever? Either way, he can't be trusted by either side. We are fairly sure that his silvery cape is made of Demiguise fur.

Lestranges

We expect them to escape from Azkaban with, or without, the dementors' help. Extremely dangerous and fanatical – as they were willing to go to Azkaban rather than denounce Voldemort. In the Pensieve, Harry saw the Lestranges, Crouch, and a fourth person (a male) sent to Azkaban. Voldemort did not mention that fourth person to the circle of the Death Eaters. Was that because he was innocent, because Voldemort didn't want to give away his identity, or because he has already escaped...? Who was this mystery prisoner, where is he now, and who's side is he on?

Gilderoy Lockhart

His memory possibly could be cured already, and/or he could be under control of someone. He may have already been busy as the spokeswizard for the Dark Force Defense League in Rita Skeeter's article.

Longbottoms (Neville's Parents)

We suspect that they may have been able to recover had it not been for St Mungo's. We think they are being prevented from getting better. If only we could get the true information about what they saw – but we fear that won't happen as long as they're in St Mungo's.

Lucius Malfoy

He apparently has already bought his way into Fudge, the Department for Disposal of Dangerous Creatures, St Mungo's, we have seen he can sway the school governing board, and he even may be able to influence the print media. Can his money control greedy goblins? How far has he infiltrated the Ministry and the rest of the wizarding community? Will Lucius Malfoy be content to have a puppet of his as Minister of Magic, or will he try to become Minister of Magic, himself? Does his money reach into the Muggle world? Because of his money and influence, he will certainly be a central figure in Voldemort's plans.

Minerva McGonagall

Minerva (Athena) is the Ancient Greek goddess of war, and thrives in a battle environment. She was depicted as strong, clever, and always seemed to prevail in both mortal and immortal conflicts. She also had the ability to create clever disguises for others. What kind of disguises might Minerva McGonagall be able to "switch" onto people? Then there's her Gaelic last name, which means "son of the most valorous one." Based on her namesake, the Professor seems fairly invincible.

Severus Snape

We know Snape spied for Dumbledore last time, and we are being led to believe he is doing it again. Does he spy by putting people into trances? Does he have a *network* of spies? As a former Death Eater, Snape could "take over Hogwarts," pretending once again, to be a Voldemort supporter (or he might just work undercover at night).

Celestina Warbeck

Based on her name and the other evidence about her favorite charity (St Mungo's), Celestina probably isn't who she seems. She could be highly dangerous due to her large (and possible blindly loyal) fan following.

Percy Weasley

Percy may really turn-in a member of his own family... or at least it might look that way. If he is like Sir Perceval, it could be tragic! Based on the legend, he may even cause a death and or mess up a rescue operation. HP Sleuths might want to go on a quest for information about the legend of the Holy Grail. All those "interrogations" that they put Percy through concerning Mr. Crouch may not have been just questions. It took Hedwig way too long to come back with Percy's reply to Ron in Book 4, and then the response was so curt – it sounded a bit like Crouch Sr. Could a Voldemort insider have used that opportunity to obtain sensitive information from Percy, or even have put him under the *Imperius Curse*? Something odd's going on with Percy. Unfortunately, his true personality makes it difficult to recognize if something is wrong. We may not know now, until the end, if he is acting of his own free will.

Creatures to Watch If There Is a War

Dementors

They will probably turn-over Azkaban to Voldemort. Do they already have orders to go after Harry? (They did try to get rid of him once already.)

Ghosts

Will they spy for their respective houses? Will Myrtle leave her bathroom to help? Ghosts can be very useful – they go right through walls, and they certainly cannot die (although they can be petrified). Would Moaning Myrtle be heroic? Would that settle her restless spirit?

Giants

Will Hagrid and Mme Maxime convince them to side with Dumbledore? There may be a split between the "good" and "bad" giants.

Gnomes

J.K.R. mentioned in an interview with Scholastic.com, that gnomes leave craters of dirt where they have eaten the plants, meaning that gnomes around the house is a tip-off that wizards live there. That may be dangerous for wizards trying to hide from Voldemort. Mr. Weasley might want to reconsider keeping those pests around. Has Harry noticed any gnomes at any of the houses on Privet Drive? Is the Dursley's garden free of gnomes?

Goblins

Will they stay neutral or will they side with the "highest bidder"? How will Bill Weasley factor into this? In fantasy, goblins are famous for being ruthless fighters. Now this could get nasty. Prof. Binns specifically mentions "bloody and vicious goblin riots." Why were they rebelling? There have been a lot of goblin rebellions. Why so many and what caused them? Are any of the "rebels" still around? Have the problems been resolved? If the goblins do not remain neutral and side with Voldemort, the consequences could be devastating for the "good guys."

House-elves

Will they all stay loyal to their "Masters" this time if their masters are evil? How will Dobby help (master) Dumbledore? Will Winky now accept Dumbledore as her master? Will either of them go to the Weasleys? How will they be treated by the other house-elves? House elves have powerful magic so the 100+ house-elves at Hogwarts will be a tremendous asset to the "allies."

Peeves

Will he take sides, or will he just disrupt *anyone* who is in Hogwarts?

— Organizations to Watch If There Is a War —

Dark Force Defense League

This is another organization from which we have not seen anything good. Our first impression of it was from its "honorary member," Gilderoy Lockhart (would any reputable organization make Gilderoy an honorary member?). We then had a "representative" state in Book 4 that Harry might have a violent personality. It is possible that Gilderoy, himself, was responsible for that commentary, which would mean that Gilderoy is the only "member" we have met so far (maybe there is *only* one member and that this is another one of Gilderoy's marketing ploys?) However, we have not heard of his recovery, so either someone "helped" Gilderoy make that statement, or it was another League member. The Dark Force Defense League seems like a shady bunch anyway. We suspect that, if they exist, they are in reality, a "Dark Force Users Group." They are probably using the "Defense" image to cover up their real evil intentions. So far, our opinion of the Dark Force Defense League is reserved skepticism.

Ministry of Magic

This is probably one of the most nerve-wracking of all the cliff-hangers from Book 4. We already know Voldemort had spies there before, and we already know that there are still Voldemort's spies in the Ministry (Macnair). What is going on at the Ministry? How *well* has Voldemort already infiltrated it? What happened when Bill went to tell Mr. Weasley about Dumbledore's instructions? Who else did they tell, and who did they recruit? Did they tell Percy? Did they tell Amos Diggory? What was the reaction? Arthur Weasley will be watched very carefully now by Voldemort's insiders, so he (and anyone he and Bill have recruited there) will have to be extremely careful. If they do anything that looks at all threatening to Fudge or Voldemort's supporters, then he is in mortal danger. ☹ According to a J.K.R. interview with Scholastic.com, the Ministry is not informed and does not know in advance of any Muggle-born wizard children. That may be important if children become targets (like Harry was).

Muggle Ministry

We do not know how much the general Muggle world will be affected during this war, but it will be important to monitor that. We know that England has sent troops off to Afghanistan, but we do not know if they are only fighting Muggles in that area. We also know from Book 3 that Fudge has at least one connection at the Muggle Ministry who he can contact if he wants to communicate with Muggle leaders.

Puddlemere United

Oliver Wood may have to dodge more than Bludgers when playing for this Quidditch team. We know that Celestina Warbeck sings their anthem, and we are aware that she is probably untrustworthy. At least we have Oliver in there on our side, but the problem is, there are not enough clues to figure out if the whole team is already corrupt or not. What we do know is that it could get very dangerous for poor Oliver who only wants to play Quidditch and doesn't know what he just got himself into....

St Mungo's

Everything we have seen of St. Mungo's so far gives us goosebumps. We know that St Mungo's is a favorite charity of both Celestina Warbeck and Lucius Malfoy. We also know that they were not up-front about admitting that they had no information about Barty Crouch Senior's supposed "illness," which helped everyone cover up that he was not really sick. They were very quick to offer an "expert" who (without examining him) readily diagnosed that Harry could be suffering from psychological problems. Worst of all, poor Neville's parents are in there supposedly because they are insane from the effects of the *Cruciatus Curse*, and that just brings up visions of "a Cuckoo's Nest." J.K.R. said in an interview with the BBC that Gilderoy Lockhart is in there right now, himself. What fiendish plots might be hatching at St Mungo's?

The WWP Orb (We show it...You interpret it)

(HARRY POTTER AND THE ORDER OF THE PHOENIX)

These are the most spellbinding clues from within the books and from J.K.R. interviews/chats. But what will actually happen? What do HP Sleuths think?

Wizards and Muggles in the WWP Orb

Headmaster Dumbledore

Dumbledore told Harry outright that he can become invisible without a Cloak. We also are convinced that he can see through Invisibility Cloaks. His shining silver hair/beard, plus his talents with invisibility, lead us to believe he is part Demiguise. We also suspect he has other ways of letting him see things other wizards can't. His hair used to be auburn (similar to Lily Potter), so we have to consider a possible link there.

Most importantly, he was the Transfiguration Professor back when Harry's parents and Voldemort went to school. Add that to J.K.R.'s statement that she intentionally used a name for him that means *bumblebee*, and we see that Professor Dumbledore can most likely transform into a bee (or even multiple forms like Merlin).

Dumbledore's resemblance to Gandalf, Merlin, and all the famous wizards of fantasy is obvious. Then there's all that banging. Sort of makes us jumpy. Reminds us a bit of the drums at Moria in *The Fellowship of the Rings* by J.R.R. Tolkein. Could he "pull a Gandalf" on us? *Lord of the Rings* fans will remember what happened there....

Mrs. Arabella Figg

Mrs. Figg was confirmed by J.K.R. to be a wizard. She has probably been watching over Harry all this time. Could she even be part of a *Fidelius Charm*? What is her relationship to Perkins from Arthur Weasley's Department? One possibility is that she and Perkins are the same person. Remember Mr. Weasley borrowed a tent from Perkins that looked like Mrs. Figg's house, and even smelled like cats? Is Polyjuice Potion being used by her? If so, that would mean drinking that yucky Polyjuice Potion all day. They could also be using *Switching Spells* or other "disguises." Mrs. Figg's cats are probably magical or even transfigured in some way. Considering how many times Harry was forced to sit and look at pictures of Snowy, Tibbles, Tufty, and Mrs. Paws, he should be able to recognize them by now! Will Mrs. Figg be the female Defense Against the Dark Arts teacher that J.K.R. mentioned during a chat on AOL?

Hermione Granger

In an interview with Time Magazine, J.K.R. said that she is "surprised" no one is usually concerned about Hermione. J.K.R. informs us that she considers Hermione to have a lot of "vulnerability." J.K.R. took Hermione's name from Shakespeare's "The Winter's Tale." This is a key clue! It is highly likely that Hermione's fate will parallel that character (more twist endings). HP Sleuths may want to bone-up on their Shakespeare.

RESTRICTED AREA

✳ **Neville Longbottom**

A tobacco plant called Longbottom Leaf was the hidden link that exposed Sauruman's plot to take over the Shire. Neville is assuredly a missing link in J.K.R.'s mystery. He, therefore, has the potential of becoming one of the most important characters in the story (did anyone mention that to Matthew Lewis?).

Based on the clues and evidence from Book 4, we are now sure that Neville's memory problems are the result of a *Memory Charm*. His *Memory Charm* was probably cast when his parents were tortured. They either cast too great a spell, or the normal spell was too strong for an infant. Either way, poor little Neville's memory was permanently damaged. What terrible secrets must he have witnessed that would have caused someone to put a *Memory Charm* on an infant? Neville is probably holding key to the identities of his attackers and their evil deeds in that leaky cauldron of his head. We would have huge clue about the traitors, if only Neville could remember.... Unfortunately, we learned from Voldemort that breaking *Memory Charms* is not safe.

✳ **Remus J. Lupin**

(see also James Potter)

In the legend of Romulus and Remus, Remus was killed by his brother (or his brother's followers).

Remus Lupin is actually dead. The Remus J. Lupin we know is actually James Potter switched into Lupin's body with a *Switching Spell*.

J.K.R. is dropping hints all over the place about the Lupin septology mystery. She has made it clear there is something very special about Lupin. When asked who her favorite characters are, J.K.R. always specifically mentions that she loves Lupin. In interviews, such as with the BBC, she says it was Lupin that made Book 3 so important for her to write.

The Book 1 evidence is:

- How did Dumbledore get James' Invisibility Cloak, and how did Hagrid get the key to the Potter's vault?

The Book 3 evidence is:

- UNlike everyone else, Lupin never stared at Harry's scar or mentioned his eyes or resemblance to James. (Ch. 5)

    Lupin simply addresses Harry by name as if he was already very familiar with him.

- Lupin seems to be able to read Harry's mind   (Ch. 8)

    We have found that characters appear to do that when they have "inside" information, or a close relationship with each-other.

- Harry tells Lupin that when a dementor gets near him, he hears his mum being murdered by Voldemort. On hearing this, Lupin had made "a sudden motion with his arm, as though to grip Harry's shoulder, but thought better of it." (Ch. 10)

384

Lupin may be relating to Harry's emotions or his own, but he is trying to distance himself from Harry. There is no reason why he should stop himself from just gripping Harry's arm if he were Lupin. Something here is affecting him, too.

- ☾ Trelawney said that Lupin "positively fled when I offered to crystal gaze for him – "(Ch. 11)

    He's obviously afraid of exposing something. We might have thought he was just afraid that she might discover he's a werewolf, however, we learned that the whole staff already knew of that.

- ☾ When Harry tells Lupin he is hearing his mum's voice louder, Lupin looks "paler than usual." Harry then tells Lupin how he hears his dad's voice for the first time trying to hold off Voldemort so his mother could escape. "'You heard James?' said Lupin in a strange voice." (Ch. 12)

    Hearing about Lily didn't make him sad, it made him "pale." Why would Lupin react oddly to Harry hearing James? Because of the odd circumstances – he realized it wasn't James saying it.

- ☾ Professor Lupin, who was "both shaken and pleased," comes over to congratulate Harry on his spectacular Patronus. (Ch 13)

    Lupin was "shaken" from seeing what we later learn is James' own Patronus.

- ☾ Professor Lupin enters the room in a "shower of red sparks." (Ch 17)

    A true Gryffindor...

- ☾ "I certainly don't want Harry dead...." "An odd shiver passed over his face." (Ch.17)

    That's not just a teacher or friend saying that.

- ☾ Lupin: "now that we could all transform." (Ch 18)

    Why wouldn't he say "Now that *they* could all transform"?

- ☾ Lupin has "no hesitation" about what Harry's father would think (Ch 18)

    Why is he so sure about what Harry's father would **think**?

Harry's father, James, is now stuck inside the body of one of his closest (but dead) friends. He has had to live like this for 12 years, hiding from Voldemort and his followers. James is now, for all intents, Remus Lupin (complete with the werewolf transformations). He is unable to reveal his identity (especially now that Voldemort has been seen again), and is paranoid that his own emotions will make him weak and he will let the truth slip. He so badly wants to touch his son, but he doesn't dare (sob!).

(See the James Potter listing in this section for how this happened.)

✳ **Warlock Perkins**   (see Mrs. Figg)

Peter Pettigrew

Peter Pettigrew (Wormtail/Scabbers) probably did not blow up that street of Muggles in front of Sirius. Sirius said that Wormtail blew it up with just his wand behind his back. Maybe Wormtail used Dark magic, but that still seems a bit too powerful for a weak wizard like Pettigrew (remember McGonagall did say he was "hopeless" at dueling). He might have had some help, and the wand behind his back could have been a signal. We know that Fudge was the first on the scene; and that his is really good at covering things up. Who really killed all those Muggles?

Also, we expect Voldemort to still have control of Wormtail's new hand – which would make for an interesting dilemma if Harry ever has to ask Wormtail to spare him as he once did for Wormtail.

You see, Wormtail - Voldemort can still control that hand. Just one little waver of your loyalty, and you may become the victim of your own hand.☺ Now we really hope Dean Thomas doesn't see that! Of course, knowing J.K.R., it will probably come down to Dean vs. the crawling hand. Hope he's been practicing with his boggart....

Harry Potter

Everything points to Harry being a direct descendent of Godric Gryffindor.
- ☾ He is a Leo (Gryffindor Lion)
- ☾ His wand sent out red and gold sparks (Gryffindor colors) when he first tried it.
- ☾ His parents lived in Godric's Hollow
- ☾ Everyone comments about his bravery
- ☾ In Book 2, Dumbledore said "Only a true Gryffindor" could have conjured Godric's own sword.

His green eyes may also tie him to Slytherin:
- ☾ The Sorting Hat wanted to put Harry into Slytherin House
- ☾ His mother also had green eyes – is she somehow a direct descendent of Salazar Slytherin?
- ☾ Harry is a Parselmouth.

That could be one reason Voldemort wants to Kill Harry (just like Justin Finch-Fletchley said in Book 2).

What power might those green eyes hold? In an interview with the BBC, J.K.R. admitted that they probably will have a special power. We also noticed that the movie posters for the first movie show Harry giving us a very strange look – as if he were doing magic with his eyes. Although Dumbledore believes Harry's Parselmouth is due to the scar, we believe in Rule #4 (sorry, Headmaster). Could it be that no-one – except Voldemort, knows this? Being a direct descendent of *two* very powerful wizards would give Harry the potential to become one of the most powerful wizards of all time. Is this why Voldemort so fears Harry?

As to whether or not J.K.R. will have Harry die in the end, there is no definitive information, but we do know something. In an chat on Barnes&Noble.com back when she had just finished Book 3, J.K.R. actually said that in Book 7, Harry will get to use magic outside of Hogwarts. Of course, she may have changed her mind since then, but we know that she has had the overall outline of all 7 books since she finished Book 1, so this is probably reliable. However, we still cannot know for sure if, once he gets out of Hogwarts in his final year, he survives. He may have a final conflict with Voldemort....

James Potter

(see also R. Lupin)

Prongs lives! WWP believes that *all four map-makers* **did** appear (in some form) on the Hogwarts grounds that night in Chapter 21 of Book 3! We are convinced that Harry's father **was** there too!

What probably happened to James and Remus:

Thinking that they had doubts about the reliability of Black (their Secret Keeper for the *Fidelius Charm*), James and Lupin must have taken *one extra* precaution. Using a *Switching Spell*, they managed to switch identities. This was done without the knowledge of *anyone* else (with the possible exception of Lily). We doubt that even Dumbledore (who never knew they were Animagi) had been told.

After the switch, Lupin (looking like James) stayed at their house, while James (looking like Lupin) left.

Voldemort attacked, and Lupin (looking like James) was killed. Having no body to switch back to, James was now stuck inside the body of werewolf Remus Lupin.

With everyone thinking he is Lupin, James is (at least for the moment) safe from Voldemort, who is convinced he is dead. Even though James has to live the painful life of a werewolf, at least he is not being hunted by Voldemort or his followers. Therefore, Sirius (who he now knows is innocent of betraying him) may be the only one he will trust with the information.

The reason James and Lupin had to go to that extreme is, of course, still unknown and is at the heart of this entire septology mystery. We have been told that, for some reason, Voldemort wants to annihilate all of the Potters. There is something important about keeping James and Harry alive.

Now we understand why J.K.R gave us all those hints. Knowing about this makes the mystery even more excruciating! The suspense is worse than ever!

(See the Remus J. Lupin listing in this section for evidence.)

RESTRICTED AREA

✦ Lily Potter

There is definitely something very important about Lily's green eyes. One possibility is that she is somehow descended from Slytherin (and not even been aware of it, herself). Additionally, those eyes probably contain some kind of power. Everyone claims Lily is "Muggle-born" but we do not know for sure (Rule #4). Was Lily adopted by Muggles, or was Petunia adopted by wizards hiding-out as Muggles? We know there is more to Lily's background.

✦ Professor Quirrell

Quirrell might be back. Read it again carefully. Dumbledore only said that Quirrell was "left to die" by Voldemort, but no one ever confirmed that he did, indeed, die. Harry almost died too – but Dumbledore saved Harry. Did Dumbledore also manage to save Quirrell? Don't forget, according to Dumbledore's comment to Harry at the Pensieve, there is someone besides Voldemort who is "getting stronger". Voldemort thinks Quirrell died, but he sure didn't stick around to help, did he?

✦ Rita Skeeter

Rita (the original) may be dead. Was she the victim of the murder Wormtail was to commit? We know she's a scandal reporter and isn't very nice, but she's gone further than just making controversy. We think she has been either replaced by an imposter (Polyjuice or other spell), or is being controlled. Remember, she is always sucking on her acid-green quill. In an interview on the BBC, J.K.R. remarked that there is something more in Rita besides venom. She's not all Rita. If she has been replaced, it may be by the fourth prisoner we saw at Crouch Junior's trial. Rita seems too masculine, and that prisoner was a male. Those rigid blond curls of hers remind us a bit of Gilderoy, but nothing else matches. We'll just keep on the lookout for 3 gold teeth.

✦ Severus Snape

There are overwhelming signs that Snape is a vampire. Do we believe it? Yes. Do we have proof? No, but there is bloody good evidence. Even Madam Pomfrey may not know – remember, Snape went to Filch for help when he was wounded by Fluffy.... J.K.R. has dropped many hints about Snape:

- ☾ He lives in a dungeon
- ☾ He's always up at night
- ☾ Ron's little joke about Snape "turning himself into a bat or something."
- ☾ He has "sallow skin"
- ☾ Quirrell (who mentioned, at the Leaky Cauldron, that he was going to buy a book on Vampires) described Snape as "flitting around like an overgrown bat."
- ☾ Just like Snape had assigned an essay on werewolves to expose Lupin, Lupin then assigned an essay on Vampires (as payback?).

If there is a potion for werewolves, could there be a potion for vampires as well? Could this be part of Snape's problem? But then why would Snape not relate to Lupin instead of hating him? Because J.K.R. never makes anything that easy....

Fred & George Weasley

Don't be fooled by these goof-offs. They are exceptionally talented wizards. Fred and George probably did some time-traveling to hedge their bet with Bagman at the World Cup. Their next project is bound to be significant. Those two may be jesters, but they are also very enterprising. We can only imagine the havoc they could (will) create if they use their talents on devious devices to thwart their enemies. (Voldemort has no idea what he's in for...)

Creatures in the WWP Orb

Firenze

There is most likely some kind of link between Firenze, the Centaur from Book 1, and Florence (the person Bertha Jorkins caught being kissed) from the Pensieve in Book 4. The name "Firenze" is the Italian name for Florence. Notice that Firenze is much friendlier to humans than other centaurs. Is it possible that Florence might have been turned into a centaur and that both are the same person? What do the stars say?

Spells and Magic in the WWP Orb

The Big Switch
(Priori Incantatem)

- Book 4, Ch 34 -If James is not really dead, and it was actually Lupin who came out of Voldemort's wand, then that could explain the reason why the shadows would have switched places in the original editions of Book 4 (did we say "switched"?). First of all, given that nothing is as it appears, we don't know for sure that Lily *was* the last to die. Even if she was, Lupin (who looks like James) can come out and say "your mother wants to see you." However, **knowing** that James is still alive, Lily would **never say** "your father wants to see you." So that really should never have been switched, but J.K.R. may be more devious than we realized. Switching shadows, switching Editions, and all that *Switching Spell* stuff were probably clues. Trick or Treat!

Mirror of Erised
Niaga rorrim taht ees ylbaborp lliw ew

Poisons

Harry was likely poisoned in Book 4 by the Acromantula and did not even notice it. Harry seems to be more immune to things than most people - including an apparent immunity to poison.

RESTRICTED AREA

✳ Switching Spells

We just don't know very much about *Switching Spells* (yet) – except that they are quite important, they are common, they are generally easy to do, and that Neville still has trouble with them. We suspect that Lupin may have been subjected to them, and we wonder if various body parts of some main characters may also have some relation to *Switching Spells*. Just another way to make it very difficult to know in the world of magic whether what you see is really what you get....

✳ Time Travel

In a chat on AOL, J.K.R. refused to comment about whether Harry will time-travel again. Does anyone dispute that was a Rule #2? We are fairly sure that Fred and George can, and have done it at the World cup in Book 4.

✳ Use of Magic

J.K.R. was definite in a chat on Barnes&Noble.com that magic will surface in wizard kids before age 11 in almost all cases. However, she reveals that there will be an exception where a character, faced with a dire situation, does perform magic! Who will that be? We think the most likely will be Filch. Petunia would be a candidate, but we're not convinced she's a blood relative. If she is, then even Dudley could be possible (snicker). Regarding Dudley, J.K.R. also gave us a hint in another Barnes&Noble.com chat that Harry has not yet used magic on Dudley (!).

Clothing in the WWP Orb

✳ Dobby's Socks

It is very likely that there will be something special about those socks that Dobby made for Harry. He is a powerful little elf, and since he knitted them personally, they could very likely contain magical properties! Could those properties have been spotted by Crouch when he said "nice socks" to Harry at the Yule Ball?

✳ Mrs. Weasley's Sweaters

Even if she has not done so previously, we feel that Mrs. Weasley will probably put something magical into those sweaters of hers for year 5.

✳ Woolly Dressing Gowns

Perhaps it's just coincidence that both Dumbledore and this witch have woolly dressing gowns? Where was the Headmaster during the World Cup? What do HP Sleuths think?

Hogwarts in the WWP Orb

✳ Is this the "end of Hogwarts"? In Book 2, Professor McGonagall was afraid it was when she thought another student (Ginny) had died. She was basing it on something

Dumbledore had "always said." Now Cedric has died, so is it the end? The problem is, Gilderoy Lockhart cut her off (Rule #2) just as she was explaining what Dumbledore had told her about that. What makes us most nervous are everyone's comments that everything's fine "*as long as we have Dumbledore.*"...

✳ We know from a interview with J.K.R. on the BBC that some of the Hogwarts Professors have spouses. We also are told by J.K.R. that it is key to the plot!

✳ J.K.R. said, during an interview with SouthWestNews.com, that Harry might get to see the other (2) house common rooms.

✳ In an interview with the BBC, J.K.R. mentioned a room at Hogwarts which has special powers. All we know is that it is one of the rooms from Book 4 and that Harry hasn't found out yet about it's special powers.

How to analyze a J.K.R. hint: Make NO assumptions and think creatively. A room from Book 4 does not mean anyone actually entered the room. So what rooms are mentioned in Book 4? (We don't count Dumbledore's "disappearing room" joke.) What do HP Sleuths think? Here's a quick list – can HP Sleuths come up with any others?

Astronomy tower
- Bathrooms (Prefects, Myrtle's, all others)
- Classrooms
- Great Hall
- Room across from Great Hall
- Room behind Great Hall
- Gryffindor Common Room & Dorm
- Hospital ward
- Kitchens
- Library
- Owlery
- Slytherin Common Room
- Staff Room
- Teachers' offices (Dumbledore's office, Filch's office, all others)
- Trophy Room

What would be the "magical properties"? If it's the kitchens, they may be able to transport from there to anywhere in the castle (which is how Dobby gets around). If it's the Gryffindor common room, there is a Grandfather Clock in there. The Prefect's bathroom is not only cool, but we are under the impression that J.K.R. (who has said she likes to read in the bathtub) would give that luxurious tub special powers. Then there's the Astronomy tower, which is still a void to us..... HP Sleuths can have fun exploring the castle.

About Book 5 and Beyond

Statistics

Working Title - ***Harry Potter and the Order of the Phoenix*** - by J. K. Rowling

Facts & Statistics for Book 5:
- ☾ Projected Release Date Summer 2003

Facts & Statistics for combined Books 1-4:
- ☾ Overall sales for the first 4 Harry Potter books has topped 130 million copies
- ☾ The Harry Potter books have been printed in 42 languages (including Albanian!)

RESTRICTED AREA

— Key Characters That We Are Likely To See In Book 5 —

RESTRICTED AREA

WIZARD KIDS

Susan Bones
- (see Fawcetts and Bones)

Lavender Brown
- Hopefully, we will find out why she was sorted into Gryffindor

Cho Chang
- Does Harry get to know her more now?
- Does Harry tell her what happened that night?

Vincent Crabbe
- Can he or Goyle be "duped" by a clever wizard?

Colin Creevey
- Where was he going with those grapes the night he was petrified?
- The Creevey brothers would be exceptionally loyal to Harry
- We are speculating that the Creevey brothers may have elf blood or other small, powerful creatures in their heritage

Dennis Creevey
- We vote for important role and smart little wizard

Fleur Delacour
- Does she visit Hogwarts again (or maybe Bill)?
- Does Ron get to pursue a personal relationship with her?

Miss S. Fawcett
- (see Fawcetts and Bones)

Seamus Finnegan
- Extremely logical
- Close friend of Dean Thomas
- Banshees are his boggart

Florence
- We were told about her for a reason – who was she, and who was she kissing?
- Is she alive, and if so, where is she now?
- Does she have any relationship with the Centaur, Firenze?

Hermione Granger
- According to a interview with the BBC, her birthday is September 19
- Portable, waterproof fires are her specialty
- Hermione has neat handwriting
- Her boggart is that she would fail in her studies

Gregory Goyle
- Supposed to the most dense of the students – Harry thought he might flunk out

Lee Jordan
- Similar personality to Fred and George, plus similarly as resourceful
- With Bagman gone, they'll need an announcer!
- If he can't get an announcing job, Fred and George will probably need someone to help them with their inventions (as long as it doesn't include being a guinea pig!)

Viktor Krum
- Does Hermione go visit him?
- Does he come back to Hogwarts where he likes it better?
- Does he have a bird species or water creature blood in him?
- Potential Ron-Krum-Hermione triangle

Neville Longbottom
- Key link to the whole mystery
- Neville was sorted into Gryffindor for a reason
- Neville's water heritage may be important
- Friend to Ginny Weasley

Draco Malfoy
- Like Father, like son, like Voldemort

Parvati & Padma Patil
- ☾ Twins, but sorted into two different houses
- ☾ Parvati's Boggart is a mummy

Harry Potter
- ☾ Probably a direct descendent of Godric Gryffindor
- ☾ Harry is right-handed
- ☾ Harry is tied to Voldemort through dreams and through his scar (which acts as a Voldemort detector)
- ☾ Harry can talk to snakes (Parselmouth)
- ☾ Has his mother's eyes

Dean Thomas
- ☾ Extremely logical
- ☾ Good at drawing and forgeries!
- ☾ Severed hands are his boggart (Keep him away from Wormtail!)

Fred & George Weasley
- ☾ What devious products and plots are they hatching?
- ☾ Watch out for those fake wands!
- ☾ Best not to eat anything they offer you

Ginny Weasley
- ☾ We think she will have an important role in Book 5 (no longer a weak character)
- ☾ Friend to Colin and Neville

Ron Weasley
- ☾ According to a chat with BBC Online, his birthday is March 1
- ☾ Bet Ron gets the "spotlight" this time!
- ☾ Ron's handwriting is an untidy scrawl
- ☾ Ron's boggart is a spider

Oliver Wood
- ☾ Recruited by Puddlemere United Quidditch team

RELATIVES

Mr. Crabbe, Mr. Goyle, & Nott(?)
- ☾ Are Crabby and Goyle Senior as dumb as their offspring?

- ☾ Is this Mr. Nott or the student at Hogwarts?
- ☾ Voldemort says they did not do well last time – wonder what they did to mess up? Hope they're still vulnerable

Amos Diggory & Wife
- ☾ Hope they forgive Harry – we need them on our side!

Uncle Vernon Dursley
- ☾ Stupid, bullying git – but **very** brave

Aunt Petunia Dursley
- ☾ Stupid, bullying git

Cousin Dudley Dursley
- ☾ Watch out Duddykins – J.K.R. has hinted that Harry might use magic on you...Would Harry do that to get back at Dudley, or to protect him?

The Fawcetts & Boneses
- ☾ Murder victims of Voldemort last time – like Harry, their children, Miss S. Fawcett and Susan Bones, are in Hogwarts now... We assume they will be on our side

Fridwulfa
- ☾ We may meet Hagrid's mum – based on what we know of Hagrid, she is probably a good giant and she might have left only out of fear or deep hurt (she did marry a Muggle)

Mr. & Mrs. Granger
- ☾ Probably affected – maybe even recruited!

Longbottom Relative
Neville's Parents
Mr. (Frank) & Mrs.
- ☾ They know who attacked them – if only they could tell us
- ☾ They are in St Mungo's

RESTRICTED AREA

Longbottom Relative
Neville's Gran
- Weird lady – we know nothing else about her

Longbottom Relative
Neville's Great Uncle Algie
- We expect he has friends in wet places

Lucius Malfoy
- Evil, corrupt, sneaky, and definitely not nice!
- Will he go for power or stay "behind the scenes" – manipulating others?

James Potter
- We know that what he did for a career is some kind of clue
- His wand was good for Transfigurations
- His Animagus and his Patronus are stags
- See Remus J. Lupin

Lily Potter
- Her wand was good for charm work
- Her maiden name was Evans

Mr. Arthur Weasley
- Our key ally inside the Ministry... Arthur is as important to the Ministry as Dumbledore is to Hogwarts

Bill Weasley
- Our hero! Where's the treasure, Bill?

Charlie Weasley
- Charlie's hot! (Especially when he's got one of them Dragons next to him.☺) Dragons may not make good pets, but they sure make a great defense!

Mrs. Molly Weasley
- Gryffindor doesn't make them any better! Remember – she can be a "sabertooth tiger" (she can even control Fred and George!)

Percy Weasley
- Would he truly turn in his own family, or is he already being controlled, against his will, by someone?

TEACHERS & STAFF

Professor Binns
- How will his knowledge of the Goblin Rebellions help?
- Does he know about secret passages, rooms, and/or treasures?

Albus Dumbledore
- He can become invisible without a Cloak
- He is not afraid to use Voldemort's name
- He speaks other languages
- He has loopy handwriting
- He has long fingers

Argus Filch
- He is extremely loyal to Hogwarts
- He may be the one J.K.R. said would use magic late in life
- According to the WB Web site, he supposedly knows the background and whereabouts of all Hogwarts artifacts

Professor Flitwick
- Does he have any "connections" with elves?
- He was supposedly dueling champion

Rubeus Hagrid
- Do cats make Hagrid sneeze?
- Hagrid's house is Gryffindor
- Hagrid's handwriting is a scribble

Madam Hooch
- Bet she can really fly!

Professor Karkaroff
- Where is he, and will Voldemort catch up with him?
- Is he the one Voldemort thinks is the "traitor" or the one "too scared to return"?

Gilderoy Lockhart
- Gilderoy may not be gone... (wish we could forget him)
- J.K.R. stated in an interview that he's at St Mungo's
- J.K.R. would not say whether or not he will return

Remus J. Lupin
- ☞ Not afraid to use Voldemort's name
- ☞ Sirius is staying with Lupin in Book 5
- ☞ What does that J. stand for?

Mme Olympe Maxime
- ☞ Will she go with Hagrid ?

Deputy Headmistress Minerva McGonagall
- ☞ Dumbledore trusts her implicitly as his Deputy

Professor Mad-Eye Moody
- ☞ J.K.R. has definitely confirmed in a chat on Barnes&Noble.com [bn.com] that the real Mad-Eye Moody will be back, and that we will like him even more than the fake one!

Madam Irma Pince
- ☞ Watch who's checking things out

Madam Pomfrey
- ☞ What else will they bring into the school (she did ask)? What can be worse than 3-headed dogs, dragons, and dementors? Shudder...

Professor Sinistra
- ☞ What dark secrets await in Prof. Sinistra's Astronomy tower?

Professor Severus Snape
- ☞ Keep an eye on the batty, sallow-skinned Snape who hangs out in dungeons
- ☞ What is his secret, dangerous task?

Professor Sprout
- ☞ Watch out for her Venomous Tentacular

Professor Sibyll Trelawney
- ☞ Any new predictions?
- ☞ What was her first (and only other) correct prediction?
- ☞ Is she linked to the Bloody Baron?

OTHER HUMANS

Ludovic (Ludo) Bagman
- ☞ Goblin trouble
- ☞ He is currently in hiding, so we may not see him again until Book 6 or 7, but we will list him just in case

Ali Bashir
- ☞ He has found at least one customer for his flying carpets

Sirius Black
- ☞ Not afraid to use Voldemort's name
- ☞ What will Lupin and Sirius plot?

Penelope Clearwater
- ☞ Will she be highly faithful to Percy, or deceptive and deadly?

Barty Crouch, Junior
- ☞ Can dementors regurgitate souls?
- ☞ Bet he won't appreciate what Fudge did to him, after all his loyal work

Mrs. (Arabella) Figg
- ☞ J.K.R. stated that we will learn all about Mrs. Figg in Book5 ☺
- ☞ In what way is she related to Warlock Perkins in Mr. Weasley's department?

Nicolas & Paranelle Flamel
- ☞ If Flamel is Dumbledore's partner, he and Perenelle could be called upon for help before they die

Mundungus Fletcher
- ☞ Not yet sure if we're glad he's on our side... Remember he tried to hex Arthur Weasley from behind his back! Probably just the ornery type

Colonel Fubster
- ☞ J.K.R. says he's a Muggle; we say we want him on our side

Cornelius Fudge
- ☞ Inept, or traitor?

Lestranges
- ☞ Watch out for the Lestranges!
- ☞ Will they break out of Azkaban?

RESTRICTED AREA

RESTRICTED AREA

Macnair
- Highly dangerous – positioned inside the Ministry and supporter of Lucius Malfoy
- If Voldemort has his way with Macnair, heads will roll....

Mr. Ollivander
- Remembers every wand he sold
- Ancient looking and skeletal with moon-like eyes
- Long fingers

Warlock Perkins
- What's a Warlock?
- How well does Perkins know Mrs. Figg?

Peter Pettigrew (Wormtail)
- Wormtail will kill (he killed Cedric for sure)
- He still owes Harry one for saving his life
- Is there any significance to his "tattered ear"?
- Why did he bite the finger of the son of a fellow Death Eater (Goyle) in Book 1?

Rita Skeeter
- Something odd about Rita
- J.K.R. confirms that Rita will be back – We're just not sure who "Rita" is

Celestina Warbeck
- Most likely a fraud and in league with St Mungo's

Voldemort
- Voldemort senses lies and smells guilt
- Dumbledore was transfiguration teacher of Voldemort

CREATURES & ENTITIES

Avifors
- They're in the Wizards of the Coast Trading Card Game, so we could see them later...

Aragog & Mosag
- J.K.R. comments about Aragog in a chat on Barnes&Noble.com was only that he'll be back – she wouldn't give any other information (That tells us that he has and important role, and that he might play a "good guy" this time)

Bloody Baron
- Are any HP Sleuths brave enough to ask how he got so bloody?

Buckbeak (Beaky)
- Good boy! Give him a treat!

Chameleon Ghouls
- Can't even trust a suit of armor....

Centaurs (Ronan, Bane, & Firenze)
- J.K.R. has sort of come out and said in an interview with the BBC that Firenze will be back ☺
- Is there a link between Firenze and Florence in the Pensieve?

Crookshanks
- Nice kitty...Can you protect our Hermione?
- He's part Kneazle and Sirius says he's one of the "most intelligent of his kind"

Dementors
- Where do they come from? Are they created and if so, by whom?
- How do they communicate?
- Will they turn Azkaban over to Voldemort?
- Remember that the lights go out when they enter a place

Dobby, the house-elf
- Dobby is powerful and can appear and disappear inside of Hogwarts
- He has long fingers
- He has a thing about socks

Fang
- Big bark; big coward – but we love him

Fawkes
- Warm body, warm song, warm heart

Fat Lady Portrait
- Hope she is brave enough to protect Gryffindors

Fluffy
- Hagrid really likes his pets, so Fluffy must be somewhere where Hagrid will be seeing him again

Ford Anglia
- It's the turquoise transporter! We still want to know if anyone was behind the wheel...
- Is it "alive" and can it think for itself?
- What kind of spell did Mr. W put on it?

Goblins (Griphook)
- Many rebellions against wizards
- They run Gringotts
- They have long fingers
- Don't mess with them

Hedwig
- How does she find Sirius?
- Where are her relatives?

Hogwarts Lake Squid
- The giant squid appears to be friendly – Fred and George tickle it's tentacles, and Colin Creevey thinks it rescued Dennis when he fell in; however, Harry seems to be fearful of it

Incarcifors
- They're in the Wizards of the Coast Trading Card Game, so we could see them later

Kelpies
- These are deadly water creatures and we know Hagrid spotted some in a Hogwarts well (should have sicked one on Gilderoy...)

Lethifold
- J.K.R. describes them as being the most fearsome of creatures

Merchieftainess Murcus
- Hogwarts' underwater defenses

Moaning Myrtle
- Seems a bit "denser" than most ghosts
- A true wandering spirit – she could show up anywhere there's water

Nifflers
- We bet Bill keeps a lot of these guys around

Norbert
- He is Hagrid's favorite, and a fave among readers, so we are betting that we will see Norbert again – the questions is, will he recognize "mommy" Hagrid?

Mrs. Norris
- Give her a kick for us (uhh...no, we didn't mean that)
- She is probably part Kneazle
- If Filch is loyal, his kitty is too

Peeves, the Poltergeist
- Why is he still at Hogwarts? Maybe we'll find out in Book 5

Pigwidgeon
- The little owl who could....

Unicorns
- There have to be more unicorns (of course)
- Ron's wand has a unicorn hair – is there anything special about those who have unicorn cores?

Weasley Ghoul
- Is he a guard dog, or a hazard?

Winky, the house-elf
- What will Winky do?

Bits and Rememberits

These are clues and unsolved mysteries from the previous book that HP Sleuths should keep in mind as they read Book 2. Keep alert for more evidence....

Rememberits

Running Bits That May Be Clues

Body Parts
- Noses
- Eyes
- Ears
- Feet
- Heart
- Stomach
- Hands and Fingers
- Untidy and/or long Hair

Creatures
- Slugs
- Spiders
- Beetles, Cockroaches, and Scarabs
- Flies and Bugs in general

Numbers
- The number 12 and Chapter 12s
- The number 13 and Chapter 13s

Woolies
- Socks
- Mrs. Weasley's Sweaters
- Woolly Dressing Gowns

Wonderland
- Watches and Clocks
- Hares and Rabbits

Miscellaneous
- Ogden's Old Firewhiskey
- Orphans
- Banging noises

Questions Still Bugging Us...

From Book 1

- Voldemort says he killed Harry's father first – Voldemort's a liar, do we believe him?
- How did Dumbledore get James' Invisibility Cloak, and how did Hagrid get the key to the Potter's vault?
- Did Hagrid bring the infant Harry somewhere else before Privet Drive?
- Who is Dumbledore, what does he know, and what is his past?
- Why won't Dumbledore leave Hogwarts?
- What is the history behind Lily and Petunia?
- Why did Harry not see any living relatives (like Petunia) in the Mirror of Erised?
- What is so special about Harry's eyes?
- What is Harry's relationship to *the* Gryffindor?

- Why did the Sorting Hat want to put Harry into Slytherin?
- Why did the Sorting Hat take so long with Seamus and Neville?
- Why did Harry not remember the dream about Quirrell's turban?
- Why did Filch bandage Snape's leg instead of Madam Pomfrey?
- Who gave Norbert's egg to Hagrid?
- What was that "faint whispering" Harry heard in the Hogwarts library?
- Who is the Ravenclaw ghost?
- Who was the ghost Harry and Ron saw on their way to the mirror?
- Can ghosts see through Invisibility Cloaks?
- Where did Percy get Scabbers (and why was Ron allowed to take him to school)?
- Who planted Harry's letters in the eggs?
- Why can't Dumbledore tell Harry why Voldemort wanted to kill him?

From Book 2

- What did everyone who was petrified actually see, and what were they all doing when they saw the Basilisk?
- How did both Hermione and Penelope become petrified with one small mirror?
- Why was Colin Creevey wandering around at night with grapes?
- Why did the name T. M. Riddle sound familiar to Harry?
- Is there a link between Harry and Slytherin?
- Why did Lucius Malfoy call Harry's parents "meddlesome fools" - what did they find out?
- What is it that Dumbledore "always said" about the "end of Hogwarts"?
- Why does everyone make different noises when appearing/disappearing?
- What else can/does the Sorting Hat do?
- What do wizards do with frog spawn?
- Why did the Ford Anglia engine die?
- Why did the Ford Anglia engine restart and keep running?
- Will Gilderoy get his memory back?
- Is Voldemort the last remaining "ancestor" or "descendent" of Slytherin?

RESTRICTED AREA

RESTRICTED AREA

From Book 3

- ☾ Why did the dementors try to get rid of Harry first?

- ☾ How do dementors communicate?

- ☾ Can other wizards "talk" to animals?

- ☾ Was the male voice, in Harry's flashback, his father?

- ☾ Who are Harry's ancestors on *both* sides?

- ☾ What is the septology mystery around Lupin?

- ☾ If you can't Apparate or Disapparate in Hogwarts, then what is it that Dobby and Fawkes do to appear and disappear?

- ☾ Does the victim of a *Shrinking Solution* keep his/it's memory?

- ☾ Can Penelope be trusted?

- ☾ What happened during the goblin rebellions, and who won?

- ☾ How did Nick get (nearly) beheaded, and who (nearly) did it?

- ☾ Who/What drives Hogwarts Express and what did Lupin "discuss" with him/it?

From Book 4

- ☾ Which of the Book 4 Cliffhangers will be revealed in Book 5?

Interesting Tidbits

WHAT "THE ORDER OF THE PHOENIX" MIGHT MEAN

It seems like "The Order of the Phoenix" is a form of brotherhood that binds a select group of wizards. We suspect that those who end up with a phoenix wand core may be linked. However, if that is true, then would Voldemort belong too? We'll have to wait on that one....

It is likely that when one member of the Order is in need, the other member(s) will drop whatever they are doing to go to the aid of that member. We suspect that Dumbledore's flare to Hagrid when he saw that Krum had been stunned was the signal that they use. We believe that silvery form was in the shape of a phoenix.

The qualities of a phoenix will most likely be crucial to this group. The phoenix song, in particular, will have a special effect to help them against their enemies.

J.K.R. often mentions that her favorite creature is the phoenix. So, of course, when she was asked, during an interview with the BBC, what kind of wand she would have, she immediately specified phoenix feather, which she would like in a walnut wood.

Characters Confirmed to Appear in Book 5 and Beyond

- ☾ We will get to see the *real* Mad-Eye in action, according to a chat with J.K.R. on Barnes&Noble.com, and he is supposed to be even more awesome that the Crouch Junior version. Watch your tail, Draco....

- ☾ J.K.R. has assured us that Ron's favorite creature (NOT!), Aragog, will return.

- ☾ J.K.R. has verified in an interview on Scholastic.com, that Arabella Figg is, indeed, **the** Mrs. Figg from the Privet Drive neighborhood.

What We Are Told Will Happen in Book 5

- ☾ Book 5 is supposed to start out like the other books, and Harry will be back to school (where more fun awaits), according to J.K.R. in an interview with the Houston Chronicles.

- ☾ J.K.R. also said, during an interview with Entertainment Weekly, that Harry will go off to visit another magical place during Book 5.

WWP's Rules of CONSTANT VIGILANCE!

Never let your guard down with J.K.R. These are The Rules to remember (unless your memory is as bad as Neville's). Rules for HP Sleuths:

1) **If she reinforces it, she means it (and wants us to remember it).**
2) **If she suddenly interrupts something, she's hiding a key clue!**
3) **There's no such thing as a coincidence.**
4) **Don't take a character's word for it.**
   > Corollaries
   > **4a) Hermione is usually right (except when she gets emotional)**
   > **4b) Ron is usually wrong (except when he makes a joke about it)**

(see WWP Help Desk FAQs for full explanation)

Interesting Tidbits

Background on Ghosts

- ☞ Why do some people become ghosts in J.K.R.'s magical world? We can see that her ghosts are definitely the *restless-spirit* types, but we don't understand why it only happens to some people. According to her interview on Scholastic.com, we will find out in Book 7.

Wicked Stuff

- ☞ J.K.R. has **hinted** (that's what *she* called it in a chat on Barnes&Noble.com) that Harry will use magic on Dudley.

- ☞ According to an interview with Rainforest Books, J.K.R. says that wizards have something even *better* than an Internet that we will see in later books. (What could they be using? Let's see...mirrors, water, paintings...what else?)

- ☞ In a chat on Barnes&Nobel.com, J.K.R. revealed that one of the characters who has never used magic will surprise us by doing so in the future. (Hmmm...) We can think of Filch, (a Squib), or someone like Petunia (grimace).

Will Draco Malfoy become an Ally?

- ☞ Lots of people have hypothesized that Draco might see the error of his ways and team-up with Harry. However, in a chat on Barnes&Noble.com, J.K.R. would not give that any credence.

Will J.K.R. write another Book about Harry when she finishes Book 7?

- ☞ First of all, J.K.R. is making no promises that Harry will even live past Book 7. However, she speculated, during a chat on Barnes&Noble.com, that she might possibly consider writing more, but she is only committing to seven at this time.

RESTRICTED AREA

RESTRICTED AREA

Possible Endings to the Whole Septology

Possible Endings (Book 7) to the Whole Septology
(Based on clues through Book 4)

We see, from the Rowlinguistics, themes, and satire in her stories, that J.K.R. is a fan of many genres of literature, theatre, and film including: Classical Mythology, Literature, and Alternate Reality.

She also seems to appreciate intricate plots and, especially, the "twist ending." We will speculate on some possible endings to the entire Epic Mystery (end of Book 7), using the clues she has given us so far through Book 4.

The following are just a few of WWP's theories (the more we think, the more crazy scenarios come to mind):

Invaders from Mars Scenario

It was all a dream...(But it's now going to happen for real...)

Book 1 *does* start with a sleeping infant and then Harry waking up...

Alice in Wonderland Scenario

Was it all a dream?

There are plenty of references:
- Hares and Rabbits
- Clocks and watches
- Dormice
- Tiger-Lily
- Child turned into pig
- Crazy Knight
- Life-size animated chess pieces

A Christmas Carol Scenario

It was all a dream – but the choices you make will determine which part of the dream comes true

There are some references:
- Peppermint Humbugs
- Ability to go back into a memory
- The theme that choices make you what you are
- Time-Turner special effect

Sci-Fi Scenario

You will never know what reality or is who is in control - because the aliens are

Wizards may not be originally from Earth

Space-Time warps all over

Scenes reminiscent of *The Prisoner* TV series

Dumbledore and Voldemort – Time Lord Scenario

Dumbledore moves around in different time-spaces, amusing himself, while trying to thwart the diabolical plans of "the Master"

There are plenty of references:
Dumbledore has soft spot for Muggles
TARDIS-like environments
The master's TARDIS
Time-travel
Dr Who vs. The Master
The Fourth Doctor's unlocking tool

Terminator II Scenario

Voldemort (Harry) is given a chance to go back and stop himself before he causes a global disaster

There are strong arguments for this one:
This one best explains Dumbledore's comment that he cannot **yet** tell Harry why Voldemort wants to kill him (because Harry may not be able to deal with the guilt).

One possibility is that Voldemort could have been "re-born" (as Harry).

Another is that someone else has sent one of the characters back to stop Voldemort.

Wizards Movie Scenario

Someone is a (long-lost) twin, brother, or relative Scenario

There are so many physical similarities between Voldemort and Harry/James, or Dumbledore (auburn hair) and Lily, or between other characters.

What other warped scenarios can HP Sleuths dream up?

RESTRICTED AREA

Reality Check

Due to J.K.R.'s precise writing style, plus her well-developed world and character pro-files, we are able to spot clues and predict events, as she has challenged us to do. She has carefully designed her magical world and adheres to strict "rules" (just as she explains in interviews). Her mysteries are so well implemented that we can solve riddles in a world, which defies our own physics.

However, we have only followed the trail she has left for us, as we have no special insight into what will actually happen. We are having a great time trying to find the clues and hypothesize what she might do. Nonetheless, J.K.R.'s works are so complex and intricate that nothing is ever certain until it is published (and even then, watch out for twists and red herrings!)

If J.K.R. finds out that HP Sleuths are on her trail, she might raise the stakes and change the rules again – as she is not only brilliant, but also in control of this game.☺

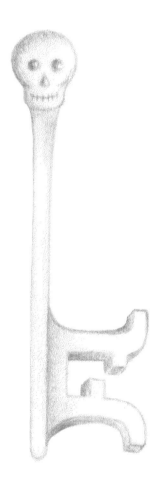

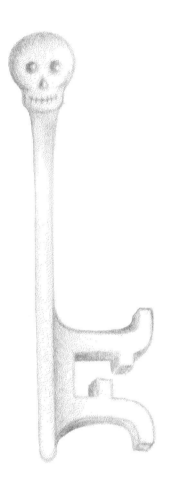

Bibliography

Chats and Interviews with J.K.Rowling
> **America Online**, October 19, 2000
> **Barnes&Noble.com**, March 19, 1999
> **Barnes&Noble.com**, September 8, 1999
> **Barnes&Noble.com**, October 20, 2000
> **BBC**, Fall 2000
> **BBC Online**, March 12, 2001
> **CBC Newsworld**, July 18, 2000
> **Entertainment Weekly**, September 7, 2000
> **eToys.com**, Fall 2000 (not dated)
> **Houston Chronicle**, March 20, 2001
> **Raincoast Books**, March, 2001
> **Scholastic.com**, February 3, 2000
> **Scholastic.com**, October 16, 2000
> **SouthWestNews.com**, July 8, 2000
> **The Sydney Morning Herald**, October 28, 2001
> **Time Magazine**, October 30, 2000 - Vol. 156 - No. 18

Official Harry Potter Publications
- *Harry Potter and the Philosopher's Stone*, Bloomsbury Press, 1997.
- *Harry Potter and the Sorcerer's Stone*, by J.K. Rowling, Scholastic, Inc, 1997.
- *Harry Potter a l'Ecole des Sorciers*, by J.K. Rowling, translated from English by Jean-Francois Menard, Gallimard Jeunesse, 1998.
- *Harry Potter and the Chamber of Secrets*, by J.K. Rowling, Scholastic, Inc, 1999.
- *Harry Potter et la Chambre des Secrets*, by J.K. Rowling, translated from English by Jean-Francois Menard, Gallimard Jeunesse, 1999.
- *Harry Potter and the Prisoner of Azkaban*, by J.K. Rowling, Scholastic, Inc, 1999.
- *Harry Potter et le Prisoner d'Azkaban*, by J.K. Rowling, translated from English by Jean-Francois Menard, Gallimard Jeunesse, 1999.
- *Harry Potter and the Goblet of Fire*, by J.K. Rowling, Bloomsbury Press, 2000.
- *Harry Potter and the Goblet of Fire*, by J.K. Rowling, Scholastic, Inc, 2000.
- *Fantastic Beasts and Where to Find Them*, by Newt Scamander, Obscurus Books (U.S. Publisher, Scholastic Press, 2001) for Comic Relief U.K.
- *Quidditch Through the Ages*, by Kennilworthy Whisp, Whizz Hard Books (U.S. Publisher, Scholastic Press, 2001) for Comic Relief U.K.
- *Conversations with J.K. Rowling*, by Lindsey Fraser, Scholastic, Inc, 2000.
- *Harry Potter and the Sorcerer's Stone*, Warner Bros. Pictures, 2001.

Literature Sources
- *The Hobbit*, by J.R.R. Tolkien, Ballantine Books, 1937.
- *The Fellowship of Ring* (the trilogy Part I of *The Lord of the Rings*), by J.R.R. Tolkien, Ballantine Books, 1965.
- *Chronicles of Narnia*, by C. S. Lewis, Harper Collins Publishers Ltd., 1998.
- *The Annotated Wizard of Oz*, by L. Frank Bauhm, edited by Michael Patrick Hearn, W.W. Norton & Company, 2000.

- *Alice in Wonderland*, by Lewis Carroll, edited by Donald J. Gray, W.W. Norton & Company, 1992.
- *Shakespeare A to Z*, by Charles Boyce, Dell Publishing, 1990.
- *The Unabridged William Shakespeare*, edited by William George Clark and William Aldis Wright, Running Press, 1989.
- *The Iliad* and *The Odyssey*, by Homer
- *The Little White Horse*, by Elizabeth Goudge, Puffin Books, 1946.
- *Nancy Drew* mysteries, by Carolyn Keene
- Jane Austen's novels

References
- Mythology references by Irad Milkin, Michael Grant & John Hazel, and Edith Hamilton
- *Who's Who in Classical Mythology*, by Michael Grant & John Hazel, Oxford University Press, 1996.
- *Dictionary of Classical Mythology*, by Pierre Grimal, Penguin Books, 1990.

Film and TV
- *Dr. Who* TV Series (Tom Baker as the Doctor – Adric companion), British Broadcasting Company (UK), PBS (USA).
- *The Prisoner TV Series*, ITC Incorporated Television Company, Ltd., 1967.
- *Wizards*, animated film by Ralph Bakshi, Twentieth Century-Fox, 1976.
- *Star Trek, Deep Space Nine* TV Series, Paramount Pictures

HP Slueth Notes

WWP's Rules of Constant Vigilance!

Never let your guard down with J.K.R. These are The Rules to remember for HP Sleuths:

1) If she reinforces it, she means it (and wants us to remember it).

2) If she suddenly interrupts something, she's hiding a key clue!

3) There's no such thing as a coincidence.

4) Don't take a character's word for it.

Cut here for your official HP Sleuth bookmark.